MEDIEVAL KNIGHTHOOD
IV

# MEDIEVAL KNIGHTHOOD
## IV

*Papers from the fifth*
*Strawberry Hill Conference*
*1990*

EDITED BY
CHRISTOPHER HARPER-BILL AND RUTH HARVEY

THE BOYDELL PRESS

First published 1992 by The Boydell Press, Woodbridge


The Boydell Press is an imprint of Boydell & Brewer Ltd
PO Box 9, Woodbridge, Suffolk IP12 3DF, UK
and of Boydell & Brewer Inc.
PO Box 41026, Rochester, NY 14604, USA

ISBN 0 85115 319 4




ISSN 0967–8069
Medieval Knighthood

(Formerly ISSN 0959–6453: The Ideals and Practice
of Medieval Knighthood)




The paper used in this publication meets the minimum requirements
of American National Standard for Information Sciences –
Permanence of Paper for Printed Library Materials, ANSI Z39.48–1984

Printed in Great Britain by
St Edmundsbury Press Ltd, Bury St Edmunds, Suffolk

# CONTENTS

# ILLUSTRATIONS

The plates are grouped together after page 240

# PREFACE

The fifth Strawberry Hill conference on medieval knighthood was held at St Mary's College from 9–11 April 1990. The papers there delivered are here printed substantially as delivered, although mention should be made of the excellent range of slides with which Adrian Ailes illustrated his lecture on heraldry.

As usual, the thanks of the organisers and editors are due to many individuals and institutions. For permission to print illustrations and diagrams in this volume we are grateful to the Bodleian Library, English Heritage, the Society for Medieval Archaeology and the Royal Commission on the Historical Monuments of England. Dr Richard Barber and his staff at Boydell and Brewer have once again been models of helpful efficiency at every stage of production.

At St Mary's we are indebted, as always, to the Bursar and his staff for their assistance, and most especially to Sheila Peever for her excellent catering. Above all, however, everybody who has attended this conference over the years would surely wish to join in thanks, regrettably for the last time, to the Principal, the Very Reverend Desmond Beirne, C.M., who is about to move on to wider responsibilities within the Province. He has constantly encouraged the holding of this, as of other conferences, not least by his generous hospitality to participants. We hope he may feel that his support has been justified.

C.H-B.
R.E.H.

# ABBREVIATIONS

| | |
|---|---|
| *Anglo-Norman Studies* | *Anglo-Norman Studies: Proceedings of the Battle Con-ference*, ed. R.A. Brown (to xi), subsequently by M. Chibnall, 14 vols, Woodbridge 1979 etc. |
| *ante* | *The Ideals and Practice of Medieval Knighthood*, ed. C. Harper-Bill and R. Harvey, 3 vols, Woodbridge 1986 etc. |
| *Antiqs. Journ.* | *The Antiquaries Journal* (Society of Antiquaries of London) |
| ANTS | Anglo-Norman Text Society |
| BL | British Library |
| BM | British Museum |
| CBA | Committee for British Archaeology |
| *C Ch R* | *Calendar of Charter Rolls*, 6 vols, HMSO, 1903 etc. |
| *CCR* | *Calendar of Close Rolls* 67 vols, HMSO, 1902 etc. |
| *CFR* | *Calendar of Fine Rolls*, 32 vols, HMSO, 1911 etc. |
| *CIPM* | *Calendar of Inquisitions Post Mortem*, 16 vols, HMSO, 1904 etc. |
| CNRS | Centre National de la Recherche Scientifique |
| *CPR* | *Calendar of Patent Rolls*, 60 vols, HMSO, 1901 etc. |
| *Ec HR* | *Economic History Review* |
| *EHR* | *English Historical Review* |
| FP | Magdalen College, Oxford, Fastolf Papers |
| GDB | Great Domesday Book |
| HMC | Historical Manuscripts Commission |
| HMSO | Her Majesty's Stationery Office |
| JF | *Jordan Fantosme's Chronicle*, ed. R.C. Johnston, Oxford 1981. |
| *Journ. BAA* | *Journal of the British Archaeological Association* |
| LDB | Little Domesday Book |
| *Med. Arch.* | *Medieval Archaeology* |
| MGH | Monumenta Germaniae Historica |
| OMT | Oxford Medieval Texts |
| OV | Orderic Vitalis, *Ecclesiastical History*, ed. M. Chibnall, 6 vols, OMT 1968–80 |
| *PBA* | *Proceedings of the British Academy* |
| *PL* | *Paston Letters and Papers of the Fifteenth Century*, ed. N. Davis, 2 vols, Oxford 1971–76 |
| *P and P* | *Past and Present* |

| | |
|---|---|
| RCHME | Royal Commission on the Historical Monuments of England |
| *Rot. Hund.* | *Rotuli Hundredorum*, ed. W. Illingworth and J. Caley, 2 vols, 'Record Commission', 1812–18 |
| RS | Rerum Brittanicarum Medii Aevi Scriptores, 1858–1911 (Rolls Series) |
| SCH | *Studies in Church History* |
| TE | *Testamenta Eboracensia*, 6 vols, Surtees Society, 1836–1902 |
| TRHS | *Transactions of the Royal Historical Society* |
| ZfdA | *Zeitschrift für deutsches Alterum* |

In citations, place of publication is London unless otherwise stated.

# INTRODUCTION

As has become the custom, the papers given at the fifth Strawberry Hill conference on medieval knighthood cover a wide area, both territorially and chronologically. Some common themes do, nevertheless, emerge.

One group of essays deals with the embellishments of lordship, either architectural or heraldic. Ann Williams examines the residences of the precursors of the Anglo-Norman lordly and knightly classes, demonstrating that while there were certainly no castles in England before the advent of the Normans, the term *burh* should not be restricted to those royal townships built 'to shelter all the folk', but rather also describes the homes of thegns which were designed to give protection against marauders, but neither to serve as administrative centres nor to be the focal points of resistance to the king.

Surveying the complex architectural history of Bodiam Castle, Charles Coulson exposes the myth of its strategic importance as a bastion against the incursions of French invaders of the south coast. If the intention was military, the execution was extraordinarily incompetent, and this is hardly a credible proposition. Rather the aim was purely symbolic, the self-conscious architectural statement of an *arriviste* who had successfully infiltrated the inner recesses of royal patronage; the combination of lapidary magnificence and military ineffectiveness was almost tongue-in-cheek.

A far more practical intention is suggested by Adrian Ailes for the origins of heraldry in the twelfth century. It was not that any substantial changes in armour had made it necessary to devise some novel means of recognition, but rather that contemporary modifications in arms and accoutrement provided new vehicles for identification, by means of devices on lance-pennons, surcoats and shields, by means of which participants both in tournaments and in battle might be known. This means of self-expression towards the end of the twelfth century both became hereditary and was displayed on those seals with which the knightly class increasingly authenticated written instruments.

The second group of papers concern those ideals which motivated the aristocracy of western Europe, or at least groups amongst them, from the late tenth to the fifteenth centuries – although Peter Nobel, in his examination of some thirteenth-century romances, suggests that various perversions of knightly conduct did not always attract condemnation even from those authors conventionally believed to have propagated the chivalric ethos. The study of other literary sources, however, and also of legislation, suggests that such cynical realism was an aberration. Reviewing the Peace movement which originated in southern

xiii

France at the turn of the tenth and eleventh centuries, Jane Martindale emphasises the initiative of the Poitevin dukes of Aquitaine. The violence condemned was not perpetrated exclusively by *equites* or *milites*, but by bands of undifferentiated predators. The theme of the conciliar decrees was not simply the protection of the clergy, but also the condemnation of those members of the clerical order who themselves committed violence, or indeed were fornicators. She also focuses upon the counterpart to the ideal of divine peace, an evolving concept of 'sacralised war' necessarily waged by a lawfully constituted ruler intent on the creation of order.

Holy war is one of the main themes of Konrad's *Rolandslied*, analysed by Jeffrey Ashcroft, who stresses the spiritualisation in the German version of the *chanson de geste*. Konrad emphasised to his patron, Henry the Lion, perhaps unrealistically but in the spirit of St Bernard of Clairvaux, the holy and religious nature of the *Drang nach Osten*, but he constantly urged also the need for unanimity in unswerving, if reciprocal, loyalty to God's earthly vicar, the emperor – a theme which mirrors that of the *Gesta Frederici*, but an aspiration which ultimately was to prove fruitless as relations declined drastically between Henry and Barbarossa.

Feudal discord was the occasion of the composition of Jordan Fantosme's *Chronicle*, which has hitherto been much examined in terms of style, but has received little attention as a political tract. Matthew Strickland analyses the work as a reflection of the mentality of the Anglo-Norman knightly class bestriding the northern border. Again the constant theme is loyalty, which had proved an elusive concept while Henry II and the Young King were at war and when many lords held lands in both England and Scotland. Jordan provided a *speculum principis* for the young Henry, emphasising the way in which his ally William the Lion had been led astray by the evil counsel of newcomers and *iuvenes*, but he wrote also a *speculum militis*, advocating respect for the church, loyalty to the knight's lawful lord, and the need for practical wisdom in the conduct of war.

An emphasis on military prudence was, almost three centuries later, a main theme of the writings of Stephen Scrope and his circle, which revolved around his step-father Sir John Fastolf. After a fascinating account of the complex psychological relationship between these two men, Jonathan Hughes examines their cultural milieu, strongly influenced by classical learning filtered through works with which they had become familiar during the English occupation of northern France. In their concentration on rationalism and free-will, rather than on the dictates of religion, and also in their belief, even in the worst years of the war, in the imperial destiny of their homeland, this group is seen as an important element in the development of the English Renaissance, which has itself been characterised as 'the Indian summer of English chivalry'.

# The Knight, Heraldry and Armour:
# The Role of Recognition and
# the Origins of Heraldry

ADRIAN AILES

The popular image today of the medieval knight is incomplete without his shining armour and heraldic shield. To these one may add his crest towering high upon his helmet, his emblazoned banner, and, covering his faithful war horse, a richly embroidered caparison. It is a striking image, one that has to a great extent been created and moulded by fictional literature beginning with the earliest Old French epics and courtly romances of the twelfth century. It reached its apogee in Sir Walter Scott's masterpiece, *Ivanhoe*, and in this century Hollywood has perhaps completed the picture by actually recreating the image in the flesh.

For much of the Middle Ages and for many of the more wealthy knights this rather romantic portrait in terms of arms and armour was in fact not all that far from the truth, at least not for those special occasions such as tournaments. When armed for battle or tourney knights were usually covered *cap à pied* in armour. From the eleventh century this consisted of a knee-length mail hauberk and, covering the head, a mail coif and nasal helmet. During the course of the twelfth century leg defences appeared as did the pot helm, which completely covered the face. The introduction of plate armour and bascinet or crested great helm resulted in the gradual decline of the shield as a means of defence. This in turn reduced the role of shield designs as a means of recognition, but from the middle of the twelfth century knights had worn surcoats over their body armour which often repeated either their own arms or badge or those of their lord; indeed, such garments were literally 'coats of arms'. At first, the surcoat was long and loose-fitting, but it was gradually replaced by the skirted, and then tight-fitting, jupon. By the time of Bosworth Field at the very end of the Middle Ages it had evolved into the more elaborate and often very colourful heraldic tabard.

1

For how long, however, had this seemingly inseparable link between a knight and his coat of arms existed? Knights – that is, the highly trained and heavily equipped cavalrymen of the Middle Ages – first came into prominence in the ninth and tenth centuries, whereas armorial bearings, those ordered, stylised, perhaps stereotyped hereditary shield devices, did not emerge for another two hundred years. Moreover, it has commonly been held that coats of arms were first adopted as a means of identifying the knight, unrecognisable in his armour. The difficulty with this theory is that for some time before the advent of heraldry knights could not be identified when equipped for combat. Was there, then, some particular development in a knight's armour and accoutrements between the middle of the eleventh century and the middle of the twelfth century that made him even harder to recognise and thus forced him to adopt some permanent means of identification when in battle or tourney?

Before considering the role that recognition played in the origins of armory it is worth asking just how useful heraldry was to prove as a means of identification. The answer, it seems, is that on the whole it was remarkably successful. From its inception it provided an indispensable means by which knights in armour could be recognised, or indeed, as we shall see later, appear in the guise of another or incognito. Examples are numerous. According to his verse biography the newly knighted William Marshal, one day to become Regent of England, was recognised at a tournament in 1167 by his heraldic shield. This, says the *Histoire*, bore the device of Tancarville, the Norman household in which William was then serving.[1] In another tournament scene, this time from a fictional work of the late 1170s, a number of knights are identified by their shields, all of which are blazoned in detail.[2] Throughout the Middle Ages heralds recognised those entering the lists by means of their coats of arms; only then could they announce the combatants' names and, at the end of the day, proclaim the victors. Their specialised knowledge extended to the battlefield. On the morning after the Battle of Crécy in 1346 Edward III commanded two of

---

[1] 'Sis escuz est de Tankarvile'; *Histoire de Guillaume le Maréchal*, ed. P. Meyer, 3 vols, Paris 1891–1901, line 1478; S. Painter, *William Marshal*, Baltimore 1933, 24. William, then aged about 22, had been a member of the household of his 'cousin germain', William de Tancarville, the Chamberlain of Normandy, since he was 13 or 14 (David Crouch, *William Marshal*, London 1990, chapter 2). Richard I was recognised on Crusade by his banner ('Itinerary of Richard I', in *Chronicles and Memorials of the Reign of Richard I*, ed. W. Stubbs, 2 vols, RS 1864–65, i, 307, 319 and 415) and his nephew, the German emperor Otto IV, at Bouvines 1214, by his eagle shield and banners (Ph. Mousket, *Chronique Rimée*; passage trans. in Georges Duby, *The Legend of Bouvines*, Oxford 1990, 211).

[2] Chrétien de Troyes, *Le Chevalier de la Charrete [Lancelot]*, ed. M. Roques, reprinted, Paris 1978, lines 5773–802, 5816–24; passage quoted in full in G.J. Brault, *Early Blazon*, Oxford 1972, 26–27. For recognition by shield device in two late 12th-century works see Jehan Bodel, *La Chanson des Saisnes*, ed. A. Brasseur, Geneva 1989, 2 vols, *Redaction* AR lines 4026–27, and Renaut de Beaujeu, *Le Bel Inconnu*, ed. G.P. Williams, Paris 1929, lines 5920–31.

his knights, Sir Reginald Cobham and Sir Richard Stafford, to go out to the battlefield 'taking with them three heralds to identify the dead by their arms and two clerks to write down their names. They were amazed at the number they found'.[3]

Perhaps the best, certainly the most poignant, example of a fully armed knight being recognised by his shield device comes from the pen of that industrious chronicler and monk from St Albans, Matthew Paris, writing in the middle of the thirteenth century. He describes how, in 1250 on the night before her son William Longespée was killed on Crusade, Ela, abbess of Lacock, had a vision. In this 'a knight completely equipped in armour was received into the heavens, which opened to receive him; and as she knew the knight's shield by the device [picturam] on it, she enquired in astonishment who the knight was who ascended to heaven and was received by the angels to such glory whose arms [spolia] she recognised, and the reply was made to her in a clear and distinct voice, "It is your son, William" '. The story is obviously apocryphal, but nevertheless it illustrates graphically the unique role heraldry played in helping to identify even close relatives when clad entirely in mail.[4]

Indeed, not to wear one's coat of arms in battle could have devastating consequences. At the Battle of Bannockburn in 1314 Gilbert, earl of Gloucester and last male heir of the great house of Clare, is supposed to have perished because he entered the fray without having first donned his chevronny surcoat.[5] At Worringen in 1288 Count Reinald of Guelders was taken prisoner but then released, having first been stripped of his coat of arms to avoid further recognition by his captors. However, he was quickly recaptured by four Brabant knights unaware of his identity.[6]

During the Middle Ages heraldic devices were so successful in identifying knights, otherwise unrecognisable in their armour, that they actually created problems of their own. A knight had only to swop his armorial surcoat and shield for those of another to be safely taken for that person; or he could assume entirely bogus arms and thus appear icognito. Contemporary literature, particularly the Arthurian romances, abound with such incidents, which were not unknown in real life.[7] At the Battle of Bouvines, a century before Bannockburn,

3 Froissart, Chronicles, trans. G. Brereton, Harmondsworth 1978, 95; Froissart, Chroniques, ed. G.T. Diller, Geneva 1972, 739. For heralds and warfare see Sir Anthony Wagner, Heralds of England, 1968, and P. Adam-Even, 'Les fonctions militaires des hérauts d'armes', Archives Héraldiques Suisses lxxxi, 1957, 2–33.
4 Matthew Paris, Chronica Majora, ed. H.R. Luard, 7 vols, RS 1872–1883, v, 153–54. In the Chanson des Saisnes the queen, Sebile, does not recognise her lover Baudoin, disguised in captured arms, until he removes his helmet (ed. Brasseur, Redaction AR line 3177).
5 See the refs cited in the note to line 183 of The Bruce by Master John Barbour, ed. W.W. Skeat, 2 vols, Scottish Text Society, Edinburgh 1884, ii, 268.
6 J.F. Verbruggen, The Art of Warfare in Western Europe during the Middle Ages, trans. S. Willard and S.C.M. Southern, Amsterdam 1977, 247.
7 See for example, Chrétien's Lancelot, lines 5575–6058, and his Cligés, ed. A. Micha, reprinted Paris 1970, lines 4552–922 and p. xvi (written c.1176); The Romance of Tristan by Beroul, ed.

3

Eudo, duke of Burgundy, swopped his surcoat (though not his shield) for the coat of arms (*la cote à armer*) of the much feared knight, William de Barres, whose deeds of derring-do had gone before him as far as Syria. When the duke's enemies saw the terrifying spectacle of the great 'William' approaching they steeled themselves for the worst. Fortunately for them the ducal imposter did not live up to his borrowed arms and they were duly spared.[8] Edward III, in the manner of all good Arthurian knights, seems to have been particularly partial to fighting incognito. At the Dunstable Tournament of 1334 he appeared in the arms of a certain 'Monsieur Lionell'.[9] His choice of alias was doubtless inspired by the Lionel of Round Table fame as well as by the lions on his own (genuine) royal arms. On the same occasion, he and his knights also fought in the arms of Stephen de Cosyngton and Thomas Bradestone.[10] At a later tournament in Dunstable in 1342 the King fought as an ordinary knight (*miles simplex*) and in 1349 he fought at Calais under the banner of Sir Walter Manny, again 'armed simply as any other knight'.[11]

Even ships, towns and whole armies might be disguised under the banners or behind the shields of the enemy.[12] In Chrétien de Troyes' *Cligés*, written about 1176, the hero and his men enter the besieged town of Windsor dressed in the captured arms of the enemy.[13] The same trick was attempted by the Saracens during the siege of Damietta in 1250. According to Matthew Paris the besieged Crusaders, having discovered their enemy's ploy, were grieved to see the enemies of Christ rejoicing 'clad in the armour and bearing the standards and painted devices [*cognitionibus picturatis*] which they knew so well'.[14] At the battle

    A. Ewert, 2 vols, Oxford 1970, lines 3985–4019 (written *c.*1160), and especially Brault, p. 30, and *Arthurian Literature in the Middle Ages: A Collaborative History*, ed. R.S. Loomis, Oxford 1959, 358 and refs cited there.

8  'Anonyme de Béthune' (written after 1220) in *Receuil des historiens des Gaules et de la France*, ed. L. Delisle, xxiv, pt II, Paris 1904, 750–75 (p. 769); trans. in Duby, *Legend of Bouvines*, 196.

9  Juliet Vale, *Edward III and Chivalry*, Woodbridge 1982, 68.

10  Ibid.

11  Malcolm and Juliet Vale, 'Knightly Piety', *History Today* xxxvii, 1987, 16, Froissart, *Chroniques*, ed. Diller, 870. At a tournament in Dartford Edward III fought under the banner of William de Clinton (R. Barber and J. Barker, *Tournaments: Jousts, Chivalry and Pageants in the Middle Ages*, Woodbridge 1989, 32).

12  'Itinerary', 91–92, Roger of Howden, *Chronica*, ed. W. Stubbs, 4 vols, RS 1868–71, iii, 112, cf. *Arab Historians of the Crusades*, ed. and trans. F. Gabrielli, 1957, 200; Paris, *Chronica Majora*, iv, 306.

13  *Cligés*, lines 1815–39; cf. *La Chanson des Saisnes*, ed. Brasseur, *Redaction* AR lines 3128–82 and especially the note to line 3172 in vol. ii.

14  Paris, *Chronica Majora*, v, 162. According to Jean de Waurin (d.*c.*1474) at dawn on the day of the battle of Wakefield, 30 December 1460, Lancastrians under Sir Andrew Trollope appeared before the town claiming to be reinforcements and displaying the earl of Warwick's badge – a ragged staff; the duke of York came out to greet them and was duly attacked (Jehan de Waurin, *Recueil des Croniques et Anchiennes Istories de la Grant Bretaigne, a present nommé Engleterre*, 5 vols, ed. W. and E.L.C.P. Hardy, RS 1864–91, v, 325–26; A. Goodman, *The Wars of the Roses*, 1981, 42).

of Evesham in August 1265, the Lord Edward (later Edward I), having defeated Simon de Montfort's son at Kenilworth the previous day, likewise rode forth under the freshly captured banners of his enemy. Simon's scout, Nicholas – 'he was his barber, a man skilled in the knowledge of arms' – told the earl, 'Look, soldiers are coming from the north and, as far as I can see in the distance, the banners are yours'. By the time Nicholas had taken a second look however, the royalists had raised other banners so that this time he saw those of Edward, Gloucester and Mortimer.[15]

Another problem brought about by the success of heraldry as a means of recognition was that coats of arms had a nasty habit of exposing their owners to mortal danger. It was crucial to be seen and recognised by one's own men, but armorial bearings could also single out their wearers for special attention by the enemy. When Robert the Bruce and his men were caught by Aymer de Valence in a surprise attack at Methven, near Perth, in June 1306 the Scots hurriedly covered their blazons with white cloth so that individuals could not be recognised.[16] Some leaders were so worried at being given away by their arms that, according to the military historian J.F. Verbruggen, they simply did not wear them in battle.[17] We do know that some dressed others in their own coat of arms to act as decoys. Before the battle of Poitiers in 1356 John II is said to have disguised nineteen decoys in the French royal arms.[18] In Shakespeare's version of the battle of Shrewsbury fought in 1403, which he based on Holinshed, Sir Walter Blunt appears 'semblably furnish'd like the king himself'. He is promptly slain by Douglas in mistake for Henry IV. Hotspur informs Douglas that 'the king hath many marching in his coats' upon which the gruff Scotsman declares, somewhat grandiosely, that he will annihilate 'the entire royal wardrobe'. Even when the poor man does eventually reach Henry, similarly clad in the royal arms, he is still unsure whether this is the king.[19]

There were other problems connected with heraldry as a means of recognition. Its very popularity ensured an increasing multiplicity of arms. (This is probably the reason why, from the mid-thirteenth century, heralds began to record shields on long rolls of arms.) It must have become virtually impossible to

---

15 *The Chronicle of Walter of Guisborough*, ed. H. Rothwell, Camden Society lxxxix, 1957, 200; Antonia Gransden, *Historical Writing in England, c.550–c.1307*, 1974, 470.

16 Walter of Guisborough, 368, Michael Prestwich, *Edward I*, 1990, 507.

17 Verbruggen, *Art of Warfare*, 240; here he states that Duke John I of Brabant wore his arms, sable a lion or, at the battle of Worringen (1288) 'for unlike many princes of his day who gave their insignia to one of their knights so as to escape recognition, the duke wore his arms himself'. At the battle of Steppes (1213) John's great-grandfather and predecessor, Duke Henry I put on a plain suit of mail and handed over his lion banner and surcoat to a trusty follower, Henry of Holdenburg, who perished on that account (ibid., 70, and Charles Oman, *A History of the Art of War in the Middle Ages*, 2nd edn, 2 vols, 1924, i, 451).

18 Froissart, *Chronicles*, trans. Brereton, 129.

19 Henry IV Part I, act v, scenes III and IV; see *First Part Henry IV*, ed. A.R. Humphreys, Arden Shakespeare Series, 1960, 151 note to lines 7–8 and 175–76 for Holinshed's account; see also C.W. Scott-Giles, *Shakespeare's Heraldry*, 1950, 86, 97.

recognise every shield in the heat and dust of battle. Mistakes did occur. At the battle of Barnet, fought on a foggy Easter Sunday in 1471, 'the earl of Oxford's men had upon them their lord's livery, both before and behind, which was a star with streams, which was much like King Edward's livery, the sun with streams; and the mist was so thick that a man might not profitably judge one thing from another; so the earl of Warwick's men shot and fought against the earl of Oxford's men, weening and supposing that they had been King Edward's men; and anon the earl of Oxford and his men cried 'treason! treason!' and fled away from the field with 800 men'.[20]

Damage to shields, surcoats and standards often rendered the devices upon them unrecognisable. War was, and alas still is, a messy and unholy business. In Chrétien's *Erec et Enide*, written about 1170, Kay cannot recognise Erec, because 'there were no distinguishing marks to be seen on his arms [*armes*]: he [Erec] had received so many blows from sword and lance on his shield that all the paint work had come off'.[21] The contemporary Old French poet Ambroise relates how, at the taking of Daron on the Third Crusade in May 1192, Stephen de Longchamp's banner 'went in first, but it was severely rent and not entire, but cut and slit'.[22] At Bouvines the knights' surcoats, it is said, 'have been so cut up and ripped into a thousand shreds . . . that each combatant can barely distinguish his friends from his enemies'.[23] And a century later at Bannockburn, according to Barbour's *Bruce*, the shields were so defiled with blood that their devices could no longer be made out.[24]

In short, heraldry as a means of recognition was not perfect. But it was without doubt a vast improvement on the preceding situation. As a means of recognition armorial devices and later personal badges and livery were maintained right up until the end of the Middle Ages.[25] Heraldry greatly assisted in ensuring that men knew who and where their leaders were and that, hopefully, they were still alive. They could thus follow them more easily and look to them for commands and direction. Common insignia also instilled amongst both knights and footmen a sense of esprit de corps within the various contingents and must, therefore, have helped maintain morale and cohesion in the confusion of battle and tourney. The practice appeared early. In the *Roman de Troie*,

20 A Chronicle of the First Thirteen Years of the Reign of King Edward IV by John Warkworth, ed. J.O. Halliwell, Camden Society 1st series x, 1839, 16.
21 Erec et Enide, lines 3947–56; Chrétien de Troyes, Arthurian Romances, transl. D.D.R. Owen, 1987, 53.
22 Ambroise, L'Estoire la Guerre Sainte, ed. G. Paris, 1897, lines 9313–15.
23 Oeuvres de Rigord et de Guillaume le Breton, ed. F. Delaborde, 2 vols, Paris 1882–85, 'Philippiad', Liber XI lines 183–88 (written in 1220s); trans. in Duby, Legend of Bouvines, 200.
24 Bruce, i, 329; ii, 268.
25 For the increasing popularity of livery and personal badge as a means of recognition see Malcolm Vale, War and Chivalry, 1981, 96–98. For examples of the badge see Edward IV's French Expedition of 1475, ed. F.P. Barnard, Oxford 1925; and of livery see Michael Prestwich, The Three Edwards: War and State in England 1272–1327, 1980, 144, 192, 239, and cf. Froissart, trans. Brereton, 245.

written *c*.1160–*c*.1180, the men of Remus, king of the Cicones of Thrace, cover their helms, surcoats, saddles and shields 'in the same colour for thus it pleased their lord so that they could recognise each other in the great battles where they would be and that it would be said and told what they had done'.[26] And, at the close of the Middle Ages, according to *Gregory's Chronicle*, just before the second battle of St Albans in 1461, every lord's man within the meisne of Queen Margaret, wife of Henry VI, bore 'their lord's livery that every man might know his own fellowship by his livery'.[27]

How, then, had knights been able to distinguish each other before the adoption of armorial bearings? The problem had certainly existed beforehand. At the battle of Sherstone in 1016 Edmund Ironside had to doff his helmet to prove to his men he was still very much alive.[28] In a much more famous episode at Hastings Duke William was forced to do likewise.[29] Indeed, the ducal family seems to have had a particular problem when it came to being recognised in battle. In 1051 envoys of the young Duke William had to explain to Geoffrey Martel, count of Anjou, who was spoiling for a fight, what sort of accoutrements their master was accustomed to wear in battle so that Geoffrey would recognise him.[30] In a mêlée outside the besieged town of Gerberoy in 1079 William's own son Robert unknowingly unhorsed him wounding his father in the arm. Only when William spoke did he recognise the king and realise his *faux pas*.[31] A similar misfortune befell the Conqueror's second son. In a skirmish fought in 1091 Rufus was unseated by a soldier who admitted, somewhat rashly, to having mistaken the king for a mere knight. Again, it was only when the king made his feelings vocal that he was recognised.[32]

[26] *Le Roman de Troie par Benoit de Sainte Maure*, ed. L. Constans, Paris, 1904–12, 6 vols, lines 6713–28. See above for William Marshal bearing his master's arms in 1167. For the multiple use of identical arms see *Expugnatio Hibernica: the Conquest of Ireland by Giraldus Cambrensis*, ed. and trans. A.B. Scott and F.X. Martin, Dublin 1978, 168 (describing an incident in 1176); Gautier d'Arras, *Ille et Galeron*, ed. Y. Lefreve, Paris 1988, lines 5753–60 (written 1167–78); the Joshua Initial (fo 69; *c*.1150–*c*.1180) of the Winchester Bible (C.M. Kauffman, *A Survey of MSS Illuminated in the British Isles iii, Romanesque MSS*, 1975, cat. no. 83); the Carmen de Bello (*c*.1197) by Peter of Eboli (being Codex 120/ii of the Civic Library of Berne), and the later references cited in Paul Adam-Even, 'Les usages héraldiques au milieu du XIIe siècle', *Archivum Heraldicum*, A° lxxvii, Bulletin 2–3, 1963, 18–29 (p. 28).
[27] 'Gregory's Chronicle', in *Historical Collections of a Citizen of London in the Fifteenth Century*, ed. James Gairdner, Camden Society n.s. xvii, 1876, quoted by Rodney Dennys, *Heraldry and the Heralds*, 1982, 115–16. The inclusion of livery and badges on the Salisbury Roll (*c*.1463) testifies to their importance in the 15th century.
[28] William of Malmesbury, *De Gestis Regum Anglorum*, ed. W. Stubbs, 2 vols, RS 1887–89, i, 215.
[29] William of Poitiers, *Gesta Guillelmi ducis Normannorum et regis Anglorum*, ed. R. Foreville, Paris 1952, 190; David M. Wilson, *The Bayeux Tapestry*, 1985, pl. 68.
[30] William of Poitiers, 40; William of Malmesbury ii, 288. For the date see D.C. Douglas, *William the Conqueror*, 1964, 59, n. 7.
[31] Florence of Worcester, *Chronicon ex Chronicis*, ed. B. Thorpe, 2 vols, 1848–49, ii, 13; Simeon of Durham, 'Historia Regum' in *Opera*, ed. T. Arnold, 2 vols, RS, 1882–85, ii, 208.
[32] William of Malmesbury ii, 364.

That knights in the days just before the introduction of heraldry were truly unrecognisable in their armour is well illustrated by an episode from a contemporary chronicle, the *Gesta Stephani*. It describes how in 1136 a force under Judhael of Totnes was able to mix unnoticed among the royal camp then in Exeter besieging the castle. At the appropriate moment they were quickly whisked into the stronghold by a sudden sortie of the garrison. The chronicle adds that Judhael's party were able to mingle with King Stephen's men beforehand 'for, among so many clad in mail, it was impossible easily to distinguish one from another'.[33]

The way in which knights did recognise one another and distinguish friend from foe in these pre-heraldic days was, it appears, by means of flags and war cries. Significantly, the words for both, *enseignes* and *signa*, were both later used for armorial bearings, and both flags and war cries did, of course, continue to act as an indispensable means of recognition throughout the Middle Ages.

For centuries flags and standards had existed in many shapes and forms. Usually they were simple in design and easily recognisable. Before the introduction of heraldry two types were used for recognition. First, there were those standards and other great ensigns which preceded armies on the march and which in battle provided a focal point for men to rally under and regroup; examples include the famous Dragon standard of the English depicted on the Bayeux Tapestry and the sacred Oriflamme of St Denis of France mentioned in that remarkable Old French epic, *The Song of Roland*, written down in about 1100.[34] Secondly, there were those personal banners and flags that closely accompanied leaders and presumably provided the only sure means by which they could be identified as being both present and alive. At Hastings, for example, Harold fought alongside his jewelled banner of a fighting man.[35] The Christian leaders, Bohemond and Baldwin used individual banners of a single colour on the First Crusade, and the Norman kings of England certainly possessed royal standards.[36] Although such flags were personal, there is no evidence that they

---

[33] *Gesta Stephani*, ed. and trans. K.R. Potter, rev. R.H.C. Davis, 1976, 37; this part of the *Gesta* was written *c*.1148.

[34] Wilson, *Bayeux Tapestry*, pl. 71; strangely none of the early sources mention the Dragon (J.S.P. Tatlock, 'The Dragon of Wessex and Wales', *Speculum* viii, 1933, 223–35 (225); *La Chanson de Roland*, ed. F. Whitehead, Oxford 1970, line 3093). Compare the *angelus* – St Michael's standard – used by the Saxon rulers of Germany in the 10th century (see the refs cited in K. Leyser, 'The Battle at the Lech', *History* l, 1965, 1–25 (18)), and the notorious Raven Banner of the Vikings (*Anglo-Saxon Chronicle*, trans. G.N. Garmonsway, 1972, 'E' version sub anno 878, 77 and note 5; N. Lukman, 'The Raven Banner and the Changing Ravens', *Classica et Medievala* xix, 1958, 133–51).

[35] William of Poitiers, 224; William of Malmesbury ii, 302.

[36] Fulcher of Chartres, *A History of the Expedition to Jerusalem 1095–1127*, trans. F. Ryan and ed. H.S. Fink, Tennessee 1969, 99, 158; William II: Orderic Vitalis, *The Ecclesiastical History*, ed. and trans. M. Chibnall, 6 vols, 1969–80 (henceforth OV), v, 247; Henry I: ibid., vi, 29, and Stephen: Henry of Huntingdon, *Historia Anglorum*, ed. T. Arnold, RS 1879, 271; see also A. Ailes, *The Origins of the Royal Arms of England*, Reading 1982, 44–50.

were hereditary or that their designs were repeated on their owners' shields; they were not, therefore, heraldic in the strict sense of the term.

As far as war cries are concerned, when shouted in unison, these also had the double effect of terrifying the enemy and boosting morale within the ranks. In *The Song of Roland* the leaders, Charlemagne and Baligant, despite carrying decorated shields, only recognise one another when each shouts his war cry.[37] In his Arthurian *Brut* (completed in 1155) the Anglo-Norman poet Wace, doubtless reflecting the practices of his own day, describes a battle of ancient times in which men could not distinguish friend from foe 'save only by the cry they shouted'.[38] The chronicler-monk Orderic Vitalis, writing from his abbey of St Evroult in Normandy at the beginning of Stephen's turbulent reign, relates how, in 1119, Frenchmen hiding in a storehouse ran to the archbishop of Rouen's 'castle' shouting out the English royal battle cry, but once inside changed it to 'Montjoie!', the French *cri de guerre*. They then duly expelled the surprised inhabitants making it possible for the French king to enter the town.[39]

Thus, in the pre-heraldic days of the ninth, tenth and eleventh centuries flags and war cries were the only sure means of identifying knights completely clad in mail. From about 1100, however, the situation dramatically changed. Previously shield designs such as those depicted on the Bayeux Tapestry had been haphazard, random and presumably of little or no consequence. They were simply decorative.[40] From the beginning of the twelfth century this ceased to be the case.[41] Henceforth, shield designs appear to be more orderly, even

---

[37] *Roland*, ed. Whitehead, lines 3564–66.

[38] *Le Roman de Brut de Wace*, ed. Ivor Arnold, 2 vols, Paris 1938–40, ii, lines 12037–40.

[39] OV vi, 217.

[40] For shields on the Tapestry see J.R. Planché's, *The Pursuivant of Arms*, 3rd edn, 1873, 23–24, W.S. Ellis, *The Antiquities of Heraldry*, 1869, 164–70, and Ailes, *Origins of the Royal Arms*, 84 note 9.

[41] For the origins and early development of heraldry see especially L. Bouly des Lesdain, 'Études héraldiques sur le XIIe siècle', *Annuaire du Conseil héraldique de France* xx, 1907, 185–244 and his 'Les plus anciennes armoiries françaises (1127–1300)', *Archives Héraldiques Suisses* v, 1897, 69–79, 94–103; J. Marchand, 'L'art héraldique d'après la littérature du Moyen Age, Les origines: la Chanson de Roland', *Le Moyen Age* xlvii, 1937, 37–43; P. Gras, 'Aux origines de l'héraldique: la décoration des boucliers au début du XIIe siècle d'après la Bible de Citeaux', *Bibliothèque de l'École des Chartes* cix, 1951, 198–208; Adam-Even, 'Les usages héraldiques au milieu du XIIe siècle', M. Pastoureau, 'La Diffusion des armoiries et les débuts de l'héraldique', in *La France de Philippe Auguste: Le Temps des Mutations*, ed. R-H. Bautier, Paris 1982, 737–59; M. Pastoureau, 'L'origine des armoiries: un problème en voie de solution?', *Genealogica & Heraldica: Report of the 14th Internat. Cong. Her. & Gen. Sciences*, Copenhagen 1982, 241–54; *Les Origines des Armoiries*, ed. H. Pinoteau, M. Pastoureau and M. Popoff, Bressanone 1981, esp. the chapter 'L'Apparition des armoiries sur les sceaux en Ile-de-France et en Picardie (c.1130–1230)', by Brigitte Bedos Rezak, 23–41; L. Jéquier, 'Le début des armoiries en Suisse romande', in *Mélanges de Travaux offerts à Me J. Tricou*, Lyon 1972, 179–92; Faustino Menendez Pidal de Navascues, *Le Début des Emblèmes Héraldiques en Espagne*, Lisbon 1984, and A. Ailes, 'Heraldry in Twelfth-Century England: The Evidence', in *England in the Twelfth Century: Proceedings of the 1988 Harlaxton Symposium*, ed. D. Williams, Woodbridge 1990, 1–16.

systematic, as if responding to a new role. Simple geometric patterns, looking very much like true heraldry, appear within the first decade of the century and in the 1120s and 1130s animal charges in the classic heraldic poses emerge. It may be that such designs were conforming to new guidelines – the forerunners of the heraldic rules that later were to govern the number and use of colours and so on. These 'proto-heraldic' designs seem to have been neither mere decoration nor truly heraldic; it is not known, for example, if they were hereditary. Whatever the case, by the third quarter of the twelfth century such designs were being used consistently, and, more importantly, were being passed on unchanged to sons and successors.[42] Heraldry had been born.

How much of this was due to recognition – the need for knights to be identified when covered in mail? The evidence, though scanty, is fairly conclusive. It seems that the new shield designs appearing in the iconographic evidence, literary texts and illuminated manuscripts of the first half of the twelfth century were in many cases at least prompted by a pressing need on the part of knights for an effective means of recognition. The indirect evidence is strong. If these patterns were used, perhaps specifically adopted, for the purposes of identification, then we would expect them to hold certain qualities and to meet certain requirements. It is possible to show that this indeed was the case. Firstly, proto-heraldic designs as well as the very first true arms were, as we have noted, bold and simple. They nearly all consisted of geometric patterns or a single beast. They could thus be easily identified both at a distance and in the immediate fray of battle. It is possible that as early as the middle of the twelfth century shield designs were following the classic heraldic rule whereby only certain colours could be used, and these, moreover, could not be placed on top of each other but only on to gold and silver backgrounds and vice versa. Such a requirement must surely have come about at this early stage in the development of heraldry as a result of shields being used as a means of recognition. Black lions on blue shields or gold bends on silver would simply not have served as effective marks of identification.

Secondly, if these new designs appearing at the beginning of the twelfth century were used for recogniton, we would expect them to have been used consistently by their owners. It was no use if a man used a lion one day or on one campaign, and, say, an eagle on the next. The evidence suggests that more and more men were maintaining the same shield device. Our first known coat of arms – the Angevin gold lions on blue – was, for example, used by the same man, Geoffrey, count of Anjou, for at least twenty years.[43] Moreover, the seal

---

[42] See for example the seals illustrated in Sir Anthony Wagner, *Heralds and Ancestors*, 1978, 12. Early hereditary devices and arms on seals include the wheatsheaf of the Campdaveines, counts of St Pol, the chevrons of the Clare family and the checky arms of Warenne. See also Ailes, 'Heraldry in 12th-Century England', 6–7. In the *Roman de Troie* Pyrrhus carries the arms of his father (line 23889; Adam-Even, 'Les usages héraldiques', 23).

[43] There is chronicle reference for their use in 1128 (John of Marmoutier, 'Historia Gaufredi

evidence of the 1130s and 1140s reveals a similarly consistent approach to arms. More and more men of the aristocratic and knightly classes were at this time adopting seals on which they portrayed themselves on horseback, equipped for combat, and often carrying a shield emblazoned with their arms. These seals, and presumably the arms depicted on them, were in many cases used over several years without change. Moreover, even when there was occasion to change a seal, care was often taken to repeat the same arms on the new design. Thus the two succesive seals (c.1135 and 1146) of Ralph, count of Vermandois depict his checky coat.[44] This not only suggests that such devices were very important to their owners but that, in an illiterate age, even their portraits on equestrian seals could only be identified by the heraldry employed.

Thirdly, if these designs were used as a means of recognition we would expect them to have been repeated on their owners' armour and accoutrements wherever possible. This would at least ensure that even if the shield were damaged, or the surcoat or banner torn, a knight could still be recognised by his device. Once again, examples exist from an early period. Waleran, count of Meulan and earl of Worcester, repeated his checky arms (doubtless a differenced version of those of his uncle, Ralph, count of Vermandois) on his gonfanon, surcoat and saddlecloth as depicted on his second seal dating to about 1139.[45] Later the principal device of the shield was repeated on the horse caparison (1150s) and saddle (1190s).[46] It was also often painted on the side of the helm (1180s) and later used as a crest (1190s) which, towering above the mêlée, could be easily seen.[47]

---

ducis Normannorum et comitis Andegavorum' in *Chroniques des comtes d'Anjou et des seigneurs d'Amboise*, ed. L. Halphen and R. Poupardin, Paris 1913, 179–80) and they were presumably in use at the time of his early death in 1151 since they appear on his funerary plaque made in the late 1150s (S. and M. Nikitine, *L'Émail Plantagenet*, Nancy 1981 and *British Heraldry*, ed. R. Marks and A. Payne, 1978, 16). Unfortunately Geoffrey's seal is non-armorial (W. de G. Birch, *Catalogue of Seals in the Dept of MSS in the British Museum*, 6 vols, 1887–1900, no. 6317).

44 L. Cl. Douet d'Arcq, *Archives de l'Empire: Collection des Sceaux*, 3 vols, Paris 1863–68, no. 1010, and G. Demay, *Inventaire des sceaux de l'Artois et de la Picardie*, 2 pts in 1 vol, Paris 1875–77, no. 38; both seals illustrated in M. Pastoureau, *Traité d'Héraldique*, Paris 1979, 31.

45 Birch, *Catalogue of Seals . . . in British Museum*, no. 5666, *British Heraldry*, 16. For the date see Edmund King, 'Waleran, Count of Meulan and Earl of Worcester (1104–1166)', in *Tradition and Change*, ed. D. Greenway et al., Cambridge 1985, 165–181.

46 Caparison: seal of William FitzEmpress 1156–64 (*Fascimilies of Early Charters from Northamptonshire Collections*, ed. F.M. Stenton, Northants Record Society iv, 1930, 24–25); and 3rd seal of Roger de Mowbray c.1157 (Birch, *Cat. Seals in Br. Mus.*, no. 6219, *Charters of the Honour of Mowbray 1107–91*, ed. D. Greenway, 1972, lxx, lxxxiii). Saddle: lions on Richard I's saddle ('Itinerary', 197).

47 Helm: counterseal of Philip d'Alsace, Count of Flanders c.1181 (G. Demay, *Inventaire des sceaux de la Flandre*, 2 vols, Paris 1873, no. 139). Crest: Richard I's lion fan crest 1195 (Birch, *Cat. Seals in Br. Mus.*, no. 87) and Baldwin, count of Flanders' modelled crest 1197 (Demay, *Sceaux de l'Artois*, no. 52). It was probably for the purposes of recognition that Arnaut Guilhem de Marsan advised his readers in the 1170s to 'have the saddle-cloth made with the same emblem as the saddle and the same colour as is painted on the shield, and the pennon

Fourthly and finally, if these proto-heraldic designs and early arms were used as marks of identification we would expect some form of control to ensure that no two men could display identical arms. If they did there would be no other means of knowing which man was which. Although heralds do not appear in the extant evidence until the late 1170s,[48] the probability is that heraldry was already under some form of supervision by the middle of the twelfth century and that this was prompted by knights wishing to keep their armorial bearings personal and unique.[49]

The circumstantial evidence does then strongly suggest that the earliest proto-heraldic designs and very first arms were being used to help identify their owners in battle and tourney. The probability is that many of them were adopted primarily for this reason. And, even if they had been adopted for some other purpose, it is a fact that before long they too had taken on this rather mundane, though crucial, role.

Fortunately, there is also some direct evidence that arms were adopted specifically for the purposes of recognition. At the same time as formal geometric patterns appear in the illuminated manuscripts, we begin to read in the Old French of *connoissances* or, in the Latin, of *cognitiones* – literally, 'emblems of recognition'. Moreover, the majority of these refer to shield devices. This new use of the surface of the shield must have made such designs much more effective as a means of personal identification. It was now no longer a case of a single flag or war cry having to be shared by all. Shields were carried by individuals and were thus much more personal. It also meant, of course, a step much closer towards true heraldry – the systematic use of hereditary devices centred upon the *shield*.[51]

---

on the lance in the same way' (passage quoted in David Nicolle, *French Medieval Armies, 1000–1300*, 1991, 21).

[48] The first references are in Chrétien's *Lancelot* (lines 5537) and in his *Yvain* (ed. M. Roques, reprinted Paris 1971, lines 2204–8), both written in the late 1170s, and in the *Hist. de G. le Maréchal* (lines 977–81 [describing an event in 1167], 3485–520, 5222–29; passages quoted in full in A.R. Wagner, *Heralds and Heraldry in the Middle Ages*, 2nd edn, Oxford 1956, 130–31); the *Hist.* was written between 1226 and 1229.

[49] When in *Lancelot* (lines 5793–98), written c.1177, two knights carry identical shields the reason for this duplication is swiftly given – they are companions.

[50] The first references to *connoissances* appear in the *Roland: escuz unt genz de multes cunoisances* (ed. Whitehead, line 3090), which also contains shields of proto-heraldic patterns (quarterly: line 3867; fleury: lines 1276, 1354, 1810, 3361; party: 1299, 1600); these designs and the *connoissances* mentioned may well be the same thing. For references to *connoissances* see Lesdain, *Études héraldiques sur le XIIe Siècle*, 196–97, and Brault, *Early Blazon*, 147–48.

[51] By the second half of the 12th century *connoissances* were repeated on surcoats and pennons (*Le Roman de Thèbes*, ed. Guy Raynaud de Lage, Paris 1966–67, 2 vols, lines 3563, 3589, 5511, 8599 and 9035 [written c.1155] and Thomas, *Les Fragments du Roman de Tristan*, ed. B.H. Wind, Geneva and Paris, 1960, Fragment Douce, lines 909–12 [written c.1160]); and on caparisons: *Roman de Troie*, lines 9538–39; see references quoted in Paul Adam-Even, 'Les enseignes militaires du Moyen Age et leur influence sur l'héraldique' in *Receuil du 5e Congrès Int. des Sciences Généalogiques et Héraldiques à Stockholm*, 1960, 167–194 (170–72). They were also inherited by this date, e.g. *Ille et Galeron*, ed. Lefèvre, lines 488–90 and note to line 489.

12

That *connoissances* or *cognitiones* were used for recognition is demonstrated from an incident described by Orderic Vitalis. He writes how, after the battle of Brémule in 1119, Peter of Maule and some of the other French fugitives threw away their *cognitiones* 'to avoid recognition' and, cunningly mixing with their pursuers, shouted out the English war cry.[52] Wace states quite clearly that their very *raison d'être* and primary purpose was recognition. In his *Roman de Rou* (written betwen 1160 and 1183) he describes how at Hastings:

> The knights had . . . . . . . . . .
> Shields on their necks, lances in their hands,
> And all had made cognizances [*connoissances*]
> That one Norman would recognise another
> So that in the contention
> Norman would not kill Norman
> Nor one Norman strike another.[53]

Although he is refering to 1066 we can assume that Wace is here reflecting knightly practice nearer to his own day.[54]

If, then, some knights did adopt shield devices purely and simply to be recognised in tourney or battle, then we can suppose that something in the period just before heraldry must have prompted, perhaps even forced, knights to adopt some clear form of identification. The obvious inference is that such necessity was brought about by a change in armour.

This was not, in fact, the case. There were no major changes in armour during this period which made knights more difficult to recognise and so would force them to adopt clear and permanent marks of identification. The face guard and barrrel helm, which did completely cover the face, appeared in the 1180s and 1190s, well after the introduction of heraldry. Nevertheless, there were three significant changes in the accoutrements of knights at this time which certainly encouraged this burgeoning group of men to adorn their equipment with bold patterns and devices for the purposes of identification, thus helping solve an age-old problem. It is true (as we shall see later) that some knights may have had other reasons for adopting such designs, but it is a fact that within a few decades all such devices had taken on the role of *connoissances* – emblems of recognition.

---

[52] OV vi, 217.

[53] Wace, *Le Roman de Rou*, ed. A.J. Holden, 3 vols, Paris 1970–73, ii, lines 7679–84.

[54] Compare Jean de Meun (in the late 13th century), when translating the classical treatise on tactics by Vegetius. Breaking away from the text, which describes Roman legionaries inscribing their shields with their names and those of their cohorts, Jean adds: 'à l'exemplaire de ces faits ont les chevaliers de maintenant enseignes et bannières et cotes d'armes et escuz, et leur cognoissance dedens et par ce cognoissent ils leurs amis et leurs anemis'; passage quoted in Adam-Even, 'Les enseignes militaires du Moyen Age', 172.

The first change in the accoutrements of knights was the adoption of the couched lance. The practice was first used about 1050 near Normandy, though it only gained widespread diffusion at the turn of the century.[55] Previously the spear was either thrown as a projectile or held underarm or overarm to deliver a thrust. By couching the lance under the armpit a longer, heavier spear could be used. Since it was no longer to be thrown it could now also suppport a pennon; such a flag would have impeded its previous use as a javelin. Thus in the Bayeux Tapestry none of the lances carrying pennons are being thrown and nearly all the lances carrying pennons are held in the couched position or straight upright at rest. Along with early seals, the Tapestry also suggests that these little flags were often decorated with small roundels and crosses.[56] Although there is no evidence to suggest that such devices were used consistently or were hereditary, it may well be that in time the colours and designs displayed upon them became so closely associated with their owners, either as individuals, or in groups such as the mounted squadrons or 'conrois', that they actually helped identify them. Whether or not this was the case, such pennons must surely have acted as the precursors of the later and larger heraldic gonfanons by which men often came to be identified in battle.[57] Some of the first known arms appear on gonfanons, and it has been argued that shield devices repeated the design of the gonfanon rather than the other way round. It is also interesting to note that both com-manders and knights depicted on the Tapestry fly lance pennons. They were thus not the preserve of the higher echelons of society. In this respect they also

[55] Jean Flori, 'Encore l'usage de la lance . . . La Technique du combat chevaleresque vers l'an 1100', *Cahiers de Civilisation Médiévale* xxxi, 1988, 213–40, and Maurice Keen, *Chivalry*, New Haven 1984, 23–25.

[56] It is unlikely that the crosses and roundels decorating the lance flags of the Norman and Scottish kings as depicted on their royal seals were in any way meaningful. It is just possible that the knight depicted on the Bayeux Tapestry bearing a lance flag charged with three roundels is Eustace de Boulogne or one of his men (see Pastoureau, 'L'origine des armoiries: un problème en voie de solution?', 249). We know from other sources that three torteaux were the family device of the counts in the late 11th century and that, like similar family devices, they were later metamorphosised into the family coat of arms (ibid., 248–49). However, the evidence here is not at all certain.

[57] Although contemporary writers speak of 'gonfanons' and 'pennons' being used as rallying flags or even bearing personal devices, this is either after the introduction of armorial bearings or the term is being used very loosely and such flags might better be described as 'standards or banners' rather than as gonfanons or pennons, which we tend to visualise as mere adjuncts to the lance. It is doubtful, for example, whether 'gonfanoniers' such as Geoffrey of Anjou in *The Song of Roland* (line 106) were responsible for small lance pennons or whether the flags (both described as *gunfanun* and *enseigne*) of Thibaut of Bourges and his nephew, Esturmi, in *The Song of William* (written in the first half of the 12th century), which were trampled in the ground so that the army might escape recognition, were small lance flags (*La Chanson de Guillaume*, ed. D. McMillan, 2 vols, Paris 1949–50, lines 262–76). As the epic poems of the day were eager to relate, pennons attached to lance heads were often driven into the bodies of enemies, usually pagans – hardly a suitable use for a flag to rally under and protect.

foreshadowed the use of heraldic banners and gonfanons as ensigns of identification by greater and lesser men alike.[58]

The second change in the accoutrements of the knight that helped encourage the adoption of some permanent means of recognition actually gave its name to coats of arms. The probability is that surcoats were first adopted on the First Crusade at the very end of the eleventh century in imitation of the Saracens to prevent the armour from becoming too hot under the East Mediterranean sun or from rusting in the rain. One of the earliest references to a knight wearing a surcoat dates to 1127 and refers to an incident in the Holy land. The Arab-Syrian chronicler, Usāmah Ibn-Munqidh, relates how he fought with a Frankish horseman armed with a lance and shield and wearing a helmet and coat of mail over which he displayed 'his colours in a green and yellow silk tunic'.[59] The design was thus very probably proto-heraldic, if not armorial. Waleran's seal (c.1139) provides the earliest known evidence of an heraldic surcoat and in the *Roman de Thèbes* (written between 1150 and 1156) Melampus wears a surcoat decorated with what the author describes as his '*connoissance*'.[60] Such a large area devoted to the insignia, often personal, of the wearer or his master must have served as a vital means of recognition, particularly if the shield or banner were lost or damaged.

The third and last change occurred towards the end of the period we are considering, just as heraldry was beginning to take root. It concerns the shield. Many of those depicted on the Bayeux Tapestry are long and kite-shaped, and decorated with random designs. At their centre often lies a large prominent boss surrounded by smaller studs. Metal bands, perhaps strengthening bars, divide some shields into compartments. During the first half of the twelfth century, however, the boss tends to diminish in size, sometimes disappearing altogether. The metal rays emanating from the centre become much more fine, frequently ending in decorative *fleurs de lis*.[61] Both boss and rays are occasionally seen

---

58 Twelfth-century seals reveal a variety of men bearing pennons and gonfanons on lances, e.g. *Cat. Seals in Br. Mus.*, nos 5672, 5735, 5759, 5763, 5809, 5899, 6064, 6072, 6112, 6134, 6169, 6300, 6317, 6318, 6322, 6356, 6364, 6415, 6445, 6471, and 15662. Wace writes in his *Rou* that in Duke William's invasion army the barons bore gonfanons and the knights pennons (lines 6505–6), which might tie in better with the practices of his own day, but again too much weight should not be given to those terms, which were often interchangeable.

59 *An Arab-Syrian Gentleman and Warrior in the Period of the Crusades: Memoirs of Usāmah Ibn-Munqidh*, trans. Philip K. Hiti, 1987, 90. His adversary is surprised to find armour under the tunic.

60 *Thèbes*, ed. de Lage, line 5512. His shield is party argent and gules (lines 5513–14). William the Breton (writing in the 1220s) explains that at Bouvines the knights wore surcoats so everyone could be recognised by the signs upon them:
   Queque armature vestis consuta supreme
   Serica cuique facit certis distinctio signis. ('Philippiad', Liber XI, lines
                              183–84; trans. Duby, *Legend of Bouvines*, 200)

61 This design became known as the escarbuncle and is frequently attested to in contemporary literature. For examples see Lesdain, 'Études héraldiques', 191–92, which also contains useful

existing (somewhat uneasily) alongside or even over proto-heraldic and even heraldic designs.[62] But, as they gradually fade in importance so the broader, less encumbered surface readily lends itself to painted designs. In particular single animal charges are now given full rein.[63] It was now much more easy for knights to display upon their shields clear and permanent designs which could be used as effective marks of identification. Moreover, as we have already noted, this new use of shields provided a much more personal method of recognition than flags and war cries, and shields were to become the main medium for true heraldry.

All three changes did not make their knightly owners more difficult to recognise. What lance pennons, surcoats and smooth shields did provide was an unprecedented opportunity for individual knights (both great and small) to adorn new and relatively large surface areas of their accoutrements so that in battle and tourney they could be the more readily identified. The temptation to do so at a time when decoration, chivalric display and family symbols were becoming more and more popular with an increasingly class conscious and hereditary élite of knights would have been irresistible.

Some of those knights who did decorate their equipment for the purposes of recognition would have adopted purely arbitrary designs which they then had to use consistently in order to avoid confusion. In time such designs would have become so closely linked with these men and their families, lands and lordships, that their children would have inherited them deliberately unchanged as a proud, outward sign of their succession. Where this was the case, such designs became hereditary shield devices, in other words, heraldic. It may be that friends and followers, or cadet branches of the family, would then slightly 'difference' these designs to indicate some special relationship with the original owner.[64] Alternatively, other knights, also wishing to be distinguished in battle,

references to bosses. See also F. Menéndez Pidal, *Début des Emblèmes Héraldiques en Espagne*, 11–13, 35–38, where he suggests that the rays signify social distinction.

[62] See the bosses on early proto-heraldic designs reproduced in Gras, 'Aux origines de l'héraldique', and in the well-known depiction (c.1130–40) of the dream of Henry I by John of Worcester: Oxford, Corpus Christi Coll., MS 157, 382 (*The Chronicle of John of Worcester, 1118–40*, ed. J.R.H. Weaver, Oxford 1908). The best example of an escarbuncle placed over heraldry is on the Plantagenet Enamel (see note 43 above). Waleran's seal (c.1139) depicts a large boss on his checky shield and a similar boss decorates Roger de Mowbray's fleury shield depicted on his third seal (c.1157). Later, in the *Roman de Troie* (c.1160–80) Paris carries a shield charged with a boss and a leopard (lines 11359–60). Richard I's great seal (1189) bears a lion shield charged with a boss.

[63] For examples of mid-12th century armorial (or proto-heraldic) shields without bosses see the seals illustrated in Wagner, *Heralds and Ancestors*, 12, and the MS illuminations of Goliath in the Dover Bible (Cambridge, Corpus Christi Coll., MS 3 fo 116v) and of Pliny in a frontispiece to a copy of his Natural History (Médiathèque Louis Aragon, Ville du Mans, MS C 263 fo 10v); both illustrated in Ailes, 'Heraldry in 12th-Century England: The Evidence'.

[64] Early examples of differencing are difficult to detect as much was done by colour change and our best evidence – seals – does not reveal this. Twelfth-century examples include the Warenne Group of checkered shields and the quarterly coat of the Mandevilles (see A.R.

would have adorned their accoutrements with emblems that already possessed a fixed and hereditary character of their own; perhaps such symbols were a pun on the family name. Thus, the Campdaveines, counts of St Pol, placed their wheat-sheaf symbol on their shields so that all could see that they were Campdaveines (literally, field of oats).[65]

Some men would have chosen a particular symbol or image which was personal to them as indviduals, and which they now wanted to use for identification when in full armour. According to William of Malmesbury the poet-duke, William IX of Aquitaine (d.1126), 'a giddy, unsettled chap who . . . wallowed in the sty of vice', placed the image of his mistress on his shield declaring that he would 'bear her in battle just as she bore him in bed'.[66] He may also have hoped, of course, that the aspect of her figure would have somehow unsteadied the opposition. However that may be, as Gerald of Wales notes (in about 1218), princes usually chose to adorn their shields and banners with fierce and ferocious beasts as an index of their own ferocity; such charges it was hoped might strike terror into the enemy.[67] Peter of Blois, another member of the Angevin royal court, disdainfully points out that degenerate knights of his day were all too keen to paint images of war on their saddles and shields although that was about the nearest they got to real fighting.[68]

Not all knights would have adorned their shields, pennons, surcoats and horse caparisons in order to be recognised in battle. Some may have done so for purely aesthetic reasons. Decoration lies at the very root of heraldry. Many early patterns mirrored contemporary architectural adornment, whilst others may well have owed their existence to the bands and borders that strengthened the shield, which for some time had been gaily decorated.[69] Animal charges very

Wagner, 'Heraldry' in *Medieval England*, ed. A.L. Poole, 2 vols, Oxford 1958, i, 338–381), and the lion of England (ibid., and Ailes, *Origins of the Royal Arms*, 52–53, 60–63). Roger de Mowbray's fleury shield may be a differenced version of that of Stephen, count of Brittany, d.1137 (Ailes, 'Heraldry in 12th-Century England: The Evidence', 5). The earliest examples of adding small charges to shields to difference them stem from the 1190s (Pastoureau, *Traité d'Héraldique*, 178).

65 For these and other examples see Pastoureau, 'L'origine des armoiries', 249 and figs 2–9; see also Ignacio Vicente Cascante, *Heraldica General Y Fuentes de Las Armas De Espagne*, Barcelona 1956, *passim*, for the lion of Leon, the castle of Castille and the eagle of Navarre appearing on coins and as *signa*, before being placed on the shield.

66 William of Malmesbury, *De Gestis Regum* ii, 510; C. Warren Hollister, 'Courtly Culture and Courtly Style in the Anglo-Norman World', *Albion* xx, no. 1, Spring 1988, 1–17 (15).

67 Gerald of Wales, 'De Principis Instructione Liber', in *Opera*, ed. J.S. Brewer, J.F. Dimock and G.F. Warner, 8 vols, RS 1861–91, viii, 320–21; cf. *Roman de Thèbes*, ed. de Lage, lines 779–84.

68 'Bella tamen et conflictus equestres depingi faciunt in sellis et clypeis, ut se quadam imaginaria visione delectent in pugnis, quas actualiter ingredi, aut videre non audent' (*Petri Blesensis Barthoniensis in Anglia Archidiaconi Opera Omnia*, in *Patrologia Latina*, ed. J.P. Migne, ccvii, Epist. 94, col 296).

69 See Planché, *Pursuivant of Arms*, *passim*; F.P. Barnard, 'Heraldry', in *Medieval England*, ed. H.W.C. Davis, Oxford 1924, 201–2 and figs 190–98; Lesdain, 'Études héraldiques', 202–6; and cf. Florence of Worcester, *Chronicon ex Chronicis*, ii, 195.

probably took their cue from the stylised beasts which so often decorated silks from the East. Not everybody, it should be noted, was in favour of such high fashion. In the first half of the twelfth century St Bernard of Clairvaux, the apostle of the new *milites Christi*, lambasted the way in which the profane militia covered themselves and their horses with silk wraps and decorated their lances, saddles and shields with paint, ornaments he considered better suited to the fairer sex.[70] Although such decoration may initially have been without meaning, once again, if used consistently, it would quickly become associated with its owner and in due course become the means by which he was identified when clad in mail. If then inherited it would in time also become heraldic.

What is now termed 'peer pressure' would also have persuaded many up-and-coming knights of the need to display what were fast becoming status symbols upon their accoutrements. Such emblems provided powerful outward proof of their membership of an increasingly élite social and military class. And again, once adopted and used consistently upon shields, banners and surcoats, they too would have quickly served to identify their owners in battle and tourney, taking on an heraldic nature of their own.

Thus, in the century after Hastings certain changes in the equipment of knights prompted these men for various reasons to surround themselves with certain patterns and devices. The likelihood is that many did so principally to be recognised when armed for combat. How often, however, was such recognition necessary? For certain, Europe in the twelfth century was a society organised for war. Young men, bachelor knights, like William Marshal, were trained for combat and knightly duties, often in household groups. There were also the duties of castle-guard and accompanying and protecting one's lord on his travels. Some obligations involved serjeantry duties that might include, for example, carrying the banner of one's feudal lord.[71] Pitched battles, on the other hand, demanding some means of personal identification, were relatively scarce.[72] The odds were too high; siege and strategy were preferred. It was rather in two other spheres that heraldry as a system of identification really came into its own.

The first was the tournament. It is no coincidence that the real rise of this aristocractic and knightly sport was contemporaneous with the appearance of

[70] 'Operitis equos sericis, et pendulos nescio quos panniculos loricis superinduitis; depingitis hastas clypeos et sellas; . . . Militaria sunt haec insignia, an muliebria potius ornamenta?' S. *Bernadi Clarae-Vallensis Abbatis Primi Opera Omnia*, ed. D. Joannis Mabillon, *Patrologia Latina*, ed. J.P. Migne, clxxxii, col 923; Duby, *Legend of Bouvines*, 99.

[71] A.L. Poole, *Obligations of Society in the Twelfth and Thirteenth Centuries*, Oxford 1944, 72, and C. Warren Hollister, *The Military Organisation of Norman England*, Oxford 1965, 221 and n. 2.

[72] Duby, *Legend of Bouvines*, 112–13; Verbruggen, *Art of Warfare*, 288–89. William Marshal only took the field in two pitched battles (Crouch, *William Marshal*, 181–82). Another 'chivalric' figure, Richard I, only fought two, perhaps three, battles (John Gillingham, 'Richard I and the Science of War in the Middle Ages', in *War and Government in the Middle Ages*, ed. J. Gillingham and J.C. Holt, Woodbridge 1984, 78–91 (81)). Henry II never fought a single battle and Philip Augustus only the one (ibid.).

true heraldry, namely in the second quarter of the twelfth century.[73] Initially tournaments consisted of no more than a series of general mêlées spread over a large area and often over many days. The more chivalric 'jousting' between two individuals seems to have become the vogue in the later twelfth century, if the romances are to be believed. As far as heraldry was concerned, these knightly exercises provided a particularly fertile environment for its growth and dissemination. First and foremost they provided regular opportunities for knights and groups of knights to come together in full armour and 'do battle'. If actual battles were relatively rare then a young man in the second half of the twelfth century could participate in the next best thing – a tournament – as often as once a fortnight.[74] The fact that they were usually fought between teams – for example, the Angevins and the French or, in England, the northerners and the southerners – made it doubly important for participants, spectators and judges to know one side from the other.[75] It is thus not surprising that many of our early references to knights being identified by their arms, or indeed confusing everyone else by appearing under false colours, arise from tournament scenes.[76] Moreover, although there is as yet hardly any evidence for rules and judges, it is at this stage, in the 1170s, that heralds of arms, who were later to supervise these occasions, appear for the first time within the context of these mock battles.[77] As we have already noted, they would have needed a good knowledge of the various arms used and from an early stage would have exercised some form of control in the adoption and design of shield devices so as to avoid confusion. Tournaments also provided excellent occasions for spectacle and display, and must therefore have greatly encouraged the appearance and proliferation of bright shield devices, banners and crests.

The other context in which knights could display new devices was the seal. From the second quarter of the twelfth century, seals, like tournaments and heraldry, became something of a vogue amongst these classes and again, like heraldry, began to descend the social ladder as those below aspired to the manners and practices of their social superiors.[78] Such men naturally wished to be portrayed according to their status and position in society, namely, as a fully

---

73 Barber and Barker (*Tournaments*, 16) point to the fact that between 1125 and 1130 there is a sudden crop of tournament references in chronicle sources; our first known coat of arms dates to 1128. For tournaments in the 12th century see Duby, *Legend of Bouvines*, 84–97 and Crouch, *William Marshal*, 174–78 and bibliography, 211–12.

74 Crouch, *William Marshal*, 175.

75 Teams often fought in tightly knit groups or 'conrois'. In the second half of the 12th century bands of men fought under knights banneret (such as William Marshal) – commanders who could raise their own heraldic banner.

76 See above pp. 2–4.

77 See refs to *Lancelot*, *Yvain* and the *Hist. de G. le Maréchal* in n. 48 above.

78 Richard de Lucy (d.1179), Henry II's justiciar, complained that 'in former times it was not the custom for every petty knight (*quislibet militulus*) to have a seal which is appropriate only for kings and great men' (*The Chronicle of Battle Abbey*, ed. and trans. E. Searle, 1980, 214); cf. the passage in a grant by Geoffrey de Mandeville (d.1166), 2nd Earl of Essex: 'Istam cartam

armoured knight on horseback – hence the familiar equestrian seal of the Middle Ages. Here again, though, as in the tournament, one knight could look very much like another, unless distinguished in some way. Moreover, it was especially important in an illiterate age that the seal owner be easily identifiable to all. The problem was greatly alleviated by ensuring that the knight depicted bore a unique personal device (be it a pre-existing family emblem or something new) by which he could be recognised. Indeed, by the end of the twelfth century a single shield of arms on its own had, in some cases, come to be used either as a counterseal or instead of the equestrian portrait of the owner-knight.[79] This was the first time that arms were to stand in the place of their owners. Seals thus provided another excellent opportunity for either adopting a shield device for the first time or for further displaying one's coat of arms. They also brought armorial bearings into the non-martial world of women, and later bishops and merchants.[80] Their precision of detail also allowed for greater sophistication in the design of arms, so that combinations of two or more coats on a single shield to denote some form of alliance could now be prominently displayed in military and civilian life.[81]

The origins of heraldry thus owe a great deal to knights in the twelfth century needing some form of identification in the tournament, battle or on their seals. The evidence, particularly the increasing use of more systematic designs which could be readily identified in battle and the references to 'connoissances' (literally emblems of recognition) in contemporary texts, bear this out. For at least one mid-twelfth-century writer identification was clearly the raison d'être of these new cognizances or distinguishing marks. That these developments occurred in the twelfth, and not the tenth or eleventh, centuries was not due to changes in armour making knights more difficult to recognise. Rather they were the result of a number of factors coming together for the first time. Recognition was certainly one of these, probably the most important one. The ability of

feci signari sigillo dapiferi mei . . . donec sim miles et habeam sigillum, et tunc eam firmabo proprio sigillo' (quoted in Barnard, 'Heraldry', 204).

[79] For the introduction of the 'armorial seal' see Brigitte Bedos Rezak, 'L'Apparition des Armoiries sur les Sceaux en Ile-de France et en Picardie', 27–29, and idem, 'Les Sceaux au Temps de Philippe Auguste' in La France de Philippe Auguste, ed. R-H. Bautier, 721–36 (728–29); Ailes, 'Heraldry in 12th-Century England', 8–9; Léon Jéquier, 'Début et développement de l'emploi des armoiries dans les sceaux', XV Congreso Internacional de las Ciencias, Genealogica y Heraldica, Madrid 1983, 317–43 (335–36), but cf. Pastoureau, 'La Diffusion des Armoiries et les Débuts de l'Héraldique', 741 and n. 12.

[80] Rohese, sister of Gilbert de Clare, first earl of Hertford, was using a seal charged with the Clare chevrons after 1156 (Birch, Cat. Seals in Br. Mus., no. 13048; British Heraldry, 16); for the use of arms by bishops and merchants see Pastoureau, Traité d'Héraldique, 49–51, and D.L. Galbreath, Manuel du Blason, revd L. Jéquier, Lausanne 1977, 43–52.

[81] Examples, however, are late. The composite coats of Robert de Pinkney (1195) and William de Mauleon (1199) may be examples of the combination of two coats on a single shield (Cat. Seals in Br. Mus., no. 12646 and Sir Christopher Hatton's Book of Seals, ed. L.C. Loyd and D.M. Stenton, Oxford 1950, no. 351). For 13th-century examples see Galbreath, Manuel du Blason, 218–220.

20

knights now to 'decorate' new and relatively large surface areas of their accoutrements, and to display the results regularly in tournaments and on seals,
quickly ensured the popularity of these designs as an effective means of identification. It is true that some knights may have had other reasons for displaying
such devices, but whatever the initial reason for their appearance in individual
cases, within a matter of decades they had all taken on the role of identification.
Within an equally short space of time their potential as indicators of class, status
and connections, both family and feudal, helped bring about their hereditary
use well beyond any military functions they originally served. That, however, is
another story.

# 'Si waren aines muotes': Unanimity in Konrad's Rolandslied and Otto's and Rahewin's Gesta Frederici

JEFFREY ASHCROFT

Konrad's German adaptation of the *Chanson de Roland*[1] provides a focus for debate about the feasibility and the propriety of interpreting medieval literary narrative as a contribution to the political and ideological consciousness of its audiences.[2] For several reasons there might seem to be secure grounds for attributing such a function to the *Rolandslied*. Major themes: sacral kingship and feudal loyalty, holy war to convert the heathen and expand the universal dominion of the Christian Roman Empire, have political resonance already in the Old French source.[3] Konrad translated the ancient *geste* of Charlemagne into German in the period of the second half of the twelfth century when the

1   *Das Rolandslied des Pfaffen Konrad*, ed. C. Wesle, 2nd edn by P. Wapnewski, Altdeutsche Textbibliothek lxix, Tübingen 1967 (quoted henceforth as *RL*); *La Chanson de Roland*, ed. F. Whitehead, Oxford 1946 (quoted henceforth as *Ch*). K.-E. Geith, 'Zur Stellung des *Rolandsliedes* innerhalb der Überlieferung der *Chanson de Roland*', in J. Heinzle, L.P. Johnson & G. Vollmann-Profe, eds., *Wolfram-Studien XI: Chansons de Geste in Deutschland. Schweinfurter Kolloquium 1988*, Berlin 1989, 32–46, shows that Konrad's source manuscript mediated between the α and β branches of the *Roland* transmission.
2   F. Ohly, 'Zum Reichsgedanken des deutschen *Rolandsliedes*', ZfdA lxxvii, 1940, 189–217, rightly rejects older readings of the poem as Welf propaganda but insists too emphatically on its religious inspiration and functions. The interpretation of the *Rolandslied* as a work which articulates contemporary political and ideological values is exemplified by E. Nellmann, *Die Reichsidee in deutschen Dichtungen der Salier- und frühen Stauferzeit*, Philologische Studien und Quellen xvi, Berlin 1963, and M. Ott-Meimberg, *Kreuzzugsepos oder Staatsroman? Strukturen adeliger Heilsversicherung im deutschen 'Rolandslied'*, Münchener Texte und Untersuchungen zur deutschen Literatur des Mittelalters lxx, Munich 1980.
3   The testimony of Gui de Ponthieu, William of Malmesbury and Wace suggest the adaptability of the feudal and chivalric values of the *Chanson* for the Normans in 1066. See D.D.R. Owen, 'The Epic and History: *Chanson de Roland* and *Carmen de Hastingae Proelio*', Medium

Carolingian model of *sacrum imperium* had central significance in the political and ideological programme of the emperor Frederick I.[4] If, as is now generally assumed, Konrad's poem dates from around 1170, it followed hard on the canonisation of Charlemagne at Frederick's instigation.[5] Its patron, Henry the Lion, duke of Saxony and Bavaria, was the most powerful and controversial of Frederick's magnates. He presumably acquired a manuscript of the *Chanson de Roland* through his marriage in 1168 to Mathilda, daughter of Henry II of England. In commissioning or in listening to 'his' version of the story, it is not likely that Henry was inattentive to the significance of Charlemagne as a legitimising model of kingship or forgetful of his own claim to Carolingian lineage; nor that he failed to associate the synthesis of holy war to expand the Christian empire and crusading chivalry in the Bernardine mode, which is one major thrust of Konrad's adaptation, with his own prime enterprise in the 1160s and 1170s, the conquest, colonisation and conversion of Slav territories to the east and north of his ancestral duchy of Saxony – itself first conquered and converted by Charlemagne – which since 1147 had possessed the aura and sanction of crusade.[6]

Konrad in any case makes the connection for his patron in the epilogue to the poem:

> daz si sin ie gedachten,
> daz man iz fur brachte
> in tutische zungin gekeret,
> da ist daz riche wol mit geret.
> [. . .]
> Nune mugen wir in disem zite
> dem chuoninge Dauite
> niemen so wol gelichen
> so den herzogen Hainrichen.     (*RL* 9031–9034, 9039–9042)

That they [Henry and Mathilda] took pains to procure it
[*scil.* 'the book which was written in France', lines 9022–

*Aevum* li, 1982, 18–34. For political interpretations of the *Chanson* with bearing on the subject of this essay, see K.-H. Bender, *König und Vasall: Untersuchungen zum Chanson de geste des 12. Jahrhunderts*, Studia Romanica xiii, Heidelberg 1967, and E. Köhler, '*Conseil des barons' und 'Jugement des barons'. Epische Fatalität und Feudalrecht im altfranzösischen Rolandslied*. Sitzungsberichte der Heidelberger Akademie der Wissenschaften, Philosophisch-historische Klasse 1968, iv.

4 See Heinrich Appelt, 'Die Kaiseridee Friedrich Barbarossas', in Gunther Wolf, ed., *Friedrich Barbarossa*, Wege der Forschung ccxc, Darmstadt 1975, 208–244.

5 Although Konrad gives Karl the attributes of a saintly king-confessor, he does not accord him the title *sante*. See the discussion by D. Kartschoke, *Die Datierung des deutschen Rolandsliedes*, Stuttgart 1965, 158–167.

6 For a general account of Henry, see K. Jordan, *Heinrich der Löwe*, Munich 1979. On his crusading activity, see F. Lotter, 'Die Vorstellung von Heidenkrieg und Wendenmission bei Heinrich dem Löwen', in W.-D. Mohrmann, ed., *Heinrich der Löwe*, Veröffentlichungen der Niedersächsischen Archivverwaltung, Heft xxxix, Göttingen 1980, 11–43.

9023] and have it turned into German, brings honour to
the empire. [. . .] Now in this age we can compare no-one
with King David so appropriately as Duke Henry.

Discreetly, perhaps since his patron was not the exclusive claimant to the
mantle of Charlemagne around 1170, Konrad here promotes Henry's claim to
embody Carolingian virtues: as *novus David* he acquires an honorific title which
since Charlemagne denotes the monarch, in particular the wearer of the imperial crown, as typological fulfilment of ideal theocratic kingship.[7] What jus-
tifies this claim is first and foremost Henry's prosecution of holy war to conquer
and convert the Slavs:

> got gap ime di craft
> daz er alle sine uiande eruacht.
> di cristen hat er wol geret,
> di haiden sint uon im bekeret:
> daz erbet in uon rechte an.   (RL 9043–9047)

God gave him the strength to defeat all his foes. He has
exalted Christendom and converted the heathen. This is
his rightful inheritance.

These lines in the epilogue refer back to and quote the opening passage of the
*Rolandslied* in which Konrad attributes Karl's assured place in the presence of
God to the fact that

> . . . er mit gote uoberwant
> uil manige heideniske lant,
> da er di cristin hat mit geret   (RL 13–15)

---

7   E. Nellmann, 'Karl der Große und König David im Epilog des deutschen *Rolandsliedes*', ZfdA
xciv, 1965, 268–279 (reprinted in R. Schnell, ed., *Die Reichsidee in der deutschen Dichtung des
Mittelalters*, Wege der Forschung dlxxxix, Darmstadt 1983, 222–238). Lines 9050–9052 quote
the earlier twelfth-century poem *Lob Salomos* (lines 150–152), which are themselves a
paraphrase of Revelations 22:5, and thus allude to the explicit comparison of Karl with
Solomon in the description of the reception of Genelun's envoys at his court, lines 671–673.
The epilogue also appears to borrow formulations from the obituary to the emperor Lothar
III, Henry the Lion's maternal grandfather, in the *Kaiserchronik* (ed. E. Schröder, MGH,
Deutsche Chroniken I, lines 17165–17181). See also G. Vollmann-Profe, *Geschichte der
deutschen Literatur von den Anfängen bis zum Beginn der Neuzeit*, ed. Joachim Heinzle, Bd. 1:
*Von den Anfängen zum hohen Mittelalter*, Teil 2: *Wiederbeginn volkssprachiger Schriftlichkeit im
hohen Mittelalter*, Königstein/Ts 1986, 134–135. Arnold of Lübeck, *Chronica Slavorum*, MGH,
Scriptores rerum Germanicarum, 1868, 193, compares Henry, *cultor pacis*, with Solomon in
his obituary of the duke. The seven-branched candelabra probably donated by Henry to his
new cathedral in Braunschweig in 1170–1180 has been held to betoken an imitation by
Henry of Solomon's gifts to the Temple. See P. Bloch, 'Siebenarmige Leuchter in christlichen
Kirchen', *Wallraf-Richartz Jahrbuch* xxiii, 1961, 55–190.

25

with God's help he subdued many a heathen land and
thereby exalted Christendom.

Henry, *nepos Karoli*[8] and *alter David*, renews in his own age the Carolingian
*dilatio imperii*.

That Carolingian history in vernacular epic narrative could offer Konrad's
patron and contemporary audiences a legitimising precedent and an exemplary
model for the Wendish crusade on the marches of the empire, finds support in
the principal historiographical source for Henry's campaigns, the *Chronica Slavorum* of Helmold of Bosau, written in the same years as the *Rolandslied*.[9] Helmold
sees the Saxon wars of Charlemagne, 'most glorious of all the courageous propa-
gators of Christian faith . . . who have laboured for God in Northern parts', and
Otto the Great being continued and brought to a triumphant climax by Henry
the Lion:

> More than all the dukes before him, more even than the renowned Otto,
> he has broken the might of the Slavs [. . .] the whole domain of the Slavs
> [. . .] is by God's grace transformed into one colony of Saxons where the
> numbers of churches and servants of Christ multiply.[10]

Also common to the vernacular epic and the Latin chronicle is the integration
of twelfth-century crusading chivalry into the ancient tradition of imperial holy
war. Konrad affixes the badge of the cross to Karl and his warriors, lards their
exhortations before and during battle with the idiom of crusading sermon and
chronicle and depicts them as Bernardine *novi milites*. Helmold subjects Henry
the Lion to the expectations of a crusading prince once he has taken the cross in
1147 and helped force upon St Bernard the diversion of the North German
crusaders to the lands beyond the Elbe.[11] The major chronicler of Henry's later
years, Arnold of Lübeck, describes how the duke celebrated his triumphal status
as pacifier and converter of the heathen by undertaking an armed pilgrimage to
the Holy Land in 1172.[12] The synthesis of *dilatio imperii* and *peregrinatio crucis* in

---

8   As Henry is termed in the dedicatory poem of the Helmarshausen Evangelistary. See U.
    Victor, 'Das Widmungsgedicht im Evangeliar Heinrichs des Löwen und sein Verfasser', *ZfdA*
    cxiv, 1985, 302–329.
9   Ed. H. Stoob, Freiherr-vom-Stein-Gedächtnisausgabe, Darmstadt 1973 (henceforth identi-
    fied in quotations as CS). See J. Ashcroft, 'Konrad's *Rolandslied*, Henry the Lion, and the
    Northern Crusade', *Forum for Modern Language Studies* xxii, 1986, 184–208.
10  '. . . gloriosissimus [. . .] et in fronte statuendus eorum, qui pro Deo in partibus aquilonis
    laboraverunt': CS 3, 42; '. . . qui protrivit robur Slavorum super omnes duces, qui fuerunt ante
    eum, plus multo quam ille nominatus Otto [. . .] Omnis enim Slavorum regio [. . .] nunc dante
    Deo tota redacta est veluti in unam Saxonum coloniam, et instruuntur illis civitates et
    oppida, et multiplicantur ecclesiae et numerus ministrorum Christi': CS 109–110, 378–382.
11  See Lotter (n. 6, above).
12  Arnold, *Chronica*, 10–31. Henry appears to have hoped for a military deployment, as crusader
    rather than mere pilgrim, in the Holy Land until dissuaded by King Amalric and the

epic and chronicle is evidence of a similarity of concern on the part of clerical poet and clerical historian. Certainly, Helmold is frequently highly critical of Henry's failure to measure up to ideal models and the expectations of the Church. (Among contemporaries he was a byword for arrogance, avarice and ruthlessness towards friends and foes alike.)[13] Only in the later 1160s does Helmold depict Henry successfully combining his territorial ambitions with the effective propagation of the faith and thus finally responding to a long struggle by the Church in Saxony to influence his perception of the aims and methods of the Slav wars.[14] The synthesis of imperial theocracy and chivalric crusade is realised less problematically in Konrad's epic in the form of an ideal prescription for his patron, offering him an exemplary identity as the proponent in his own age of the fusion of Carolingian traditions with a crusading piety of Bernardine stamp, *novus David* and *novus miles*.

The clerical historian Helmold, who dedicates his chronicle to the canons of Lübeck and to the memory of his teacher Gerold, its first bishop, (CS Praefatio) has a more critical attitude to Henry the Lion, frequently at odds with the Saxon Church, than the clerical poet Konrad, writing at the direct commission of Henry and Mathilde, shows in his panegyrical epilogue. However, poet and chronicler show a like concern to urge upon Henry the Lion a sense of Christian mission, informed by Carolingian historical example and contemporary crusading ideology. Their common ground is explicable not only in terms of education and clerical affiliations[15] or possible common audiences and readership,[16] but

Templars. See E. Joranson, 'The Palestine Pilgrimage of Henry the Lion', in J.L. Cate & E.N. Anderson, eds., *Medieval and Historiographical Essays in Honor of James Westfall Thompson*, Chicago 1938, 146–225; H.E. Mayer, 'Die Stiftung Herzog Heinrichs des Löwen für das Heilige Grab', in W.-D. Mohrmann, ed., *Heinrich der Löwe* (see n. 6, above), 307–330.

13 See H.W. Wurster, 'Das Bild Heinrichs des Löwen in der mittelalterlichen Chronistik Deutschlands und Englands', in W.-D. Mohrmann, ed., *Heinrich der Löwe* (as n. 6, above).

14 Jordan, *Heinrich der Löwe*, especially Chapter 4; Lotter, 'Heidenkrieg und Wendenmission' (both as n. 6, above).

15 Konrad admits in lines 9080–9083 that he first translated his Old French source into Latin, then into German. The significance of his Latin-orientated culture for an understanding of the ideological concepts and vocabulary of the *Rolandslied* is as yet little explored. See D. Kartschoke, '*in die latine bedwungin*. Kommunikationsprobleme im Mittelalter und die Übersetzung der *Chanson de Roland* durch den Pfaffen Konrad', *Beiträge zur Geschichte der deutschen Sprache und Literatur* cxi, 1989, 196–209.

16 While Helmold dedicates his Chronicle to the canons of Lübeck, it is unlikely that this, the major narrative of the first half of Henry's reign, was not also received at the ducal court. Konrad's poem, as lines 9031–9034 confirm, was primarily intended to be read to his patrons at court; the early manuscript copy A belonged to the Hospitallers in Strasburg and, especially in its modernised version by Der Stricker, the poem was popular with the brothers of the Deutschorden (see B. Schumacher, 'Die Idee der geistlichen Ritterorden im Mittelalter', in H. Beumann, ed., *Heidenmission und Kreuzzugsgedanke*, Wege der Forschung vii, Darmstadt 1963, 374f.; P. Strauch, *Die Deutschordensliteratur des Mittelalters*, Halle 1910, 29; H. Finger, 'Untersuchungen zur Geschichte der Bibliothek des Deutschen Ordens in Mergentheim. Teil I', *Gutenberg Jahrbuch* lv, 1980, 325–54), and as a quasi-hagiographical text the work may have been employed as refectory reading matter in monastic contexts (see F. Ohly, 'Zum

also in terms of similarities in the functions of chronicle and epic. For Konrad, it is evident, the story of Charlemagne and Roland is historical validation, proto-type and exemplar for Henry the Lion's fulfilment of his Carolingian inherit-ance and his conduct of the office of Christian ruler and crusader.

Given that the comparison of historical epic and chronicle sheds light on shared ideological suppositions and functions, it seems permissible to ask what common ground may be established between the *Rolandslied* and a further major historiographical work of the 1160s, in which Henry the Lion plays a less central but still significant role: the *Gesta Frederici* of Otto of Freising and Rahewin. This is the major contemporary testimony to the ideology of empire and its realisation in the political programme of Frederick Barbarossa. My paper takes as its focus and point of comparison a theme: unanimity as an exemplary component of the relationship between king and nobles in the Christian *res publica*, which has salient importance both in key passages of the *Rolandslied* where Konrad significantly departs from or expands his source, and in the passages of the *Gesta Frederici* where Otto and Rahewin depict the relationship of Frederick I and Henry the Lion.

Unanimity in the New Testament, pre-eminently in the Pauline Epistles, ex-presses the fraternal solidarity and likemindedness, *unanimes, una voce*, of the early Christians (Romans 15:5–6, cf. I Corinthians 1:10, Galatians 3:26–28, Ephesians 4:4–6, Philippians 1:27, 2:1–4, I Peter 3:8). When Konrad cites Psalm 132 as a typological prefiguration of the unanimity of crusading chivalry:

> Dauid psalmista
> hat uon in gescriben da:
> 'wi groze in lonet min trechtin,
> di bruderlich mit ain ander sin!
> er biutet in selbe sinen segen,
> si scuolen iemir urolichen leben',     (RL 3453–3458)

> David the psalmist wrote of them: 'How great a reward
> my Lord gives to those who live together like brothers.
> He bestows his own blessing upon them and they shall
> live joyfully for ever more',

he not only invokes the biblical imperative of unanimity but also shows his awareness of its specific place among the virtues of the spiritual and literal *militia dei*. The suppression of individual will is an aspect of obedience as required of

---

Dichtungsschluß *Tu autem, domine, miserere nobis*', *Deutsche Vierteljahrsschrift* xlvii, 1973, 26–68). J. Bumke argues against polarisation of the 'clerical' and the 'secular' in assessing the genesis and functions of vernacular literature in the twelfth century: *Höfische Kultur*, Munich 1986, 683.

the monk by the Rule of St Benedict.[17] The chronicle literature of the First Crusade, in formulating crusading chivalry as a 'novum militiae genus [. . .] qua gemino pariter conflictu infatigabiliter decertatur, tum adversus carnem et sanguinem, tum contra spiritualia nequitiae',[18] sees unanimity both as a spiritual response to the call to imitate Christ and as the military duty of warriors serving their God in battle. Thus when the crusaders, in Robert the Monk's account of the sermon at Clermont, respond with one voice to Urban II's appeal, the Pope bids them show the same solidarity in warfare by turning their call 'Deus vult' into a unanimous battlecry.[19] The *Gesta Francorum*, depicting the same response to Urban's sermon: 'Franci audientes talia, protinus in dextra fecere cruces suere scapula, dicentes sese Christi unanimiter sequi vestigia', then shows this fraternal unity in action: 'Estote omnimodo unanimes in fide Christi et sanctae crucis vexilli victoria'; 'nostrique unanimiter invaserunt Turcos, qui omnes stupefacti arripuerunt fugam'.[20] Here as in other respects Bernard of Clairvaux brings the concepts and formulation of the dual *militia dei* to their ultimate refinement. Of the Templars he demands: 'Dicas universae multitudinis esse cor unum et animam unam, ita quisque non omnino propriam sequi voluntatem sed magis obsequi satagit imperanti'. The Rule of the Templars subsumes the Benedictine requirements of obedience and abnegation of self-will; Psalm 132 forms part of the rite of reception into the order: 'Et le frere chapelain doit dire que l'on dit, Ecce quam bonum [et quam iucundum, habitare fratres in unum]', and the assumption of the entrant knight into the brotherhood of the order is sealed with the kiss of peace, as Konrad's warriors too exchange it: 'ain ander si chusten. / daz pace si ainander gaben' (*RL* 5782–5783).[21]

Unanimity as an insistent theme in the *Rolandslied* forms part, it seems clear, of Konrad's injection of crusading piety into the chivalric ethos of the *Chanson de Roland*. There is much evidence in the text that the writings of St Bernard were a particularly important source for him.[22] While precise routes of transmission are impossible to reconstruct, Bernard's role in the designation of the Slav campaigns as a crusade in 1147, the interest in the military orders apparent in Germany as a result of the participation of German knights in the Second

---

17 *Benedicti Regula*, ed. R. Hanslik, Corpus Scriptorum Ecclesiasticorum Latinorum lxxv, Vienna 1960, chaps 4–5 and 71, pp. 29–38, 161–162.

18 Bernard of Clairvaux, *De laude novae militiae*, in J.P. Migne, *Patrologia latina*, clxxxii, 921C.

19 *Historia Hiersolimitana*, in *Recueil des historiens des croisades, Historiens occidentaux* iii, Paris 1866, 729C–D.

20 *Anonymi Gesta Francorum*, ed. H. Hagenmeyer, Heidelberg 1890, I,3; IX,7; XVII,6.

21 *La Règle du Temple*, ed. H. de Curzon, Paris 1886, 168 & 345. The *pax tecum* was of course also a familiar part of the Roman rite and of monastic liturgical practice. See F.-W. Wentzlaff-Eggebert, *Kreuzzugsdichtung des Mittelalters*, Berlin 1960, 94f.

22 Wentzlaff-Eggebert, 91–98; for detailed analysis of echoes of crusading sermons and chronicles in the poem, see H. Richter, *Kommentar zum Rolandslied des Pfaffen Konrad. Teil I*, Kanadische Studien zur deutschen Sprache und Literatur vi, Bern/Frankfurt 1972.

Crusade proper,[23] and the growing general dissemination of the ideals of crusade in the second half of the twelfth century, form the general context of Konrad's reception of the concepts and idiom of redemptive chivalry. However, some more specific forces can be discerned. It is possible that the first German benefactor of the Templars had been the emperor Lothar III, Henry the Lion's revered grandfather,[24] whose ancestral castle of Süpplingenburg in Saxony may have been donated to the order as early as 1130.[25] Henry the Lion certainly had close dealings with the Templars and made donations of arms and money to the order during his pilgrimage to the Holy Land in 1172.[26] The Templars' only North German properties were in Saxony and the Welf family retained a continuing affiliation with the order.[27] Margrave Albrecht the Bear had donated Werben on the Elbe to the Hospitallers in 1160.[28] Manuscript A of the *Rolandslied*, written in the last third of the twelfth century, belonged to the library of the Hospitallers in Strasbourg. In Der Stricker's modernised early thirteenth-century reworking, Konrad's poem figures prominently in library catalogues of the Teutonic Order.[29] Such historical evidence bears out that Konrad's spiritualisation of the chivalric ethos of the chanson de geste has a definable locus in twelfth-century Saxony and in the concerns of his ducal patron.

The consistent stress on unanimity, common purpose and collective commitment as a motor of decision and action is a new emphasis in the German poem. None of the passages in which Konrad refers to *ainmuot* and its cognates has a direct correspondence in the extant manuscripts of the *Chanson de Roland*. The thematic significance of unanimity is established immediately in the expository section (*RL* 1–360) which represents Konrad's most extensive and revealing expansion of his source. Here Karl receives from God's angel the divine com-

---

[23] H. Prutz, *Die geistlichen Ritterorden*, Berlin 1908, 308–310; K.W. Klein, *Die Ausbreitung des Johanniterordens in Oberdeutschland bis zum Jahre 1317*, Freiburg i.B. 1922, 14f.; J. von Pflugk-Harttung, *Die Anfänge des Johanniter-Ordens in Deutschland*, Berlin 1899, 6; M. Schüpferling, *Der Tempelherren-Orden in Deutschland*, Bamberg 1915, 87f, 240f.; H. Lüpke, *Untersuchungen zur Geschichte des Tempelordens im Gebiet der nordostdeutschen Kolonisation*, Bernburg 1933, 10f.

[24] Invoked by Henry in charters (see *Die Urkunden Heinrichs des Löwen*, ed. K. Jordan, MGH, Die deutschen Geschichtsquellen des Mittelalters, 1949, e.g. nos. 48 and 81), in the 'coronation miniature' of the Helmershausen Evangelistary (see *Evangeliar Heinrichs des Löwen. Vollfaksimile des Codex Guelf. 105 Noviss. 2° der Herzog August Bibliothek in Wolfenbüttel*, Frankfurt 1989, fol. 171v), and on the dedicatory inscription of the altar to the Virgin in Braunschweig (see H.-H. Möller, 'Zur Geschichte des Marienaltars im Braunschweiger Dom', *Deutsche Kunst- und Denkmalpflege* xxv, 1967, 107–118).

[25] Prutz, *Ritterorden* (as n. 23, above), 335.

[26] Mayer, 'Die Stiftung Herzog Heinrichs' (see n. 12, above). Mathilda's father Henry II of England paid an annual fee to the Templars from 1172 as part of his penance for the murder of Thomas Becket.

[27] Prutz, 235; Lüpke (see n. 23, above), 10f.

[28] Lüpke, 11.

[29] See n. 16 above.

mission to undertake a missionary war, *bellum deo auctore*, against the pagans in Spain. Of his obedient response, as 'gotes dinistman' ('God's vassal', lines 31, 55), there is no question. But he observes the feudal procedures by consulting his paladins,

> . . . zwelf herren,
> di di wisistin waren,
> die sines heres phlegeten.
> [. . .]
> si waren guote chnechte,
> des keiseres uoruechten.   (*RL* 67–69, 71–71)

> twelve lords, who were the wisest of his military leaders
> [. . .] brave knights who were the emperor's champions.

Their unanimous consent to the expedition expresses a double sense of allegiance, as *fideles dei et regis* to Karl as *keiser* and to God:

> 'ia hat iu got hie gegebin
> ein uil uolliclichez lebin;
> daz hat er umbe daz getan,
> sin dinist wil er da uon han.
> swer durch got arbeitet,
> sin lon wirt ime gereitet,
> da der keiser allir hiemele
> uorderet hin widere,
> daz er iu uirlihin hat'.   (*RL* 91–99)

> 'God has given you abundance on earth and for that now
> requires His service. Whoever takes on hardship for God
> receives his reward there where the emperor of all heaven
> demands back what He has conferred on you'.

In turn the twelve summon their vassals and give them the free choice of rendering help.

> si redeten alle gemeinlichen
> si ne wolten in niemer geswichen;
> swaz si durch got wolten bestan,
> des ne wolten si nicht abe gan.   (*RL* 141–144)

> All spoke with common voice that they would never
> yield from their side and would not go back on their
> commitment to God.

When the great army assembles, having adopted the badge of the cross, Karl promises divine reward to all who have left 'wip oder kint [. . .] hus oder eigen'

31

('wife or child, house or lands', lines 184–185) for God's sake. The warriors must pledge not only military arms but their spiritual commitment:

> 'habet stetigen muot,
> habet zucht mit guote,
> wesit demuote,
> wesit got unter tan,
> uwir meisterschefte unter tan;
> welt ir also uol komen,
> so uindit ir dar ze hiemele daz lon
> der ewigin genaden'.   (RL 214–221)

> 'Be firm of heart, keep good discipline, be humble and
> obedient both to God and to your commanders. Do this
> to your utmost and you shall find in heaven the reward of
> eternal grace'.

Archbishop Turpin elaborates these injunctions of the crusading homily[30] into an ambitious programme of militant piety for the 'heiligin pilgerime' ('holy pilgrims', line 245) reminiscent of Bernard of Clairvaux's *De laude novae militiae*:[31]

> 'trinket den kelh den er tranc,
> eret daz uil heilige cruce;
> mine uil libin lúte,
> minnet sibin tagezit,
> daz retet der kuoninc Dauid:
> ir scult spade unt fru sin,
> so erhoret uch min trechtin.
> uwer spise si gemeine,
> daz herze machet reine'.   (RL 258–266)

> 'Drink the cup that [Christ] drank, honour the holy cross.
> Dearly beloved brethren, worship God seven times a day,
> as King David admonishes: serve Him night and day, that
> the Lord may hear you. Let your food be plain and com-
> mon to all, and purify your hearts'.

It emerges already from Konrad's new introductory section that unanimity acquires its imperative force through the interaction of three allegiances. The theocratic role of Karl, whose kingship embodies the temporal rule of God as *rex regum* ('cheiser allir chuoninge', line 2), enforces on his subjects the require-

---

[30] See the biblical and homiletical parallels cited by Richter, *Kommentar* (see n. 22, above), 79–86.
[31] Richter, 99–102.

ment of unquestioning loyalty to the heavenly king through his earthly *vicarius*. Precisely the traitor Genelun expounds this to the heathen:

> 'sinen boten uon himele
> sendet er zuo dem kuonige;
> der gebiutet ime die hereuart.
> so ne ist des nehein rat,
> wir enhelfen ime da zuo.
> [. . .]
> got ist selbe mit ime'.   (*RL* 1797–1802, 1808)

'[God] sends His angel from heaven to the king and commands him to wage war; so there is no question but that we support him [. . .] God Himself is with him'.

At the same time Karl is scrupulous in consulting his barons and they in gaining the consent of their men 'daz irz willeclichen tuot' ('that you do it of your own free will', line 213). The vocabulary of feudal co-operation is as pervasive in the *Rolandslied* as in the *Chanson de Roland*. As we shall see, Konrad is also aware of and exercised by the potential for tension and conflict between the descending and the ascending themes of royal power and the conceptions of allegiance which these involve: authority deriving simultaneously from theocratic sacrality and from the 'willing' consent of vassals. In his opening depiction of the mobilisation of imperial holy war, which defines a model valid for the poem as a whole, Konrad uses the crusading vow as the third and overriding bond which secures the whole nexus of allegiances. The warrior's service is solicited by the emperor and fulfilled through fealty to him; but it is simultaneously a free act of commitment to God, a personal *imitatio Christi* to be rewarded not in *dulce France* but in heaven. Unanimity of response is doubly motivated and enforced, by the sacral character of Karl's royal sanction, which requires his subjects to be *fideles dei et regis*, and by the direct reciprocity of the knights' personal bond of fealty with God, which renders the king less the direct focus than the filter of allegiance. There is obvious potential for tension and conflict here too, once not only the king but each individual warrior is 'gotes dinistman' (and Konrad indeed bestows this epithet both on Karl as *rex in vice dei* and on crusaders collectively and severally).[32] In the initial paradigm, however, Konrad is at pains to show how theocratic sanction, feudal loyalty and crusading vow complement and reinforce one another.

This conception of politico-religious allegiances, ideologically more complex than we find in the *Chanson de Roland*, meets a first test of its viability in the council episode (*RL* lines 891–1749), where, in the traditional story,

---

[32] E.g. lines 31, 55, 801 (Karl); 3063, 4101, 4405 (warriors). See R.A. Wisbey & C. Hall, *A Complete Concordance to the Rolandslied*, Compendia iii, Leeds 1969.

Charlemagne seeks the advice of his barons as to how he shall respond to the offer of the pagan king Marsile to render tribute and hostages in return for the withdrawal of the French army from Spain pending the eventual baptism of Marsile and his people. In the Old French poem there ensues a tensely narrated debate (*Ch* 157–341). Roland argues vehemently against the acceptance of peace terms and for a renewed military offensive. Ganelon urges trust in Marsile and accuses Roland of arrogance and folly. He finds support from Naimes and the general assent of the barons. The question is then whom to send as envoy to the heathen court to convey Charlemagne's peace terms. Naimes, Roland, Oliver and Turpin all volunteer and the emperor rejects them. Roland proposes his stepfather Ganelon, to the acclamation of the barons. Ganelon's confident assertion of the sincerity of the heathen desire for conversion is revealed as duplicity: he accuses Roland of betraying him out of lust for his wealth and expects to die at the hands of the treacherous Marsile. He declares formal *diffidatio* and vows revenge on Roland.

Konrad expands the council scene roughly fourfold and substantially recasts it. Of course he cannot alter its fundamental nature and purpose as 'le cunseill que mal prist' ('the ill-fated council', *Ch* 179), but he is palpably concerned to minimise the damage it does to his image of the Christian *res publica* and its exemplary functioning. In the first place he modifies the context of the council episode. In his depiction of the reception of the heathen envoys at Karl's court, he presents a grandiose typological portrait of the emperor, supreme like Solomon above all kings of the earth ('sit Salomon irstarph,/so ne wart so groz herschapht,/noch ne wirdet niemmir mere', lines 671–673) and in his awesome appearance an image of Christ in majesty.[33] As in the *Chanson de Roland* he is prepared to consider Marsilie's offer, but here the interview with the envoys is abruptly broken off as the heathen defenders of Corderes make a surprise attack only to be routed by the Christian besiegers led by Roland. In this way Konrad chooses to underline the ultimate invincibility of the emperor and the duplicity of the heathen as an immediate prelude to the council scene. This begins with Karl's invocation of the Holy Spirit on his barons in their assessment of Marsilie's intentions. Whilst in the French source Charlemagne simply states a dilemma: 'Mais jo ne sai quels en est sis curages' ('But what his purpose is I cannot tell', line 191), Karl expects the council to anticipate God's redemptive providence:

> 'nu ratet gotes ere.
> ia ne suoche ich nicht mere
> wan daz wir so gedingen
> daz wir gotes hulde gewinnen'.  (*RL* 906–910)

---

[33] For an exhaustive discussion of the typological symbolism of the portrait, see Richter, *Kommentar*, 140–165.

'Now consider what befits God's honour. For I want no
less than that we so proceed as to win God's grace'.

The ideal expectation here too is unanimity in the collective service of God and
emperor. The ideal of course is unattainable: Genelun's treachery has to happen,
for the story (and ultimately the divine purpose) requires it. But the council still
becomes, as far as Konrad can contrive it, a demonstration of solidarity and
commitment to holy war. Roland here also speaks first, repudiating Marsilie's
deceit, rejecting the lure of heathen tribute and restating his vow of self-sacrifice
as a warrior of Christ. Far from Roland being a lone voice, Olivir, Turpin and
Naimes give him ardent support: Karl as 'uoget uon Rome' (lines 960, 973)[34]
must enforce his universal Christian dominion; all reject heathen gold and
pledge, in Turpin's words, to labour in God's vineyard till they have earned the
wages of salvation.[35] Even the ascetic bishop Sante Johannes,[36] who offers to
preach the faith to the heathen as a test of their sincerity, demands their
conversion as a precondition of the army's withdrawal from Spain.

So it is Genelun who breaks the pattern of unanimity by attacking Roland for
bloodlust – now quite implausibly – and by urging the simple acceptance of
Marsilie's offer. Having exculpated the barons as far as the constraints of the
story allow, Konrad has to let his depiction of Karl take the damage that
necessarily accrues for the flawed outcome of the council. Roland's restrained
riposte:

'der rat geuellet mir uoble:
man nimt iz ane gotes ere
unde geruwet uns hernach uile sere'.   (RL 1151–1153)

'[Genelun's] advice does not please me. To accept it will
ill serve God's honour and we shall come to repent it'.

provokes the emperor's unaccountable anger. The unanimity of all save Genelun is not good enough:

'tuot iz durch gotes ere
uñ gesamnet iuch einer rede,
die uns der heilige geist gebe'   (RL 1161–1163)

---

[34] The term is a vernacular equivalent for *advocatus* or *defensor ecclesiae Romanae*. As imperial
title in the *Rolandslied* it stresses the universal character of Karl's theocratic kingship. See
Nellmann, *Reichsidee*, (as n. 2, above), 120–123, 130f., 176; Richter, *Kommentar*, 206f.;
Ott-Meimberg, *Kreuzzugsepos*, (as n. 2, above), 139–142.

[35] Lines 978–990, in which Konrad draws on the tradition of homiletic exegesis of the parable
of the vineyard, Matthew 20:1–16. See Richter, *Kommentar*, 210–214.

[36] The figure of Bishop St John is unique to Konrad's version. On the various attempts to
suggest historical prototypes, see Kartschoke, *Datierung*, (as n. 5, above), 129–140, who
identifies him as Johannes Scotus, an Irish missionary martyred in Mecklenburg in 1066.

'For the sake of God's honour, find one common voice as
the Holy Spirit may inspire us'.

Karl suspends the formal council and has his barons withdraw into a private
consultation. Genelun now restates the argument for a retreat on Marsilie's
terms in a more reasoned way, though it is still unanimously rejected by all the
rest. The solution to their impasse – what had in the *Chanson de Roland* seemingly been the preference of all but Roland from the very start: to send an envoy
to test Marsilie's sincerity – emerges now as a compromise which Turpin puts
forward and which at last commands truly unanimous support. With this,
Konrad does manage in some sense to square the circle: the ideal of unanimity is
preserved and a proposal emerges, not tainted as it is in the Old French poem by
being Genelun's, and which leaves the integrity of Roland, Olivir, Turpin and
Naimes unimpaired, a device which also fulfils the narrative requirement of
ensuring that the truth of the heathen peace plan is tested. The crux is of course
who the envoy shall be, and Konrad can now follow his source quite faithfully as
Karl rejects the candidatures of Roland, Olivir and Turpin, and accepts Roland's
– here wholly guileless – nomination of Genelun.

It cannot be denied that Konrad largely vitiates the dramatic tension of the
debates in the *Chanson de Roland*. There the council scene is a contest of
distinctively profiled, in some sense individualised figures, who perhaps also
embody in a formalised way real tensions between competing conceptions of
royal and baronial power.[37] Unanimity effaces the characters of the *Rolandslied*,
so that their speeches and debating positions becomes essentially interchangeable. The difference is one of intention, not narratorial incompetence. Konrad's
device of a second consultation of the barons, which produces the saving but
fateful compromise, imposes a new reading on the ancient story. It crucially
modifies the depiction of Genelun. From the start he is isolated among Karl's
advisors; when all the rest advance crusading zeal and service of the sacral
emperor as their key arguments for rejecting Marsilie's peace, Genelun's eagerness to avoid further hostilities emerges no longer as expedient caution, which
others can share, or even merely as cowardice, but as betrayal of the divine
mission entrusted to Karl and unanimously endorsed by the chivalric crusaders.
Already in the council scene he is implicitly a Judas whose personal vendetta
against Roland cannot be dissociated by niceties of feudal law from his allegiance to Karl.[38] Beyond the exigencies of plot, Konrad's deeper intention in
his reshaping of the council scene is – consistent with his introductory exposition – to present a paradigmatic image of sacral kingship in concert with
baronial loyalty, and to fuse the theme of imperial holy war, *dilatio imperii*, with
the chivalric ideology of crusade.

---

[37] See Bender, *König und Vasall*, and Köhler '*Conseil des barons*' (n. 3, above).

[38] Genelun is explicitly a Judas in lines 1925, 1936, 6103. For a much fuller discussion of the
issues of law and treachery in the *Rolandslied*, see Ott-Meimberg (as n. 2, above), 116–210.

The interpolated separate consultation of the barons which hatches the fateful compromise is a neat narratorial device, in that it detaches the emperor himself from a decision which, though rational enough from a tactical point of view, sets in motion the events culminating in the tragedy of Roncevaux. However, it may also be evidence of Konrad's awareness of actual forms and conventions of royal counsel in the twelfth century and of their ideological significance. In a recent study of counsel in the political practice of the early Middle Ages, Gerd Althoff shows how historiographical sources depict the formal councils of rulers from Carolingian times into the twelfth century as occasions geared to the ritual establishment of a *consensus fidelium*, an ideal unanimity, to the prestige of the participants and to the public demonstration of concord.[39] Debate and dispute had no place in the formally convoked *colloquium publicum* of kings and their counsellors. Disagreements and controversies were dealt with by means of the informally convened *colloquium secretum* which preceded or supplemented the *Hoftag* whose function was to display, not first achieve, the consensus of the realm. Karl's anger at the failure of his barons to present him with a unanimous response to Marsilie's démarche is thus understandable as his reponse to a breach of constitutional propriety, a failure to achieve a demonstration of concord and consensus vital to the legitimation of Karl's sacral kingship and to the repeatedly professed function of the council, the maintenance of the *honor dei*.

In a second pivotal episode Konrad's concern with unanimity involves him in a fundamental reshaping of the story as transmitted by his source. This is perhaps the most famous moment of all in the *Chanson de Roland*, when the rearguard of Charlemagne's army, covering its retreat from Spain, is attacked by a numerically overwhelming pagan army. Repeatedly (laisses 79–87) Oliver pleads with Roland to sound the horn Olifant which will summon the emperor back to their rescue. Roland refuses. A vassal must suffer gladly for his lord, to call for help would be to admit cowardice and forfeit renown; the pagans are in the wrong, the Christians are in the right; God cannot wish to see France dishonoured:

> 'Fier de [la] lance e jo de Durendal,
> Ma bone espee, que li reis me dunat!
> Se jo i moerc, dire poet ki l'avrat
> . . . . . que ele fut a noble vassal'.   (Ch 1120–1123)

> 'Strike with your lance, and I with Durendal, my trusty
> sword that the king gave me. Should I die, let him who
> acquires it say: "This belonged to a noble vassal!" '

---

[39] G. Althoff, '*Colloquium familiare – Colloquium secretum – Colloquium publicum*. Beratung im politischen Leben des früheren Mittelalters', *Frühmittelalterliche Studien* xxiv, 1990, 145–167.

The narrator comments:

> Rollant est proz e Oliver est sage,
> Ambedui unt merveillus vasselage.
> Puis que il sunt as chevals e as armes,
> Ja pur murir n'eschiverunt bataille;
> Bon sunt li cunte e lur paroles haltes.    (Ch 1093–1097)

> Roland is valiant and Oliver is wise. Both are marvellous
> in their courage. Once armed and mounted neither will
> shirk battle for fear of death. Both counts are fine men
> and noble their speech.

These words do not so much seek to judge motives, let alone allocate blame for the disaster to follow, but to celebrate two valid perceptions of warrior virtue which coexist in epic tension, in rivalry yet complementing each other. Certainly, as Oliver's prediction of slaughter is borne out, he savagely condemns Roland's 'folly' and lack of *mesure* (lines 1723–1726), though these charges are seemingly refuted or compensated by the heroism of the last stages of battle and Roland's apotheosis in his death scene.

Recent commentators tend to absolve Roland of 'démesure' at least to the extent that it might constitute a tragic flaw or a moral culpability.[40] However, it does seem that Konrad, in adapting the story for his German audience, was aware of a collision between the disparity of heroic roles and values which Roland and Oliver play out in the debate about sounding the horn and his own concern to promote the theme of unanimity of purpose amongst the crusading warriors. Here as in the council scene he is prepared to let an ideological consideration override and, from a literary narrative point of view, jeopardise what audiences then as readers now must have recognised as a vital component of the traditional story – albeit subtle to the point of ambiguity. Our perception of Roland's refusal to sound the horn in the German version is affected firstly by modifications of the broader context of the episode. Roland is no longer the commander of the rearguard of the retreating army. Konrad goes beyond the strict terms of Charlemagne's truce with the heathen as laid down in the message which Genelun delivers to Marsilie:

> 'er heizzet dir waerlichen sagen:
> enphahest du di cristinlichen ee,
> daz dine marche alle mit fride ste.
> er lihet dir halbe Hyspaniä,
> daz ander teil scol Ruolant haben'.    (RL 2031–2035)

---

[40] For a recent summary, and extension, of the debate, see R.F. Cook, *The Sense of the Song of Roland*, Ithaca/London 1987, 62–74, 147–159.

'He bids you be told in truth, that if you accept the
Christian faith all your borders shall be left in peace. One
half of Spain he will bestow as your fief, Roland shall
hold the rest'.

(translating *Ch* 470–473). Now however, where the *Chanson de Roland* has
Charlemagne invest Roland with his bow, as symbol of his military charge to
cover the army's withdrawal (lines 766–782), Karl designates Roland as viceroy
of Spain, to exercise imperial overlordship of Marsilie's subject kingdom. He not
only invests Roland with the banner appropriate to feudal tenure of a marcher
county (line 3181) but has him 'enthroned and crowned over Spain to the
honour of Christ' (lines 3149–3151). Thus Roland's charge is to hold the land
in suzerainty, to represent Karl's universal sacral authority. The enhanced stress
on the imperial theme is promptly complemented by a restatement of the
crusading commitment of Roland and his knights as he musters his army:

> . . . zwaincec tusent man,
> an den nichtes gebrach.
> swa iz in dar zu geschach
> da si gote scolten dinen,
> da ne gesunderote si niemen.
> si furten uaile den lip.
> si gerechten sich in alle zit
> durch den heiligen gelouben ersterben.
> durch got wolten si gemarteret werden.   (*RL* 3246–3254)

> Twenty thousand men without flaw. Whatever oppor-
> tunity arose for them to serve God, no-one would part
> them from each other's side. Avid for self-sacrifice, they
> were ready at every moment to die for the holy faith, to
> suffer martyrdom for God.

Roland fixes the badge of the cross on his splendid armour (lines 3332f.). As the
pagan hosts appear, the army prepares for battle and certain death in unanimous
commitment to self-sacrifice:

> si heten alle ain muot.
> ir herce hin ze gote stunt.
> [. . .]
> daz raine opher si brachten
> do si daz cruce an sich namen.
> ze dem tode begonden si harte gahen.
> si chouften daz gotes riche.
> sine wolten ain ander nicht geswiche:
> swaz ainen duchte guot,
> daz was ir aller muot.
> Dauid psalmista

hat uon in gescriben da:
wi groz in lonet min trechtin,
di bruderlichen mit ain ander sin!
[. . .]
ain zu uersicht unt ain minne,
ain geloube unt ain gedinge,
ain truwe was in allen.
ir nehain entwaich dem anderen.
in was allen ain warhait.

(RL 3420–3421, 3446–3456, 3459–3463)

All were of one mind, their hearts were fixed on God . . .
They proffered a pure sacrifice when they took the cross
upon themselves. They hastened to greet death, to purchase God's kingdom. They would not desert one
another: what seemed right to any one had the consent
of them all. David the psalmist has written of them: how
great a reward my Lord gives to those who live together
like brothers . . . one hope and one love, one faith and
one assurance, one trust was common to all. None left
the other's side, they shared a single truth.

Accordingly, when Olivir addresses Roland (lines 3845–3869), it is not to
raise questions of tactical expediency. He praises God for the opportunity of
redemptive sacrifice. And God's help is assured so that the overwhelming numbers of Marsilie's army are of no account:

'owol ir guten knechte,
welt ir ain muote sin,
ia hiluet iu selbe min trechtin.
si habent den tot ander hant'.   (RL 3860–3863)

'Brave knights, if you will be of one mind, the lord of
hosts himself will aid you. [The pagans] shall suffer certain death'.

Now comes the appeal for Roland to sound the horn, summon the emperor and
save the lives of his vassals. It is reduced to a single plea of just six lines, and
Olivir's speech has itself supplied the counter-argument which Roland duly
picks up:

'daz muoz nu allez an gote gestan
[. . .]
di haiden sint uor gote uirtailet;
so werdent abir mit bluote gerainet
di heren gotes marterare
[. . .]

40

wi salic der ist geborn
den got da zu hat erchoren,
daz er in sinim dinste beliget,
want er im daz himilriche zelone gibet.
[. . .]
got wil siniu wunter hi erzaigen,
der guote Durndart sine tugent erscainen'.

(RL 3870, 3879–3881, 3885–3888, 3897f.)

> 'Let all that rest with God . . . Before Him the pagans
> stand condemned, whilst these noble martyrs shall be
> washed clean with blood . . . Happy the fate of that man
> whom God chooses to let die in His service, for He shall
> give him heaven for his reward . . . God will here reveal
> His wondrous power and my good sword Durndart its
> keen edge'.

The secular preoccupations of vassal loyalty, family and personal honour in the Old French source are rigorously suppressed. What is remarkable in Konrad's remotivation of Roland is, however, just as much the disappearance here of feudal allegiance to Karl as sacral emperor which, as we have seen, otherwise forms an essential component of the nexus of loyalties. With his investiture as viceroy in Spain, Roland appears to become himself the focus of communal allegiance. During the long battle description there is a drastic recession of references to Karl, whereas in the *Chanson de Roland* Charlemagne continues to be frequently invoked.[41] Indeed, between Karl's departure from Spain and his summons to avenge Roland and the fallen of the first battle, nine out of ten references to him by name, and four out of six references to him as *keiser*, are made by the pagans. Roland on the other hand is twice accorded the title *voget* otherwise reserved for Karl in his sacral status as *vicarius dei*. Both of these occur in scenes which depict a kind of acclamation:

> di cristen riefen alle samt:
> 'owol du herre Ruolant,
> uoget der Karlinge,
> durch soteniu gimme,
> aller riter ere'    (*RL* 5975–5979)

> The Christians cried with one voice: 'Hail, prince
> Roland, lord protector of the Franks, jewel purified in the
> fire, glory of all knights'.

(see also lines 5360–5366). As 'uoget der Karlinge' he stands in Karl's stead,[42]

---

[41] E.g. *Ch* 1254, 1350, 1377, 1444, 1560.
[42] In its sense of 'defender of the Franks' this occurrence (cf. also line 5365) stands midway

41

and the jewel image further recalls the emperor who as saintly king-confessor is 'sam daz durch sotene golt' ('like gold refined in the fire', line 943). This second acclamation prefaces Roland's decision to sound the horn and recall Karl's army (line 5995ff.) and serves to offset the imputation of guilt for the lost battle which Olivir levels against him.

In the Olifant episodes Konrad again departs quite radically from the traditional pattern of the epic story as he inherited it from his source. His imposition of exemplary unanimity on the dispute of Roland and Oliver drastically reduces the impact of these climactic moments in the narrative of the *Chanson de Roland*. Konrad's depiction of the first battle of Runzeval and the apotheosis of Roland (lines 6771–6949) give a vastly enhanced prominence to his vision of a crusading *nova militia*. In this central section of the poem a conception of Christian chivalry is developed which begins to acquire an autonomous impulse and validity, no longer so firmly anchored in the older patterns of imperial universalism which were seen to characterise Konrad's introductory exposition and the council episode. In the Olifant episode and in the battle depiction in general unanimity has an imperative value as the expression of a direct commitment of the warrior nobility to redemptive chivalry. Nonetheless, in the *Rolandslied* as a whole, and with Karl's return to inflict final defeat on Marsilie and the heathen emperor Paligan, to convert Spain and absorb it into the Christian *imperium*, Konrad is manifestly concerned to integrate the theme of crusading chivalry firmly into the framework of imperial theocracy.

The epilogue of the *Rolandslied* (lines 9017–9094) provides us with a specific and explicit historical context in which to interpret Konrad's promotion of the ideal of crusading chivalry and his integration of the imperial and crusading themes. Here he celebrates his patron Duke Henry the Lion of Saxony as the supreme contemporary proponent of missionary war and Christian expansion in the tradition of Charlemagne and Roland. Imperial lineage (line 9047), conquest and conversion of the heathen on the Eastern marches of his Saxon duchy (lines 9043–9046), are vital components of Konrad's celebration of Henry, as they are of the duke's prestige in the accounts of chroniclers in the 1160s and 1170s.[43] There is evidence from as early as 1108 of a linkage between the centuries-old traditions of imperial holy war against the pagans in North-East Germany and the ideology of crusade; the diversion to the Saxon wars of a substantial part of the German crusading effort in 1147, in which the young Henry was involved, demonstrates the ready connection in German minds

between the references to Karl's theocratic status as 'uoget uon Rome' (960, 973, 1380, 1566, 2010, 7653), and those to God as 'protector' of Olivir in battle (4252) or to Karl as 'uoget witwen unde weisen' ('protector of widows and orphans': 2862, 8690). The acclamation seems to convey more than a tribute to Roland's military leadership. See also n. 34 above.

[43] See Helmold, CS, and Arnold of Lübeck, *Chronica*.

between crusade and older traditions of *dilatio imperii*.[44] Certainly, the reality of Henry's Slav wars did not always measure up to the poetic ideal. The chronicler Vincent of Prague alleged of the Wendish Crusade of 1147 that 'the Saxons fought more to seize lands for themselves than to strengthen the Christian faith'.[45] Of the year 1149 Helmold of Bosau writes: 'on all the campaigns the young duke has fought thus far against Slavia, there was no mention of Christianity but only of money'.[46] Konrad's intense spiritualisation of the crusading holy war and, for instance, his insistence that heathen financial and material tribute should not be an inducement to the *milites dei*[47] may betray some of the inherent tensions between his patron's territorial ambitions in colonial Transalbinia and the Church's expectations of his Christian mission. The promotion in the *Rolandslied* of the theme of unanimity, often against the grain of the epic story, Konrad's welding together of imperial theocracy and baronial fealty, with the crusading commitment cementing this synthesis, may also carry a critical subtext. Despite Konrad's eulogy of Henry's harmonious relationship with his vassals (lines 9055–9063), the duke was renowned for his ruthlessness in securing his dynastic and feudal interests within the duchy of Saxony and was in frequent conflict with his Saxon vassals, who conspired and rose against him more than once in the 1160s – and by whom he was to be arraigned and condemned in 1180.[48] However when Konrad was composing his poem around 1170, his depiction of unanimity and concord in the Christian empire, and its betrayal by the self-seeking Genelun, may have served not least to remind Henry that however powerful he made himself in his Saxon territorial state, his status was conditional on a relationship of reciprocal support with the German emperor. From Frederick I's investiture of Henry with the two duchies of Bavaria and Saxony in 1156 at least until Henry's refusal to reinforce Frederick's army in Lombardy in 1176, the duke's support for the emperor's Italian campaigns and throughout the papal schism was prompt and valued. In return Frederick I endorsed and facilitated Henry's development of his Saxon duchy and his conquests beyond the Elbe into a territorial state unprecedented in the German empire.[49] Within the colonial lands Frederick granted Henry the right to invest bishops and effectively to exercise imperial powers in extending the *imperium christianum*.[50]

---

[44] See Ashcroft, 'Konrad's *Rolandslied*, Henry the Lion, and the Northern Crusade' (as n. 9, above), 192–194.

[45] *Annales*, MGH Scriptores 17, 663.

[46] 'In variis autem expedicionibus, quas adhuc adolescens in Slaviam profectus exercuit, nulla de Christianitate fuit mentio, sed tantum de pecunia': CS 68, 238–240.

[47] See Ashcroft (as n. 9, above), 199–201.

[48] See Jordan (as n. 6, above), especially chapters 5 and 9.

[49] See P. Munz, *Frederick Barbarossa: A Study in Medieval Politics*, London, 1969, especially 338–346; F. Opll, *Friedrich Barbarossa*, Gestalten des Mittelalters und der Renaissance, Darmstadt 1990, 228–240.

[50] Jordan (as n. 6, above), 39–42, 48–53.

This reciprocity of emperor and territorial prince is an important theme and a structuring leitmotif in another large-scale expression of imperial ideology from the third quarter of the twelfth century: the *Gesta Frederici* of Bishop Otto of Freising and his secretary Rahewin.[51] The work is of course the crucial historiographical source for the early years of Barbarossa's reign; but more than that, together with Otto's earlier *Chronica*, the *Historia de duabus civitatibus*, the *Gesta Frederici* present a grandiose ideological interpretation of the Christian Empire in – as Otto greets it – the new dawn of joy and peace which banishes the dark night of discord in the City of God.[52] The 'tragic' vision of terrestrial history in the *Chronica* has its corrective in the *Gesta*, now that with Frederick's accession 'things have changed for the better, the time to weep yields to the time to rejoice, a time of war to a time of peace'.[53] Concord within the Christian state, the harmonious co-operation of Empire and Church, are the fundamental themes of Otto's and Rahewin's panegyrical biography of Barbarossa. Especially significant is the role which Frederick I himself played as patron and recipient of the *Gesta*. The work was effectively an imperial commission, and Frederick supplied Otto, at his request, in 1157 with a summary of main events since his election which indeed provides the basis for the first two books of the *Gesta*. The work is then an authorised official portrait and in some measure represents Frederick's aims and actions as he wished them to be seen.[54]

Book I of the *Gesta* recapitulates the events from the last years of Henry IV to the election of Barbarossa which Otto had already described in the penultimate book of the *Chronica*. There the reign of Conrad III appears as a time of irremediable crisis, in which Conrad's conflicts with the Welfs in Bavaria and Saxony are a prime source of the 'present woes' in the empire, and a symbol of the universal chaos which leads Otto to predict that 'the world could not long endure, by reason of the multitude of our sins and the stinking corruption of this most unsettled time'.[55] In the *Gesta*, Otto significantly revises his account of Conrad's reign. While it remains an age of conflict and the frustration of hopes, as even the Second Crusade is vitiated by the discord of the Christian princes, through it there now runs a golden thread of hope: the tragic theme of the

---

[51] Bischof Otto von Freising und Rahewin, *Gesta Frederici seu rectius Chronica*, ed. F.-J. Schmale, Freiherr vom Stein-Gedächtnisausgabe, Darmstadt 1974 (quoted henceforth as GF).

[52] Otto von Freising, *Chronica oder Historia de duabus civitatibus*, ed. W. Lammers, Freiherr vom Stein-Gedächtnisausgabe, 5th edn, Darmstadt 1990. On Otto's philosophy of history and the relationship of the two chronicles, see Schmale, introduction to the *Gesta Frederici*, 1–15; E.F. Otto, 'Otto von Freising und Friedrich Barbarossa', and J. Spörl, 'Die "Civitas Dei" im Geschichtsdenken Ottos von Freising', both in W. Lammers, ed., *Geschichtsdenken und Geschichtsbild im Mittelalter*, Wege der Forschung xxi, Darmstadt 1961, 247–278 and 298–320.

[53] 'Cum igitur rebus in melius mutatis post tempus flendi tempus ridendi, post tempus belli tempus pacis modo advenerit . . .': GF, Prologus, 118.

[54] GF, 83–88, and Schmale, Introduction, 1–26; Opll (as n. 49, above), 7f.

[55] '. . . et exhinc provincia nostra multis malis suiacere cepit': *Chronica* vii, 24, 542; 'presertim cum tam ex peccatorum nostrorum multitudine quam tumultuosissimi temporis feculenta improbitate haut diu stare posse mundum putaremus': VII, 34, 558–560.

*mutatio rerum* is countered by the rise of the Staufer culminating in Conrad's deathbed committal of the royal insignia to the young Barbarossa.[56] Unanimity is the keynote of Frederick's election to the German crown 'by general demand and with the consent of all princes'.[57] And this unanimity has for Otto of Freising a very particular connotation and value: the profoundest reason for the unanimous assent was, he surmises, the fact that Frederick belonged by birth to both of the families, Staufen and Welf, which had so frequently been in rivalry with each other and disturbed the peace of the realm; God's providence, which looks to peace for the future, now places Frederick 'like a cornerstone to repair the enmity of these two dynasties'.[58]

The price of Welf electoral support must have been undertakings on Frederick's part to endorse Henry the Lion's claim to Bavaria, and throughout Book II of the *Gesta* the 'conflict between his own flesh and blood'[59] – between his Welf cousin Henry the Lion and his Babenberg uncle Henry Jasomirgott, incumbent of the Bavarian duchy – provides in Otto's narrative a test-case of Frederick's success in restoring the peace and honour of the empire. At the Reichstage in Würzburg in 1152, at Bamberg, Regensburg and Speyer in 1153, at Goslar in 1154 and at Regensburg in 1155, it is Henry the Lion who faithfully attends and awaits the emperor's mediation, Henry Jasomirgott who absents himself or obstructs the restoration of order and concord.[60] Otto candidly reveals one urgent motive which impels Barbarossa to press for a settlement at Goslar:

> Frederick had striven now for almost two years to resolve the quarrel of the two princes who were so closely linked to him by ties of blood; he was moved by the young duke's [Henry the Lion's] pressing desire to recover the patrimony long withheld from him and in any case he needed him as knight and comrade in arms in the arduous campaign that lay ahead.[61]

And indeed Henry's loyal and militarily important contributions to Frederick's Italian campaigns between 1154 and 1160 recur as a subsidiary but telling theme in both Otto's and Rahewin's accounts to provide an emblematic expression of

---

56 GF i, 71, 278–280.
57 'ab omnibus Fredericus Suevorum dux [. . .] petitur cunctorumque favore in regem sublimatur': GF ii, 1, 284.
58 '. . . quod utriusque sanguinis consors tamquam angularis lapis utrorumque horum parietum dissidentiam unire posset': GF ii, 2, 284–286.
59 'controversia, que inter eius carnem et sanguinem [. . .] agitabatur': GF ii, 7, 292.
60 GF ii, 7; ii, 12; ii, 45; ii, 48; ii, 57–58.
61 'Itaque Fredericus, dum iam fere per biennium ad decidendam litem duorum principum, sibi, ut dictum est, ex propinquitate sanguinis tam affinium, laborasset, tandem alterius instantia, qui in paternam hereditatem, a qua diu propulsus fuerat, redire cupiebat, flexus, imminente etiam sibi expeditionis labore, in qua eundem iuvenum militem sociumque vie habere debuit, finem negotio imponere cogebatur': GF ii, 12, 302.

45

*pax* and *concordia*.[62] In fact, Otto does not single out Henry the Lion for his part in the first Italian expedition, and for his valour in the skirmishes in Rome after Frederick's imperial coronation, as do Otto Morena and the *Carmen de gestis Frederici*, or more predictably Helmold of Bosau.[63] However the final arbitration of the Bavarian question at the Reichstag of Regensburg in September 1156 is the event with which Otto chooses to end the second book of the *Gesta* (and, as it was to turn out, his contribution to Frederick's biography). Henry the Lion's confirmation as duke of Bavaria, balanced by the elevation of Babenberg Austria to a duchy with extraordinary privileges, sets a triumphant seal on the first phase of Barbarossa's reign:

> From that day forth until the present one such joyful peace smiled on the whole transalpine empire that Frederick was not only hailed as imperator and augustus but rightfully called father of the fatherland.[64]

In his continuation of the *Gesta*, Rahewin takes up with still more enthusiasm the portrayal of Barbarossa as 'non regni rector sed unius domus, unius rei publice paterfamilias'.[65] In the second Italian campaign he depicts how Henry, 'nobilissimus dux', distinguishes himself through his 'love for the holy Roman Church and for the honour of the empire';[66] Rahewin reports how Pope Hadrian IV cites the mediation of 'our beloved son Henry duke of Bavaria and Saxony' in the aftermath of the Besançon *beneficium* dispute.[67] While Henry gives loyal support to the emperor in the developing conflict with Rome, he appears in the *Gesta* as a proponent of reconciliation. When Barbarossa urgently needs reinforcements against Milan early in 1159, he sends urgent messages to 'Duke Henry of Bavaria and others, bishops and princes of the empire, reminding them of their fidelity and appealing to their readiness  to preserve the state of the empire'.[68] Henry's response is as ever prompt and he plays a prominent role in ending the bitter siege of Crema. It is in this context of the arrival of Henry, escorting the empress Beatrix, to join Frederick in Italy, that Rahewin pays his most elaborate tribute to the duke. A panegyric culled largely from Sallust

---

[62] See especially GF ii, 58; iii, 16; iii, 24; iii, 26; iv, 46.

[63] Otto Morena, *Libellus de rebus a Frederico imperatore gestis*, ed. F.-J. Schmale, *Italische Quellen über die Taten Kaiser Friedrichs I. in Italien und der Brief über den Kreuzzug Kaiser Friedrichs I.*, Freiherr vom Stein-Gedächtnisausgabe, Darmstadt 1986, 54; *Carmen de gestis Frederici*, ed. I. Schmale-Ott, MGH Scriptores rerum Germanicarum, lines 2943*ff.*; Helmold, CS, 81, 280.

[64] 'Porro tanta ab ea die usque inpresentiarum toti Transalpino pacis iocunditas arrisit imperio, ut non solum imperator et augustus, sed et pater patrie iure dicatur Fridericus': GF ii, 58, 390.

[65] GF iii, 17, 428.

[66] 'ob amorem sancte Romane ecclesie et honorem imperii': GF iii, 24, 446–448.

[67] '. . . commonitionem dilecti filii nostri Heinrici Baioarie et Saxonie ducis': GF iii, 26, 452.

[68] '. . . advocat et ducem Baioarie Heinricum aliosque tam episcopos quam proceres imperii, commonens eos fidelitatis sue, ne desertores regni [. . .] velle se probare ipsorum benevolentiam circa statum imperii conservandum': GF iv, 28, 578.

highlights his courage and chivalric accomplishments, his stern self-discipline and moral rigour:

> He preferred to be good rather than merely appear so. The less his taste for fame, the more he accrued it [. . .] having received the duchy of Bavaria from the emperor, once acquainted with the nature and customs of its people, he established peace throughout the land, making himself popular with the virtuous and inspiring fear in the wicked . . .

This is an exemplary image of Christian chivalry and lordship, combining physical bravery and moral virtue, the *fortitudo* of a Roland and the *sapientia* of an Oliver.[70] All this has little value for the historical assessment of Henry, still less so what follows: Rahewin's adaptation of Sallust's contrastive character sketches of Cato the Younger and Julius Caesar to fit Henry the Lion and Welf IV – Rahewin had earlier applied the same classical identikit to Rainald of Dassel and Otto of Wittelsbach.[71] Nonetheless, this reclothing of imperial paladins in classical garb has a serious ideological function: Otto of Freising has Barbarossa reject the condescension of the Roman citizens before his coronation with a scornful assertion of the *translatio* of Roman virtue to the Franks:

> [. . .] to quote the words of one of your own writers: 'Once, yes once there was virtue in this republic'. Once, I say. If only we could say as truthfully as willingly 'now'! [. . .] Would you like to see again the ancient glory of Rome? The dignity of its senate? The order of its encamped army? The strength and discipline of its chivalry, bold and invincible as it enters battle? Then look at our state! All that is now ours.[72]

---

69 '. . . esse quam videri bonus malebat. Ita, quo minus appetebat gloriam, eo magis illam assequebatur. [. . .] Is, recepto ab imperatore, ut supra dictum est, ducatu Baioarie, ubi naturam et mores hominum cognovit, multa cura, multo consilio in tantam claritudinem brevi pervenerat, ut, treuga per totam Baioariam firmata, bonis vehementer carus, malis maximo terrori esset . . .': GF iv, 46, 602. Acerbus Morena gives a more sober portrait of Henry, describing his physical appearence, stressing his wealth and power, and referring to his imperial lineage, *Libellus* (as n. 63, above), 188–190.

70 See Wurster (as n. 13, above), 410. The combination of these virtues makes for an ideal hero and ruler – more commonly they are presented as contrasting qualities of two juxtaposed characters: E.R. Curtius, *European Literature and the Latin Middle Ages*, London 1953, 170–176.

71 Compare GF iv, 46, 602–604 and iii, 22, 440. The primary source is Sallust's *Bellum Catilinae* liii–liv.

72 '. . . ut tui scriptoris verbis utar: Fuit, fuit quondam in hac re publica virtus. Quondam dico. Atque o utinam tam veraciter quam libenter nunc dicere possemus! [. . .] Vis cognoscere antiquam tue Rome gloriam? Senatorie dignitatis gravitatem? Tabernaculorum dispositionem? Equestris ordinis virtutem et disciplinam, ad conflictum procedentis intemeratam ac indomitam audaciam? Nostram interue rem publicam. Penes nos cuncta hec sunt': GF ii, 32, 346.

In this perspective, Rahewin implies, Henry as loyal supporter in Frederick's Italian wars is a prime embodiment of the *romanum imperium christianum*. The ideological thrust of this passage is not fundamentally different from that of the portrait at the very end of the *Gesta*, where Rahewin paraphrases Einhard to depict Frederick I as a curly-haired, red-bearded Charlemagne *redivivus*.[73]

With this, the *Gesta's* contribution to Barbarossa's *imitatio Caroli*, we return to a framework of symbolic reference which Otto's and Rahewin's biographical chronicle shares with Konrad's *Rolandslied*. There is in fact no strong reason to presume that Konrad had access to the *Gesta Friderici*. Although the work is for us a pre-eminent documentary source and indisputably the finest piece of historiography in its time, however tendentious, its contemporary influence appears to have been slight. The presentation copy which went to the imperial court can scarcely have failed to meet with Frederick's approval as an unsurpassable tribute to his theory and practice of kingship. Yet the further dissemination of the *Gesta* seems to have been surprisingly restricted. From Freising itself the manuscript tradition extends only to a handful of monasteries in Bavaria and Austria.[74] There is no evidence of its transmission to North Germany. The old assumption that Konrad was a Bavarian and composed the *Rolandslied* in Regensburg no longer looks so self-evident as it once did; the locus of the poem is Henry the Lion's Saxon domain, not Bavaria which he visited infrequently and briefly and where his territorial and political stake was slender.[75] My reasons for linking the *Gesta* and the *Rolandslied* do not in any case rest on the assumption of direct influence or borrowing of ideas. Sufficient for my contention is the common presence of Henry the Lion in the two works and the comparable role in them both of the concept of unanimity in the Christian empire.

The intertextual allegories of the *Gesta* – Henry the Lion as Sallustian Cato, Frederick Barbarossa as Einhard's Charlemagne – are examples of the way in which it provides readable clues to the decoding of its ideological subtext. So the function of Henry the Lion in Barbarossa's grand imperial design, as Otto and Rahewin chronicle it, is readily perceived: he acts as a symbol and test case for the unity and political harmony which underpin the emperor's programme of reasserting imperial rights in Italy. We may note the lack of reference to what in hard political terms was the quid pro quo for Henry's compliance: Frederick's acquiescence in Henry's state-building in Saxony and its colonial territories. A comparable decoding of the *Rolandslied* would be inappropriate. Despite the

---

[73] GF iv, 86, 708–712, based on Einhard, *Vita Karoli*, 21–26.

[74] Schmale, GF Introduction, 58–71.

[75] See E. Nellmann, 'Pfaffe Konrad' in K. Ruh, ed., *Die deutsche Literatur des Mittelalters. Verfasserlexikon*, 2nd edn, v, Berlin 1984, 115–131; A. Kauf, 'Heinrich der Löwe und Bayern', in W.-D. Mohrmann, *Heinrich der Löwe* (as n. 6, above), 151–214. In a forthcoming essay I intend to present new documentary evidence about the historical identity of Pfaffe Konrad and his affiliation to the court of Henry the Lion.

evidence in the epilogue that Konrad was aware of the contemporary resonances of the epic story and concerned to convey them to his patron and audience, we cannot impute to him the intention of constructing a political allegory. All the same, as his promotion of the theme of unanimity illustrates, Konrad understands history as *exemplum* and his poem can function as an ideological model. By casting Henry in the role of the new David of his age (lines 9039–9042, 9066–9068), heir to the Carolingian tradition of *dilatio imperii* and exponent of crusading chivalry, Konrad presents him, in the *gesta* and the literary personae of Karl and Roland, with a forbiddingly ideal and authoritative image of lordship and Christian knighthood, which provides both an exemplary mirror for the ideological goals and pretensions of Henry's military and political ambitions and a tribunal before which the reality of his achievements might be judged.

There are penalties and ambivalences in Konrad's undertaking and indeed in the whole enterprise of poetry with such a contemporary political dimension. In his recasting of the council scene and the Olifant episode, Konrad deploys his ideological point only by compromising the aesthetic integrity of the epic as the *Chanson de Roland* embodies it. Even for his patron Henry the Lion there may have been loss as well as gain in having Konrad furnish him with a version of the great epic designed to promote German ideals of imperial holy war and the Baltic crusade. Konrad's extreme idealisation of theocratic kingship and redemptive chivalry, the very impeccability of motivation which he imposes on Karl and Roland, may create representative images which accrue to the prestige of the Welf duke, but they also prescribed a standard against which contemporaries might measure their actual perception of Henry's lordship in Saxony and Slavia. Comparison with the *Gesta Friderici* suggests that Konrad's modifications of his source in the *Rolandslied* reflect and promote a mutually advantageous co-operation of Staufen emperor and Welf duke in the 1150s and 1160s, one reflex of which is the value both works place on unanimity in the Christian *res publica* between emperor and feudal magnates, between warriors in the cause of the sacral empire. But the centripetal momentum of the theme of unanimity coexists in some tension in the epilogue of the *Rolandslied* with the assertion of Henry's claim to Carolingian succession, a theme with centrifugal potential implying a renewal of Welf claims to royal status and a challenge to the permanence of the allegiance of Henry to Barbarossa, so important to Otto of Freising's vision of the new dawn of peace and concord under Frederick I.[76] The

---

[76] On Henry's pretensions to royal status, see J. Fried, 'Königsgedanke Heinrichs des Löwen', *Archiv für Kulturgeschichte* lv, 1973, 312–351. The significance of his Welf dynastic consciousness and his new status as territorial magnate for Konrad's poem and its epilogue is illuminated by Vollmann-Profe (see n. 7, above), 134–137. According to Sigebert of Gembloux, *Chronographiae Auctarium Affligemense*, ed. P. Gorissen, Verhandelingen van de Koninklijke Vlaamse Academie voor Wetenschapen, Letteren en schone Kunsten van Belgie, Klasse der Letteren xv, 1952, 143, Frederick I designated 'duos imperatores, filium Konradi predecessoris sui et post eum Heinricum ducem Saxoniae' in the event of his possible death at the siege of Milan in 1160.

fragility of royal and princely unanimity was rapidly to reveal itself in the 1170s. Henry the Lion did not join Frederick's expedition to Italy in 1174; when in early 1176 Frederick's parlous military situation impelled him to appeal to the duke for reinforcement, Henry refused. Historians' accounts of the meeting at Chiavenna are undoubtedly coloured by hindsight, such as the apocryphal story which has Barbarossa kneeling in supplication before Henry, and the ducal steward Jordan of Blankenburg dissuading his master from helping the emperor up from his knees with the words: 'Let the imperial crown lie at your feet, one day it will rest on your head'.[77] Though the significance of the encounter at Chiavenna should not be exaggerated, it did mark a swiftly developing divergence of interest between emperor and territorial prince which culminated in Henry's trial and banishment by feudal peers who were unanimous in condemning him.[78] When offered participation in Barbarossa's imperial crusade in 1189, as an act of rehabilitation, Henry declined, preferring to stay in banishment.[79] The *Rolandslied* offered a poetic role model for Henry in 1180 as it had done ten years earlier: not now the loyal Roland but the unfaithful Genelun.

[77] The anecdote occurs in two early thirteenth-century sources, the chronicle of Burchard of Ursberg and the *Sächsische Weltchronik*. See Jordan, *Heinrich der Löwe* (as n. 6, above), 189; Opll, *Friedrich Barbarossa*, 118, 235f.; Munz, *Frederick Barbarossa*, 307–310 (both as n. 49, above).

[78] Jordan, 194–213;

[79] Arnold of Lübeck, *Chronica* iv, 7, 128.

# Some Analysis of
# the Castle of Bodiam, East Sussex*

CHARLES COULSON

## I. THE SIGNIFICANCE OF BODIAM

The castle of Bodiam, blandly ensconced in its lily-pond of a moat, is well-known, but can scarcely be said to be well-understood.[1] It represents the popular ideal of a medieval castle and its inheritors from the Marquis Curzon of Kedleston, the National Trust, style it simply '*the* favourite castle' in their tourist leaflet, and 'everyone's fairy-tale castle' in their 1985 Guide.[2] That it has had so compelling and so enduring an impact, not least today six centuries since it was

* A brief summary of this paper appears in *Fortress*, X August 1991, entitled 'Bodiam Castle: Truth and Tradition'.

[1] Dr W. Douglas Simpson commented that 'few English castles have been more thoroughly studied or more extensively written about', since 1831: 'The Moated Homestead, Church and Castle of Bodiam', *Sussex Archaeological Collections* (hereafter SAC) lxxii, 1931, 69–99 (hereafter Simpson 1931). The present paper enlarges upon my note 11 (p. 76) in 'Structural Symbolism in Medieval Castle Architecture', *Journ. BAA* cxxxii, 1979, 73–90. Acknowledgement is gratefully made for the benefits of discussion of a résumé of this paper to Michael Clanchy, Richard Eales, Anthony Emery, Richard Gem, Robert Higham, Lawrence Keen, John Kenyon, Beric Morley, Michael Prestwich, Derek Renn, Andrew Saunders, Nigel Saul, Arnold Taylor, Michael Thompson. For communicating in November 1990 full details of the landscape survey done in 1988 by the Royal Commission on the Historical Monuments of England my special thanks are due to Paul Everson of RCHME Keele, (National Archaeological Record, Southampton, NAR no. TQ 72 NE1; also *Med. Arch.* xxxiv, 1990, 155–7 (hereafter RCHME i and ii)) and their very generous help in providing the specially drawn site plan (Fig. 2) and 'viewing platform' detail (Fig. 3), together with photographs (Pls 7, 10, 15) where indicated, is most gratefully acknowledged. Mr Everson also discusses the landscaping aspects in CBA *Research Report* no. 78, 1991, *Garden Archaeology* ed. A. E. Brown, esp. 9–10. For less tangible but great benefits I am indebted, as always, to the late Otto (R. C.) Smail.

[2] Anne Yarrow, *Bodiam Castle*, Norwich 1985 (1985 Guide) contains an excellent brief treatment of the domestic and seignorial aspects. Curzon's book (*Bodiam Castle*, 1926) was good

51

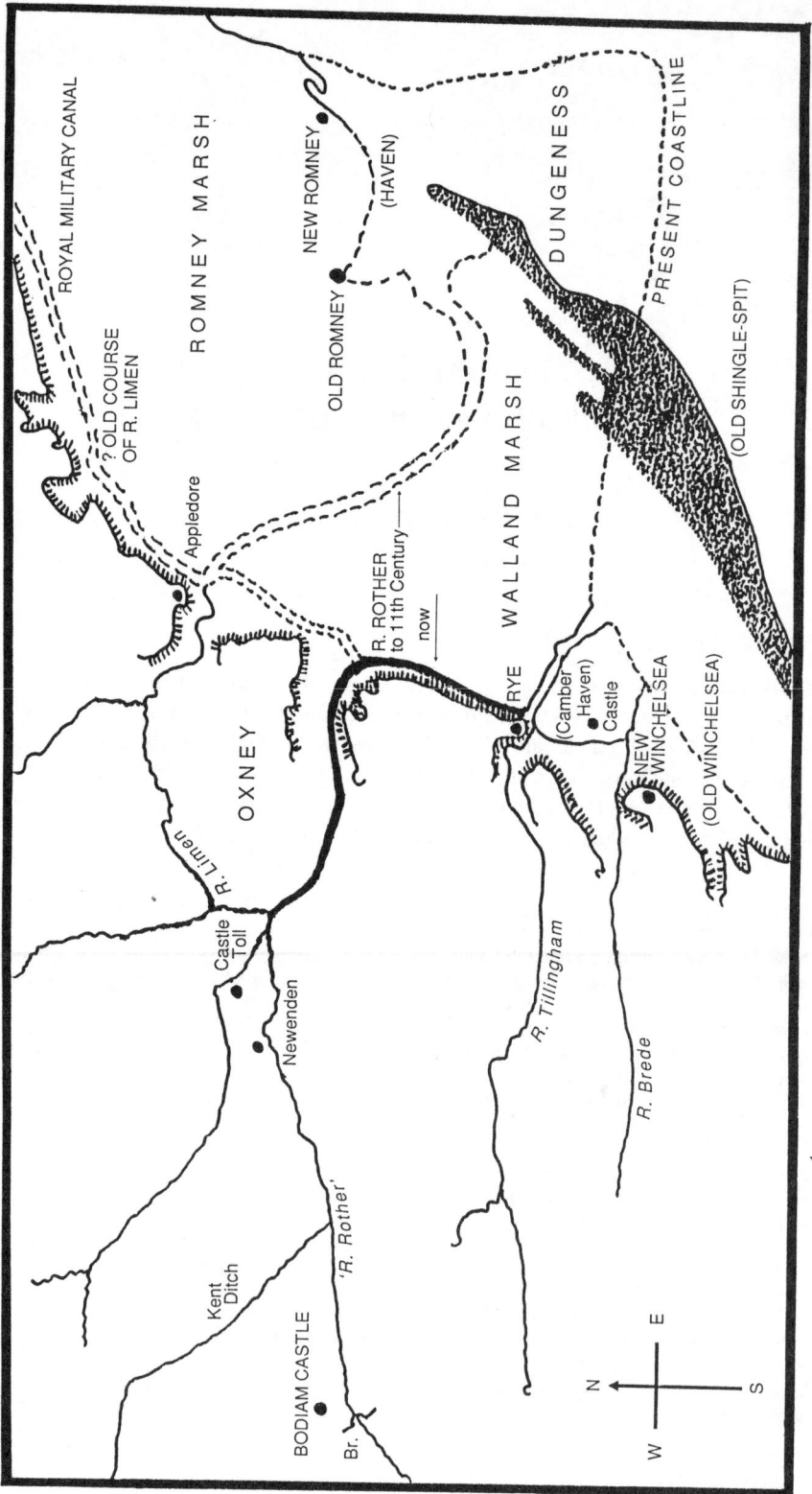

ROYAL MILITARY CANAL

R O M N E Y   M A R S H

NEW ROMNEY

(HAVEN)

DUNGENESS

PRESENT COASTLINE

? OLD COURSE OF R. LIMEN

OLD ROMNEY

(OLD SHINGLE-SPIT)

Appledore

R. ROTHER to 11th Century

now

W A L L A N D   M A R S H

OXNEY

RYE

(Camber Haven) Castle

NEW WINCHELSEA

(OLD WINCHELSEA)

R. Limen

Castle Toll

Newenden

R. Tillingham

R. Brede

Kent Ditch

'R. Rother'

BODIAM CASTLE

Br.

N
W — E
S

1          5          10 MILES

completed, triumphantly proves its success. In the modern literature of castle studies it has held a special position which would have pleased Sir Edward Dallingridge, who sought and duly obtained licence, in October 1385, to build what has also been called 'the most spectacular private castle of the decade'.[3] The fairy-tale cannot be sustained and questioning analysis rather than enthusiastic advocacy is our present purpose. The equivocation of Bodiam comment, finely balanced between lurking ugly disbelief and uninhibited romantic enjoyment, to be found almost universally in all kinds and levels of work, must be resolved.[4]

The building remains profoundly significant in a perhaps surprising variety of ways. It has been assumed to be the most notable (indeed, virtually the sole) exception to the scenario of post-Edwardian (military) 'decline', and it is certainly something of a test-case for the understanding of licences to crenellate. These royal patents (or charters), ostensibly authorizing the construction of stone walls and battlements (and occasionally of other fortifications), usually phrased as additions to an existing dwelling, come formally into being with the commencement of enrolment under King John and last until the early Stuart period. From c.1200 until 1578 over 500 sites were licensed (some several times), nearly half of them (217) during the reign of Edward III.[5] They have traditionally been regarded as prohibitive in purpose, reluctantly conceded, and thought to bear the imprint of a supposed royal disfavour towards noble

for its date and circumstances (cp. Curzon and H.A. Tipping, *Tattershall Castle*, Lincolnshire, 1929, *passim*). He bought Bodiam in 1916, conserved it and left it to the Trust in 1925. A new Guide by D. Thackray is understood to be in preparation. The form *Dallingridge* is adopted in preference to the variant medieval phonetic spellings (*viz.* Dalling Ridge near East Grinstead) approximating to *Dalyngrigge*.

3   D.J. Turner 'Bodiam, Sussex: True Castle or Old Soldier's Dream House?' (274), *England in the Fourteenth Century: Proceedings of the 1985 Harlaxton Symposium*, ed. W.M. Ormrod, Woodbridge 1986, 267–77 (hereafter Turner).

4   Recent comment remains 'military' in emphasis or equivocates e.g. R. Allen Brown, *English Medieval Castles*, 1954, 95–6; slightly modified in *English Castles*, 1976, 144–6; C. Platt, *The Castle in Medieval England and Wales*, 1982, 114–8; D.J.C. King, *Castellarium Anglicanum*, Kraus International, 1983, 469 hereafter King; M.W. Thompson, *The Decline of the Castle*, Cambridge 1987 (hereafter Thompson), 17, 36–7, 111, penetrates more deeply but substantially adheres to the traditional view (*pers. comm.* 6 October 1990).

5   Coulson 1979 (n. 1 above); more generally, 'Hierarchism in Conventual Crenellation: an essay in the sociology and metaphysics of medieval fortification', *Med. Arch* xxvi 1982, 69–100. Since a study of *Royal English Licences to Crenellate, c.1200 to 1578* is in preparation for the Boydell Press, source references and discussion of this material have been kept to a minimum.

---

*Figure 1.*

Sketch plan showing position of Bodiam Castle in relation to changes in the coastline in the neighbourhood of Romney Marsh since Saxon Times.
(Adapted with kind permission from B.K. Davison, *Med. Arch.* xvi, 1972, 124)

castellation.[6] It has also been implied that they are prescriptive, implementing some national defence plan. This latter is the particular claim made for Bodiam; namely that the licence, in saying that the new castle was for 'the defence of the adjacent countryside' and for the 'resisting of the king's enemies', in effect, 'designated what was otherwise a privately-owned residence and stronghold as forming part of a coastal or second-line (sic) national defence scheme' (see Fig. 1). Its construction is further attributed to the danger of French raids and to the loss of 'control of the Channel' between 1372 and 1387.[7] If the licence were indeed, as W.D. Simpson has claimed, the result of central and royal *dirigisme* and granted only for these reasons of public benefit, then it would truly be unique.

Very fortunately, the building itself offers the most eloquent testimony since it is entirely of one period and almost entirely of one build. Far from standing alone against the weight of the general evidence (of licences to crenellate most notably), both the structure and the historical circumstances of Bodiam Castle when re-examined are found to concur. The nearly complete remains and the very suggestive documentary evidence corroborate each other. The militant array of walls and towers, which primarily concerns us here, is almost intact. The interior, although stripped out, still retains substantial traces of the lodgings and apartments, but the outer shell being virtually undamaged it is possible to address directly the key issue which has focused controversy, namely the degree of its 'seriousness as a fortification'. The debate goes back to the early commentators and still continues as a live issue. Some reconsideration may achieve a certain general clearing of the ground and restore to the fellowship of chivalry a long-lost brother, redeemed from the ranks of the military.

## II. THE PROBLEM OF BODIAM

It will be sufficient to mention the principal existing views to show the extent and nature of the central problem of interpretation and to illustrate the equivocation referred to.

---

[6] The view is ubiquitous but see the summary by Daniel Williams 'Fortified Manor Houses', *Trans. Leicestershire Archaeological and Historical Society* i, 1974–5, 1–16. For an early denial see W. Mackay Mackenzie, *The Medieval Castle in Scotland*, London 1927, appendix A; and recently, Richard Eales 'Castles and Politics in England, 1215–1224', *Thirteenth-Century England*, ii 1988, esp. 39–40; and 'Royal Power and Castles in Norman England', *Ideals and Practice of Medieval Knighthood* iii 1990, *passim*.

[7] Simpson 1931 (84–5 *et passim*) citing the sack of Rye by Jean de Vienne in 1377, attacks on Rye and Winchelsea, 1380, etc. The fashion for 'military' explanations has received apparent support from the terms of the 1385 licence, which have been taken uncritically with rare exceptions e.g. T.F. Tout's weighty dubiety (see note 74 below), *Chapters in the Administrative History of Medieval England*, 6 vols, Manchester, 1920–33, iii, 411 n. 1; also J.R. Maddicott, *Past and Present*, Suppl. i 1975, 64–5.

The authority of G.T. Clark still stands high. He began his monographs in the 1830s and was incautious only when unduly influenced by E.A. Freeman, to whom he dedicated his collected papers, published in 1884 as *Medieval Military Architecture in England*. He was able to employ the services of record-searchers but his work does somewhat lack historical context.

When dating masonry from stylistic or structural signs alone he was most careful not to make attributions earlier than the mid-twelfth century and resisted the strong expectations for Anglo-Saxon castles of masonry. On stonework he was impervious to the pressures of contemporary fashion, but he did succumb notoriously in thinking some earthwork mottes to be pre-Conquest.[8] His description (1874) of the *assiette* of Bodiam shows him at his best.'A sort of platform was selected upon the sloping ground, about thirty feet above the river (Rother)'s level and in it was excavated a rectangular basin, 180 yards north and south, by 117 yards east and west, and about seven feet deep (see Fig. 2). To the east the containing bank was wholly artificial, formed of the excavated material, as was also the case with the contiguous parts to the north and south . . . . In the centre, or nearly so, of the excavation was left a rectangular island of rather above half an acre in area, raised artificially about four feet . . . (giving) a wet moat from thirty-five to sixty-five yards broad'.[9] Clark was struck by the defensive incongruity of the post-medieval sluice then used 'for the occasional emptying of the moat' (originally quite frequently needed for cleaning out the silt and issues of the garderobes) and thought that 'probably something of the sort was originally constructed, though it would, of course, be concealed (*sic*)'. Realism nevertheless required him to remark that 'the fact is, however, that a few vigorous workmen could at any time have cut through the bank in a few hours, and thus have deprived the castle of one of its defences' (see Pls 1, 2, 4, 8, 9, 16). Enchantment resumed its sway next sentence with – 'the mud, however, until dry would be an even better protector than the water'.[10]

---

8 George Thomas Clark was a civil engineer and scholar who had worked with Brunel (see King xii). His prefatory chapters to his collected papers (1884, next note) incurred the ire of J.H. Round (anonymously but typically in *The Quarterly Review* clxxix, 1894, 27–57; and more aggressively, *Archaeologia* lviii, 1902, 313–40, targeting also Freeman) and of E. S. Armitage (*Early Norman Castles of the British Isles*, 1912, *passim*). See also J.M.B. Counihan, 'Castle Studies in England and on the Continent since 1850', *Anglo-Norman Studies* xii, 1988, *passim*. But Clark's reputation rests solidly on his pioneering castle monographs.

9 *Medieval Military Architecture*, 1884 i, 239–47, reprinting *Archaeologia Cantiana* ix 1874, cv–cxvi. The 'basin' was actually partly excavated and partly levelled up with the spoil (see Pl. 7). The Royal Commission 1988 landscape survey (*RCHME* i, 4) gives the moat as on average 115m. x 155m. and the water depth as about 2m. The central 'platform' is slightly to the S of centre of the tapering rectangle of water (see Fig. 2).

10 There are now concrete capped overflows in the centre of the S bank and near the NE corner (lately replaced by a restored spillway). Cleaning was evidently done by cutting the bank. There was no morass but only eighteen inches of silt on the firm bottom in 1970, accumulated since the 1920 emptying. Sewage in a latrine shoot did not deter the French in 1204 at Château-Gaillard. Laying brushwood and planking was standard procedure, normally countered by deep ditches. Simpson 1931, 88, dismissed Clark's objection (although Curzon

55

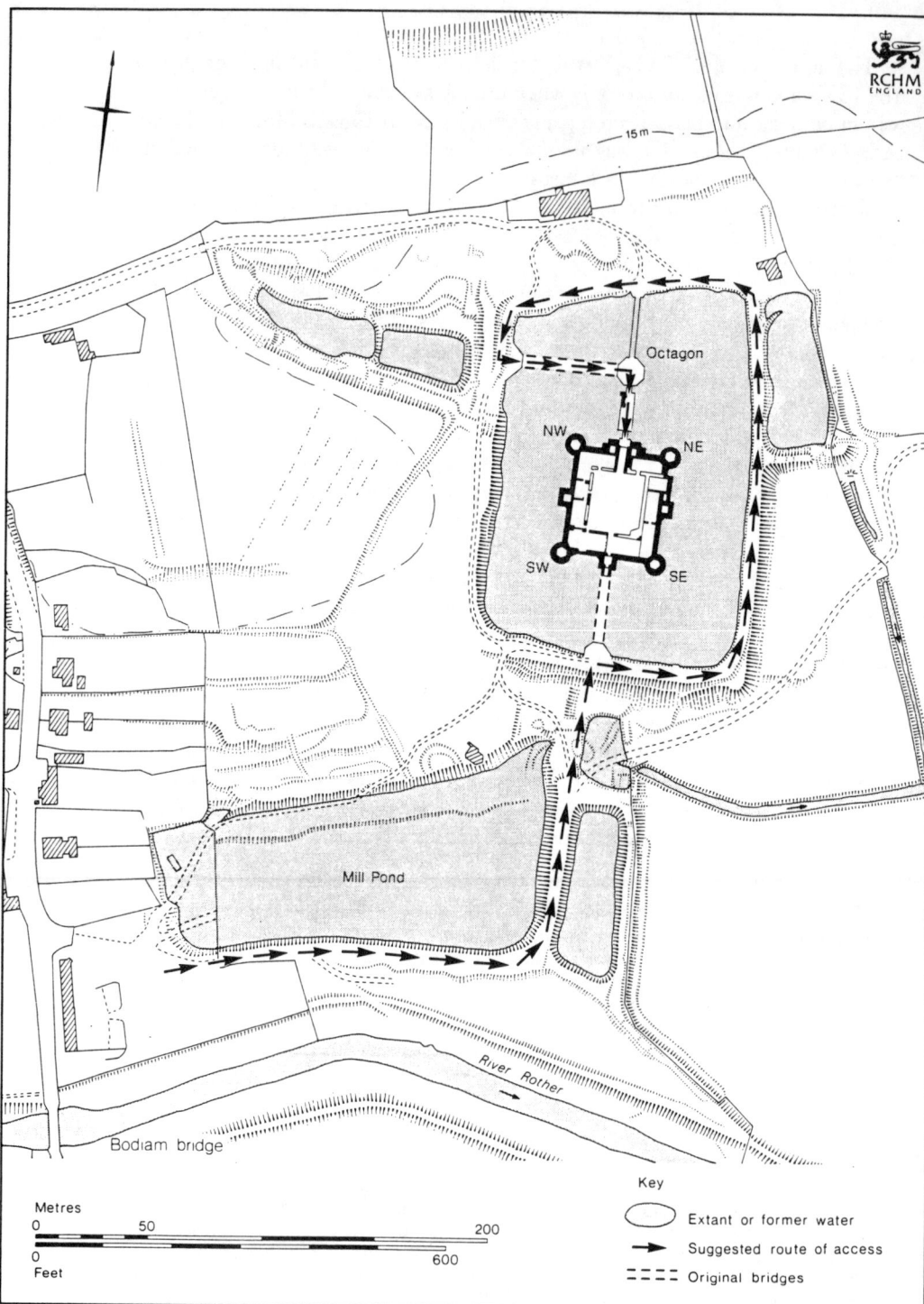

15 m

RCHM
ENGLAND

Octagon

NW    NE

SW    SE

Mill Pond

River Rother

Bodiam bridge

Metres
0        50                                          200
0                                              600
Feet

Key

Extant or former water

Suggested route of access

Original bridges

With much careful factual detail and some very illuminating asides, Clark then turns to the building on the 'platform'. The rectangle, exclusive of tower-projections, measures 152 feet north and south, by 138 feet east and west (184 by 171 feet overall).[11] The curtain walls are forty feet and a half high from moat to parapet copings and six and a half feet thick at the bottom, the round or 'drum' angle towers being twenty-nine feet in external diameter. Aesthetically the ensemble of 'eight mural towers, four cylindrical and four rectangular' (but the Main Gate is rectilinear *rectius*) provides, in Clark's words, 'an agreeable variety to the outline'. It would be naive to suppose this effect was accidental (see Pl. 10). Proportions are assisted also by the stair turrets to the towers (dummies covering the stair-wells) which are 'crested with miniature battlements in the late-Perpendicular manner'. Clark faithfully describes the gunloops found only in the Main Gate, but has difficulty in believing the reputed

had accepted it) and argued that 'to cut through the bank' (about six feet thick at the top) 'would scarcely be an easy job, or one of a few hours, under the full command (*sic*) of parapets and towers lined by the finest archery in Europe'. Such archers (had Dallingridge been able to pay them) would not have been allowed to skulk at an inland site remote from the threatened coast (see Fig. 1). Any attackers would also possess archery and might be numerous.

11 RCHME i, 4. Clark did err in saying there are chain-holes in the upper corners of the Main Gate 'drawbridge' rebate. As with the Postern, this is precluded by the location and dimensions of the portcullis slot, in any case (see Pls 3, 11). The building may still have been ivy-clad in 1874. Its small scale is shown by Colchester 'keep' (about 154 by 113 feet excluding projections); Caerphilly inner ward (about 200 feet internally) and Beaumaris (about 175 by 190 feet internally). Expanding Bodiam's dimensions by a third, or slightly more, would give it the 'Edwardian' size its designer conveys by careful proportioning. Clark surely knew of the licence to crenellate (terms summarized by J.H. Parker, note 14 below) but curiously was not misled or influenced (i, 240).

---

*Figure 2 (opposite)*

Bodiam castle, site and landscape plan. (RCHME, Feb. 1991, Crown Copyright reserved)

'The earthworks surrounding Bodiam castle form an elaborate and contrived setting for the building, of a coherence not previously perceived. Most striking is the use of sheets of water to create a staged landscape, not only to be passed through but to be viewed from above . . .' (C. Taylor, P. Everson and R. Wilson-North, *Med. Arch.* xxxiv, 1990, 155–7, including the plan on which the above is based, specially adapted by great courtesy of the Royal Commission on the Historical Monuments of England, by P.M. Sinton)

*Notes*

1 Since 1988 the NE moat sluice has been restored by the National Trust, together with the NE overflow pond.

2 The principal route of access proposed above supplemented the direct NW approach along the side of the two NW ponds, not marked here.

3 The 'viewing platform' (Fig. 3) lies about 750 feet NNW from the N margin of the main moat.

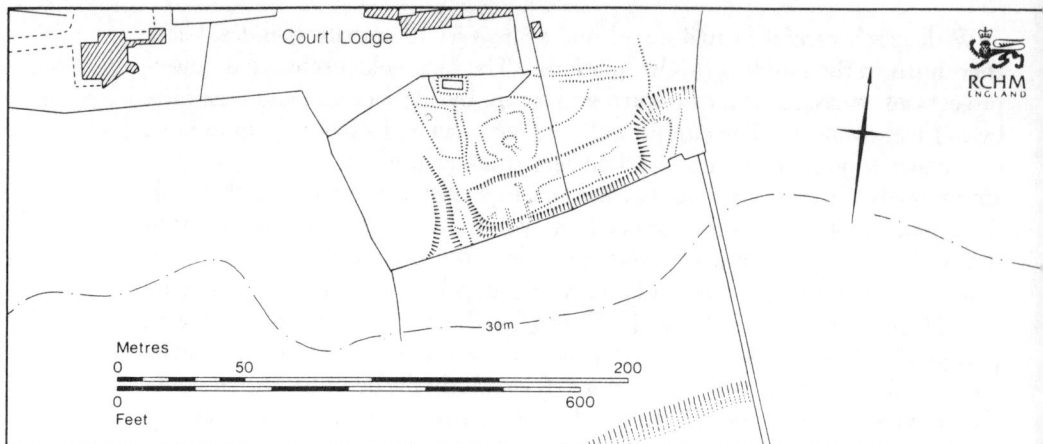

*Figure 3*
Bodiam castle, 'viewing platform' or belvedere. (Crown Copyright reserved)

'On the crest of the high ridge (about 750 feet) to the N of the castle, and some 30m (nearly 100 feet) vertically above it, is an earthwork known as the Gun Garden . . . interpreted following limited excavations in 1961 as a medieval building platform . . . The earthworks consist . . . of broad terraces backed by what may be the sites of buildings . . . obviously ornamented and grand in scale. It is most likely to have been a garden or pleasance . . . but it must surely also have functioned as a viewing platform for the landscaped setting of the castle below. Whether it . . . was physically linked to the castle is now unclear . . .' (C. Taylor, P. Everson and R. Wilson-North, *Med. Arch.* xxxiv, 1990, 155–7: p. 156 is the complete original plan of the entire site, including the viewing platform here treated separately by kind agreement of RCHME)

defensive purpose of the round holes in the vaults of the gate passage. These so-called 'murder-holes' occur in both chambers of the Main Gate passage, where the vaults are fallen, and in the intact vault of the Postern gate passage. 'The openings', he says, 'are, of the central boss, six inches, and of the others, four inches diameter. These apertures can scarcely have been meant for defence; they are too small, and do not command the four corners of the passage . . .'. Fantasies involving boiling oil and molten lead (hazardous even with a stone ceiling) are summarily dismissed but without any alternative explanation being offered.[12]

The rest of his description is devoted to the halls, chambers and 'domestic' offices of the manor-house enveloped by the walls and filling every interior space, including the towers. He concludes with the shrewd comment that 'the

[12] The brick flooring (probably nineteenth century) to the chamber over the passage complicates measurement, but the central hole is seven inches diameter and the others about six inches. All are now blocked (one with ?early-modern brick), perhaps a late medieval modification for domestic convenience. Very effective defensive holes, of different design, can be seen without the doors of Henry VIII's Deal Castle.

58

drum towers look older than their real date, their gorge walls, general proportions and arrangements, well-staircases and lancet and often trefoiled windows, savouring of the Edwardian period' and contrasting, he feels, with the Perpendicular mood of the interior details. Despite some doubts caused by the unpracticality of the putative though vanished right-angled trestle bridge approach to the Main Gate *via* the Octagon (in fact, an authentic feature), 'Castle Clark's' main conclusion firmly annexes Bodiam to his province. 'It was', he declares, 'a castle, not a manor-house, nor palace'.[13] Whether this view reflects a sensitive or contemporary understanding of what such a castle truly was (let alone a fair assessment of the actual structure) must be questioned, but it was the verdict also of John Henry Parker in 1859 in still less acceptable form. For Parker, Bodiam 'is altogether more of a castle than a house; it was habitable but built chiefly for defence'. Somewhat more perceptive, of atmosphere at least, is his comment that 'the windows in the towers are small, narrow and round-headed, just like Norman or Early English'.[14]

Not remotely subtle or sympathetic is the paper published in 1903 by the local antiquarian Harold Sands, in the *Sussex Archaeological Collections*. We find here a military rationale of the most undiluted variety, but strenuous advocacy makes light of the difficulties. Mr Sands' work is a bizarre tribute to the militant aura which the unknown designer so cleverly created. The position, fourteen miles up the now shrunken but just tidal river Rother from Rye, lying ten and a half miles inland from the nearest coast by Hastings, possesses, we are told, 'considerable strategical advantages'.[15] The 'higher ground' which, in fact en-

---

[13] Clark's 101 other monographs nearly all deal with much earlier and major castles, to which he tried to assimilate Bodiam. His reservations are the more telling, as a result, and his omissions more understandable. Subsequent general surveys of castles have regrettably discarded his careful case-study method and popular synthesis has (D.F. Renn, *Norman Castles in Britain* 1968, and King, excepted) been repetitively superficial.

[14] J.H. Parker (and T. Hudson Turner) *Some Account of Domestic Architecture in England . . .*, 3 vols in 4, Oxford 1851–9, iii, 312–4 (still basic; cp. M.E. Wood, *The English Medieval House*, 1965). Parker published the first 'List of Licences to Crenellate from the Patent Rolls' (iii 401–22). Seriously incomplete though it is, his preliminary comments are percipient. Unfortunately William Stubbs and many since took him as proof of the existence of some restrictive policy and system of royal licensing; and not of crenellating but of fortifying (note 6 above).

[15] H. Sands, 'Bodiam Castle', SAC xlvi, 1903, 114–33 (p. 115); the 1985 Guide (caption to first photograph) claims a harbour and an estuary in 1385. The actual estuary S of Rye was in constant danger from the coastwise drift of shingle (later to form Dungeness; see Fig. 1). The fourteen miles of now partly canalised meandering stream, now crossed by six bridges, some doubtless once fords, flowing from Bodiam to Camber (on the Haven, now inland, in the late fifteenth century; see *Med. Arch*, viii 1964, 259) was not a waterway to compare e.g. with the Arun or the Medway. Bodiam administratively represented the upper extremity of the port of Winchelsea e.g. in the 1400 enquiry into the improper shooting of ballast, blamed for blocking the (seaward) channel (*CPR 1399–1401*, 346). In 1349 a dam at *Knellesflote* allegedly blocked the upper river (Nigel Saul, *Scenes from Provincial Life: Knightly Families in Sussex 1280–1400*, Oxford 1986, hereafter Saul, 164). It was clearly quite narrow. The small rivulet at Bodiam combines with four others (now the Kent Ditch, two miles downstream;

tirely overlooks the site especially on the western side, 'was not', we are assured, 'within the range of the offensive weapons in use at the time of its foundation' (see Pl. 10). This reads oddly since Sands' own drawing shows the ground level at bowshot, or 220 yards radius from the castle to the west, to be about ten feet above the tower tops and nearly thirty feet above the curtain parapets (see Pl. 7). Crossbows, longbows, mechanical artillery in the form of mangonels and trebuchets, as well as rapidly developing cannon, were all in use in the 1380s.

the Newmill Channel; the Royal Military Canal, of c.1800; and the Union Channel) before flowing around the dominant bluff of Rye, with its coeval Ypres Tower, and (in 1385) into the enclosed basin of Camber Haven. The upper part at least could easily be barred (e.g. by piling as was quite customary on the coast) at many points (notably at Newenden, four and a half miles below Bodiam) but the river gave access to no attractive inland target, nor would French raiders have preferred slow and small barges to swift horses or direct marching had deep invasion ever been attempted. The late fourteenth-century water-table may have been slightly higher but John Leland was told 'the water is a little brakkische' at Bodiam bridge, just above the castle, which suggests not, if sea-level has not changed. He reported also very credulously that 'the fresch water or ryver' flowed eastwards to Appledore, which it had ceased to do by the end of the twelfth century at the latest (see below). Traditions of the old river 'Rother' *alias* Limen long outlived the reality, and still survive. It had flowed to the sea at Old Romney or perhaps to Lympne and Hythe at the eastern end of the Marsh (*The Itinerary . . . in or about 1535–1543*, ed. L. Toulmin Smith, 1964, v, 62–3, 68). He seems to have picked up a folk tradition of the era of the Danish raids when Newenden and Appledore stood on true estuaries and were easily accessible to seaborne raiders, as Rye (and, to a lesser extent, (New) Winchelsea) continued to be (see *Med. Arch.* xvi, 1972, 124 map). The text typically adopts the Bodiam tradition of 'blocking French raids up the Rother'; also ibid. viii, 1964, 81–6). Dallingridge's fiction may itself have been prompted by local folklore. The 'ancient ship' found in 1823 (sixty-four feet long by fifteen feet beam) six miles below Bodiam (Sands, 117–8) being undated and relating probably to the old river course E to the Romneys, is no proof of late fourteenth-century 'navigability', particularly of the sinuous and shallow upper reaches; nor, in any case, could Bodiam interdict passage unless a large field-force was based there. Only in full-scale invasion could Bodiam be reached. In Leland's time this was a real fear but he treats Bodiam as of no relevance, for this it could neither resist nor stop. Turner (271–2, Fig. 1) relies on a more than necessarily conjectural sketch map of the coastal region not, as he believes, as it was in the late fourteenth century but in fact as it was in the ninth or tenth century. The once great port town of Old Romney, chiefest of the Cinque Ports but by then decayed, Turner's map would place not high and dry far inland but some miles out to sea (and its contemporary successor New Romney, like some *Lyonesse*, still more deeply submarine). Even for the Danish era, it exaggerates the probable breadth of the ancient estuary S of Oxney. Turner, while attempting to allow for more recent work, has only carried to extremes the fantasy Sands and Simpson have propagated, amalgamating local folklore with a credulous acceptance of Dallingridge's meretricious licence. Ancient swamps and marshes, like secret subterranean passages, are powerful myths. The present course of the Rother was created, about ten miles downstream of Bodiam, by choking and silting of the old course, diverting the river S to Rye and (Old) Winchelsea. Recent work strongly indicates this in fact occurred, not in the great storms of 1287 as is customarily held, but 'by at least the late twelfth century': T. Tatton-Brown, 'The Topography of the Walland Marsh Area . . .' in *Romney Marsh: Evolution, Occupation, Reclamation*, ed. J. Eddison and C. Green, Oxford 1988, 105–111 (ref. due to R. Eales); cp. M. Beresford, *New Towns of the Middle Ages*, 1967, 15, on Old Winchelsea. Maritime access, but for barges only, from Yarmouth, is rather more plausibly advanced for John Fastolf's Caister by Simpson and H.D. Barnes (*Antiqs. Journ.* xxxii, 1952, 33–52), but a touch of the same curious aquatic obsession may be present here too.

Those 'murder-holes' in the gate passages (despite Clark, from whom much detail is taken unacknowledged) were for 'thrusting down posts to stop a rush . . . or for casting down that favourite medieval defensive agent, powdered quicklime'. Froissart does mention this, but for external use only.[16]

We are told that between the two cheek-walls outside the Postern entry there was once the pit of a lifting bridge, the outer end supposedly spanning a gap between the masonry abutment and the trestle-bridge crossing the moat. Remains of this bridge and of a similar long fixed timber catwalk to the Octagon in front of the main entrance were investigated in 1919–20 and in 1970 when the moat was again emptied for cleaning. Although none of the characteristic traces of a *pont à bascule* occur in the masonry of either entry or of the Barbican (the recess framing the Postern doorway in particular contradicting the notion) each bridge had a lifting span at its outer end instead (see Pls 2, 3, 9, 11). This, in the case of the Main Entry at least, was not quite original but a contemporary afterthought. The gaps afforded some defence but scarcely beyond a symbolic and ceremonial interruption of the access. Simple removable spans of timber are all that the little platforms, or revette aprons, in front of the Main and Postern entries (and of the Barbican) can have allowed. These are far removed from the massive combined bridge and doorway-closures of Caerphilly and elsewhere, where a pit received the inner counterbalanced end. Harold Sands, however, confidently believed in his 'drawbridges' and even advanced the view 'that originally there was a line of exterior defences, possibly and not improbably in stone, and certainly in wood, running partially or entirely round that part of the outer edge of the bank which retains the waters of the moat' (i.e. on the south and east sides). Sands unfortunately had in mind not so much the dauntless and gallant *escarmouches* and *appertises d'armes* at the 'barriers' so beloved of Jean Froissart, as his own personal vision of a warlike fortress armed at all points. In the sketch plan he attached he omits this imaginary outer defence but transforms the two half-piers to the trestle-bridges on the north-west (main entrance) and south (postern) banks into full-blown and large octagonal tower foundations. Still more visionary, among his other suggestions, is that the Rother level and its 'navigability' were such as to permit a large dock for sea-going ships below the site immediately to the south (assimilating Bodiam to

<hr/>

16 See the valuable summary by J.R. Kenyon, 'Early Artillery Fortifications in England and Wales: a preliminary survey and reappraisal', *Arch. Journ.* cxxxviii, 1981, 205–40; Sands, fig. 26 *et passim*; *Chroniques . . . de Jean Froissart*, ed. J.A.C. Buchon, 2nd edn enlarged, Paris 1835, 4 vols, e.g. i 91 (siege of Aubenton, 1340). Simpson's citations (1931, 90) do not relate to gate passages. Definite examples of water shoots are exterior, placed to soak the doors (e.g. Caerphilly, inner face of main east gatehouse; Leybourne, Kent; see S. Toy *The Castles of Great Britain*, 1953, 239–40). Richard II's Bloody Tower, London, has similar vault-holes as also has contemporary Donnington. Voice-communication for the porters, or surveillance and intimidation, are possible, but not shooting. 'Eyes' in vault-bosses are found in other contexts.

Beaumaris).[17] Equally aberrant is his idea that the angle towers 'were probably covered by high conical roofs, not being large enough to carry engines'. Their structure indicates otherwise, to go no further. Elsewhere Sands shows he is aware of the cultural and domestic elements in the castles of this era but no attempt is made to reconcile them in a fashion true to the period and its works. The image of an anarchic Middle Ages, 'red in tooth and claw', is not easily relinquished.

It is worth persisting a little longer with this most unsatisfactory paper, which compounds its errors by both plagiarizing and denigrating G.T. Clark (by picking a quarrel, chiefly on the garderobe chamber doors), because it demonstrates (albeit in ludicrous extremity) the kind of literal-minded, materialistic anachronism which has prevented Bodiam Castle from being properly appreciated, or its ethos comprehended. Sands regarded it essentially as a military fort, citing the thirty-three remaining fireplaces, several ovens and twenty-eight garderobes as proof 'that the castle was intended to be manned by a large garrison, certainly not less than a hundred men'. While emphasizing the powers of the contemporary longbow (but entirely ignoring these at the disposal of an attacking party), Sands could still pass over without remark the entire absence of arrow-loops throughout the place, whether in the merlons of the parapets or elsewhere (see e.g. Pl. 4). He saw the chief defence of the castle as lying in 'the passive strength afforded by the moat, the external barbicans, and the machicolations above the gates'. In reality, the structural solidity of Bodiam is spurious within and without.

Anachronistic popularization is the last accusation seemingly to be made against Alexander Hamilton Thompson, but his very solid work focused expressly on 'military architecture'. He also took literally that tendentious phrase in the licence and believed that 'the defensive nature of the works at Bodiam is very clearly apparent, not only in the strength (sic) of the walls, the height of which is equal to the height of the walls at Harlech, but in the provision made for the defence of the approaches'. The facts of contemporary siegecraft he omits. He likens the moat to that of late-thirteenth century Leeds (Kent),

---

[17] See note 15. Romantic imagination has also made a 'tilt-yard' of the large embanked area to the SSW (see Fig. 2). This was another enclosed pond well above river level, probably a mill-pond to supply which the local springs were supplemented by a new leat from Salehurst (note 84; RCHME i, 9–11). These outer ponds, to the S above the Rother and to the NW, and E of the moat were 'water features all intended to enhance the visual appearance' (RCHME ii). Sands elsewhere (e.g. 'Some Kentish Castles' in *Memorials of Old Kent*, eds Ditchfield and Clinch, 1907, 150–237) shows great realism. On Bodiam he equivocates between fantasy (e.g. that the interior had timber platforms for projectile engines, 122) and the sober locating of the castle at some (ill-defined) stage between the Tudor manor house and 'the sterner forms of military architecture of Norman times'. Many good comparisons are drawn, and siegecraft is carefully discussed (129–30), but this pragmatism succumbs to the seduction of Bodiam. Even Sidney Toy, 213, describes the moat as 'fed from the river'. Of the fallacy of regarding castles 'strategically', even in Palestine, the classic refutation is R.C. Smail, *Crusading Warfare*, Cambridge 1956, ch. I. For the bridges see note 32 below.

praising the careful revetting of 'the islands in the lake' but does not grasp the major differences, notably the crucial weakness of the purely earthen banks which at Bodiam pound it up (see Pls 4, 7). Whereas the revetments protected the foundations and earth infill from the erosion of the water, almost stagnant though it is, the retaining banks on the south and east have neither lining nor core of masonry.[18] This is not he sort of misjudgement which an engineer, like G.T. Clark, or an architect with strong historical insights, is likely to commit. Hugh Braun in his 'little book' *The English Castle* (1936) characterizes Bodiam as 'a fortified manor-house' (surely the essential nature of castles, at whatever level) and rightly praises it as 'one of the most perfect . . . as well as possibly the most beautiful' example of the *genre*. As usual, he then tags on a discussion of the alleged danger of French raids, which supposedly made Bodiam different, relying again on the licence, chiefly supported by a superficial impression of the apparently elaborate defences. Braun, like Clark and also Parker, remarks on its 'looking much more like a castle of a century earlier', but he goes much further than they in treating these fourteenth-century castles in general as 'toy for-tresses', attributable to the 'fashionable craze' for chivalry. The last of the 'real castles', in his eyes, was Beaumaris in Anglesey, begun in 1295 and still unfin-ished twenty years later. Despite their affinities of plan, the later 'so-called castles', he declares, or 'more properly fortified manor-houses . . ., would not have stood up to a trebuchet and the artillery of the Civil War crumpled them up like a pack of cards'. His view is uncompromising: 'Nothing would suit such marvellous persons as these . . . lords and ladies but that they must live in castles. The fact that there was very little need for such was a small consider-ation; those who had not already a (more or less obsolete) castle had to see about building one as soon as they could afford it and acquire the necessary (*sic*) licence'.[19] Christopher Hohler has since then (1966) condensed Braun's view, shorn of qualification, into the trenchant judgement that Bodiam, 'though planned in accordance with sound military principles (*sic*) is . . . really an old soldier's dream-house and could never have played a significant part in a late-

---

18 A.H. Thompson, *Military Architecture in England during the Middle Ages*, Oxford 1912, 322–7, 338; cp. the criticism of 'the military point of view', as a whole, and Thompson in particular, for defining (232) a castle as 'a military post which may include one or more dwelling houses within its walls', by Mackay Mackenzie, appendix B, on the modern concept of 'the keep'. For Thompson the Bodiam licence had for its 'main object . . . to provide against a French attack upon the ports of Rye and Winchelsea (*sic*) at the mouth of the Rother . . .' (cp. Fig. 1, and note 15 above). Comparison with the great dams at Leeds, Caerphilly, Kenilworth, and also at London would have been corrective. Commonsense would too. The Bodiam embank-ment is structurally barely adequate even without hostile interference (*pers. comm.*, 24 June 1970, Mr L.E. Hole). The revetments of the outer bridge piers are not quite original, it seems (note 32 below).

19 H. Braun, *The English Castle*, 1936, 102 *et seq*. Licences were acts of royal patronage, patents of architectural nobility. Braun's comment on Beaumaris may in purely 'military' terms have some justification but culturally and historically it has none. It is a strange and widespread modern arrogance to reject so many places contemporaries called 'castles' as though we better understood their true nature.

63

fourteenth century war'.[20] With the latter point it is impossible to disagree, but Bodiam should not be dismissed as mere *braggadocio* on that account. The middle ground must be explored. Hohler's view is still very much the minority opinion. But there is a compromise hypothesis, that advanced by Dr W. Douglas Simpson of Aberdeen in the 1940s.

Simpson argued in a closely-related group of papers in 1939–46, that 'bastard feudalism' decisively affected the later castles.[21] It is an attempt to construct a socio-economic explanation (in this case strongly tinged by the Tudor 'feudal anarchy' myth and by revivalist militarism) which constitutes the most sustained effort so far to bring to bear upon a series of buildings, in a systematic manner, many of the wide range of relevant issues. Simpson devoted a long paper (1931) to Bodiam and contributed in 1961 a Guidebook on the castle for the National Trust. His doctrine has persisted in steadily more diluted guise.[22] For the enemy without, by and large, Simpson substituted the enemy within – potentially restive and mutinous household troops, on whose disaffection the pay packet allegedly exercised less restraint than had formerly the personal loyalty to their lord of men who were his feudal dependents, doing him unpaid service during brief periods of warfare. Architecturally the case depends on proving that the quarters assigned by the scheme (often on flimsy evidence) to these retainers were defensibly separated from those of the lord's family (in the restricted and modern sense), which goes far beyond the expression of degrees of rank and differences of use effectuated by ordinary doors, stairways, ante-

---

[20] The quadrangular towered plan is not exclusively 'military'. Hohler's phrase has provoked but if indeed 'a man is not on oath in lapidary inscriptions', captions should also be excused. (C. Hohler, 'Kings and Castles: court life in peace and war', in *The Flowering of the Middle Ages* ed. Joan Evans, 1966, 140).

[21] Most notably 'Bastard Feudalism and the Later Castles', *Antiqs. Journ.* xxvi, 1946, 145–74; also 'Castles of Livery and Maintenance', *Journ. BAA*, 3rd ser. iv, 39–54 with some extra material. Simpson did not apply the interpretation to Bodiam in 1931. In 1935 it was still evolving ('The Affinities of Lord Cromwell's Tower House at Tattershall', *Journ. BAA* xl, 177–92) but was nearly developed by 1938–9 ('Warkworth: a castle of Livery and Maintenance', *Archaeologia Aeliana* xv, 1938, 115–36; 'Dunstanburgh Castle', ibid. xvi, 1939, 31–42; 'Belsay Castle and the Scottish Tower Houses', ibid. xvii, 1940, 75–84; 'The Castles of Dudley and Ashby de la Zouche' *Arch. Journ.* xcvi, 142–58). The architectural relevance at least of the phenomenon (recently e.g. C. Carpenter, 'The Beauchamp Affinity: a study of Bastard Feudalism at work', *EHR* xcv, 1980, 514–32; cp. G. A. Holmes, *The Later Middle Ages*, 1962, 27–30, 165–7) is by no means generally accepted (e.g. Stewart Cruden, *The Scottish Castle*, Edinburgh 1960, 87–91). Patrick Faulkner (note 25 below) had no need of the hypothesis.

[22] Changes of tone and detail are found between the 1961, 1975 (Catherine Morton) and 1985 Guides. The large room in the NW range has been 'Stables?', 'Garrison', and again 'Stables'. The 1975 text keeps 'retainers' (e.g. 16) but the Plan has 'Servants' Hall'. In 1961 and 1975 (16, 17) 'that necessity of all good (*sic*) castles the dungeon' is put in the NW Tower basement but 1985 admits 'the lake water' would flood it, suggesting instead the two cavities (inaccessible; lit by loop-lights) under the porters' chambers in the Main Gate, which are equally implausible.

chambers and passages.[23] Also, the pronounced trend at this time towards greater privacy for the lord and his closest companions affected even monasteries and has to be allowed for. In fact, at all periods, separate defensibility of component units (essentially the 'keep' concept) is, to the 'military' interpreter, frustratingly unusual. The whole thesis in short presents innumerable difficulties. Standing or long-term garrisons, for one thing, were prohibitively expensive in whatever manner they were remunerated, nor are mercenary soldiers confined to the era of the 'Hundred Years War'.[24]

Simpson's attempt at Bodiam to link contemporary society to the architecture must still be commended. His insistence that Bodiam Castle 'is a strong fortress erected, as the terms of its licence show, to subserve national military needs', cannot, however, be accepted. His presumption of dominant military purpose must be compared with the very careful analysis done on the interior by P.A. Faulkner, who has convincingly shown that providing suites of lodgings for persons of varying rank is the clue to much castle-planning in the later thirteenth century and in the fourteenth. At Bolton in Wensleydale this technique is particularly illuminating.[25] At Bodiam, Simpson asks us to 'note that the retainers' quarters (the western range) are completely isolated (sic). They communicate neither with the gatehouse (Main Gate) at their own end nor with the lord's suite at the other' (unless the bold retainer were to stroll across the courtyard). The well, which Clark was unable to find in 1874 (nor any piping, as at Leeds, from an exterior spring) and which Sands expected in the central courtyard has been located, by Simpson, in the basement of the SW Tower where it serves 'both the Lord's Kitchen and the Retainers' Hall'. This, he feels, is important as 'the water supply . . . is under the lord's control' – which conjures up some intriguing visions of rival scullions warring over the water-pots. Faulkner's analysis of the entire surviving accommodation, focusing especially

---

[23] Most clearly formulated by Simpson in 1946, (note 21 above) 151–2. Internecine Scottish *ambiance* may have contributed. The theory was even stretched to Edward Stafford's Thornbury, Gloucs. (licensed 1510). At Doune Castle, Perths., (ibid 148) his whole case depends on a single door closure, between the Servants' Hall and lord's suite (cp. his excellent 'The Tower Houses of Scotland', in *Studies in Building History*, ed. E.M. Jope, 1961, 229–42).

[24] Space precludes discussion here. Separately defensible sections (e.g. Château Gaillard) or units were valuable anyway for prolonged defence against external enemies, as Caerphilly abundantly but most exceptionally shows (e.g. C.N. Johns, *Caerphilly Castle*, HMSO Cardiff 1978, 51, 68 *et passim*). The 'keep-gatehouse' here, at least, is a reality. On privacy see Wood (note 14 above), 129–36; also M. Girouard, *Life in the English Country House*, 1978, 30 quoting Langland *c*.1362, and ch. 3 *passim*

[25] Simpson appreciates the aesthetics of the seignorial rôle but Faulkner consistently follows the practicalities through to the details of the building; P.A. Faulkner, 'Domestic Planning from the Twelfth to the Fourteenth Centuries', and 'Castle Planning in the Fourteenth Century', *Arch. Journ.* cxv, 1958, 150–83; ibid. cxx, 1963, 215–35 (Bodiam, 230–4). His comments command acceptance in almost all respects, notably that the customary duplication (e.g. of Halls) was to provide separately for the occasionally resident lord and the permanent manorial staff.

on access-linkages, is wholly to be preferred to Simpson's internecine variety of militarism, and it alone makes sense of the ways in which the tower chambers communicate with the interior and with the wall-walks (allures) of the curtains.[26]

The architectural grandeur and powerful effect of Bodiam are, however, beyond dispute and are justly extolled by W. Douglas Simpson (1961) and epitomized by the heraldic displays on the two gate towers (see Pls 2, 11). The difficulty lies in discerning how far the visual impact and the symbolic significance inherent in battlemented panoply have affected particular features and exaggerated them in the familiar contemporary fashion whereby art enhanced structural function. Working the same transformation upon the defensive elements of fortification, such as the crenellation, flanking towers, archery loops (absent here), portcullis and drawbridge, can so perfectly integrate the military and the psychological that separately analysing the contribution of each becomes very difficult. The wisest course is to resist the temptation to write off any feature as 'sham', or to take any element as purely 'functional' (by which 'defensive' is intended normally). It is an artful combination which expresses, and most deliberately evoked for contemporaries, all the complex seignorial associations of the medieval castle-image, which included the deterring (and, if necessary, the defeating) of attack at whatever level was appropriate in the personal, local and wider circumstances. Given that the age of Richard II was one of the most sophisticated and cultured of the whole era of medieval European civilization, it would be as well to jettison the crude dichotomy implicit in the assertion that Bodiam is 'a late but genuinely military castle, no mere residence'.[27] It is a gross anachronism in any medieval period but especially in this (see Pl. 15).

---

[26] Simpson (1931, 91–2) admitted he was puzzled by the seemingly haphazard presence or absence of wall-walk doorways. The present 'well' seems to be only a cistern, despite the 1985 Guide (7). Pollution from the 'lake', to which its level corresponds, would be a danger. The soldiery Simpson believed Dallingridge kept here figure alternatively as 'his well-tried free companions' and as the unruly mercenaries upon whose existence his 1946 thesis depends (e.g. 161). The notion that some French commando raid might hunt down their old adversary here is most imaginative (1985 Guide, 1).

[27] 1975 Guide 9. It is simplistic to regard the 'noble display' of the south front, and to write (truly) of the north side 'as one of the noblest façades (sic) of medieval military architecture' ('. . . the Great Gatehouse, broad lofty and browbeating') as meaning that they necessarily therefore constitute 'a formidable fortification' (Simpson 1961, 6, 9), although they might be acceptably described as 'a grand parade of feudal pride' (see Pls 8, 10). Wholly to be preferred is the sensitive analysis by Beric Morley of fourteenth-century castle design, Essays in Memory of Stuart Rigold, ed. Alec Detsicas, Kent Archaeological Society, Maidstone, 1981, 104–13.

## III. THE STRUCTURAL EVIDENCE OF THE CASTLE PROPER[28]

Because the wider questions of location and historical context are best dealt with in concluding, and flow from considering the exterior and its *assiette*, we will examine first the significant details as seen from within, in order to address the central issue of this paper, namely the precise sense in which it may be affirmed that Bodiam is truly a castle.

### Interior Impressions

The preservation of the building is remarkably complete, having suffered no apparent damage when surrendered in 1483 nor during the Civil War, when so many castles were vindictively dismantled and disfigured. Opportunistic pre-Victorian quarrying for the worked ashlar, and the effects of time, are alone visible. Fortunately, building stone is quite readily available in quarries scattered across the area (Wadhurst stone). Much of the interior, where some of the internal walls and partitions may have been of timber and plaster, and an uncertain but considerable amount of masonry, have disappeared, although a great deal still remains.[29] The embankments pounding up the lake for some space of time may have been breached and left with the water drained off, but

---

28 Warm acknowledgement is due for invaluable help to Mr J.H. Past, custodian, and to Mr L.E. Hole, the contractor, in June 1970, and to the late Derek Cassleton-Elliott of Vinehall Farm, Robertsbridge, for his intermediary good offices. Any unattributed information in this and the following section IV is due to them. Other details derive from examination mostly in August and October 1989. All are easily verifiable with no more equipment than un-prejudiced observation.

29 Edward's son, John Dallingridge, died in 1407 and another John in March 1443 (*CCR 1441–7*, 94–5). Bodiam, not held in-chief, passed to the Lewknors. In the Buckingham revolt, November 1483, a commission significantly including Richard Lewknor, obtained its surrender (*CPR 1476–85*, 370). The large calibre integral cast-iron bombard found in 1919 in the moat was not a garrison weapon being much too large to fit the Main Gate gunloops. If a relic of the supposed attack, it cannot have been used since there is no visible damage, unless to the (largely vanished) Barbican. The interior may have been partially gutted, as happened then to Buckingham's own Maxstoke (J.D. Mackenzie, *The Castles of England . . .*, 2 vols 1897, i, 360), but Bodiam stayed in some sort of occupation until the early seventeenth century. It fitted Simpson's thesis to believe the tradition of a Civil War siege (1931, 97–8) nominally on the strength of an alleged cannon battery, near the top of the slope overlooking the north front, 'known of old as the Gun Garden or Gun Battery Field'. Found to be medieval in 1960 the royal Commission interpret this as 'a viewing platform for the land-scaped setting of the castle below' (*RCHME* i, 13–5; ii, *passim*; (see Fig. 3); and *Med. Arch.*, vi–vii, 1962–3, 334–5). Bodiam does not figure in the list of 150 known Parliamentary 'slightings' (including Bolton, Donnington, Maxstoke, Sterborough, and Wressel, all comparable) compiled by M.W. Thompson (138–57, appendix 3). There are no apparent defensive modifications, despite allegations (e.g. 1975 *Guide* 13: the SE Tower ground floor lights needed no enlargement; traces are equivocal and in the wrong place for flanking (see Pl. 5); no other lights have been tampered with) and wild assertions e.g. that the 'towers were later provided with gun-ports for covering-fire all round the castle by adapting arrow-loops' (*sic*), among other embroidery in P. S. Fry, *The David and Charles Book of Castles*, 1980 91, 190–1.

this was clearly not part of any 'slighting'. Only the most conveniently accessible stonework has been taken, namely most of the northern Barbican, much of the domestic ranges and all the parapets of the curtains except for the north and south-east (see Pls 6, 15). The destruction has been mild and freestone detail has not generally been wrenched out.[30] The towers have largely been spared: the summits of the Main Gate, of the NE, NW and SE angle towers almost entirely so; and of the rectangular mid-wall towers the East Tower is largely unscathed and the others (apart from the Mid-West Tower) have lost little more than some of the merlons of their parapets. The machicolated portions of parapet would have been especially easy to destroy. Even the dainty and attractive stair turrets are intact, and most of the elegant chimneys. The 'defences' are barely touched, the Main Gate gunloops being unmodified and in pristine condition. The only conspicuous medieval alteration is the supplementary portcullis chamber built onto the inner ground floor of the Main Gate, extending the passage inwards to meet the interior building alignment. The details show this was a contemporary afterthought, which with the cheek walls and platform added outside the Postern Tower form the chief exceptions to the masterly foresight with which the whole closely-combined scheme has been carried out. The consistency of detail and in the dimensions of standard features (e.g. doorways, stairs and windows) is most notable. Preparatory earthworks (principally to the moat) could have begun at the time of the licence in October 1385, and the masonry revetments and foundations at the start of the next building season. The variety of coloration of the ashlar suggests batches of material of diverse provenance. It is economically employed (see e.g. Pl. 5). In all, with the limited means at Dallingridge's disposal and allowing for competition for the services of peripatetic masons, a quite prolonged construction period is indicated, perhaps as much as eight 'seasons'. Such mild gaucheness and crudity of execution as is visible in the lintels to some allure doorways, and in the construction of the lesser arches in general, strikes the eye only because of the contrast with the careful plugging of the putlog (scaffolding) holes, the

Cannon on the wall-tops are most improbable (Kenyon, 1981, 209). Stone chips (from the original construction) were found in the moat in 1970, but no traces of any attack.

[30] Signs were found in 1970 that grass or rushes had grown on part of the area, at a level about eight inches below the modern slime of lily detritus (Curzon?) and about ten inches above the original bed. The masonry taken was all accessible from the interior. In 1778 the pond was full (print, 1975 *Guide*). Clark noted (1874) that 'enough, and not too much, has been done to arrest the effects of time and weather. The repairs have been well executed, and in Wadhurst stone, the proper material . . .' (Clark i, 240). Certainly, they are not now evident. Simpson (1931, 96–9) argues over-ingeniously that 'slighting', not quarrying, was responsible. Even 'penal slighting', to punish Lord Thanet, would not have spared the 'defences'. But he may be right to ascribe the direct northern earthen causeway (rather questionably replaced by a timber cat-walk recently) to the late medieval period (see Pl. 9). Of his alleged widening of the main entrance for carts by cutting away the basal jamb mouldings, however, there is no conclusive sign (see Pl. 14). The hub not the cart tyre required the greatest width in any case, and leaves distinctive marks.

elegant parapet crestings, nicely moulded corbels to the machicolation (particularly of the Main Gate) and the charmingly proportioned and sturdy mouldings of the single-light exterior windows to be seen everywhere.[31] For reasons of
safety and covenience some parts of the castle are not ordinarily accessible. The
upper chambers of the Main Gate can be inspected but not its summit, nor the
eastern ground floor. The only usable portion of wall-walk is that linking the
Main Gate to the NW Tower, all levels of which are open, as also is the case
with all but the upper floor of the Postern. Otherwise, only the 'basements'
(ground floors) can be seen closely, but these limitations do not materially affect
the present investigation.

## The Postern Tower, Doorways and 'Programme'

The Postern is a scaled-down version of the main entrance, lacking any gunloops and with one portcullis chase instead of three. The doors at the inner side
of the entry chamber open directly into the Screens Passage (see Pl. 3). The
chamber vault and its 'murder holes', in the bosses at the intersections of the
ribs, are all intact. It is, in all, a lightly-protected private access, or more
probably, a 'tradesman's entrance', conveniently placed to supply the adjacent
kitchens. Indeed 'Postern' is a misnomer, but traditional. Exteriorly, the straight
wooden trestle-bridge once debouched upon the narrow space between the low
cheek walls. Around the archway into the tower is the emphatic square recess
which might ordinarily be taken for a drawbridge rebate. It closely resembles
that on the Main Gate, but neither there nor here is there any sign of a pit, nor
any trace of chain holes in the spandrels.[32] The portcullis groove is of reasonable

---

[31] The thesis of defence crisis has tended to predicate speedy construction, just as belief in a
'slighting' fitted the military interpretation, although Curzon (to whom Simpson normally
defers) thought the construction 'took several years' (Simpson 1931, 89). Notably, all parts
went up at once, not defences first and apartments later. Dallingridge's means were piecemeal
and diverse, and his local and national preoccupations considerable, especially as a royal
councillor from 1389 until shortly before his death c.1394 (notes 83, 84). 'Wadhurst stone',
from a number of local quarries, is a coarse but enduring material varying from pale buff to
greenish light grey. Many standard items, such as newel-stair treads (about ten and a half
inches high except in the upper Main Gate where of twelve inches riser), windowheads and
jambs, were supplied ready-made from the quarry. The sporadic use of lintels reinforces the
'job-lot' impression. Lesser arches made of large soffit-hollowed bed-tilted blocks, not radial
voussoirs, are normal at this period. Masons' marks hve been found on some underwater
ashlars. On building seasons and duration see J.G. Edwards, 'Edward I's Castle-Building in
Wales', PBA xxxii, 1944, esp. appendix I; D. Knoop and G.P. Jones, The Medieval Mason,
Manchester 1949, 131–4; L.F. Salzman, Building in England down to 1540, Oxford 1952,
passim.

[32] 'Meutrière' is the French Romantic modernism but for an archery loop ('archère' rectius for
arbalisteria or archeria); see E.E. Viollet-le-Duc, Dictionnaire Raisonné de l'Architecture Fran-
çaise . . . art. 'Meutrière' for details of loops. Base timbers (e.g. sleeper beams) of the main
trestle bridge were found in 1920, and in 1970 on the Postern approach (see Pl. 2) by David
Martin (Hastings Area Archaeological Papers i, 1973; summarized Med. Arch. xv, 1971, 148;
and more fully, with context, by S.E. Rigold, 'Structural Aspects of Medieval Timber Bridges'

size for a thin oak grating, similar to the fragment remaining in the Main Gate. No traces of any winch can be found.[33] The only other closure to this gate passage are the doors at either end, the inner archway opening onto the Screens Passage (with the fine triple service doorways still intact on the left hand side), the outer closed by an old, but not original frame and (vaguely linenfold) panel, two-leaf door, set in a rebate four and a half inches deep with the hinge-hooks still in place. No trace of the normal defensive closure, by means of one or two substantial timber bars set in a deep hole and drawn across to engage in a socket in the opposite jamb, can be found. Indeed, none of the Bodiam doorways, not even the defensively vital ones (such as the access to the staircase from the entry chamber), are so provided. Closure was effected by small (metal) bolts mounted on the door, engaging in small shallow sockets. It is of purely domestic character nor can arrangements now gone explain it: even a pivoting bar on one of the leaves of the original Postern door, engaging not in the jambs but in a bracket on the other, would be very weak in such an exposed position.

Hinge-hooks and depths of rebates give the rough thickness of doors, and also of window shutters. Here the hinges seem mostly to have been set in wooden plugs fixed in cut-out sockets, and many have disappeared. But the resultant recesses cannot be mistaken for drawbar holes. Doors and shutters universally were evidently of planks on fragile battens, seldom exceeding two inches in thickness and mostly under one inch in all.[34]

The Postern passage chamber is generously lit by two windows of the type

(p. 77), *Med. Arch.* xix, 1975, 48–91). Both at first were uninterrupted but (probably soon) altered to provide lifting spans to new stone-encased semi-octagonal abutments, i.e. such defences as these approaches possessed are not attributable to the 1385–6 coastal-defence crisis. Both were carefully dismantled, the N bridge (?) when the causeway was built (the N side of the gap is revetted, see Pl. 9). The cheek walls to the Postern were also after-thoughts (not bonded), the result being a diminutive version of Warwick's barbican, or those of York and Alnwick town walls (see Pl. 1). Even when there was no actual drawbridge, such square recesses around portal archways become standard symbolism, e.g. the brick gatehouse at Rye House, Herts. (licenced 1443; *C Ch R* vi, 38); Maxstoke (1345) has 'murder holes' but again no drawbridge to its recess. The obligatory portcullis slit occurs and also provision for parapet crenel-shutters (Binney note 41 below, pls 9, 10).

[33] The Postern portcullis chase (see Pl. 3) measures five by four and a half inches, slightly slimmer than the remains (seen by Clark in 1874 and probably medieval) at the Main Gate (chases four by three inches and six by four and a half inches deep) which consist of halving-jointed (oak) bars, iron plated and secured with rivetted-over wrought-iron nails. All the other chases are empty. They show no wear and may never have been fitted with gratings (built *in situ* or inserted from above, where space allows).

[34] Clearances between hinge-hooks and rebate face seldom indicate doors more than three quarters of an inch (2 cm) thick even allowing for strap-hinges fixed directly to planking itself nailed to battens or to a complete frame. Traces of brick blocking in the jambs of the inward Postern passage doorway cannot have been bar-hole and socket. Minor adaptations, some in brick, show the continued convenience of the house into the Jacobean period, although Leland disliked its archaism. His dismissive reference suggests he did not inspect it ('an old castle', *Itinerary* iv, 68), cp. the appreciative 1538 survey of Warkworth, Northumberland (Turner and Parker iii, 204).

standard throughout. These look along the adjacent curtains but can in no sense be termed 'loops', still less 'slits', the unaltered example being thirteen inches wide by twenty-six inches high, with traces of iron bars, shutter rebate and hinges (see Pl. 1). In the castle as a whole four basic types of outward window can be distinguished. They illustrate the 'programme' to which the designer was working. Any fortification was advertised as such. The *signa fortericie* such as crenellation, towers, moats, drawbridge and portcullis, of course, but also the arrow-slits, or later the gun-loops, were made evident. Whereas the message of power and deterrence compelling respect was a by-product in works of conspicuous solidity and defensive efficiency (e.g. major castles), magnates of lesser motivation or more modest means, needs and social pretensions chose to convey it by the studied exaggeration of features of defensive origin, which have been called 'the vocabulary of fortification'. This lesser class of building is best termed 'militant architecture'. When this embroidery of the substance develops (with no obvious point of transition as Bodiam shows) into outright mannerism and hyperbole (as at Herstmonceux), other means than physical force have clearly taken over that message of power and status. Contemporaries knew the language and would have read aright those Bodiam windows. It is the modern observer who may be deceived.[35]

## The Windows and Loop-Lights

The window openings are, then, as eloquent as the doorways. Originally they were equipped with shutters and bars, except only for the narrow loop-lights to the garderobe chambers. Little original ironwork remains, but the indications at the accessible windows show they were protected by a vertical bar and up to five horizontal (saddle) bars in the largest, to prevent illicit entry. Many are within quite easy reach from a boat or raft (see e.g. Pl. 5). Some have traces of incised glazing grooves (on one side only) but they are shallow, with no sign of lead cames, and probably one of the sixteenth- or seventeenth-century refinements. Originally there may well have been small glass panes set in the shutters but not in the few surviving, probably early-modern replacements. Outward and inward windows are treated indifferently. Shutters cannot much have exceeded three quarters of an inch in thickness, most being half an inch thick, that is slightly thinner than the doors. They too were secured by sliding metal bolts of small

---

[35] Cp. Turner, 277 and consider Louis d'Orléans castles of Vez, La Ferté Milon and Pierrefonds whose documentation and *construction de prestige* are analysed by Jean Mesqui and Claude Ribéra-Pervillé in *Bulletin Monumental* t. 138, iii, 1980, 293–345, esp. 320–3). At a humbler level, and for *signa fortericie* see C.L.H. Coulson 'Castellation in the County of Champagne . . .' in *Château Gaillard Etudes . . .* ix–x, Caen 1982, 347–64. For the Breton gentry see M. Jones *et al.*, 'The Seigneurial Domestic Buildings of Brittany . . .', *Antiqs. Journ.* lxix, 1989, 73–110; also the important discussion by Thompson ch. 5. ('A Martial Face'), which concentrates attention on the fifteenth century but discusses illuminatingly the 1360–90 additions at Warwick.

dimension. Some of the open effect of these plentiful apertures was modified by the shutters, by which light and draughts were regulated, but the powerful contemporary crossbow particularly, or the English longbow, would find in them little obstruction.[36] Disregarding the various forms of window-head and mould-ings, the four types referred to are: the standard, medium size in the towers and curtains, exemplified by the Postern gate chamber; secondly, rather smaller 'basement' lights, most readily seen in the SE Tower (five and a half inches wide by twenty-eight and a half inches high, minimum opening) and in the SW ('Well Tower' two and a half inches wide by twenty-five inches high, exception-ally, and having no splay at all to the outer thirteen inches of their jambs, making them quite useless for shooting); and thirdly, the large and multi-light special purpose windows of the Lord's Hall and Chamber, in the SE curtain and of the Chapel (see Pl. 15). Finally, and of the most interest for defensive poten-tial, because most flank the curtains in good enfilading positions and open through relatively thin walls, are the loop-lights to the latrines and some of the stair-wells.[37]

The positioning of the windows in the tower rooms should first be noted. It is quite unrelated to flanking (the defensive *raison d'être* of projecting towers), being upon the outward half of the perimeter so as to get the best light, leaving the thickened junctions with the curtains to accommodate the vice stairs. Essentially, above the ground floor each of the drum towers contains three storeys, each chamber provided with three of these windows, a fireplace and a compact garderobe closet opening off a short passage, the stair being on the opposite side. Very skilful planning was required to fit all this, and suitably proportioned openings for each, into the limited space, even with walls only six feet thick. Descending privy shoots (discharging below the moat surface) and ascending fireplace flues are the verticals determining the placing of the win-dows which, where possible (for structural and visual advantage) are staggered, although many do vertically coincide (see Pl. 4). The effect is admirable. Wall-masses everywhere predominate and yet excellent illumination, well distributed and balanced, is achieved. The window seats are on the sill aprons to make the

---

[36] The late fourteenth century windlass-crossbow was formidable and widely used and could outrange the longbow (R. Payne-Gallwey, *The Crossbow*, 1958, 20–30, 90–1 *et passim*). The combination of crossbowmen (behind their *pavises*), archers, trebuchets, mangonels and cannon in contemporary sieges is clear in MSS, e.g. H.W. Koch *Medieval Warfare*, 1978, 80, 149; notes 39, 41 below; also E.E. Viollet-le-Duc, *Dictionnaire du Mobilier Français* vi, 215–21 art. 'Pavois'.

[37] Despite wish-fulfilment assertions, the windows along the most vulnerable west side are not smaller but conform to the general pattern of their type. The medium size in the Postern Tower is thirteen by twenty-six inches (ground floor), ten by forty-nine (first floor); in the Sacristy (next the Chapel) ten by thirty-five; N Tower ten and a half by forty-eight generally. The Well (SW) Tower basement lights (not 'loops') are the only examples here to suggest even remotely the *soupirail* type, raked steeply to light and ventilate foundation-pit chamber-s. The dove-cot in the SW Tower summit is convenient for both kitchens (oddly, Sands did not claim this was for carrier-pigeons to send messages in time of siege).

most of the limited space and the arched heads to the splayed recesses are most elegant and attractive. The voids are as large as harmonious proportion allowed. The skin of this house may be a castellated one, but John Harvey's comment is very just that 'the building is certainly not the work of an unaided country contractor'. Domestic convenience and a certain modest elegance prevail throughout.[38] Lacking niches (the jambs are simply splayed) and without rake to the sills, these windows would scarcely be usable even by a crossbow-man and in no way resemble defensive slits. Experiments at Whitecastle (Gwent) have shown that archers (and a crossbowman with slightly better success) were able at twenty-five yards distance from the walls to put nearly a third of their arrows (or bolts) through slits a mere one and a half to two inches wide. Even with the slight protection of shutters, the entire interior of Bodiam Castle would be exposed and men crouching behind the merlons of the parapets above would be scarcely less vulnerable. Had they been there at all, Edward Dallingridge's 'trusty companions in arms' would have been hard-pressed even by a band of peasant archers with their war-bows in which so many were well-practised.[39]

The last resort of the military analyst looking for archery loops would be those apparently very well-placed garderobe closet and stair loop-lights, set in the flanks and squinch walls of all eight towers (see Pls 6, 15). Perhaps here a covert 'active defence' might lie concealed, much as the *bourgeoisie* (and clergy some-

---

[38] Bodiam, though castellated with such *panache*, has an almost *bourgeois* cosiness quite absent from such grand magnatial lodgings as John of Gaunt's hall-suite at Kenilworth. J. Harvey (*Henry Yevele*, 1940, 41, 80) believed that 'the position of Dalyngrigge (i.e. at Court) and the simple powerful (*sic*) design of the castle, strongly suggest Yevele as the architect'. He was involved at Cooling and at Canterbury (cathedral nave and city walls) and the 'gatehouse' at Saltwood has 'the appearance of being Yevele's'. In Harvey's *The Perpendicular Style*, 1978, 107, these buildings are definitely ascribed 'to Yeveley or to his associates' on 'various combinations of structural evidence and records'. Yevele, it must be stressed, was a large-scale omni-competent contractor and not especially a 'military' architect. A very capable site-supervisor or Master Mason must have been in day-to-day charge at Bodiam if Harvey is right, for Yevele, like Dallingridge, can have spent very little time here.

[39] Dr Derek Renn and Peter Jones ('The Military Effectiveness of Arrow-Loops', *Château-Gaillard* ix–x, Caen 1982, 445–56) confirmed also how such niched loops were used in defence (cp. Viollet-le-Duc, note 32 above). Whitecastle's mid-thirteenth-century loops have long slits with the rare refinement of staggered cross-slots (here it is argued for wider view rather than field of fire, cp. Viollet-le-Duc). These may have raised the success-rate, but the rubber tips fitted to the arrows, to avoid damage to English Heritage property, would have reduced it. A standard thirteenth-century arrow loop measuring one and a half inches by (say) seven feet long presents about 130 square inches. The smaller medium Bodiam windows are a compact area of about 340 square inches, implying a seventy-five per cent success-rate at the very least shooting from the bank. The modern crossbow tested by Renn and Jones did slightly better. French galleys were manned by crossbowmen (notes 36, 41). By the mid-fourteenth-century, *via* transitional forms (e.g. Swansea; Llanblethian; Lewes barbican; Bishop's Palace, Wells), the crosslet-oillet (or cruciform) loop, with circular expansions to the end of each arm (horizontal as well as vertical) had been evolved. Amberly (note 76; licensed 1377) has an inept and showy compromise form. On defensive loops see also H.G. Leask, *Irish Castles and Castellated Houses*, Dundalk 1951, 20, for a careful description of the features distinguishing them from ventilation slits.

times) wore steel caps under their bonnets and jacks under their peaceful cloaks. If so Bodiam could perhaps plausibly be labelled, as some have suggested, 'fortified manor-house', a category imagined to be a sort of lesser castle. The arbalist, after all, was used from many a cramped space, given sufficient lateral clearance for its short (by the 1380s, steel) bow. It was aimed and discharged like a modern hand-gun, the stock to the shoulder, and the crossbowman could dwell on his aim and snap-shoot. Longbows were much more demanding.[40] Many of these inconspicuous stair and latrine-ventilating loops, by minor design changes, could so easily have been of defensive value. Their standard exterior dimensions are two and three quarter inches wide by fifteen inches high, but even when the lintel to the opening is at or above eye-level shooting out of them is virtually impossible because the sill is much too high and is horizontal. No longbowman could use them and an acrobatic crossbowman would have the greatest difficulty. The NW Tower shows the rejected opportunity to perfection and also, on its first and second main floors, has windows which perfectly command the Barbican and causeway to the Main Gate. The lower position especially would have been perfect for an enfilading gunloop, but the architect has chosen to put these in conspicuous but very poor positions frontally in the Main Gate (see Pl. 13).

The real preoccupations are shown by the very large Chapel, Chamber and Lord's Hall windows to the east and south-east, which demonstratively flaunt their vulnerability. The effect from outside, nicely set off by the elegant chimneys peeping over the battlements (not yet quite in the ostentatious Tudor manner), is of palatial comforts peering through the castle walls – an enticingly veiled hint of the seignorial conveniences within. Putting them here (they could well, in fact, have opened on the Courtyard) where they overlook the Rother meadows, gave more light and a better view. It enhanced also the scenic effect of the open aspects of the site (see Pls 7, 15). On the other side, facing the dull, steeply-rising ground to the west and north, they would have spoiled the cultivated effect of the elongated entry and frowningly sombre Main Gate, preceded by its Octagon and Barbican (see Pl. 10). Their placing may be discreet, but it is not defensive; it is on the south and east that any attacker would

---

[40] Viollet-le-Duc, *Mobilier* v, arts. 'Arbalète', 'Gambison'; vi art. 'Jacque'. Clergy and *bourgeoisie* were not of the legitimate arms-bearing class, unlike the gentry or (on special summons) the peasantry and urban levies (e.g. permission, 1347, for Philippe V to a Toulouse merchant for him and two attendants to be covertly armed: *Actes du Parlement de Paris* ii, ed. H. Furgeot et al., Paris 1960, 201 no. 7560). It is very remarkable that, despite the importance in English warfare of the longbow, its special requirements behind walls (very long, shallowly-raked sills; overhead space *etc.*, e.g. Caernarvon, mural gallery to Menai Strait) are very rarely met, loops continuing to be of crossbow type. The late fourteenth-century rebuild of Bothwell, Lanarks., with its 'French' crossbow loops (short, double-ended slit; deep internal niche), continuous curtain and tower machicolation, and drawbridge 'à flèches' (as at Herstmonceux) is a most instructive comparison showing deep differences of circumstances and response (e.g. Cruden, ch. 8; cp. B. J. St. J. O'Neil, *Castles and Cannon*, Oxford 1960, esp. pls 3–10 of gunloops).

cut the moat bank and the steepness of the further slope spoils visibility of the crucial ground from the wall and tower tops.[41]

## Parapets, Machicolation and Planning

Of the eight towers the parapets are conveniently accessible only with the Postern and NW towers, and of the curtain allures solely the NW. Such, however, is the consistency of details and dimensions, and so closely does the summit machicolation of the Postern Tower replicate that of the Main Gate, that the evidence is tolerably complete. Crenellation, whether to plain or overhanging parapets, has always been the essential mark of castellated architecture and was retained when other 'emblems of fortification' (such as the emphatic archery loops of the later thirteenth century) went out of vogue. Similarly, chemical artillery created at once a new military practice and a new aesthetic mode, which is reflected by the gunloops flaunted by the Main Gate. Machicolation, which is of more recent pedigree, was here a mannerism, put where it is to differentiate the two gate towers, giving them an up-to-date appearance, and to heighten the contrast with those archaic-looking drum and mural towers, and also with the 'Edwardian' aspect of the windows, which so struck J.H. Parker and G.T. Clark (see Pls 9, 16). At Scotney, coeval and nearby, Roger de Ashburnham opted for machicolated drum towers and the effect is strikingly different.[42] Whereas the mason-technique at Bodiam is true to

[41] The placing of the chapel window (of severe but up-to-date Perpendicular design) is strongly reminiscent of the Clintons' Maxstoke, a castle which almost disdains pretence (plates in M. Binney, *Country Life*, April 11, 18, 1974, 842–5, 930–3). The chimneys in elaborate brickwork (some dummy) added by the Howards to Framlingham have their antecedents here, although Clark (i, 246, cp. 242, 245) resisted the implications. The concave southern counterscarp, down to the Rother (see Pl. 7), is not well 'commanded' (*pace* Simpson 1931, note 10 above, cp. Kenyon, 1981, 209). Pavises were regularly used to screen crossbowmen particularly. Defenders would be exposed at windows or crenels. The defenders of Poole *c.*. 1405 against Don Pero Niño's Castilian raiders are said to have used house-doors 'propping them up on stakes and sheltering behind them in the battle . . . for fear of the arbalests which used to kill many of them' (*The Unconquered Knight – a Chronicle of the Deeds of Don Pero Niño, Count of Buelna*, trans. and ed. Joan Evans, 1928, 124–5. My thanks are due to Richard Eales for drawing my attention to this text). Behind such a barricade, direct and plunging 'fire' would eliminate any active resistance while the bridges were stormed and doors stove in or the bank was cut, even in full daylight. Escalade would quickly overwhelm the place. The fall at this time of so many English-held fortresses in France to brutally effective siege methods, seconded now by cannon, is the reality of contemporary warfare (note 61 below).

[42] Simpson's very penetrating comments on the aesthetic aspects consort with vagueness on the military. He justly remarks (1931, 92) that 'French fashion' at this date would have prescribed machicolation all round (e.g. Charles V's Bastille, Paris). Confining it 'to the gatehouses is a characteristically English mannerism' (but cp. Nunney). Also 'Bodiam's plan is entirely within English evolution' (ibid. 85–6), although the internationalism of European culture must still not be underrated, especially in this phase of the Wars. Such token castellation as Maxstoke did not satisfy Dallingridge's generation. Simpson was able to measure the downward-looking apertures (*machicoulis*) of the Main Gate parapets (see Pl. 6). They compare closely with those of the Postern (about twelve inches broad; from two feet six

its date, the ashlar blocks being nearly square, little longer in the bed than in the perpend (which is economical usage but less well bonded), the machicolation does make its desired point. Recessing the wings of the Main Gate precluded flanking loops but emphasized the agglomerated corbel clusters to the doubled corners. The canting off of the corners nicely reduced an otherwise awkward and disproportionate diagonal projection (see Pl. 8). Using flattish three-centered (almost segmental) arches to carry the parapets, in place of semicircular, was very modish and enhances the counterpoint of rectilinear mid-wall towers to cylindrical angle towers. It is a studied and ingenious compound, cleverly blended, made to seem all rather larger and somewhat more ancient than it really is. Nostalgia and topicality are neatly juxtaposed. Machicolation, if needed at all, would be more useful on the projected angles, and on the gate towers it is an outward display, frontally threatening but neglectful or indifferent to covering the curtain allure doorways below (see Pls 6, 16). Round fronts to the west and east mural towers would have been more solid, with less 'dead ground'; and why was the broad but shallow Main Gate crammed into the short side of the rectangle when it could have strengthened the long side confronting the western slope? No satisfactory answers can be in structural or military terms. Although now obscured by trees, the aesthetic effect of the castle, set in its lake and once surrounded by lesser pools, is fully apparent in the semi-aerial view from the hill to the north (see Pl. 10; Figs 2, 3). That this was fully intended cannot for an instant be doubted.[43]

Details and dimensions of the parapets tell us less than do the windows. Proportions overall are very satisfying and, again, largely consistent, although

---

inches up to three feet six inches long between corbels). Bold chamfering of these corbels (and of arrises throughout) gives a solid effect heightened by delicate drip moulds at the base of the parapets of the other six towers by way of contrast. Crenellation is the oldest of symbols; it denoted the *corona* of the Roman *praefectus castrorum*. It occurs much earlier in Egyptian and Assyrian bas reliefs and is ubiquitous in medieval borough seals. The *formulae* equating crenels with fortification in English licences to crenellate became standard from *c.* 1264, with Hood Castle, Yorks. (*CPR 1258–66*, 342; P. Connolly *Greece and Rome at War*, 1981, 244; Y. Yadin *The Art of Warfare in Biblical Lands*, 1963, 228, 390–1). No real improvement or radical departure in gunloop design from arbalist patterns occurs until the 'gunport' type of splayed rectangular embrasures was evolved, mainly for harbour defences (e.g. Kingswear, Devon, O'Neil, 1960, Pl. 10a). Cp. the heraldic cross *pommée*, closely resembling the crosslet-oillet loop form (C. Boutell, *English Heraldry*, 1907, 56–7).

43 Bodiam's is much more elegant than (Yevele's) outer gatehouse at Cooling whose small drum towers look top-heavy with their full-sized machicolation. At Saltwood and Canterbury West Gate solecism is avoided by machicolating only the parapet between the frontal turrets. Donnington omits the feature entirely. The lesser Cobham seat at Hever by Tonbridge (licensed 1383, *CPR 1381–5*, 326) also has a very crowded main front, but the rectangular plan of the (altered) gatehouse (partly machicolated) simplified the difficulty. Archaisms in medieval architecture do occasionally break the normal tendency to ruthless modernization (e.g. naves of Canterbury and Winchester cathedrals). Yevele's nave at Westminster respected not the details but the effect of Henry III's work. Atavistic allusion, it seems, can be imitative or conceptual; specific (great towers at Tattershall and Ashby de la Zouche) or more general, as at Raglan.

the north curtain parapets receive specially dignified treatment. Modern con-crete platforms rather disfigure the Postern and NW Tower summits but the parapets of the latter are intact, with some reinstatement of original stones. Corbels and beam-sockets below indicate low-pitched, leaded timber roofs whose narrow wall-walk-cum-gutter discharged rainwater *via* the plain-cut spouts just below the string-course. Allowing for the thickness of the concret-ing, merlons were about six and a half feet high over the roll-moulded coping and are six feet eight inches wide, crenels being two feet one inch, their plain flat sills being (originally) about two feet seven inches high. The crenel-to-merlon ratio (1:3.1) gives an admirably solid, indeed atavistic, effect, confirmed by omitting vertical mouldings to the sides of the embrasures. Nor do they occur on the up-to-date machicolated parapets of the two gates, which also conform to the severe mien displayed everywhere by plain chamfers and mouldings, in the windows most conspicuously.[44] Dimensions of the Postern parapets are similar, in both cases giving just adequate cover. Here the machicolation can be inspected; the slot between the corbels is thirteen inches deep, lacking any water-drip or arrow-deflecting moulding (see Pl. 2). As noted, it does not com-pletely wrap around the flanks of the tower, only the external and most visible portion, not the crucial curtain-junctions below (nor the rear), being covered.[45] It all 'doth protest too much' with splendid mendacity.

No incongruity obtrudes because proportion is so well kept, but these parapets are no more than thin and weak screen-walls, just over one foot thick and constructed of large blocks stood on edge. The long coping stones afford some stiffening and bond to the merlons, but what strength there is depends on the cohesion of the mortared beds and perpends. Any greater thickness would

[44] St Giles church tower has equally-spaced crenels and merlons both being coped (as are the north curtains of the castle) which is an ecclesiastical variant, also probably due to Dalling-ridge (Simpson 1931, 82). Outward roll-mouldings gave horizontal emphasis and could stop or deflect arrows, as could vertical rolls framing embrasures (e.g. Eagle Tower, Caernarvon, *c.* 1320). Both were soon ubiquitously adopted in miniaturized ornament style; cp. the com-promise adopted by the stair-turret crowns, Pls 10, 15). The full French flowering of castel-lated symbolism with exuberant tall chimneys, pinnacles, roof crestings, bartizans, échauguettes and tall conical roofs (which make Bodiam seem most reticent) is shown in the *Très Riches Heures* pictures of Jean de Berri's castles (e.g. Saumur, *Flowering of the Middle Ages*, 134; cp. R. Morris, *Cathedrals and Abbeys of England and Wales*, 1979, 29 for alternative trans. of the *Sir Gawain and the Green Knight* extract. This is an important contemporary aesthetic statement).

[45] On the sectioning function of towers and defence of their lateral doorways see Viollet-le-Duc, *Architecture . . . art.* 'Tour'. The concrete roofing (marked '1962') to the Postern does not encroach upon the wall-walk (cp. NW Tower) permitting accurate measurement. The surviving merlons are five feet three inches high, plus fourteen inches of coping. Crenels are again twenty-five inches wide, the flat sills three feet four inches from the floor. These dimensions are kept to the bare minimum for proportion's sake. Modern stature cannot exceed medieval averages by more than three to four inches, and headgear must be allowed for. For machicolation in France, of all types, see Viollet-le-Duc *art.* 'Mâchicoulis' esp. figs 9 'D' and 12 'P'. Bodiam has no hourding holes although *bretasches* were still very much in use (Viollet-le-Duc, art. 'Hourd').

have thrown out the delicate illusion of 'Edwardian' scale. Ashlar-faced rubble-concrete, though much stronger would have looked impossibly gauche. The stair-turrets, however, give the game away (human occupants could not be dwarfed). There is one to each of the eight towers. Their ostensible character as watch-towers masks their real function of covering the six feet six inch diameter stair wells. Below parapet level, hexagonal expansions, where the gorge wall merges with the curtain, contain the stair (except with the NW and E mid-towers, and the Main Gate). Above, the octagonal dummy caps are skilfully set upon the broader mass below (see Pls 6, 15). Internally they are covered over by saucer domes in small rubble but exteriorly they are turrets, battlemented in miniature as though they were accessible and usable *échauguettes*.[46]

The height of the walls, however, is no illusion; the accommodation within and outward show both dictated it. Although little thicker than structural stability required, grappling hooks and ladders from boats or rafts below would doubtless target the windows. The distance to the parapet tops would be about forty-eight feet if the moat were drained. But the omission of bow-slits from the merlons of the parapets is conspicuous, and evidently as deliberate as the design of the garderobe loop-lights (even Maxstoke had shutters to its crenels). The much grander construction of the North Front curtain parapets clinches the matter. They are one and a half times the normal thickness (i.e. eighteen inches), but the merlons are narrower (four feet nine inches) probably to fit three crenels into the short length. Dallingridge intended, perhaps, ceremoniously to man the walls, for important visitors, along the NW curtain which overlooks the angled main approach (see Pl. 8). The height of these merlons is also less than usual (five feet ten inches overall), doubtless to counter the disproportion (even to make his 'honour guard' more visible) and the standard-width crenels uniquely have coped sills. Where artifice is so subtly contrived, even minor variations from standard treatment must be given considerable weight. The north front is very much the showpiece of the whole place. The door from this allure into the Main Gate, it may be remarked at this point, opens outwards and has no defensive development, although the quarters supposedly occupied by 'the garrison' were in the adjoining range. From the wall-walk here the platform over the vault of the inward extension of the entry

---

[46] Some sort of stair-top hutch just would not do! Access could only be by ladder (as Sands realized) from the main summit, but four of the surviving six turret-tops are domed and could not be walked on, nor is there any gap in the sketchy (maximum waist-height) parapet. The clear aerial photograph in P. Johnson, *The National Trust Book of British Castles*, 1978, 133, shows flat platforms to the E and W mural towers' turrets only. Lofty watch-turrets were a favourite conceit (royal apartments, Conway). They magnify Bodiam most powerfully (see Pl. 10). Stairs are not unduly steep despite contraction of the castle's lateral scale even in the upper storeys of the Main Gate (twelve inch risers, cp. many church-tower stairs). Rubble infill and large rough blocks compose the stair-wells. Only in the NW Tower, where the stair-well intercepts the east-side allure doorway, has an awkward mis-alignment had to be overcome (note 48 below). Such infelicities are rare here.

passage, with its 'murder holes' strikes an incongruous note. The upper chamber itself, under a lean-to roof, was reached by an afterthought stairway, also not internally defensible.[47]

## The Main Gate and Gunloops

Here it is the gunloops which chiefly require attention and are not the least ambiguous feature of the castle. Entering from the NW curtain allure (no defences and no machicolation overhead), the first feature is a garderobe chamber of high rank (ribbed vault) lit by the familiar pattern of loop-light. On the opposite (east) side of the Gate is a matching example. Even a contortionist crossbowman could not use these slits. The Gate block is a screen-like structure, frontally imposing but without depth.[48] From the chamber above the entrance, on the second floor, opens the upper of two small 'gunloops' which are contrived diagonally in the re-entrant angle of the outer recess of the entrance archway (see Pl. 11). Seen from outside, they would appear to be most cunningly placed to look north-westwards, over the trestle-bridge to the Octagon, and to cover the low Barbican roof and part of the causeway linking it to the gate below. They are part of a telling façade: the eye travels upwards, past the iron-plated and powerfully symbolic portcullis, to the thin screen-wall arch above, framed within the emphatic (but meretricious) drawbridge rebate; then pauses to absorb the trio of armorial shields (Dallingridge flanked by de Wardedieu and Radynden) in a row beneath the large and solemn central window, surmounted in turn by Sir Edward's helm with unicorn crest and mantle displayed (perhaps once all coloured). To this theme of chivalric panache the 'gunloops' in question provide a corroborative hint of ruthless force; the one adjacent to the row of heraldic shields, the other above it, not far beneath the framing arch with its sectioned slot (machicoulis or *assommoir*), which doubles

---

[47] Insofar as the remains indicate; this and the wing-walls outside the Postern are of somewhat cruder masonry (note 32 above). The segmental inner archway and rough adaptation of the two moulded capitals to take formeret and diagonal ribs of the additional vault suggest on-site extemporization. The gate-passage otherwise would have debouched unceremoniously on whatever chamber was to have completed the range on this side (much as the Postern entry does into the Screens Passage). Chancellor Richard Scrope's Bolton was not so fastidious, but an enemy who won through to the small inner courtyard would be trapped, facing defended doorways all around. Exteriorly his towers and walls are much higher, and more solid, well beyond reach of ladders. Bolton, however, afforded quite as good accommodation and was as well adapted to its northern environment as was Bodiam to the softer conditions of the south, for all that Bolton has no moat.

[48] Both allure doorways, to the NW Tower and to the W side of the Main Gate, had to be awkwardly screened to adjust the levels *via* short flights of stairs, an expedient rare at Bodiam and avoided on the other side, so probably inadvertent (see Pls 8, 13). Prominent gatehouses, some pre-dating the 'Edwardian' fashion, in many fourteenth-century cases produced what David King (1983) has aptly called 'gatehouse castles' (e.g. Boarstall, 1312; Bywell, and Donnington). Bodiam's debt to this tradition is less apparent because the Main Gate does not monopolize attention to the same extent.

the threat from the machicolation high overhead. Here are all the elements of the medieval castle image, repeated with variations down to the Tudor age of Spenserian revivalism.[49] The gatehouses of stately red-brick Buckden Palace, among many such, and of Henry VIII's pretty little granite gun-fort of Pend-ennis at Falmouth (c.1540) display it quite as fully. But it is far harder to go behind the mask and assess the exact amount of incorporated force deemed necessary to give to the symbols of noble status in contemporaries' eyes the physical substance appropriate to the personal and local situation: to establish how forcible was the force; who was meant to be impressed, deterred, and, if necessary, defeated by it – and precisely how. *Kunstgeschichte* alone cannot do it, and nor can any purely 'military' rationale (see Figs 2, 3).

Examination of the two 'gunloops' does, in this case, provide limited, prosaic but quite clear answers. The upper specimen measures on the outer face twenty-six inches by three and a half inches broad in the slot, apart from the small circular oillet expansion at the foot. Through this loop the further part only of the approach, beyond the Octagon, and part of the path around the NW corner of the moat can be seen, but the sill is horizontal, putting the near approaches out of the line of sight.[50] The splay is very narrow and the traverse for any weapon extremely restricted, observations equally true of the loop on the floor

---

[49] Leland has much of Tudor attitudes as well as of the then condition of castles' repair (Thompson, 171–8) e.g. Harringworth is 'a right goodly manor-place . . . buildid castelle-like'; Bagworth had 'ruines of a manor-place, like castelle building'; Shirburn was 'a strong pile or castelet'; contemporary Pendennis and St Mawes are still 'castle or fortress' simply; Warwick is 'magnificent and strong', always admired; whereas the structurally insignificant upstart Fulbrook is 'a praty castle made of stone and brike' which 'was an eyesore to the Erlis that lay in Warwike Castle, and was cause of displeasure betweene each Lord'. Even the crenellated close of Lichfield was (most percipiently) 'somewhat castle-like'; Bolton was 'a very fair castelle', and Chideock 'a castle or a fair house'. Such views are very close to the later medieval aesthetic, concentrating on scenic quality and seignorial allusion. Leland also had an interested eye for portcullis grooves e.g. Sleaford, Denbigh and Tenby town (*Itinerary* i, 13, 20, 114–5, 196, 200; ii, 40–1, 46–8, 99, 102; iv, 27, 108; and ii 26–7; iii 97–8, 116–7).

[50] Poor translation, loose expression and low standards of proof vitiate the art-historical treat-ment by A. Tuulse, *Castles of the Western World*, 1958. The diagonal embrasure is very narrow, the horizontal bed about thirty-three inches from the floor and three inches below the bottom of the oillet (about five inches diameter); i.e. a very small gun on a shallow trunk might conceivably have used it, but only firing dead ahead and horizontally, since the sighting-slot is parallel-sided and the oillet is a cylindrical hole about seven inches deep and but slightly bevelled on the outer and inner arrises (in Canterbury city wall the contemporary gunloops, many in good enfilading positions, have larger oillets 'piercing' much thinner blocks which, despite generally poor condition where unrestored, were evidently splayed or heavily bevelled). By propping up the trunk and packing the charge with wadding a slight downward deflection would be possible, which the high position of many such loops (e.g. Carisbrooke barbican) necessitated; but the target here at least would be wholly out of sight without extraordinary contortions (cp. Kenyon, 1981, 209). A stock-mounted shoulder-held gun, like a crossbow, would have had some potential but not the contemporary 'firework on a pole' type of gun (Koch, 132, 159, 200–1; all fifteenth century; Viollet-le-Duc, *Mobilier* vi, 325–33). See discussion of the problem by D.F. Renn in *Med. Arch.* viii, 1964, 226–8 on the Southampton Arcade.

below, opening off the portcullis chamber, which differs but slightly in dimensions. The embrasure is again of the habitual contemporary gunloop pattern, 'pierced' through a thick (seven inch) frontal plate which interiorly projects from the plane of the splay of the jambs, virtually precluding alternative defensive use. The general inefficiency of this pattern is at its worst at Bodiam. The faults are found also in the ground floor gunloops as well as in the double-oillet 'dumb-bell' shaped loops on either side of the entry (see Pls 12, 13, 14). The design gravely restricts the angle of vision. Both of the diagonal upper floor loops must, in fact, be regarded as no more than spy-holes enabling the porter, and perhaps occupants of rank, to make ready for new arrivals, spotted approaching the entry to the north west – surely with due ceremony, herald and trumpet; scarcely 'in manner of war'. They are, in short, porter's lodge squints in the guise of miniature gunloops, a topical allusion like the machicolation.[51]

From the accessible western ground-floor chamber opens the largest pattern of the gunloops, regarded by the 1975 Guide (after Simpson, 1961) as 'grim reminders of the new weapon cannon, that would sound the death knell of the feudal castle'. That it manifestly did nothing of the kind is less to the present point than that, Bodiam being supremely well-planned, any lack of skill, if these loops ought to represent 1380s state-of-the-art technology, deserves to be pondered. The architect was certainly no country practitioner; nor was his patron some rustic *hobereau*. There are four of the larger loops of the 'inverted keyhole' type, all placed frontally, not in flanking positions but, at any rate, where horizontal fire was theoretically possible. The two largest examples are located in the advanced portions of the towers, and a smaller version in each of the recessed wings (see Pls 8, 12). Of these four, that in the (inaccessible) east wing

---

51 Apart from very rare 'espringald' embrasures (e.g. Tortosa, Palestine) only bow-loops were previously known. Their deep splays would resist the blows of mechanical artillery. Comparison disposes of any possibility that early gunloops (see for examples O'Neil, 12–3, showing the exaggerated plate-front at Bodiam) were built to resist heavy impact breaking away the facing stones. Fronts are thicker, with the usual slight chamfering of the exterior arrises (of slit and oillet) but nothing suggests fear of bombardment was a factor, despite their especially massive character here (see Pls 13, 14). The studiedly ambivalent message is still more pronounced in the most conspicuous pair looking onto the platform outside the main doors. The parallel-sided slot and oillet run through no less than ten inches (three and a quarter inches wide, six and a quarter inches diameter respectively). The interior is gravely exposed by such wide openings approachable closely from without. A cannon here with its muzzle laid into the foot-oillet would strike its partner directly opposite if fired. The 'dumb-bell' pattern vaguely apes the crossbow slit (e.g. Bothwell, note 40 above) but owes more to symbolism than to utility. The gunloop type of plate-fronted embrasure (notably since the slot facings project obstructively from the splay-plane) was, in addition, highly inconvenient for crossbows and still more for the longbow and yet this is the normal and ubiquitous pattern until the later fifteenth century. J. R. Kenyon argues that the elaborate cruciform-oillet loops to the Great Tower at Raglan were for ventilation only and light, and that some of the other oillets of gunloop type were purely psychological (*Essays in Honour of D. J. Cathcart King*, Cardiff 1987, 164–5, *et passim* 161–72). Outward guise and covert personality in medieval art were often tenuously connected. The same mentality was equally at work in its castellated architecture.

of the Gate could not bear on the approaches at all, and its larger fellow only with great difficulty, being originally largely masked by the Barbican. None flank the curtain walls in any way. Had they done so the problems of lack of lateral traverse would be less crucial. The pair on the western side, between them would seemingly cover the eastern (inner) part of the trestle-bridge and a little of the Octagon platform, most of which is concealed by the Barbican. Internal inspection, however, heavily damages the apparent efficacy even of the western pair. The smaller loop opens off a typical small cramped garderobe chamber, which its function was clearly to light and ventilate. Dimensions, design and purpose are all closely comparable to the diagonal squints on the upper floors, although the splay is less narrow. Admitting any secondary function is difficult, but it could conceivably be used by an archer. Lateral space, on one side, is insufficient for an arbalist. Essentially, it is a loop-light with an oillet foot, simulating the external appearance of a gunloop of the type familiar since c.1370.[52] Its larger fellow, in the 'Guard Chamber' (*recte* Porters' Lodge), because of its greater internal space and size, was undoubtedly usable by a small cannon fixed to a 'trunk' bed. Its excellent condition is not likely to be due to Curzon, more probably to its never having experienced the shock or smoke of gunpowder. Vertically, including the ten inch diameter oillet, it measures twenty-seven inches, the sighting slot being three and a quarter inches wide, both again bevelled on the exterior edges but lacking splay to the outer seven inches. Scarcely any deflection of the gun would be possible; fortunately so since, to the right, any shot fired would strike the frontal turret on the flank of the Barbican. Sir Edward must have intended having a saluting base whence to greet honoured guests with his own personal *Crakkys of Warre* firing 'blank', for which this one gunloop would be quite adequate (see Fig. 3).

The details of the 'dumb-bell' loops on either side of the entry show that a display of aggression, not any real vindictiveness, was in the designer's mind. Indeed, their width seriously exposed the interior to a bowman outside (see Pls 13, 14). Clearly also, the architect and his patron did not expect the vital doorways, opening from the gate passage on either side (itself lacking two-leaved doors to the putative portcullises) to be in any danger of being hostilely kicked in, to judge from the feeble bolt sockets in the jambs and the thinness of the doors, disclosed by the hinge-hooks. From the opposite door is reached the

---

[52] The earliest loops were apparently plain circular handgun (?) apertures set in splayed recesses, datable to 1365 (D. F. Renn, *Arch. Journ.* cxxv, 1968, 301–3). If Simpson is right that the earthen causeway (until recently) linking the Octagon to the north bank was a medieval modification which the dismantling and salvaging of the bridge timbers tends to support (notes 32, 60), then the western gunloops soon became equally inapt to close defence of the entry. The two 'gunloops', to the privies opening off the Porters' Lodges, are placed lower down than the other garderobe lights and convey an outward illusion of defence which the latter eschew (see Pl. 12). Any more might have been unduly pretentious for a *nouveau riche* cadet, albeit of an old knightly family (Turner, fig. 2, showing an 'inverted keyhole' gunloop has been printed upside down).

stair, giving direct access to the rest of the Gate, but even here there are no drawbars, nor were there any, still more surprisingly, to the main outer two-leaved doors, presently represented by a pair of respectable, but not remarkable, solidity. Behind it, the bravado of double portal chambers, 'murder holes' and three portcullises, is mere *rodomontade* when the lateral doors are so weak. There is no 'military' logic in trebling the main closures while leaving a short and direct approach to a weak back door (Postern) which entirely lacks elaboration. But there is powerful psychological sense nonetheless: it is closer to Jean Froissart (and perhaps also to Franz Kafka) than it is to Vegetius or to the Sieur de Vauban.[53] The fairy-tale element is here, allusive and romantic.

## IV. THE MOAT, SITING AND CIRCUMSTANCES

At the outset of this discussion we referred to the common opinion that Bodiam Castle is significant chiefly as an exception to a discerned general trend of 'decline' since the great days of Edward I. It is seen as a sort of Paul of Tarsus castle: one born out of due time, and thus not quite worthy to be called a castle; and yet fully one really, and a belated vindication of a certain materialistic view of medieval civilization. Indeed the 1985 Guide tells us that 'it was one of the last English medieval castles to be built, the final flowering of 300 years of castle design'. This is profoundly wrong: not so much for ignoring such a place as Raglan; nor even the awesome power of siegecraft, which had long since defied the utmost art of the military engineer; but because it disregards the whole medieval and sub-medieval procession of castellated architecture across five centuries and more of European cultural and social history. Bodiam's true importance and its authentic castle-character consist in its exalting of the castle-image *Anglice modo*, exploiting all the demonstrative opportunities available, while (most interestingly of all) spurning even a covert or secondary defensive capability. 'Fortification' was most surely metaphysical as well as material; a matter of imagery and symbolism, not just of technology. It comprehended the soldierly imperatives of Woolwich Arsenal and of the Ecole Militaire, but also transcended them.

Second only in the esteem of the gentry to crenellated walls, fine towers and

---

[53] The 'psychological warfare' element cannot be supposed to involve actual deception: contemporaries were not (for long) fooled by spurious gunloops, but they did assert the power of the owner, expressed according to the new aesthetic, which thus deterred (Coulson, 1982(1), 84–91; cp. on the 'psychology of gun warfare', Renn, Med. Arch. viii, 1964, 226–8; Kenyon 1981, 217; Turner, 277). The pristine condition of all the gunloops notwithstanding, G.T. Clark's assurance (note 30 above) covers the risky era of 'restoration' (c.1820–60). Fixed lines of fire, slowness of loading and haphazard performance must have made early guns in such loops far inferior to contemporary 'espringalds' even against fixed siege engines. Lack of lateral range could only be mitigated by gunloops in enfilade positions.

lodgings of ashlar masonry, in central and southern England, came water-filled moats. No modern rationalization of this phenomenon in terms of defence against mining, or from violent (but hydrophobic) bands of brigands can satis-factorily account for it. It was a fashion which began early. Thus the Stafford-shire knight William of Caverswall (licensed to crenellate here in 1275) caused an epitaph to be inscribed on his tomb-slab proclaiming to posterity that it was he who 'erected the castle, with dwellings, moats and works of masonry'. His boast provoked the spleen (though the castle of Caverswall was quite modest) of some unknown, who retorted with this scrawled translation and jibe, apparently in the Tudor period:

> 'William of Caverswell here lye I,
> That built this Castle and the pooles herebye':
> William of Caverswell here then mayest lye
> But thy Castle is down and thy pooles are dry.[54]

Bodiam and Dallingridge have been more fortunate. His out-lying pools are likewise dry but not the principal pond (see Fig. 2). His own, and his castle's credit (however misconceived) have stood high. It would have afforded him no little grim amusement to find his extravagant conceits so credulously received.

## Moat and Siting

The 'lake' has been drained twice this century, by Curzon and in the summer of 1970. It is a revealing experience to see the castle without its mirror of water.

---

[54] Tudor architectural emulation pursued similar ideals. No fortress which could be assaulted outright was likely to be mined, making the moat defensively superfluous. My thanks are due to Dr John Blair for sending me a copy of his 'Caverswall (Staffs.): on exceptionally early indent', *Bulletin of the Monumental Brass Society* xxxv, Feb. 1984; reconstructed *sic* – *Hic jacet Willelmus de Kavereswelle Miles + castri structor eram domibus fossisque cum cemento perficiens operam – nunc claudor in hoc monumento.* Last recorded in 1291, he 'appears as an unexcep-tional member of the knightly community, executing the usual round of duties as commis-sioner and justice' (Blair). The moated 'quadrangular castle, with four small towers and a gatehouse' (King 1983) was initially rebuilt as a castellated late-Elizabethan mansion, rather resembling Lacock Abbey (M. Girouard, *Robert Smithson . . .*, 1966, reproducing 1686 en-graving; also Mackenzie 1897, i, 390–1). On the supposed causal linkage between moats and lawlessness see note 80 and e.g. C. Platt, *Medieval England*, 1978, 111–5, 266–7; D. Wilson, *Moated Sites Research Group, Report* 9, 1982 (and *Reports* 1973–86 *passim*) but the 'prestige' explanation receives emphasis e.g. in *Medieval Moated Sites* ed. F.A. Aberg, C.B.A. *Research Report* no. 17, 1978 9–13; a large proportion of licences to crenellate concern such *gentilhom-mières* and motives of social *arrivisme* predominate. Places regarded as 'major' castles (though equally powerless to resist mechanical artillery) might be so engendered, whether built by the aspirant knighthood (Barnwell, Northants c.1264) or by careerists at their name-place or patrimony (Anthony Bek's, Somerton, Lincs., 1281; Acton Burnell, Salop., licensed 1284). Moats in literature also figure strongly (e.g. *Langland*, trans. Coghill, 1959, 47; *Sir Gawaine and the Green Knight*, note 44; and even *King Richard II*, Act ii, scene i.). As a curtilage 'fence' to demarcate a gentry seat they were unrivalled and probably more cost-effective than a wall in most situations.

The seven or eight feet of extra height add something but also transform the proportions, showing how small the place really is (see e.g. Pls 15, 16). The fine continuous plinth is completely uncovered but illusion and magic are gone. The sense of remoteness and intangibility of walls and towers reflected by still water also glorifies Queen Isabella's favourite residence of Leeds (Kent) and Warin de Lisle's Shirburn (Oxon., licensed 1377) and many a Continental *Wasserburg*. Moats conventionally segregated the lord's own courtyard from the manorial offices and *basse cour*, dignifying the castle proper, but they had their draw-backs.[55] In this case, lack of through-flow of water to scour out the sewage would have necessitated quite frequent cleansing while the house was in occupation. In 1970, having emptied the water *via* the two modern sluices on the south and north-east, about 15,000 cubic yards of silt, partly decayed lily humus, covering the bed about eighteen inches deep, were scraped off with mechanical diggers and dumped in the meadow to the SE. The castle was left, in the words of *The Times* headline to its photograph (6 May 1970) 'high, dry and defenceless' – and here is the crucial issue: in the contractor's estimation, about a dozen labourers using only picks, spades and shovels), starting work at dusk, would be able to cut completely through the retaining embankment at almost any point along the S and E sides before daybreak. His opinion, indeed, was that the water must regularly have been emptied in this way for cleaning while the house was inhabited. Probably this was done near the newly-restored overflow slightly north of the mid-point of the east bank, where it is flanked outside by an embanked area, now again a pond, from which the water would have been conducted by a ditched channel into the southern ponds, or directly into the river (see Fig. 2). At this point of the moat a channel was left where the bank merges into the slope. Scour could be minimized by gradually deepening the cut in the bank which here would be least likely to do damage. Since the bank is not 'clayed' (water-proofed with a lining of puddled clay) but composed of the impermeable heavy loam, which overlies the sub-stratum of compacted fine grey cohesive sand, no re-proofing would be needed when the breach was partially re-closed with packed earth. It would be such a simple operation that no proper sluices or reinforcements of the bank to accommodate them were thought desirable by the builder or designer. The features of this pool link it with the

---

55 In Germany the fashion lasted well into the eighteenth century (K.E. Mummenhoff *Wasser-burgen in Westfalen*, Berlin-Munich 1958, *passim*; E. Thomson and G. baron von Manteuffel-Szoege, *Schlösser und Herrensitze im Baltikum*, Frankfurt, 1963, with many early engravings). Descriptions of manor-house complexes, particularly dower and co-heiress partitions, often show that a moat divided the 'chief messuage' from its appendages. The jurors give no hint of defensive factors being involved, even when 'drawbridges' and 'gatehouses' are among the features. Examples 1352–70 are Woking, Surrey; Conington, Hunts.; Barton, Cumbria; Mul-barton and Brundall, Norfolk; Shenley, Bucks.; Slaugham, Sussex; *CIPM* x nos 46, 484; xi, no. 317; xii nos 79, 348, 404). Valuable barns, stables and byres usually lay outside such protection as the moat afforded. At Bodiam all the 'offices' (e.g. stables and dovecot) were apparently fitted into the one enclosure, which, to modern eyes, (falsely) enhances its 'castle' character.

ubiquitous manorial mill-ponds, fish-stews and growing fashion for ornamental lakes rather than with proper 'water defences' with their stone-cored or revetted substantial earthwork dams. The springs, moreover, which feed it and break out all along the northern and western margin of the basin, are not streams, and a simple small pipe once sufficed for the overflow. In 1970 it took six months to restore the water to its normal level. This was quite a dry summer but in the fourteenth century it would have been much the same at this elevation.[56]

The site, nonetheless, does offer some exceptional advantages. Defensively most awkward, being a terraced shelf partly cut into the hillside and partly built up, the creation here of a relatively wide moat and subsidiary ponds was so greatly facilitated and rendered so inexpensive by natural features that its disad-vantages were quite unimportant (se Pls 7, 10; Fig. 2). Strategic reasons for the location are inherently most implausible. They alone would not have caused the old manor-site, probably the 'moat' close to the parish church to the NE, to be superseded. Rather, the exceptional qualities of the new position must have been decisive. Having married the de Wardedieu heiress and established his tenure of Bodiam manor by begetting a son by her, Dallingridge would have desired a dwelling of dignity and visual impact commensurate with his fortui-tously prominent status in the county and reflecting his rôle in the national politics of Richard II's regency. It would fittingly crown his long career in royal service and perpetuate his family renown. Numerous castles were built for such reasons. Overlooking the Rother valley, conspicuous to the South and East, it would have prominence and 'prospect' lacking at the old 'homestead moat', which lies near the tributary valley bottom, slightly higher up but tucked away behind the ridge north of the new castle. The village has no nucleus, apart from St Giles church.[57] Although the Rother marshes would afford excellent water

[56] The RCHME (note 1 above) view the majority of the water-holding and other earthworks around the moat as medieval and probably part of the original conception, including the 'viewing platform', *alias* 'Gun Garden' (Figs 2, 3). The spring flow, allowing for seepage, need not have exceeded the present, to maintain this extensive system. The abutments of Bodiam bridge (documented 1313), two and a quarter miles above the junction with the stream of the Kent Ditch, do not suggest the water-table has been more than slightly higher (see note 15 above). Stone brought here by water (as it probably was) came evidently by barge, not by ship, and perhaps to the wharves once just downstream from the Bridge. The supposed spring-catchment basin in the NW slope is regarded by RCHME as the lower of two partly artificial ponds, possibly forming a cascade, flanking the NW entrance roadway (not marked in Fig. 2). They describe the earthworks as 'massive' as well as extensive, but it is to be noted that the SE moat bank had to be reinforced for safety in 1970 (horizontal thrust of the water, cp. the north dam at Caerphilly). It is not much less vulnerable than that of Michelham Priory, Sussex, especially on the east side, opposite to the monks' imposing fourteenth-century gatehouse, which has also traditionally been ascribed to fear of French raids (e.g. Saul, 89).

[57] From Simpson's still valuable local survey (1931, 69–71, 73–83) a further motive for his castle's assertiveness and for the new site is inferable in that Edward shared the parish church with surviving de Wardedieus and de Bodehams. He seems only to have completed the tower. It may be that his own tomb was not there but in Robertsbridge Abbey, where his son John's

defences, a site upon the flood-plain would be both unhealthy and subject to flooding. Closeness to Bodiam bridge was evidently unimportant, nor was a change of site in conflict with the terms of the licence to crenellate. The great majority relate in terms to existing sites but a fair proportion are associated with a change of manorial *caput*. All in all, to a builder whose ambition was a place as magnificent as he could afford and capable of being conspicuously moated with the maximum economy of labour and materials, the attractions of this position despite its defensive weakness must have been both obvious and decisive.[58] Examination on site suggests that there may originally have been a natural pooling of water, breaking the surface. Traces of what may once have been reeds and rushes, showing up in 1970 as dark bands of humus and rust-coloured streaks in the firm scraped pan of silt, might be so interpreted. And the constructional sequence may reasonably be deduced. Loamy topsoil was excavated, chiefly along the western and part of the northern sides and carted across to form the southern and eastern embankments, with a little levelling up of the area to the east as well. The water-absorbent silt-pan was stripped to the nearly horizontal natural bed, no attempt being made to achieve greater depth in mid-moat, nor shallower margins to reduce the water-thrust exerted on the embankments, thin and decidedly weak though they are (see Pls 1, 4, 16). The lime mortar had to be laid in dry conditions, but the slight summer spring-flow could easily have been channelled away (or penned up with a coffer dam). In 1970 exploratory spadework indicated that the depth of the wall footings varied but did not exceed two to three feet below the bed. In the places tested in this fashion no drystone rubble packing was found beneath the bottom course of ashlar, showing that it was laid completely dry.[59] The central rectangle of shal-

(d. c.1407) probably was (1975 *Guide* 23; effigy fragment in the Castle Museum). Conspicuously independent of St Giles church, the new position would be a natural response. Excavation on the 'old manor site', 350 yards NNE of the church, at TQ 784264 and rather closer to the Kent Ditch than the castle is to the Rother, has revealed a late thirteenth-century hall with service bay and solar wing of timber on dry-stone sleeper walls, within the moat (*Med. Arch.* vi–vii, 1962–3, 335; and xv, 1971, 165–6). The excavators 'confirmed that the use of the moat was domestic and not defensive' (*sic*). Edward followed his elder brother Roger (d. c.1380 in his 70s) into the Arundel affinity and was his heir. Their father had died in 1335 (Saul 38, 67–8). J. G. Hurst does not rule out a previous manor on the castle site (*Med. Arch.* vi–vii, 1962–3, 140) but his context was one of extreme caution.

58 Licence expressed as for the *mansum manerii* even technically did not preclude such a shift and there is considerable evidence that new administrative centres were thereby seen as ratified; cp. Simpson (1931, 72) '. . . the building of a strong military castle on a site selected . . . so as to command the waterway of the Rother, up which, during the weak reign of Richard II, French naval raids were feared . . .'. It is above the castle at the bridge that any such raiders (presumably in punts or wherries) would surely disembark (and be resisted) should they come so far (and so slowly) by water. The nearest part of the castle (SW Tower) is about 340 yards distant, recessed into the shoulder of the hill and barely visible from the bridge, well beyond effective range with scant (even visual) 'command'. The river is now about 260 yards from the S front of the castle, extreme range at best (note 15; Figs 1, 2).

59 Special thanks are due to Mr L. E. Hole for conducting these trials for me. For the investigations by David Martin in 1970 see note 32. Footings on the E side seem no deeper so the

low foundation trenches could thus be laid out (almost exactly North-South) and dug with such accuracy. Stone revetments, battered inwards by about three feet in a rise of nine, encased the made-earth of the central platform and revetted the barbican and Octagon (either from the first or subsequently, on construction of the half-piers of the modified trestle-bridge responds). Elsewhere revetment was dispensed with, thanks to the steep angle of rest of the heavy loam, and if any piling was needed to consolidate the earth no trace of it has been discovered.

It was all superbly economical. Sections vertically through the central raised area show how little earth had to be moved (1961 Guide centre-fold). Only the courtyard is significantly built up. The sloping plinth at the foot of the walls, rendered by Curzon in cement to reduce erosion and water seepage is of rather cruder workmanship than elsewhere. Only the top two feet or so are normally visible (see Pls 2, 9). The design effectively resisted the pressure of the water-logged semi-plastic mass within. No subsidence has occurred anywhere and the success of the engineering, with its rigorous economy of means, speaks as highly as does the more visible architecture above water-level of the skill of the builder. Much of the visual satisfaction is attributable to the walls' rising almost sheer from the water (with no 'berm' around as at Maxstoke), but this is yet another by-product of the natural aptitudes of a site carefully chosen and skilfully exploited.

Before turning from the structure to its historical context, the purpose of the originally angled main approach should be considered (see Pl. 10; Fig. 2). Any semblance of exposing to archery the shieldless (and supposedly defenceless) right-hand-side of foot soldiers (a horseman's mount was always vulnerable), as they advanced across the trestle-bridge towards the Octagon, springs not from medieval cunning but from modern imagination. Indeed, these long outer bridges, highly vulnerable to destruction which would isolate the castle and preclude the sorties which were an essential part of an active defence, are themselves more demonstrative than defensive in nature. Everyday convenience dictated the direct and shorter approach to the Postern, and also the subsequent shortening of the main approach itself (see Pl. 9), whereby the perishable timber span was replaced by an earthen causeway, lately (1990) altered to a bridge on piles.[60] Courtly ceremony is the most likely reason.

whole central platform probably rests on the natural subsoil (corroborated by the absence of differential movement). The refinement that the latrine shafts discharge below water-level, doubtless reduced the (often very chilly) updraught and some of the smell, but far superior arrangements were being provided at Langley (Northumberland) or Southwell (Notts.); see Wood, 377–8 – garderobes grouped in turrets over cess-pits.

60 Simpson (notes 32, 52 above) cited principally as evidence of medieval alteration the stone-revetted gap left before the Octagon (see Pl. 9), although Clark believed this masonry to be modern (in spite of thinking the direct causeway original). Devious approaches are a normal device both ancient (British hill forts; Greek acropolis) and medieval. The RCHME case that they were carried here to very great lengths (Fig. 2), diverting the approach from

Affinities must lie with the already long tradition of lordly residences comprising a *basse cour*, approached obliquely to the main axis, from which in turn the *cour d'honneur* was entered. The Chantilly picture of Jean de Berri's nearly coeval castle of Poitiers shows the arrangement to perfection, including the lifting bridge section. Bishop Anthony Bek's Somerton Castle (Lincs., licensed 1281), which housed the captive John the Good; Ashburnham's nearby Scotney Castle, Broughton Castle (Oxon.), licensed in 1406 to William of Wykeham's heir, and Sir John Fastolf's Caistor by Yarmouth are the best known of very many examples in England. At Bodiam the feature may well have compensated for the lack of an outer courtyard of stables and offices. Rather inconveniently (though the castle-impression gains thereby), these had to be fitted into the main building, along with the dovecot housed inconspicuously in the summit of the SW Tower, seignorial symbol though it was.

At the outer 'barriers', having negotiated the circuitous water-girt roadways, a guest of the greatest honour would be courteously received by the Lord; conducted past the specious challenge of Dallingridge tenantry and deferential domestics, *via* the Octagon and Barbican, each point doubtless the occasion of ceremony (see Fig. 2). Lesser folk perhaps would dismount at the Octagon, the great within the inner courtyard suitably impressed by portcullis, 'murder holes' and mummery. In all things, the stately *pavanne* of chivalric encounter, along with the humdrum business of manorial administration, and the whole routine life of a knightly household, were most effectively expressed and provided for, in necessities and military ethos alike.

## Some Contemporary Considerations and Context

Campaigning in Brittany and Picardy in the 1360s, as a mature soldier of fortune, Dallingridge would have been well aware of the draconian steps taken by Charles *le Sage* as Regent of France after Poitiers (1356), and subsequently as king (1364–80), both north of the Loire and later in almost all provinces, to counter the forays of English, Navarrese and 'Free Companies'.[61] Seignorial

the bridge along and between the southern ponds, up to the moat bank, on the central axis, facing the Postern Tower, and then anti-clockwise along the E side to the NW entrance, not only agrees with all the evidence examined in this paper, but is in general analogous with e.g. the circuitous lices-entrance at Pierrefonds and with Tattershall with its double moats. Such impressive approaches, affording closer and closer glimpses of the house, fully evolved later in the parks of sub-medieval mansions culminating in the landscape gardening of the seventeenth and eighteenth centuries. A late-medieval (c. 1460) and much enlarged version of oblique approaches with moats and detached barbicans is ducal Castello Sforzesco at Milan (sixteenth-century drawing in *The Horizon Book of the Renaissance* ed. J.H. Plumb, 1961, 178), but its elements are moated-sites' vernacular.

61 The spirit of Bodiam is one of remoteness from the grim harshness of war (e.g. *Froissart* i, ch. c, shows a knightly distaste for 'scorched earth' in Hainault in 1340). Dallingridge wished, while eschewing the daintiness of Saumur, to proclaim not brutal *arrivisme* but legitimate and established social position and public service. Much material for French royal defence policy is among the *Mandements et Actes Divers de Charles V (1364–80)*, ed. L. Delisle, Paris 1874.

fortresses *en pays de guerre* were subjected to a degree of royal (central or regional) direction highly rare or quite unknown in England, although Ireland and the Scottish March offer some intimations. Exhortation was backed up by supervision of munitioning and repair, with demolition the ultimate sanction. Increasingly, direct Crown take-over of castles, towns, fortified monasteries and precincts (forts of every variety) by the local Captain or royal Lieutenant, was resorted to. Proclamations ordered the people of the *plat pays* to withdraw, 'themselves and their goods' *ès forteresses*, namely the nearest viable refuge whatever it was, free of entry or exit dues. Quite rapidly new *de facto* castellanies evolved and *guet et garde* liabilities were redefined to accord with the military realities, the judges of the *Parlement* freely over-riding traditional liens and subordinations. Places too small to accommodate refugees and chattels, moved to deny targets and subsistence to the enemy, or too weak to deter sufficiently the privateering bands attracted by such concentrations of booty; or castles and forts whose lords (increasingly subsidized from local war-taxation) could not or would not man and strengthen them, were all ordered to be entirely razed to prevent their being used as 'lodgements' and raiding bases. A considerable proportion of the castellated gentry-residences and *neufs châteaux*, which had arisen within the old *châtellenies* since the later twelfth century, must have been affected in the devastated provinces. Raid counter-measures reduced not multi-plied, fortifications. Even 'incastellated' churches, namely those occupied and munitioned as bases, might suffer. Summing up his survey of this policy Pierre-Clément Timbal (1961) comments: 'Mieux vaut, en somme, un nombre limité de châteaux solides et bien pourvus qu'une multitude de fortins inefficaces; c'est ce dont se persuade facilement le régent Charles au lendemain de Poitiers'.[62]

After 1380, under the lax confusion of Charles VI's regencies and sub-

---

*La Guerre de Cent Ans vue à travers les registres du Parlement (1337–1369)*, ed. P-C. Timbal *et al.*, CNRS Paris 1961, 105–300, cites and summarizes entries about the repair, administration and resort to castles and towns (indifferently *forteresces*). C.T. Allmand, *The Hundred Years War*, Cambridge 1988 (76–82) shows the great walled towns were the chief refuges and army bases. Philippe Contamine, *War in the Middle Ages*, trans. Michael Jones, Oxford 1984, collates details on cannon (193–207), and his *Guerre, Etat et Société à la fin du Moyen Age*, Paris 1972, deals with the military reforms of Charles V and their sequel *inter alia multa* (135–233). The success of Bodiam as a 'fortification' was not in the utilitarian sphere of the art for, indeed, 'it could never have played a significant part in a late fourteenth-century war' (note 20 above).

[62] Timbal 1961, 106–7. In England in this period we have found no such precautionary demoli-tions ordered, but only the clearance of houses and obstructions to town defences (e.g. Chichester, 1377; but also inland at Winchester, 1378; CPR 1377–81, 72, 111). Local levies to help man royal castles were ordered sporadically e.g. Hadleigh, Queenborough, Rising, Trematon, Tintagel, Restormel, Launceston (CPR 1377–81, 2, 271, 455; CPR 1381–5, 566, 600); (cp. the French *guet et garde* system); but Portchester in February 1381 had only its tiny peacetime complement (CCR 1377–81, 441–2). All Scottish March castles were loosely supervised by the Wardens but direct aid or take-over was minor and notably rare (CPR 1377–81, 80, 455; CPR 1381–5, 182, 344). Precautions concentrated on the coast, and the coastwise 'maritime lands' but extended from Newcastle-on-Tyne in the NE round to SW Wales. In contrast Irish absentee lords had long been obliged to man and maintain castles,

sequently, these powers were still exercised but tended to devolve upon the great magnates in their apanages. When in his turn Henry V set about combat- ing irregulars after Agincourt, the lieutenants in his conquests regularly had powers to take over or to demolish all fortresses which 'cannot be conveniently kept to our advantage.' Public necessity, combined with the feudal take-over powers of *rendability*, justified a royal *dirigisme*, which, in England, was rarely applied even to a few especially important and vulnerable towns.[63]

The public-defence rôle ascribed to Bodiam and the pure patriotism credited to Sir Edward Dallingridge are, in this general context, equally implausible. Close cross-Channel links serve to high-light the contrasts. Individual magnates had long been required (in England during invasion scares; in Ireland, contin- ually) to reside upon their manors within the marches, or within 'the maritime lands', but this had no apparent impact upon the pattern of crenellating, with licence or without.[64] Problems in France and crisis at home made it politic for members of the governing council to profess public spirit, and the inscription put up by Dallingridge's colleague John de Cobham upon his outer gate at Cooling (Kent, licensed 1381), boldly proclaimed his unselfishness. And his protestations do have some credibility. The site lies on the Thames estuary. The spacious inner and outer enclosures would be well able to accommodate refugees and movables and Cooling is placed just where a show of defiance might deter

against internal enemies, although exemptions were not infrequent by this period (*CPR 1377–81*, 528, 608).

63 'Rôles Normands et Français . . . par Bréquigny . . .', in *Mémoires de la Société des Antiquaires de Normandie* 3 ser. iii, Paris 1858, no. 197 (1418, bailiwick of Evreux *etc*). The noted soldier Nicholas Dagworth (October 1377) was empowered to compel the repair and defence of Irish fortresses, royal and seignorial (*Rymer's Foedera*, Rec. Comm. 1830 iv, HMSO 1869, 21–2). In 1380, John of Gaunt had a similar commission for *omnia et singula castra, villas et fortulitia* 'in the March of Scotland' (ibid. 97). Even for coastal England measures were traditional e.g. 'compelling . . . knights and esquires . . . with suitable habitations . . . (in Cornwall) to remain upon their lands during the present summer'; to arraying all able-bodied men and stopping them fleeing (Isle of Thanet) and overhauling the beacon warning system (Isle of Purbeck); *CPR 1377–81*, 166, 455, 474. In May 1380 the monks of Netley were told (or obtained authority) to arm themselves and put the abbey in a state of defence being 'situate in a perilous place upon the sea shore between . . . Southampton and the high sea suitable for the enemies' landing', details undoubtedly taken from their petition (*CCR 1377–81*, 311). The danger here was real (see next note) but such alarms were initiated more often locally than centrally and had many non-altruistic motives.

64 H.J. Hewitt, *The Organization of War under Edward III, 1338–62*, Manchester, 1966, ch. I 'defence'. Resistance depended largely on local leadership; e.g. in July 1377, John de Clinton was directed to reside at his castle of Folkestone 'near the sea'; and Archbishop Sudbury in September 1380 had his men stay at Saltwood 'upon the coast' (one mile inland) thereby exempting them from array (*CCR 1377–81*, 6, 404). The earliest approach to what Simpson in particular (1961, 3) propounds for Bodiam is apparently Richard Guldeford's licence for a coastal defence fort below Rye at Camber in 1487 (see note 15). In 1547 Sir William Paulet had a fully explicit licence and commission, including powers of distraint, to enlarge and garrison the new fort on the exposed Netley abbey site (*CPR 1485–94*, 151; *CPR 1547–8*, 66–8).

enemy galleys from landing.[65] Being cut off inland was no part of the tip-and-run strategy of harassment by coastwise raiders and even that chivalrous paragon of the species, Don Pero Niño with his Castilian galley squadron (1404–6), did not care to risk it (see Fig. 1). Works at Rochester and at Queenborough, in Sheppey, and at Hadleigh on the Essex side, from the late 1360s, and the re-walling at great cost of Southampton and of the city of Canterbury (which it would have been a great *coup*, but also a major task to take and sack), were all costly and protracted.[66] Extempore timber *bretasches*, stockades and entrenchments at landing-places, manned by local levies, and barricading of town circuits and weak spots, could respond to emergencies but have left little trace, even in the printed records. When long-term dangers did beyond doubt generate defensive building by the gentry and baronial class it is of a rather distinct type, for the most part variations on the tower-house formula. Endemic raiding, cattle rustling and abducting for ransom produced, on the Scottish March and in the Lowlands, a host of tall compact dwelling-towers, single or aggregated, sometimes with a small barmkin, their roofs sheltered by the parapets. They effectively protected the lord and his household from marauders, too hasty and ill-equipped for sieges.[67] But the architectural result lacked the castle-image,

[65] In October 1380, and again in February 1381 when Cooling was licensed, John de Cobham headed commissions to survey likely enemy landing-places around the Hoo coast 'and cause them to be fortified by the erection of pales and the repair of dykes' ('piles and trenches', 1381: *CPR 1377–81*, 577, 596, 629). In 1386 the warlike bishop Despenser of Norwich built three 'bastides' to protect Great Yarmouth but lesser measures were preferred (*CPR 1385–9*, 177, 258–9; *CCR 1385–9*, 169). His licences to crenellate next year (Gaywood, North Elmham; *CPR 1385–9*, 381) were of purely manorial type. Thanet had old entrenchments and 'turreted walls both upon and below the cliff of that island', for resisting enemy landings. In England only the Scottish March approached the French system of organized refuge. The castles of Dunstanburgh (see W.D. Simpson, *Archaeol. Aeliana*, 4th ser. xvi, 1939, 31–42) Bamburgh and Tynemouth Priory were much used. Wholesale evacuation and retreat south was occasionally resorted to after Bannockburn (1314) to escape major Scottish inroads. For this and many searching points see M. C. Prestwich, 'English Castles in the Reign of Edward II', *Journal of Medieval History* viii, 1982, 159–78.

[66] The building contracts for Cooling (incomplete; W.A. Scott Robertson, *Archaeol. Cantiana* xi, 1877, 128–44; facsimile of inscription p. 134) total only £974; manor receipts in 1300 were £26 p.a. Minor works at Rochester (1367–70) cost £2,262; the new castle at Queenborough (1361–75, for protecting the populace; *CChR* v, 211–2; 1368) cost about £20,000, and the refortification of Hadleigh (1361–70) over £2,288, which last is attributable to other causes largely (R.A. Brown, H.M. Colvin, A.J. Taylor, *The History of the Kings Works* ii, 1963, 812–3, 792–804, 665–6). Bodiam might have cost as much as Cooling although it covers only just over half an acre compared with over eight acres of usable space. C. Kightly (*Strongholds of the Realm*, 1979, 134) summarizes Pero Niño's evidence (see note 41 above) emphasizing the customary case for French raids and seeing Bodiam as 'well-equipped' to resist them, but he implies dubiety as to its exposure and rejection of access by the Rother. Sandwich, near the Stour mouth, suffered but Canterbury would have taken major overland invasion, as would Winchester and other inland towns where reactions seem to be a compound of panic and opportunistic manipulation (see discussion of the same problem by Hewitt, esp. 2–5).

[67] Just how satisfactory the tower-house formula was can be seen all over the Lowlands, Cumberland, Westmorland, Northumberland, Durham and parts of Yorkshire and Lanca-

SOME ANALYSIS OF THE CASTLE OF BODIAM

however cost-effective, and wherever security permitted the more spacious courtyard layout (castellated or otherwise) was nearly always preferred. Bodiam has the unusually demonstrative militancy common to others of its decade in slightly higher degree, but is true to its general type in all other respects.[68]

Reasoning from illusive defensive effects mechanistically back to imagined military causes has, in the case of Bodiam, led to the famous licence of October 1385 being taken at its face value, so that its subtleties have not been grasped. Because no study has been done of licences to crenellate as a whole (and only a very incomplete bare list has so far been published), many misjudgements have arisen purely from lack of contextual awareness. The construction invariably put upon this particular licence illustrates how essential is the administrative as well as the archaeological context. In four crucial respects it errs: first, in thinking of licences as prescriptive royal directions; secondly, in believing the special pleading incorporated in its terms, undoubtedly by the petitioner's own intervention; thirdly, in supposing that licences were reluctantly and selectively granted; and finally, in assuming that such allusions to local dangers are peculiar or, indeed, at all specially significant. As a *corpus* and also individually licences to crenellate are most valuable evidence, illuminating a wide range of local, genealogical and chivalric questions; but so also are the licences to create parks and warrens, to exercise hunting rights, and to divert roads for the privacy of residences, privileges often associated with castellation, licensed or unlicensed.

shire, as also in Ireland, whether in castle-style like Bolton or humble dwelling-tower like the Vicar's Peel, Corbridge. Rarely can major non-royal castle-building be ascribed to ephemeral crises (cp. Henry VIII's 1538 gun-castle scheme; Edward I's N Welsh castles, particularly the response to the 1294 uprising with Beaumaris). Commons' petitions in Parliament (often manipulated) show anxiety that the savagery of French war could come to England (e.g. 1378, commonalty of Kent) and concern that lords should stay on local defence; Scarborough asked for a naval guard (1379); Sussex wanted Bramber Castle to be kept against possible French seizure and use a a raiding-base (1388), and coastal towns (also some far inland, as Salisbury, Northampton, Bath, Norwich and Winchester) were affected by the widespread and indiscriminate furore (*Rot. Parl.* iii, 20, 30, 42, 46, 53, 63, 70, 80–1, 146, 161, 200–1, 213, 251, 255; cp. K. Fowler, *The Age of Plantaganet and Valois*, 1967, 165–72). The 'navy' was not then capable of 'controlling the Channel' (cp. Simpson 1931, 84; 1961, 3, citing the period 1372–87 between the defeat off La Rochelle and Cadzand). Major invasion ostensibly was feared but coastal harassment and opportunistic exploitation by parties at home are most to be inferred from the records. The archaeological evidence overall also supports caution if not scepticism.

68 Licensed examples, 1380–90, are Hemyock (Devon), Cooling, Sheriff Hutton (Yorks.), Farleigh Hungerford (Som.), Thornton Abbey (Lincs.). Towers are still 'castles' in Scotland. William Heron, licensed in 1338 to crenellate Ford (Northumberland) obtained supplementary lordly rights in 1340 including that he should hold it *per nomen castri* (a unique instance). Ford was a quadrangular castle, suffering with Chillingham a Scots raid in 1344; sacked in 1385 (*CPR 1338–40*, 114; *CPR 1343–5*, 409; *CChR* iv, 468–9; *Rot. Parl.* iii, 255–6). The 1415 survey listing some seventy-eight Northumberland fortresses in some cases equivocates between *turris* and *fortalicium*, but the *castra* (including *ffurde*) are mainly the more established (printed C.J. Bates, *The Border Holds of Northumberland*, 'vol. i', 1891 13–9; cp. 78–9, facsimile of 1584 *Plat*). For the 'rival' courtyard house alternative (castellated still, but distinctively) see Thompson, ch. 4; e.g. Eltham Palace, Haddon Hall (56, 61).

Licences to crenellate will not, in short, bear the political weight put upon them; nor can Bodiam's carry the elaborate structure of tendentious supposition which has been chiefly founded upon it.[69]

Dallingridge's patent has more individuality than many but adhered to the standard form, progressively modified from late in the reign of Henry III. Granted by the usual 'special grace' common to most types of gracious privilege, it authorized him 'to fortify with a wall of stone and lime the dwelling-place of his manor of Bodiam next to the sea (sic) in the county of Sussex, and to construct and make thereof a castle (castrum) for the defence of the adjacent country and for the resisting of our (unspecified) enemies'. The habitual security of tenure formula of realty grants then concludes the document.[70] Occasionally petitioners had their licences phrased to refer to the work being on a new site, but the normal wording employed here was not literally construed. Licences often marked the setting up of a new manor-site, or signalized its definitive acquisition (often without building done), or some notable step into the local or national social hierarchy by the grantee. The presumed move from the old 'moat' below Bodiam church is thus unremarkable. Juxta mare is less acceptable when the nearest coast by Hastings is ten miles and more to the south. Unlike the Bodiam apologists the licence significantly does not make any case based on proximity to the river, that erstwhile 'water of Limen' which had once flowed into the sea south-eastwards at Romney (see Fig. 1). Dallingridge preferred to exploit the prevailing fear of coastal attack, not the remoter danger of invasion.[71] Justificatory references to local dangers, as 'in', 'near' or 'upon' 'the

---

[69] Lt Col A.H. Burne's 'inherent military probability' (The Crécy War, 1955, 12) approach will not do for castles. Simpson (1961, 3) believed that 'the terms of the licence appear to be unique (though there may be similar earlier instances on the Welsh and Scottish borders)'. Turner and Parker iii, 419, gave it undeserved prominence by quotation at length. W. D. Peckham, on 'The Architectural History of Amberley Castle' (SAC lxii, 1922, 21–63) even supposed (30–1) that it would be 'very unlikely that a Bishop in the Home Counties would dare fortify first and ask leave afterwards under . . . the third Edward'. In fact Edward III's Chancery issued licences for no fewer than 217 sites, a few certainly retrospective. Amberley's was from the regency (10 Dec, 1377), as was Bishop Erghum's (1377) for ten sites in a batch, including six manors, his London inn, his palace at Salisbury and the city itself, in rivalry with the citizens (CPR 1377–81, 9, 76).

[70] The 'king' granted pro nobis et heredibus nostris, as usual, but also quantum in nobis est, i.e. without prejudice to existing susceptibilities or rights, caution common in duchy of Gascony licences but rare in English ones. Here it may possibly reflect Chancery fears of a resumption of the friction with John of Gaunt, which had caused an affray in June 1384 and Dallingridge's brief imprisonment (Saul, 28–9, 75, 92–3, 191). The vagueness of inimici nostri may not be without significance. The patent was doubtless shown off to his coterie and dependents to proclaim that Edward Dalyngrigge chivaler . . . mansum manerii sui de Bodyham juxta mare in Comitatu Sussex muro de petra et calce firmare et kernellare et castrum inde in defensionem patrie adjacentis et pro resistencia inimicorum nostrorum construere et facere [possit] et mansum predictum sic firmatum et kernellatum et castrum inde sic factum tenere possit sibi et heredibus suis in perpetuum sine impedimento nostro et heredum nostrorum aut ministrorum nostrorum quorumcunque . . . (Rot. Pat. 9 Ric II pt. 1 memb. 21; 21 October 1385, Westminster; CPR 1385–9, 42).

[71] See notes 15, 56 above (cp. the bizarre notion that via the Rother the French might sail

March of Scotland', do sometimes occur in licences and were, as a rule, copied in turn by the Privy Seal then by the Great Seal office clerks, with other details from the recipient's draft or petition; but where more precise locations are given, such as 'situated on the sea coast', they are for whatever reason accurate. Only Bodiam is not virtually on the beach. Dallingridge here too was 'drawing the long bow' and the absence of verification of claims by the Chancery, coupled with his strategic personal advantages, ensured that he got away with it. So far as the texts of the licences (duly abbreviated, enrolled and mostly as calen-dared) permit us to judge, very few petitioners pleaded public utility, and none with his effrontery, so far as castles are concerned.[72]

Such pleas are, by contrast, habitual in the case of town authorities requesting power to tax merchandise, to pay not only for fortification (murage) but equally for bridge repairs (pontage), paving and other projects of 'common utility'. Communal and civic prestige was also involved, but benefit to the local popu-lace and to the realm was regularly asserted and almost always accepted. Tax remissions confirm that the favourable administrative instinct would concede quite large cash sums with only the nominal Hanaper fee taken for all grants offsetting the loss of revenue.[73] The public advantage was frequently and most explicitly cited in a number of petitions for licence to crenellate towns, notably by Hull (1327), Rye (1369), Leominster (Herefordshire, 1402), Kingswear (Devon, 1402), Plymouth (1404), Harwich (1405), Winchelsea (1415) and Alnwick (1434), all of which at the time were in clear potential danger. Thus Rye in 1369 was licensed to be walled 'in view of the perils which may ensue', and the 1415 licence for Winchelsea (to select the two examples nearest to Bodiam) referred to the king's liking such places to be strengthened '. . . (being) on the sea coast and frontier of the king's enemies and as it were a key of those

around 'behind the Cinque Ports', Turner, 271–2). Bodiam certainly established Dalling-ridge's (largely absentee) 'presence', which might calm nerves, but it could scarcely accom-modate local refugees with their chattels (see unique Kent-Sussex coastal refuge order April 1385, note 74 below) nor resist direct assault, in case of actual invasion. Its existence in no way defended Rye or Winchelsea or Hastings (Fig. 1, pace A.H. Thompson, note 18 above). Small surprise that 'no French force ever broke its teeth upon the guarded (sic) walls of Bodiam' (Simpson, 1961 3–4); but Dallingridge did thereby show his local commitment, his leading position among the east Sussex county gentry and perhaps some 'championship of local autonomy' (Saul, 68).

72 The genuine cases put Bodiam in its true light. Nearness to the Scots is cited in the licences for Scaleby, Drumburgh (1307), Triermain (1340) and Penrith (1397, 1399), in Cumberland; also for Blenkinsop (1340, Northumberland) and for Hartley (1353, Westmorland), places all known to have suffered Scots forays. Licensed sites 'on the sea coast', or similar, are Flam-burgh (1351, Yorks.); Fish-house and Quarr Abbey, Isle of Wight (1365, see note 52); Chideock (Dorset 1370, 1380); and Mablethorpe (Lincs. 1459). Juries at inquisitions ad quod damnum (at least nominally) checked before Chancery licensed diverting water conduits or roads or creating parks and warrens. Post hoc complaints about crenellating nevertheless are remarkably rare (Marham 1271, Wells City 1341, Swine 1352, Oxford town 1381). Un-licensed Barnwell c.1264 was reported calmly in 1275–6 (Rot. Hund. 7b).

73 Occasional and emergency direct royal takeover of port-town defence (most notably

parts'. Such language is, with very few exceptions indeed, significantly absent in this period respecting castles. When it does occur the location, circumstances and surviving structures fully justify it.[74]

Of the Bodiam licence to crenellate one element remains which has been especially fruitful of misunderstanding. It is the clause *et inde castrum facere*; that is, having fortified the *mansum manerii* with a crenellated stone wall, licence 'to make thereof a castle'. It means at once much less than appears, for 'castle' was a term of elusive subtlety and the phrase occurs in five other licences of Richard II alone; but also much more, because it raises the whole question of what, in contemporary terms, constituted a 'castle'. That their usage was not ours is a fact which cannot be over-emphasized. Whereas the first point is quickly dealt with, the administrative and literary meanings of *castrum*, *castellum* and *château* are quite beyond the present scope, so a few suggestions must suffice.[75]

The immediate context of the Bodiam licence offers numerous insights. In the reign of Richard II a total of fifty-six sites was licensed, of which forty-three may be termed 'manorial' (whether in lay or clerical possession); five are conventual or ecclesiastical establishments; another seven are for entire towns or individual town houses, and the other is for the bridge-houses of Kilkenny town

Southampton e.g. CPR *1377–81*, 7, 76, 80, 448; and construction of a royal tower, 174 etc.) contrasts with the normal governmental non-interference. Certainly urban enlightened self-interest (less so with castles) had some 'public benefit', but again motives, e.g. of prestige, distort the picture (H.L. Turner, *Town Defences in England and Wales* 1971, 87–94; also appendix B and C, somewhat incomplete). Implied licence was thought insufficiently honorific in some twenty-nine cases and formal licence to crenellate was obtained (by the burgesses twenty-three; by lords six). Border towns (e.g. Shrewsbury; Carlisle) do figure continually but the underlying reality is as much one of royal response as initiative. The Council was hardly a Ministry of War or a defence-forces General Staff.

[74] He appropriated the 'defence of the adjacent country' phrase used elsewhere with discrimination (e.g. at Ford, 1340, note 68 above; Penrith, 1399, CPR *1396–9*, 524). Tout (note 7 above) commented on the peculiar wording: 'this was an excuse, or the result of panic, as Bodiam is far from the sea' (Fig. 1). Tynemouth Priory (Northumb.) 'was reputed a castle' (1388), receiving defence-aid, having been 'in time of war the castle and refuge of the whole country' (1390; CPR *1385–9*, 494; CPR *1388–92*, 194), which combines the symbolic and military senses in almost modern fashion. In the invasion scare of April 1385 (CPR *1381–5*, 553, note 71 above), believed to threaten 'the people and fortalices on the English Coast', in almost French style 'all the inhabitants . . . with their families and goods', within six miles of Dover, Rye and Sandwich and from Thanet and Oxney were ordered 'to withdraw before 3 May under pain of imprisonment to the said castle and towns'. For Rye and Winchelsea see particularly CPR *1367–70*, 224; CPR *1381–5*, 518–19, 525, 532, 588; CPR *1413–16*, 224, 273, 368–9; *Rot. Parl*. iii, 70, 201. The official strategy in 1385 was to concentrate manpower and valuables at the coastal targets, which were large enough and capable of defence. It was not to flee inland.

[75] For the castle in literature see *The Medieval Castle, Romance and Reality*, ed. K. Reyerson and F. Powe, Dubuque, Iowa 1984, *passim* (reference due to R. Eales), in particular see 147–74, M.A. Dean 'Early Fortified Houses: Defenses and Castle Imagery 1275–1350 with evidence from the S.E. Midlands', a valiant attempt to establish architectural criteria. The range of the contributions far exceeds that indicated by the title. The various styles of champagne gentry-seats in succeeding thirteenth-century fief rolls offer some illumination also (Coulson, 1982(2) 353–6). On the metaphysics of 'fortification' see Coulson 1982(1).

in Ireland. This diversity is typical and significant. Most of the manor site licences conform to Edward III's standard formula but Sheriff Hutton (Yorks., 1382), Bodiam (1385), Donnington (Berks., 1386), Harringworth (Northants., 1387), Lumley (co. Durham, 1392), and Wardour (Wilts., 1393) all contain minor variants of the *et inde castrum facere* phrase. No particular weight can be given to it. Not only are Amberley (Sussex, 1377), Bolton-in-Wensleydale (Yorks., 1379) and Cooling omitted, but of those so dignified Donnington was very weak. Harringworth has vanished but was seemingly not structurally notable, and Old Wardour is essentially a tower-house, although of unique design with a courtyard or central light-well.[76] Here, however, lurks a deep pitfall – beyond all doubt we are quite on the wrong track when we casually apply originally medieval terms of status and structural style as though they were an architectural terminology equivalent to their modern derivatives. Degrees of social rank within the *bourgeoisie*, gentry and nobility and their appropriate manifestation, preoccupied contemporaries, whereas gradations of structural strength seldom did so, even in an explicitly military context. The linkage between structure and rank is esoteric and highly elusive. Bodiam may help to clarify the problem but not if, with the Royal Archaeological Institute, we define the castle as 'a fortified residence which might combine administrative and judicial functions but in which military considerations were paramount'. The strenuous efforts to prove that Bodiam is, in Curzon's words, 'a genuine military castle' represent one of the innumerable aberrations this approach has caused.[77] Ironically, by these very criteria we could not regard Bodiam as qualifying at all, whereas by the proper standards of its own *milieu*, Bodiam by its social function and its architecture fully deserves the coveted style of 'castle' (see Pls 10, 15).

[76] Reconstruction with its bartizan turrets in B. Morley, 112. Two of the fifty-six (Penrith, Thornton Abbey) are repeated; Chudleigh and Sherburn (Rest Park) have *fortalicium* instead. Bishop Rede's Amberley (notes 39, 69 above) sited on the edge of the wide flood plain, cut through the Downs by the splendidly navigable Arun, and near the bridge (or ford), might much more plausibly have been ascribed to fear of coastal raiders (Arundel Castle could not have 'blocked' them even if heavily manned), but no such tradition has arisen here. Its licence is standard and it entirely lacks Bodiam's *panache*. The 'make a castle' licences are *CPR 1381–5*, 108, cp. 333; *CPR 1385–9*, 42, 156; *CPR 1391–6*, 188, 261; cp. *CPR 1377–81*, 377; *CChR* v, 307.

[77] E.g. C. and B. Gascoigne *Castles of Britain*, 1975, 54, for some notably imaginative Bodiam comment. The definition was for the RAI research project into the origins of the castle in England (*Arch. Journ.* cxxxiv, 1971, 2) but is almost as inadequate for the Conquest period. See e.g. Giraldus Cambrensis's description of the amenities of Manorbier (Pembs.; R.A. Brown, 1954, 177); also the emphasis on the fertile environs of rebuilt Templar Saphet, in Palestine (*c.*1240–60), as well as on its formidable defences, (V. Mortet and P. Deschamps, *Recueil de Textes relatifs a l'histoire de l'architecture . . .*, ii Paris 1929, 261–4). Literary allusions are equally clear (notes 44, 75). Resentment of social pretension seems to have been felt most keenly by the Shire gentry. The 1363 Sumptuary Laws and the 1379 graduated categories of Poll Tax payers illustrate clearly the contemporary sense of hierarchy (*Rot. Parl.* ii, 278–9; iii 57–8).

The rank and landed estate of the lord who held it and the deference he evoked quite as much as any dignity of structure, in fact, in later medieval England, conferred the title as also did popular nomenclature. Dallingridge needed to compensate for his lack of pedigree. Lords of consequence lived in 'castles', just as bishops do in 'palaces', even if on archeological grounds the comfortable *VCH* term 'homestead moat' would be applied to their mansions. Nicholas de la Beche had such a place at Beams (Berks., licensed 1338) which is styled 'castle' in the enquiries into the forcible abduction from it in 1347 of his widow Margery, the king's young son Lionel of Antwerp being in residence at the time. The *mansum* of Melbourne (Derbys., licensed 1311) had as defences only a gate-house and turreted curtain but achieved castle status in Henry of Lancaster's inquisition *post mortem* in 1361. As for the equally modest works of Moor End and Maxey (Northants., licensed 1347, 1374) royal and ducal tenure lent that dignity. Contrariwise, major and ancient feudal *capita* tended to be 'castles' regardless of their occupancy or architecture. Quite frequently also the title was popularly conferred, as at Bagworth (Leics., licensed 1318) reported by inquisition jurors in 1371 as 'a capital messuage called the castle'. Mettingham in Suffolk (licensed 1343), also structurally not very distinguished, was *castellum* in 1366 and (to our eyes more justly) so was Cooling, but only on the forfeiture of John de Cobham in 1398.[78] Occasionally there are hints that quadrangular towered and moated places as such qualified. Titchmarsh (Northants., licensed 1304) was styled *fortalicium* in 1314 and described as 'a capital messuage enclosed like a castle with water and a stone wall', in 1347 (i.e. 'in castle-fashion', not 'in imitation of a castle'). But no sort of consistency was observed. It was mostly tradition in the eye of the beholder. Sir Reginald de Cobham's Sterborough (Surrey, licensed 1341) with its erstwhile seven towers, curtain, gatehouse and moat was described (1369) as a *forcelettum ad modum castri*, but while noting its 'strong walls' the jurors were just as impressed by 'the park containing deer measuring a league in circuit'. Numerous posthumous surveys show that the appurtenances contributed quite as much as the mansion-place to the renown of a noble residence. Established castles, even decaying earthworks, still possessed a prestige which put them above later arrivals, whose aim was therefore to imply respectable antiquity, though seldom as brashly as Dallingridge did.[79]

---

[78] Earlier usage of *castrum* for major 'public' works and ancient walled towns, (e.g. as a place-name element in Anglo-Saxon England designating all kinds of former Roman sites) has constantly been neglected. 'Castle' took on subsequently strong seignorial connotations giving birth to the later medieval concept, but the laboured contrast with 'communal' and 'pre-feudal' fortification is highly suspect, e.g. in 1227 and 1317 the Salisbury cathedral clergy petitioned to 'have the stones built in their minster and houses within (sic) the castle of Salisbury (i.e. Old Sarum hillfort) for their work of (new) Salisbury' (cp. R.A. Brown, M.C. Prestwich, C. Coulson, *Castles: A History and Guide*, Poole 1980, 10–11; *Rot. Parl.* i, 174–5; *Calendar of the Chancery Warrants* i, 470–1). The CIPM refs. are ix, 236–8; xi, 92–116; xii, 51–3; xiii, 237–40; see also CPR 1408–13, 195; CFR 1391–9, 257–8; CFR 1445–52, 239.

[79] Even abandoned sites were 'the old castle' or *situm castri*. Judicial and administrative functions often continued. For Titchmarsh see CIPM v, 289–90; ix, 24–5; for Sterborough xii,

## The Enigma of Bodiam

It may now be possible to venture some explanations for the enigmatic conjunction at Bodiam of an exaggeratedly militant outward ostentation which is so deliberately contradicted by the domesticity of all the features of detail. That its defensive panoply accords with the typological evolution of the southern quadrangular castle, which flourished ever more luxuriantly during the era of its military decline, must be emphasized. What is misleading at Bodiam is the apparently purposeful assertiveness of the militant overlay, but comparison with its own generation of licensed castles, to go no further (Chideock 1370, 1380; Nunney, 1373; Claxton, 1376; Shirburn, 1377; Bolton 1379; Cooling, 1381; Sheriff Hutton, 1382; Farleigh Hungerford, 1383; Lumley, 1392; Wardour, 1393; Penrith, 1397) is corrective. Bodiam is only locally exceptional. Dallingridge's circumstances do indeed offer more clues, but hyperbole is often a symptom of irrelevance. As castles' defensive value diminished, be it against foreign invasion, riot or civil conflict as well as in *guerre à outrance*, so the integral and incorporated symbolic element was emancipated to become explicit and in time fully autonomous with a life of its own. It could then develop without imposed constraints through stages which may be represented by Penshurst (re-licensed 1392), Faulkebourne (Essex, licensed 1439), Herstmonceux, Tonford (Kent, 1448), Sudeley (Gloucs., 1458), Gidea Hall (Essex, 1466), Oxburgh (Norfolk, 1482), Athelhampton (Dorset, 1495), Thornbury (Gloucs., 1510) and ultimately by such revivalist manifestations as Cowdray (Sussex, 1533) and Baconsthorpe (Norfolk, 1561). Its energy even then was far from spent as can be seen at Hardwick, Burghley House and Wollaton Hall, Nottinghamshire. Licences to crenellate continuously chart this aesthetic progression, until they and it peter out with the advent of Palladianism late in the reign of Elizabeth. At no point were 'defence' and domesticity divorced. Seignorial symbolism kept the outward and inward aspects of the castle-image in harmony throughout and it may well be possible to show that this conjunction, embodied in the gentry residence, began very much earlier. That it was already in existence in the later thirteenth century can scarcely be denied; but more to the present purpose are the problematic effects of security-consciousness in the violent late Middle Ages.

Rather unconvincing attempts have been made to attribute the very numerous moated *gentilhommières* to the defensive rather than to the socially symbolic function of noble architecture and thereby to fit them into the ready-made military scenario as a response to the endemic problems of law and order. Burglaries of manor-houses, even in daylight and by determined bands of malefactors, were certainly not uncommon but they were obviously not deterred by the level of 'defences' typified by the castle of Beams. The sophisticated

326–9. On the Anglo-Saxon lordly display of *burh-geat* see Dr Ann Williams' contribution to this volume.

amalgam of deterrence, status-affirmation and some limited degree of physical protection, characteristic of this class of 'fortified manor-house', should not be too roughly dissected. Any single, or simple, system of explanation will certainly be inadequate.[80] The full range of analysis, certainly must be brought to the understanding of Bodiam. French practices of the *chevauchée* would have placed it very low in the category of place not requiring engines to capture. It could scarcely have resisted the bands of peasant *réfractaires*, forced into copying the tactics of the Free Companies, let alone a mass uprising or *jacquerie*; nor, to judge from English *oyer et terminer* commissions, would it have been at all secure from aggravated house-breaking. Descriptions copied from the petitions of aggrieved householders may well exaggerate. But attacks holding a place 'besieged in manner of war', described in vivid detail including the culprits suspected and stating the value of the goods stolen and the damage done, are still important evidence. Their flagrancy and mass violence are very striking. One of them details an assault in October 1381 upon the Kiriel (Crioll) family castle of Westenhanger (Kent, licensed in 1343) situated four miles inland from the coast at Hythe. The destruction of many such castles has made Bodiam seem far more special than it really was. Westenhanger was once an impressive and substantially constructed, moated, roughly quadrangular castle with a gate and seven other towers, somewhat larger than Bodiam but of comparable design and siting. The attackers, led by Sir John Cornwall, according to Lettice widow of Sir John de Kiriel, 'with ladders scaled by night and entered her castle . . ., broke her houses and chambers, searched for her so closely that she was compelled to hide in some water, narrowly escaping death thereby'. The attempted ravishment failed but the raiders stole twelve horses valued at forty li., saddlery, jewellery and other goods. One of the culprits, not accused by Lady Lettice, received pardon nearly two years later 'for having with others broken the gates, doors and windows (*recte fenestre* i.e. 'shutters') of the Lady of Kiriel's Castle of Estrynghangre and besieged her there . . .', so it was no mere sneak attack.[81]

---

[80] The almost ritualised response to violence by ineffective legal processes is analogous to that by crenellating, illustrated most clearly with conventual precincts (Coulson 1982 (1), esp. 84–92; cp. H.R.T. Summerson, 'The Structure of Law Enforcement in Thirteenth-Century England', *American Journal of Legal History* xxiii, 1979, 313–27. (I owe this reference and helpful discussion to Dr Michael Clanchy). A psychological rather than a materialistic reaction is inferable. The phenomenon of 'rogue gentry' has generated a large literature, e.g. R. W. Kaeuper, 'Law and Order in Fourteenth-Century England . . .', *Speculum* liv 1979, 734–84 (e.g. 741, *oyer et terminer* commissions 1272–1377); also, more broadly, in *War, Justice and Public Order*, Oxford 1988 (esp. ch. 2). Moat-digging (and other works) are ascribed to lawlessness by C. Platt, 1978 (note 54 above), 111–5; and 1982, ch. 5; but in Sussex the problem was absent or inconspicuous (Saul, 75). Licences to crenellate suggest a broader gamut of social motives (cp. 1371 Commons' petition to dispense with the formality of licensing *Rot. Parl.* ii, 307). Beams Castle consists today of 'the remains of a moat and some earthworks'; otherwise 'a square moat', and 'traces of an earthwork' (*VCH* Berks. i, 271; iii, 268; King, *Castellarium Anglicanum*, Berks.).

[81] Bodiam's doors would not have withstood any kind of battery. If there was warning enough to raise the lifting bridges, they could be forced or by-passed; if time to remove the bridge-spans

Jealous or opportunistic near-dwellers and the perversion of the chivalric code among the war-calloused aristocracy were a serious social problem, most certainly, but the *insouciance* of the architectural response may not be too hard to comprehend.

Even when the lord was himself in residence, gentry households would seldom have been numerous enough or equipped to fight off such attacks. Tower houses needed few defenders and suited conditions of continued lawlessness much better, but the castellar fashion of central and southern England prescribed quadrangular and gracious courtyard castles. To describe the male members of the normal knightly *familia* as a 'garrison' is to distort the realities. The *personnel* aspect quite as much as the architectural *matériel* determined what resistance could be offered. A resident force comprising a handful of porters, kitchen-hands and manorial record-keepers was totally inadequate. Nor would this skeleton staff be much enlarged on occasion by the 'riding household' of their peripatetic lord. Dallingridge's old patron, Richard earl of Arundel, in his own honourable and ancient castle of Lewes, with its modernized shell-keep and outer gatehouse, was himself not untouched by the more coordinated commotions of 1381. He obtained (February 1383) a commission of enquiry into an attack by Lewes 'insurgents', who 'came armed to Lewes, broke his closes and the gates, doors and windows (i.e. shutters) of his castle there, threw down his buildings, consumed and destroyed ten casks of wine, value 100 li. (*sic*) and burned his rolls, rentals and other muniments'. Manorial records were a natural and frequent target of the Commons in 1381. Protecting them was particularly important, but in the castellated building of the decade following the Peasants' Revolt, seignorial reassertion (as on previous occasions) is the chief discernible response, not defence precautions.[82] Restive peasants, like cannon and French

(Pls 8, 12; Fig. 2), the narrow gaps could quickly be crossed by ladder or beams to the platforms without the entries; failing which the 'lake' would be crossed or the water drained (under cover of dark if necessary) and ladders put up. Accounts of such attacks show how determined they often were. Wrenching out the bars, with rope and grapple (Pl. 5) would give easy entry particularly *via* the Chapel or Hall windows. 'Siege', as such, would not be required. Plans of Westenhanger (as it was in 1648 and 1887) in J.F. Wadmore *Archaeologia Cantiana* xvii 1887 p. 200; CPR 1381–5, 133, 319, 548. Lettice outlived her son Nicholas who died in 1380 leaving a widow and baby. Any husband could expect a lucrative administration of Lettice's dower (the castle and advowson). The Criolls held of the archbishop and had also Eynsford 'castle and manor', with lands at Mongeham and Walmer in E. Kent. The deer park at Westenhanger (now the race-course) was still famous in Tudor times (*CIPM* xv, 100–1).

82 CPR 1381–5, 259; Saul, 35. The Kentish 'insurgents' also 'broke' Rochester Castle 'and all the king's gaols in Kent' (CPR 1381–5, 409; CCR 1396–9, 171–2). They attacked properties of Sir William de Etchingham, some of the culprits being Bodiam men (Saul, 82). On the defensive capabilities, in such circumstances, of northern tower-houses see Kightly, 120–7. He well shows the value of first-floor entrances, vaulted ground-floors and summits, and of skilful flanking-loops (e.g. 158, 168–9) but (the last feature excepted) the formula is essentially that of the supremely cost-effective twelfth-century dwelling-tower (styled 'keep' by the Victorians' prejudice for 'real' castles: see Pugin's skit on 'the modern castellated mansion', in

raids, all seem to have been blandly disregarded. An alternative explanation, both peculiar and general, is obviously needed. Only the former can be attempted here.

Because time has damaged or eliminated so many of Bodiam's architectural compeers, its special quality has certainly been exaggerated. In the local context it does stand out – indeed, exactly as it was meant to do; it is a most studied *coup de théâtre* (see Fig. 2). To understand its intended dramatic impact the necessary background lies in Edward Dallingridge's standing in the county. His was an acutely rank-conscious society which prescribed to each grade by blood, acquired rank or by possessions the 'conspicuous consumption' deemed proper. So, having bruised the conventions, why does he soften the impact of his castle by giving us drawbridge recesses with no drawbridges, 'gunloops' which do not work, doors without drawbars, projecting towers which do not flank, and a fragile pond for water-defences, among less conspicuous oddities, all set in an elaborately contrived *scène* of aquatic *divertissements* (see Figs 2, 3)? Castellated fashion explains the features but does not fully account for their *bravura* nor adequately for their self-deprecation. It is a curious impressario who sabotages his own show, and yet Bodiam is militarily-speaking a piece of splendid tongue-in-cheek bluff. Its covert contradictions are so many coded disclaimers of undue social pretension, whose message, we may be sure, was perfectly clear to the audience Dallingridge and his architect were addressing. There may well have been a touch of cynical humour in all that bluster and undoubtedly much romantic self-indulgence.

The case is necessarily speculative and depends largely on the peculiar position of Sir Edward during the 1380s and early 1390s in local affairs and national politics. Dr Nigel Saul has recently illuminated the local situation and further light has been shed upon the brush with John of Gaunt in June 1383. Dallingridge was an elderly man at the time of his licence to crenellate, but aggressive and only belatedly in a position to gratify ambitions quite possibly stimulated originally by his service in the French wars (c.1340–75), as were those of other aspiring gentry, many of whom figure among the recipients of licences. His military activities there and later at home are not exceptional for men of his class and type, nor is his traditional enrichment in France more than supposition. His opportunities, however, both locally and at Court in the 1380s, were distinctly beyond the norm.[83] As also for his colleague Sir Richard

M. Girouard, 1978, 244, also ch. 2 'The medieval household' for a general discussion of domestic logistics).

[83] On 'the peerage of soldiers' see M.H. Keen, *The Laws of War in the Late Middle Ages*, 1965, 254–7. Dallingridge probably built in this spirit. The *ex spoliis Gallorum* tradition is investigated by K.B. McFarlane on Fastolf in *TRHS*, 5th ser. vii, 1957, 91–116 on Caistor. See S. Walker 'Lancaster v. Dallingridge; a franchisal dispute in fourteenth-century Sussex', *SAC* cxxi, 1983, 87–94; Saul 28–9, 43, 67–8, 75, 98n., 191 on Gaunt's attempt as lord of Pevensey to assert his rights and hold his hundred court at Hungry Hatch (near Sheffield Park, seat of Sir Roger Dallingridge, d. c. 1380). Gaunt 'met with considerable provocation from a group

Abberbury, licensed to build a castle soon after (1386, June) at Donnington, ready access to the machinery of the Chancery facilitated getting a variety of grants and favours. Ten times knight of the shire for Sussex (1379–88) and especially having been one of three shire representatives on the 1380 commission investigating abuses during King Richard's minority, Dallingridge evidently could put drafts of what he wanted to the appropriate chancery clerk, in the usual way of inner-circle courtiers. Bribes and the low Hanaper fee, paid on collection after the grant was duly engrossed and enrolled, financed the office and yielded a profit. He and his like could purchase very much what they wanted. In February 1386 he got another licence, this time to divert a watercourse (often a very sensitive issue) 'from Dalyngreggesbay in Salehirst' to Bodiam Mill (probably below the Castle). His commissions, in July 1380 to advise how and at whose expense Winchelsea might be 'fortified', and in March 1386 to see to the defence and fortifications of Rye (he was, in fact, 'in the king's company in Scotland', in June 1385) imply no particular expertise, being part of the habitual general-purpose employment by the Crown of the active gentry. Nor should the extent of his local commitment in Sussex be exaggerated. Neither he nor Abberbury, king's knights though they were, supported Suffolk at his impeachment (1386), and he defected soon after to the Appellants; but not for very long. His conduct suggests the adroit trimmer, quick to collect the benefits of privilege, by violence or sharp practice if necessary, while avoiding, so far as possible, the odium of office at a moment of especial unpopularity for the royal councillor and acquisitive courtier.[84]

of local landowners led by Sir Edward'. Bodiam Manor was held of the queen's Rape of Hastings. Arundel's temporary eclipse at Court enabled Gaunt to have Edward tried and briefly imprisoned. In July 1386, Gaunt left England for his Iberian ventures. Sussex is notable for apparent immunity from 'magnate feuding' and from 'the disruptive activities of the outlaw gangs' (note 80 above). The position of men like Sir Edward was enhanced 'by the relative absence of magnate lordship' (72). He acted as Gaunt's master forester in Ashdown Forest and abused his position with impunity. He had served under Sir Robert Knollys, and in 1367 under Lionel of Clarence (CPR 1367–70, 41). Knight of the royal household (1377), he married Elizabeth de Wardedieu and inherited his elder brother's lands c.1380. His acquisition (after July 1376) of Bodiam Manor is noted in 1381 in a transaction for the sale of timber from 'a wood in Bodyham park between Bodyham pond (was this on the present castle site? see above) and the lands of Thomas Colepepere, knight', to be taken to the sea and shipped to Calais (CPR 1377–81, 611). In 1380 he was one of the shire knights on the parliamentary commission for the reform of the king's household; Shire member in 1379–88; assiduous member of the royal council 1389–93; commissioner for peace with France 1390, keeper and escheator of London, 20 June to 22 July 1392, during Richard's dispute with the citizens (among them Henry Yevele) which office was doubtles lucrative (see Tout iii, 352, 411, 413n., 469n., 470n., 480–1; J.F. Baldwin The King's Council in England during the Middle Ages, 1913 (1969), 132–3, 300n., 489 et seq., showing he can seldom have been in Sussex; CFR xi, 49, 51. He died c.1394 (Tout; Saul '1393').

[84] Abberbury at Donnington founded also a chapel and hospital (VCH Berks iv, 96, 137, 456, 508). Edward's elder (and perhaps less assertive) brother Roger had an active career latterly in Shire politics 1360–77, dying c.1380 in his 70s. He gained the de la Lynde lands, joined the Arundel retinue and fought in France with the de Poynings in 1338–46 (Saul 36,

His career does much to explain the *éclat* of Bodiam. His chivalry moreover, was evidently of the war-hardened and brutal Robert Knollys variety, and his 'toy fortress' swaggers with assumed self-confidence, as Nunney (1373), Cooling and Wardour do also in their own way, shrugging off the facts of defeat abroad. But there is very little of France about the styling of Bodiam. Not for him the majestic Pierrefonds-type double-crowned tower summits of Guy's and Caesar's towers, added to the great baronial castle of Warwick, although modernity received the gesture of his machicolation and inverted keyhole gunloops. Bodiam fits not uncomfortably its stylistic and social niche, but a more specific context might tentatively be proposed, namely that of 'reassertive castellation', a phenomenon demonstrated by several of the licences to crenellate. Having gathered to himself family lands, heiress-wife and son, profits of office and opportunity, and having confronted the great Duke of Lancaster and King of Castile, a grandiloquent statement of his triumph very naturally followed (see Pl. 10).

The instance most local and most characteristic is the case of 'Shoford', near Maidstone. It is typical in that the circumstances suggest that the chief motive for obtaining the licence was to answer back to some slight or insult. Dalling-ridge may have suffered himself in the disturbances of 1381. Arundel, his patron, certainly did. But the offence could be any event derogatory to personal standing. Near Maidstone, in early June 1381, the house of an unpopular local official, William de Topcliffe, was 'thrown down by the common people' who

67–8). In many ways Edward succeeding as head of the family built upon his achievement. The writs of 'expenses' for his Parliamentary attendances 1379–84, at four shillings per day total nearly £60 (*CCR 1377–81*, 356, 497; *CCR 1381–5*, 133, 453; *CCR 1385–9*, 119, 495). He had also ten shillings a day as a royal Councillor 1389–93, and 100 marks *p.a.* for life and perquisites (e.g. two tuns of Gascon red wine annually). Of the thirty plus councillors he was the most 'industrious', attending e.g. for 207 days between 8 January 1392 and 21 February 1393. He is styled in the council journal *Monsire* and served with John *sire de Cobham*, Lord Lovell and John Devereux (Baldwin, note 83 above). These three all had licence to crenel-late (Cooling, Wardour, Penshurst). 'Like any other medieval licence (e.g. Mortmain), a licence to crenellate would be granted to any applicant, if he was not openly hostile (*sic*) to the Crown, and could afford it.' (N. Denholm-Young *The Country Gentry in the Fourteenth Century*, Oxford 1969, 36). Edward's licence for the mill-leat (smoothed by the subtlety that the water was to be channelled 'by an ancient dyke on his own ground to his said mill at Bodiam'), dated 3 February 1386, presumably indicates that the water-holding earthworks were then quite far advanced and the inadequacy of water for the mill was apparent. The licence cost him half a mark, good value for a lucrative sign of lordship. In the summer 1385 invasion crisis quite significantly he was exempted (June) from arraying men in Sussex in order to be with the king. He backed Arundel and the Appellants in 1387–9, and in March 1388 was one of the trusties empowered to receive oaths of loyalty from Sussex notables. In January 1389 he secured the keeping of the local alien priory of Wilmington for 100 marks *p.a.*, doubtless profitably (*CPR 1385–9*, 6, 98, 123, 405–6; *CPR 1377–81*, 566; *CFR x*, 278). Invested in Bodiam Castle these combined resources yielded lasting gains, cannily safe-guarded by John Dallingridge's cultivation of Henry of Derby which was duly rewarded after the revolution of 1399 (Saul, 70). In 1412 the Sussex lands yielded £100 *p.a.* (G. Mathew, *The Court of Richard II*, 1968, 206).

had been incited by a gang responsible for sacking several manor-houses in the area and destroying manorial documents. No licence was actually needed to rebuild but, perhaps, adding some crenellation and support from the new archbishop (successor of the murdered Sudbury) William de Courtenay, in getting it out of Chancery, all served to reassert Topcliffe's status and his association with the great and to scorn those who had humilated him.[85]

Popular resentments, smouldering among the broken promises of 1381, may be an additional reason for disclaiming motives of aggrandisement, as does Dallingridge by the wording of his licence and John de Cobham even more publicly. Impressing the knightly class risked irritiating the common people, especially by treating them like French peasantry. Cooling Castle was being completed about the time the earthworks at Bodiam were begun. Both belong to that recovery of confidence by divinely ordained authority, once the levelling doctrines of John Ball had been repressed. But there is a note of self-exculpation and unease nonetheless –

> Knowyth that be-th and schal be
> That I am mad in help of the cuntre –
> In knowyng of whyche thyng
> Thys is chartre and wytnessyng.[86]

Being worsted in his quarrel over franchisal rights of jurisdiction by John of Gaunt's local agents in 1384 must have sharpened all these motives and may well have pushed Dallingridge to the bravado of Bodiam. Its studied archaisms asserted his lineage while its touches of modernity advertised his present power. The 'frontier-castle' allusion could disregard the realities of the March; nothing more poetic than that castle in a valley can be imagined. In a region, since the decline early in the century of the Warenne power, and lacking intermediate magnates, the upper gentry in East Sussex seem to have got rather above themselves. At Bodiam, Dallingridge shared the parish church, had a park only in name and suffered from all the stigma of being a newcomer. The lordly emblems and appurtenances of deer park, minor jurisdiction and rights of free warren were esteemed as much as the castle-seat itself. Dallingridge, whether

---

[85] Probably in Mote Park, SSE of the town centre, see Coulson 1982 (1), 85–6. The cases of 'Hailes' recte Halesowen (see Zvi Razi, on abbot-tenantry friction, in *Essays in Honour of R. H. Hilton*, ed. T. H. Ashton et al., 1983, 151–67; ref. due to M. C. Prestwich), Waltham and Abingdon are also revealing monastic instances. On Lewes in 1381 see note 82 above. That the chivalrous *ambiance* exists mostly in modern preconception is argued by John Gillingham on William the Marshal's *History* (*Thirteenth-Century England* ii, 1988).

[86] See note 66 above. The plaque has *beth* (i.e. 'be-eth') and *mad in help* (not 'made'). John Harvey (1944, 39) commented that 'Lord Cobham was taking no chances of arousing hostility among the peasants by the building of the castle' (but the licence is dated 10 Feb. 1381). '... The inscription is in blue enamel on a copper plate, made in the form of a charter with strings and seal'. Except that a lead flashing has been inserted at the top as a rain-drip, this well-known (but still remarkable) manifesto (?c.1385) is in pristine condition.

bruised by his set-down or emboldened by coming off well, evidently set out to make his castle at Bodiam in compensation as assertive as a careful choice of site, an excellent architect and economical expenditure of his local and central sources of income allowed.[87] It is all 'up front'. The 'castle-in-a-lake' look is still supremely effective; in its original setting the effect must have been stunning (see Fig. 2). Perhaps he was thereby somewhat stepping beyond his proper station in life, but de facto ennoblement by arms and subsequent royal service produced similar symptoms of architectural hubris in numerous members of his class. King Richard's minority, unsettled local conditions both foreign and domestic, and the experience of 'heavy lordship' at Lancaster's hands, undoubtedly explain the building which we can examine today in its singular completeness and splendour. Its ambiguity may perhaps be resolved by borrowing from the repertoire of animal behaviourism: a gregarious intruder, conscious of his strength but reluctant to provoke resentment, sends out conflicting and simultaneous signals of aggression and of submission, at once eager to compel respect while anxious not to offend unduly the hierarchical proprieties of his own time and species.[88]

[87] See notes 52, 71, 82–4 above; also 83 for Bodiam park. That crenellation was merely one of many prestigious elements is most obvious in the licences under charter (forty-five covering sixty-six sites including six town and three castle-building jurisdictional franchises) where the 'fortification' is part of an entire complex of seignoralia (e.g. Boughton Malherbe, Kent 1363; Harringworth, Northants, 1387; Kettlewell in Craven, Yorks, 1405: CChR v, 174, 307, 427). A few by letter patent are also packages combining in one document that whole array of cherished and lucrative rights appurtenant to lordly rank in terms of which Sir Edward Dallingridge's Bodiam Castle should be analysed and understood.

[88] It has been unavoidably necessary in this paper to take issue with a good many statements which have previously gone unchallenged, have been continually reiterated, but which are clearly erroneous; and also to confront some interpretations which would appear to be poorly substantiated. The result may seem rather more combative than courteous. It is indeed the third demand of that threefold test of justified utterance which is the hardest to satisfy. 'Is it true? Is it necessary? Is it kind?' The more the others are served the more elusive becomes the last.

Further Note The latest National Trust guidebook has been published since writing (David Thackray, Bodiam Castle, The National Trust, June 1991, 60pp, numerous illustrations). Use of custodianship records has supplied valuable details of early conservation work (26–30) notably by the Fuller family (1829–64), by George Cubitt (1864–1916) and by Lord Curzon (1916–25). Interestingly, it was he who had the Main Gate 'prison pits' dug out (37). There is also a variety of useful but flawed historical material. Some telling architectural indicators such as the absence of hinges for doors to the barbican, are noted (although doors are still alleged behind the mid- and inner portcullises to the main entry) and a chapter is included on 'The Setting' (55–8) not quite fairly presenting the views of RCHME, but the work as a whole is substantially traditional, attempting to assimilate contradictory evidence mentioned selectively. A few errors seem to be entirely new (since Curzon), notably Dallingridge's age and the omission of his elder brother (genealogy, 22). To catalogue them all would risk emulating J.H. Round's pungent index entry on 'Freeman, Professor' in his Feudal England, 1895.

ADDENDUM, SEPTEMBER 1992

The 1917–25 correspondence (copy generously supplied 2. ix. 92 by Dr D.W.R. Thackray) chiefly of William Weir (architect), E.E. Bowden (site-supervisor) and Curzon, reveals *inter alia multa* that: the MOAT, contrary to the opinion quoted of L.E. Hole (1970) did need clay puddling on the S and E banks; refilling 1920–1 took over twelve months owing to poor spring-flow aggravated by leakage; the old sluice was of 'portcullis' penstock type, replaced by manhole and plugged pipe; Curzon had the lilies removed (and, less successfully, rushes from his 'Tiltyard'). BRIDGES: attempts were made to find 'pits' outside both gates; the stone-cased causeway S from the Barbican was eventually accepted as a contemporary afterthought and largely refaced (in new stone). PARAPETS were extensively re-set or reinstated with original ashlar from the moat and interior; entire 'restoration' was rejected on cost (£950 estimated). The INTERIOR was largely dug out ('excavated') then partially re-filled; efforts to find true basements (Main Gate, SW and SE Towers) as 'dungeons' were frustrated by water-seepage; the 'well' found in the SW Tower (probably *recte* a cistern for rainwater and once lead-lined) filled up as the Moat level rose (1920–1). The WORK AS A WHOLE (cost £5,780, 1919–21, by Curzon's summary) was creditably conservative once the 1917 total 'restoration' scheme, costed at £20,000, was providentially declined by Lord Curzon.

# Stephen Scrope and the Circle of Sir John Fastolf: Moral and Intellectual Outlooks[1]

## JONATHAN HUGHES

The Scrope family of Bolton and Masham, which consisted of lawyers, church-men and warriors, made important contributions to the chivalric and religious culture of the fourteenth century. As crusaders and as defendants and deponents in the Scrope Grosvenor dispute they were seen to be upholders of the codes of honour of the great lineal families who claimed descent from the time of the Norman conquest; and as patrons of recluses such as Richard Rolle and Margaret Kirkby and as leaders of the church of York they were at the forefront of the devotional changes occurring among clergy and laity.[2] Within this con-text of family history and aristocratic conventions Stephen Scrope Esq. of Castlecombe would have been considered a failure. However this neurotic, deformed, impoverished gentleman who lived in the shadow of his stepfather, Sir John Fastolf, is worthy of study not just because of his unfortunate fate, but because he was so articulate about his problems and relationships, and because he was the one member of this distinguished family to write books, two transla-tions, *The Epistle of Othea* in 1440 and *The Dicts and Sayings of the Philosophers* in 1450.[3] In his correspondence and in these works he provides evidence of the emotional sensitivity shown by some of the members of Fastolf's household and of the existence of a serious moral and philosophical dimension to their lives.

Stephen's father, Sir Stephen Scrope, was the second son of Richard, the first

---

[1] I wish to acknowledge the help and encouragement I received in the writing of this paper from the librarian and archivist of Magdalen College, Oxford; Dr J.I. Catto (who read the typescript); and Dr M. Keen.

[2] J. Hughes, *Pastors and Visionaries: Religion and Secular Life in Late Medieval Yorkshire*, Wood-bridge 1988, 13–22, 77–82, 91–92.

[3] Stephen Scrope, *The Dicts and Sayings of the Philosophers*, ed. C.F. Buhler, EETS, o.s. ccxi, 1941; Stephen Scrope, *The Epistle of Othea*, ed. C.F. Buhler, EETS, cclxiv, 1970.

lord of Bolton. Lord Bolton had been intent on preserving the bulk of the family's estates (largely acquired in the fourteenth century) for his eldest son and heir, William, and Sir Stephen only received as a patrimony the Yorkshire manor of Wighton; however, Lord Bolton arranged for the marriage of Stephen and his third son, Roger, to the Tiptoft heiresses, Millicent and Margaret, and Millicent brought to her husband, Sir Stephen, the Wiltshire manor of Castle Combe and the Oxfordshire manor of Oxendon.[4] The fortunes of the Scropes of Bolton were at their height in the 1390s: William, the royal favourite, was elevated to the peerage and made earl of Wiltshire in 1397; in the same year Sir Stephen (who was also in Richard II's service) and Millicent had their first child, Stephen (named like his father after the patron saint of the family chapel in the choir of the north aisle of York Minster), followed by another son, Roger, and a daughter, Elizabeth.[5] The decline of the family fortunes began with the deposition of Richard II in 1399. Sir Stephen was with the monarch at Flint Castle in 1399 during his surrender to Bolingbroke and had to clear himself before the earl Marshall in 1400 of a charge of conspiring to dethrone the new king.[6] In the following year Richard Lord Scrope of Bolton died and two years later his second son and heir, Roger, was also dead, leaving the control of the family inheritance (during the infancy of Roger's son and heir, Richard) in the hands of his widow, Margaret. Stephen was now the eldest surviving son of the first lord of Bolton. He entered the service of Thomas of Lancaster and was his deputy in Ireland, where he died of plague in 1408.[7] The deaths within ten years of all of Richard Lord Scrope's sons left the family's estates in the hands of the sisters Millicent and Margaret, now wealthy dowagers. Stephen's mother, Millicent, wasted little time after her husband's death by marrying in 1409 at the age of forty-one John Fastolf, a butler of Thomas of Lancaster and a servant of her former husband.[8] Almost immediately after the marriage she gave her new husband right to a life interest in all her estates, effectively disinheriting her twelve-year-old son, Stephen, which was contrary to an agreement made with Sir Stephen in 1390 by which the estates would pass on her decease to her eldest son by her first marriage. In taking this extraordinary step against her son's interests she was probably following the advice of her sister, Margaret, and

4  CPR 1369–77, 219, 251–52; CPR 1377–81, 205; CFR 1369–74, 396; BL Add. MS. 38692, fos 139–41 (Worcester's account of Millicent's betrothal); BL Add. MS. 28206, fo. 6b for division of Sir Robert Tiptoft's estates among his three daughters; see Bridget Vale, 'The Scropes of Bolton and Masham, c.1300–1450: A Study of a Northern Family, with a Calendar of the Scrope of Bolton Cartulary' York D.Phil. thesis, 1987, 126–27. See Magdalen College, Oxford Fastolf Paper (henceforth FP) 59 for Millicent's lands.
5  G. Poulett Scrope, History of Castle Combe, 1852, 141.
6  J. Webb, 'Translation of a French Metrical History of the Deposition of King Richard II, Archaeologia xx, 152; Rymer, Foedera viii, 168–70. CPR 1399–1401, 401.
7  CPR 1399–1401, 507; CPR 1399–1401, 178, 597; CPR 1409–13, 208; CCR 1409–13, 208; Raphael Holinshed, Chronicles of England, Scotland and Ireland (6 vols), London 1807.
8  Poulet-Scrope, 141; Millicent was born in 1368. For Fastolf see A.R. Smith, 'Aspects of the career of Sir John Fastolf, 1380–1459', unpublished D.Phil. thesis, Oxford 1986.

certainly learning from her experiences as a widow in the Scrope family. Margaret tried unsuccessfully to marry family servants twice, in 1405 and 1407, while her son was a minor and was vigorously opposed by her deceased husband's executor, John Tibbay.[9] The latter's murder was later organised by Margaret's second suitor, John Nixander; but Tibbay successfully kept the Scrope inheritance intact until Margaret's son, Roger, entered his majority, and from this time until Roger's death in 1420 Margaret was denied access to her dower lands.[10] This second marriage initiated a series of twists in Stephen's fortunes that were to influence the evolution of his unusual and difficult personality. Fastolf soon removed Stephen by selling his wardship to a Yorkshireman, William Gascoigne, the chief justice of the king's bench, settling on Stephen, when he came of age and married one of Gascoigne's daughters, his father's Yorkshire manor of Wighton. As was customary, the boy was to be brought up in Gascoigne's household as his ward, Gascoigne would receive the rents from his estates until Stephen's majority and Fastolf received 500 marks.[11] This was the first of a series of arrangements regarding Stephen's wardship that Fastolf made with influential judiciaries, probably in an attempt to cultivate contacts within the legal profession. The arrangement was socially acceptable, for Gascoigne was a friend of the family who as chief justice had stood by Richard Scrope, the archbishop of York, and refused to pass the death sentence on him. However Stephen was unhappy in his household and Fastolf, at the insistence of certain friends of Stephen and Gascoigne himself (who may have been concerned at the way Stephen's inheritance was being controlled by his step-father) was compelled to buy back the wardship in 1413. Around this time Stephen suffered an illness that left him disfigured for life and incapacitated him for active military service.[12] However he joined Fastolf's household and accompanied his step-father on all his military campaigns in France and Normandy between 1415 and 1421. When he came of age between 1421 and 1424 he was not allowed to enter his inheritance, but he sought to break free from his step-father's influence by joining the household of Humphrey, duke of Gloucester, selling the only manor he possessed for 500 marks to purchase the necessary horse and armour.[13] The duke, a patron of John the fourth lord Scrope of Masham, may have sympathised with the misfortunes of Stephen's family, for he promised to secure for him the lordship of the Isle of Man to which Stephen's father had a claim.[14] Gloucester in these years would have been regarded by Fastolf as being

---

9    *Testamenta Eboracensia*, ed. J. Raine and J. Raine, 1836, 1855, 1864 (henceforth *TE*) iii, 38–40.
10   Vale, 'The Scropes of Masham and Bolton, 212–17, 227, *Rot, Parl*, iv, p. 164.
11   BL Add. MS 28209, fo. 21; BL Add. MS 28206, fo. 24, 13b.
12   BL Add. MS 28212, fo. 21.
13   *Cal. Anc. Deeds* vi, 284, 287, 307.
14   In 1392 Richard Lord Scrope of Bolton (Stephen's grandfather) and his two sons, William, the future earl of Wiltshire, and Sir Stephen, had purchased the lordship of the Isle of Man. After the execution of the earl of Wiltshire in 1399 the Isle was granted to Sir John Stanley,

politically unsound because of his association with Joan of Navarre, who was accused of necromancy in 1421, and his marriage with Jacqueline of Hainault, which endangered the English alliance with Burgundy; and Stephen was persuaded by his stepfather and his mother to rejoin Fastolf's service in France, probably as a secretary or accountant: the accounts of John Halle survive for the receipts and household expenses of Stephen Scrope at Honfleur, and it is probable that Stephen was responsible for supplying troops with herrings (a trade in which Fastolf's family had connections).[15] Stephen was soon embroiled in a quarrel with the marshal of Honfleur, to which he alluded in a letter written between 1428 and 1430 where he complained about Fastolf siding with the marshal. He retaliated by returning to England to live with his mother and Fastolf responded by requiring him to pay for his maintenance; as he was unable to do so pressure was put on Stephen to find a wife; he and Fastolf looked among the articulate parliamentary class.[16] On his return from France Stephen brought a letter written by Fastolf in Rouen on 31 October 1429 to his cousin John Fastolf Esq. and Sir John Kirtling, parson of Arksey, giving Fastolf's consent and his terms for a proposed marriage between Stephen and Katherine Cobham, widow of Reginald Cobham (d.1428) the son and heir of John Cobham of Hever in Hoo, with whom Stephen's family had been involved in land transactions. Katherine was also the daughter of Thomas Fauconer, mayor in 1434 of London, from whom Fastolf had purchased the manor of Davingham in 1424.[17] Fastolf required Fauconer to purchase the wardship for 500 marks; in return he and Millicent would make over to Stephen and his wife the estate of Wighton-on-the Wold in Yorkshire.[18] The arrangement fell through, but in 1432 Stephen went to Rouen to consult Fastolf about a marriage to Margaret Doreward, and in 1432–33 Fastolf returned to England to arrange the transaction. Margaret Doreward was the daughter of John Doreward Esq. of Essex, Fastolf's estate agent, a sheriff of Essex 1432–33 and son of John Doreward, the former speaker of the House of Commons.[19] Her mother, Blanche, was the daughter of Sir John Tyrell of Essex, a speaker of the House of Commons in 1437 and a member of the king's council in 1431–32. Both families had strong connections with Humphrey duke of Gloucester;[20] and the marriage was financially as well as socially desirable: in 1436 the estates of Margaret's father, John Doreward were assessed at £255 a year, ranking him fifth among Essex proprietors below

and in 1405 Sir Stephen Scrope claimed the island as the earl of Wiltshire's brother, a claim repudiated by 1408. CPR 1388–92, 559, 64; BL Add. MS 28209, fo. 21.

[15] BL Add. MS 28212, fos 10–16v.

[16] BL Add. MS 28212, fo. 23.

[17] Ibid., fo. 21. Stephen's father, Sir Stephen Scrope, purchased the manor of Hever Cobham and it was eventually released by the trustee, John Tibbay, to Fastolf and Millicent; Smith, 'Fastolf', 7.

[18] HMC 8th Report, 268; Smith, 'Fastolf', 49.

[19] Smith, 'Fastolf', 30.

[20] Sir John Tyrell served in Gloucester's retinue with John Lord Scrope of Masham.

baronial rank.[21] Fastolf in return for his consent to the marriage demanded the payment of 500 marks for the wardship, and the burden of payment fell on Stephen, for there was a recognizance by him for £300.[22] Doreward certainly drove a hard bargain, but not as hard as Fastolf, for in July 1433 Stephen, in return for his step-father's consent to the sale of his wardship, was forced into a transaction (witnessed by his brother, Robert) to sign over his interest and any legal claim on his mother's estate during Fastolf's lifetime, thereby making his fortunes dependent on his stepfather.[23] The only compensation he received in the following month was his father's estate of Wighton which was made over to Stephen, his bride Margaret, and his father in law, John Doreward.[24] Stephen soon found himself in financial trouble over the purchase of this wardship: in 1443 Stephen and Doreward agreed to pay £20 yearly pension during the life of Millicent towards this sum of 500 marks;[25] by 1448 he had fallen into debt with his father-in-law over this wardship for he bound himself, on penalty of 400 marks, to pay Doreward by Christmas £200 in restitution of his debt, and he was bound to pay Doreward 20 marks yearly out of the estates that would accrue to him on Fastolf's death.[26] It is a measure of the financial difficulties into which Stephen fell that he manumitted wealthy villeins from bondage in 1448, including a serf of Oxendon manor, even though this was prospective as he did not have the manor at that date.[27] It is not surprising that Scrope complained about being dispossessed as a result of his being bound to Doreward in a marriage that brought him disaster, and it seems to have initiated a period of suffering. In 1433 his younger brother, Robert, died and he got further into debt. He complained to Fastolf about his having a wife, servants and children to support (by 1456 only one daughter, Margaret, survived).[28] Fastolf's only contribution was to institute a suit against Stephen and he had him outlawed for failing to appear before Justice John Juyn over for a debt of £40, for which Stephen received a pardon in Norwich in October 1442.[29] Stephen's poverty was such that he was forced to sell the wardship of his surviving daughter at a reduced price, and he was still living on the proceeds of this sale in 1452.[30] During this period

---

21 J.S. Roskell, *The Commons and their Speakers in English Parliaments, 1326–1523*, Manchester 1965, 50.
22 CCR 1429–1435, 253.
23 CCR 1429–1435, 257.
24 CPR 1429–1436, 283.
25 CPR 1429–36, 283 (records payment of £200 from Doreward and Scrope to Fastolf).
26 G. Poulet-Scrope, *Castle Combe*, 283.
27 Ibid, 283.
28 Elizabeth Clere's letter in which she refers to the arrangements to be made for Scrope's daughter and Elizabeth Paston, his prospective wife, and their future children shows that she was the only surviving child by this first marriage. *The Paston Letters and Papers of the Fifteenth Century*, ed. Norman Davis, Oxford 1976, 2 vols (henceforth *PL*), ii, 52.
29 CPR 1441–46, 116.
30 Margaret Schofield, *The Dicts and Sayings of the Philosophers*, Philadelphia 1936, 1–22.

Stephen's wife died and he resided with his mother; they were joined by Fastolf who returned from Normandy after 1439 to live permanently in England, establishing and building residences in Southwark and Caister Castle, which was habitable by 1448.[31] In 1446 Millicent died but Stephen did not enter the inheritance he had signed away to Fastolf in 1433 and found himself in a position of helpless dependence. It is not clear in what capacity Fastolf employed him; perhaps he was a secretary. During 1446 he was helping his step-father acquire property: in 1442 Fastolf had purchased the lease of a property in St Olave's parish, Southwark. On 2 March, 1446 the owner of the property, William Oliver, vicar of Hoydon, died after allegedly bequeathing his property to his attorney, Thomas Sprout. Fastolf alleged the deed was a forgery and Stephen Scrope in a signed declaration recorded that Thomas Sprout had many times confessed before Stephen that William Oliver had never made estate and enfeoffment of this property to him. Stephen and the parson of Castle Combe, John Welles, also witnessed that Sprout had confessed before them that William Oliver had been sick for a quarter of a year before his death and had never left his chamber at St Katherine's. Thanks to Stephen's testimony Sprout was undermined without resorting to the courts and Fastolf acquired a valuable property, consolidating his residential holdings in Southwark.[32]

Scrope's regular employment in Fastolf's household is also suggested by his residence in Caister, which was finally completed by 1450. According to William Paston, Stephen was residing there in 1454 in his own room.[33] During this period Stephen was searching, with his stepfather's help, for a suitable wife among the East Anglian squirearchy. One was Elizabeth Paston, the daughter of Judge William Paston and Agnes Paston, and the sister of Fastolf's friend and lawyer, John Paston. Scrope at this time was fifty and Elizabeth twenty, and the negotiations were handled in 1449 by Elizabeth Clere, a niece of Fastolf, and Fastolf himself, who was probably anxious to have a firm connection with this influential legal family, and who, according to William Paston in a letter to his brother, John, was getting impatient to bring the matter in this unlikely match to a head. Stephen, to his annoyance, was prevented by Agnes from actually seeing his prospective bride and neither Elizabeth Clere nor William Paston were very keen on the marriage and thought their ages disproportionate.[34] Elizabeth Paston, perhaps in her desperation to leave home, expressed an interest as long as Stephen's lands were free (and he assured her that his surviving daughter and her husband, a knight, would receive only an inheritance of fifty marks, and the rest of his estate would go to his sons by any marriage he

---

31 Magdalen College, Oxford, Fastolf Paper 43.
32 FP 64; Smith, 'Fastolf', 178.
33 PL i, 154. Archaeologia xxi, 263–64.
34 PL i, 154. The letter is dated 1454 but is probably a mistake, 1449 is more likely, for it is improbable that negotiations would have dragged on for five years.

contracted).[35] Nevertheless Elizabeth eventually married Robert Poynings in 1458. Another of Fastolf's associates to be involved in Stephen's marriage negotiations was his cousin and feoffee Sir Henry Inglose who, as Agnes Paston reminded her son John before 1449, was busy about Stephen for one of his daughters.[36] Inglose was an East Anglian knight of Dilham, fifteen miles from Caister, who served in France under Bedford in 1421 and was an MP for Norfolk in 1436–37. The years from 1446 (the year of Millicent's death) to 1455, when Stephen was living with Fastolf, fretting about the way his stepfather retained control of his mother's property and looking for a wife of whom Fastolf would approve, must have been frustrating; Stephen expressed some of this frustration in 1452 in a series of complaints to his stepfather about his past treatment, poverty and disinheritance. He also translated for the edification (and probably moral improvement) of his stepfather *The Epistle of Othea* in 1440 and *The Dicts and Sayings of the Philosophers* in 1450. Some measure of independence was finally achieved in 1456 when Stephen married Joan, the daughter of Sir Richard Bingham, a chief justice (like Gascoigne before him).[37] Fastolf, who had served with Bingham on a number of commissions between 1452 and 1456, saw him as a useful contact and used Stephen as an intermediary in an attempt to secure his influence in a law suit in 1457.[38] Stephen also sought his new father-in-law's help in an attempt to gain control of his maternal inheritance: in 1455, with the support of John Paston, he wrote to Fastolf on Stephen's behalf asking him to allow his stepson to farm his inheritance, as he had only the 10 marks annual allowance Fastolf granted him on his mother's death on which to live.[39] Fastolf must have seriously considered the proposal, for in the following year his lawyer, John Paston I, was talking to Scrope and Bingham about the possibility of Stephen taking over Wighton and Fastolf wrote to Paston saying 'I wold rather my sone Scrope to have it with sufficient surety'.[40] However by July 1459 Scrope was still not in charge of his inheritance and Fastolf was quarrelling with Bingham and his stepson over Wighton, empowering Paston to put the matters moved by Bingham and Scrope into Justice Yelverton's hand to bring the matter to an end.[41]

This year of Fastolf's death, and probably of the birth of Stephen's only surviving son, John, saw the stepson finally entering his parent's inheritance, the lands in Yorkshire and the West Country. He received none of the lands that Fastolf had acquired in East Anglia and Southwark, nothing from his will and he was not appointed an executor, even though he was several times at

35 *PL* i, 30.
36 *PL* ii, 31, 108–109.
37 Poulet-Scrope, *Castle Combe*, 275–76.
38 *The Paston Letters*, ed. James Gairdner, 1904, repr. Gloucester 1980, 120–21.
39 *PL* iii, (Gairdner) 54–55; BL Add. MS 28212, fo. 26.
40 *PL* ii, 166.
41 *PL* ii, 181.

Caister in the previous two years and was with the old man just before his death, shortly before which, according to John Paston I and Thomas Howys, the main executors, Sir John had changed the will leaving all his land to Paston on condition that he supervised the establishment from the estate of a collegiate foundation of Benedictine monks and paupers at Caister.[42] Stephen initially tried appealing to the Pastons for some recompense. On 3 July 1462 John Daubeney informed John Paston I, Fastolf's heir, that Scrope was sending him a request for money through Bingham,[43] and in the following month Thomas Playter informed Paston that Scrope was making daily enquiries whether Paston had answered his letter concerning a request for money that Bingham had assured him he would obtain on his coming to London. Even William Paston II, John's brother, who had his own enquiries concerning Fastolf's estate, was urging his brother to give some sort of recompense to Stephen.[44] It appears, however, that Stephen got little satisfaction from the Pastons because he was soon joining forces with Fastolf's secretary, William Worcester, and Chief Justice Yelverton in opposing the nuncupative will. He had been in Fastolf's chamber on the Saturday night before Fastolf's death and was with Fastolf at Caister on a number of occasions in the preceding months and he appeared in the house of the treasurer of St Paul's Cathedral, John Druell, on 10 June 1466 to make a deposition concerning the drawing up of Fastolf's original will (where no mention was made of Paston as the heir), testifying in Worcester's defence against the charge made by the other leading executor, Thomas Howys, that Worcester had in his opposition to the will bribed witnesses to claim that Paston and Howys had forged the will. In the following month he was a witness on the same matter to Yelverton's proctor, Nasby, testifying to Fastolf's intentions to found a college at Caister.[45]

Despite the retraction of Howys, Stephen received little satisfaction from the Pastons and had to make do with his maternal inheritance, which he had to maintain in the face of debts accumulated during Fastolf's lifetime. His poverty was such that he was prepared, against his father-in-law's wishes, to release much of the inheritance he had fought so hard to obtain, and Bingham therefore exerted firm control over his son-in-law's Yorkshire estates of Wighton, Hamthwaite and Bentley, forcing Stephen to enter a plea in the court of Chancery against him and his son John, reciting the arrangement that if Stephen died within the lifetime of Fastolf or half a year after the estate would go to his wife, Joan, and their heirs, but if Stephen outlived Fastolf by a year or more the estate would go to Richard Scrope of Bolton and his heirs. Fearful of poverty in the event of his surviving his stepfather, Scrope clearly sought to guarantee his right to sell his manors. Bingham claimed that such an arrange-

42 FP 65.
43 PL ii, 279.
44 PL i, 167.
45 BL Add. MS 28206, fo. 42.

ment was contrary to the agreement made at the time of Millicent's marriage, but he lost the case, for by 1465 Stephen controlled the estate sufficiently to grant all his Yorkshire holdings to his cousin Richard Scrope Esq. of Bolton.[46] He also relinquished his control of his maternal inheritance of Castle Combe and Oxendon in an effort to find cash, and after Fastolf's death he arranged for the release of some of his bondsmen for a fixed payment of £20, and in November 1466 he sold the wardship of his six-year-old son, John, for £200 and a life interest in the estates of Castle Combe and Oxendon, to Sir John Newborough of Bradpole and East Lulworth, conveying these lands to Newborough in trust for his son John Scrope and any daughter of Newborough he was to marry.[47] Stephen then gave up his life interest in these estates in 1467 in return for an annuity of £34 2s 4d. Stephen Scrope died in 1472 and his son, John, took over what remained of his estates when he came of age in 1481. Such a life, when viewed from the chivalric perspective of family honour and in terms of personal relationships, was not very succesful and Stephen and his friends were very articulate about his misfortunes in both of these areas.

Millicent's hasty remariage in 1409 was undertaken in anticipation of the hostility of the Scrope family, who would be expected to oppose the loss to the family name of Sir Stephen's lands; what no-one seems to have forseen was the resentment his eldest son, Stephen, would feel at being wrenched from an aristocratic lineage with which he would continue to identify. Stephen's father, Sir Stephen Scrope, had bore the arms *Azure a bend Or* differenced by a mullet ermine on the upper part of the bend. The *Azure a bend Or* at the time of Stephen's birth was one of the most prestigious coats in the country: in 1386 the honour invested in it had been celebrated throughout the English aristocracy in the Scrope versus Grosvenor law suit. By the time of Stephen's twelfth birthday in 1409 his father was dead, his mother had signed over his patrimony to her new husband, a social climber who had served as a butler and servant of the Duke of Clarence (and possibly Sir Stephen), and who wasted little time in packing his stepson off to a Yorkshire household. Unfortunately Stephen could not rely on the support of his father's executor, John Tibbay (who had defended the interests of the heir of Sir Stephen Scrope's elder brother, Roger, when his widow attempted to remarry), because at this time Tibbay was serving as chancellor of Roger's ward, Queen Joan.[48] Stephen naturally continued to identify with his father's lineage and with the Scrope family of Bolton. He had been brought up in England and Ireland with Roger Lord Scrope of Bolton's heir, Richard Lord Scrope, a ward of Sir Stephen Scrope, and Stephen served with him in France and was probably with him when he died at the siege of Rouen in 1420. Stephen also had influential aristocratic friends who sympathised with his position: a group of them interceded with Fastolf to have him freed from

---

[46] Schofield, 21; BL Add. MS 28209, fo. 23v.
[47] BL Add. MS 28206, fo. 84.
[48] Vale, 'The Scropes', 219.

Gascoigne's wardship because they felt he was being undervalued;[49] and Humphrey duke of Gloucester attempted to break Fastolf's hold over him and restore to him some of his lost family pride by retrieving for Stephen the lordship of the Isle of Man. Those involved in Stephen's marriage negotiations were prepared to overlook his physical defects and advanced years because of the prestige of his lineage. Elizabeth Clere, who was not over-enthusiastic about Stephen as a prospective husband for Elizabeth Paston, told Elizabeth's brother, John Paston I, that Elizabeth 'hath herd so much of his birth and of his condicions'.[50] Stephen's new father-in-law, Sir Richard Bingham, appealed to Fastolf to hand over to his stepson the income from his inheritance on the grounds of his poverty and 'his worshipful birth'.[51] The glamour of Stephen's immediate family history was probably best appreciated by Fastolf's secretary and surveyor, William Worcester, who in the course of tracing pedigrees and investigating the descent of land for his master developed a knowledge of heraldry, genealogy and family history. Worcester wrote a short encomium in honour of Stephen's mother, Millicent, that included an account of Richard Lord Scrope's original purchase of the wardship of the Tiptoft heiresses.[52] He would also have had an interest in some of the chivalric aspects of Stephen's family history. A chronicle compiled by William Ferriby, master of St Leonard's Hospital, York and his successor, William Scrope of Masham (Stephen's cousin), which Worcester possessed and used in his *Boke of Noblesse*, contains a sympathetic account of the execution of Archbishop Richard Scrope and a nostalgic narrative of the deposition of Richard II. According to a French eyewitness attendant on the king, Sir Stephen Scrope and Ferriby (the probable author of the chronicle) risked death to remain weeping by Richard's side as he awaited the arrival of the Duke of Lancaster.[53]

Such a family history and sense of past greatness must have contributed to Stephen's bitterness towards the man who he felt had swallowed it all up. In 1452, while he was living at Caister, he presented his stepfather with a list of grievances on this matter, a copy of which, with an estimate of his losses and a claim for reimbursement, was sent after Fastolf's death to his executors, the Pastons.[54] One related to some family heirlooms he inherited in his father's will including a sword once owned by Edward III and a collection of plate bearing the family coat of arms which he claimed Fastolf had taken.[55] Others related to lost estates and injured pride, and show that Stephen shared Dante's conviction that property was an extension of the self. He accused his stepfather of main-

[49] BL Add. MS 28212, fo. 22.
[50] *PL* ii, 32.
[51] BL Add. MS 28212, fo. 26.
[52] BL Add. MS 38692, fos 139–41; Poulett-Scrope, 262.
[53] Webb, 'Translation of History of Richard II', 152; M.V. Clarke, *Fourteenth Century Studies*, ed. L.S. Sutherland and M. Mckisack, Oxford 1937, 84–6.
[54] Add. MS 28209, fos 21, 27; BM Add. MS 28212, fo. 22.
[55] BL Add. MS 28209, fo. 22.

taining him in penury, forcing him to sell a manor in Kent to raise money to join Gloucester's service, then persuading him to rejoin his service with the illusory promise of three times the value of the manor of Wighton. He also claimed that his stepfather had sold off certain of his father's estates and feoffments to divers persons and he now had no way of finding the titles to this land. Furthermore Fastolf had for a long time had the benefit of the livelihood to which he was born, despoiling and wasting it.[56] Scrope received a dignified reply but no recompense from Fastolf and he redrafted and amplified these grievances in a suit for recompense to the executors of Fastolf's estate (the Pastons), claiming that his stepfather had against good conscience kept him from the title of yearly income of the manors of Wighton, Oxendon and Hamthwaite and had gone against his promise of giving him the manor of Wighton after his mother's death. Stephen laid an unsuccessful claim for thirty years' income from the estates that were his inheritance.[57] He was no match for a calculating business man like Fastolf or his equally hard-hearted chosen heir, John Paston, and he received no recompense from either; but Stephen had the last laugh over his stepfather in that there was one bastion of aristocratic pride to which Fastolf for all his money could not aspire, the honourable lineage. In all the acrimonious disputes between them Stephen made two telling jibes: he reminded his stepfather that he had not naturally begotten a son, and in his reply to Fastolf's claim that 'he is enheryted during his lyfe as wele as I' he reminded him that this 'were nat soo: for I am com of blode and he but be gifte of jentilnes'.[58] Both things were linked in Scrope's mind with his sense of identity, his affiliation with a great family, Scrope of Bolton, and this can be seen in the precautions he took in the 1460s for the future of his son and his estates. It was more than a fear of poverty that impelled Stephen to ensure that in the event of the failure of his own line his properties reverted to his father's line of Scrope of Bolton. In 1465 in a will deposited in the hands of Richard Beauchamp, the earl of Warwick, he left (in the event of his dying without an heir) to his cousin Richard Scrope Esq, of Bolton (who as younger son of Henry the fourth lord of Bolton held a similar position in this family to that once held by Stephen) his manors of Castle Combe and Oxendon.[59] These estates were settled the following year on his son, John, but Stephen, thinking of his own misfortunes after his father's death, forestalled his son's disinheritance in the likelihood of his death (he was seventy) and his widow's remarriage by enfeoffing his lands to trustees in November 1466 until John attained his majority, when they would go to John and his children. The Yorkshire estates however were, as we have seen, sold to

---

[56] BL Add. MS 28209, fo. 21.
[57] BL Add. MS 28209, fos 20–1; BL Add. MS 28212, fo. 22.
[58] BL MS 28212, fo. 22.
[59] TE iii, 217–19.

Richard Scrope Esq. of Bolton, who died in 1485 possessed of the manors of Wighton, Hamthwaite and Bentley.[60]

The concern felt by the Scrope family of Bolton over the loss of family pride occasioned by Stephen's misfortunes is indicated in the precautions they took over his estates. Richard Scrope did more than consolidate Stephen's Yorkshire holdings which had so long been monopolised by Fastolf; he made provisions in his will in 1484 to ensure that if he suddenly died before his wife the same fate of disinheritance and sale of wardship would not befall his expected child, and he instructed his executors that if his wife remarried she would have Wighton for the term of her life and that 'yf thys childe that my wyffe is with be a son, I will that it be maryd bee the discrecion off myn executuris; and yff it be a doughte, and my wyffe happyn to be maryd, then I will that Bentelay be sowllyd on to the behalf of my childer, yff myn executuris thynke it to be don'.[61] Richard, learning from Stephen's fate, was using his executors to ensure that the family closed ranks in the event of a widow's remarriage to ensure that the family continued to survive as a trust to ensure that the children's interests were safeguarded.

Although questions of family honour and integrity contributed greatly to tension between stepfather and stepson, emotional factors were of greater significance, and it is Stephen's complex, sensitive personality and the ambivalent relationship he had with Fastolf that is the real revelation of the correspondence of the Fastolf circle. Sir John was a self-made man and a powerful personality who inspired fear, loyalty and at times affection among his servants. Henry Windsor said of his master: 'Hit is not unknown that cruell and vengible he hath byn euer, and for the most parte without pite and mercy'.[62] When John Bockyng, another servant, presented a petition on behalf of his father, Nicholas Bockyng (also Fastolf's servant) to Bishop Waynflete for various sums Fastolf was alleged to have owed him, he claimed that the reason he had not made a claim during his master's lifetime was 'the sharp and bittre answers by the said knyghte in his grete siknesses at London and also the drede that the said Bokkyng at alle tymes hadde of the said knyght'.[63] William Worcester's letters convey vividly the difficulties of working for a demanding master and dominating personality. To John Paston I he complained that on legal matters Fastolf 'questioneth and disputyth with hys seruantes here and wolle not be aunered ne satisfyed' and in a moment of exasperation Worcester said: 'so wold Jesus one of you III or som suche othyr yn your stede mygt hang at hys gyrdylle dayly to aunswer hys materes'.[64] It was a thankless task, yet Worcester served him loyally as secretary, surveyor, physician and astrologer and was at pains to ask Margaret

---

[60] BL Add. MS 28206, fo. 42v; Poulet-Scrope, 286.
[61] *TE* iii, 297–300.
[62] *PL* ii, 145.
[63] FP 98.
[64] FP 72.

Paston in 1468 to tell her son that he 'put neuyr my maister Fastolf lyfelode yn trouble, for alle the unkyndnesse and covetise that was shewed me'. In the same letter he complained that in Fastolf's household he had to put up with the jealousy and backbiting of other servants 'of the malyciouse contryved talys that Frere Brackley, W. Barker and othyrs ymagyned ontruly, savyng your reverence of me', tales which Worcester put down to 'gelosye' and 'envyouse disposicion'; this was something which, Worcester gloomily reflected, all Fastolf's servants seemed to suffer: 'he that ys next shall be yn the same as he was yn gelosye'. The fear that all the servants had of Fastolf's temper certainly contributed towards the unhealthily competitive atmosphere. In 1454, after complaining about his lack of renumeration in Fastolf's service, he ended a letter to John Paston, 'Our lord bryng my maistre yn a better mode for othyrs as for me'. In 1456 Worcester complained to John Paston I that because he was Fastolf's secretary entrusted with carrying his master's requests to the accountants they used him as a scapegoat and blamed him for giving the wrong advice to Fastolf if they were unable to meet their master's orders. Nevertheless Worcester had genuine affection and loyalty towards a man he seems to have regarded as a father figure. William Paston wrote to his brother John in 1459, 'I understand by hym he will neuer haue oder master but his old master'. After the funeral Worcester told John Paston himself, 'Ser I am the same man as ye left me, upryght and yndyfferent for to wille and do for my maister asmoch as my sympyle power may'.[65] From 1460 to 1478 he continued to carry out what he believed to be his old master's intentions, defending his lands against rival claimants, listing his goods, and quarrelling and eventually coming to terms with the other executors.[66] To Margaret, mother of his former friend and leading opponent, John Paston I, he boasted in 1468 that Fastolf 'trusted and lovyd me'.[67] He frequently referred to him in the journal he kept in 1478 of his tour of England and Wales, and at Tavistock church in Exeter he noted some lines of poetry that probably expressed his relationship with Fastolf: 'One loves, therefore one fears/To love is therefore to fear/but the contrary holds not true'.[68] Fastolf had the type of complex personality, full of contradictions, which inspired conflicting emotions of resentment and loyalty: he could be generous and mean, idealistic and smallminded, sentimental and hard, and he certainly regarded himself as a misunderstood person: on a memorandum to a debt owed him he wrote 'for my good wille my fortune is to have trouble'.[69]

Stephen was an equally complex character. He was extremely sensitive and difficult, but trusting and with a great capacity for friendship and generosity.

---

[65] PL ii, 355–6, 162–3, 102, 162–3 PL i, 158.
[66] McFarlane, 'Worcester', 209.
[67] PL ii, 355.
[68] William Worcester, *Itineraries*, ed. J.H. Harvey, Oxford 1969, 122: 'amat ergo timet/Est amor ergo timor'.
[69] Magdalen College MS Titchwell 40.

Worcester described him as a 'gentle esquier' and his father-in-law Bingham described him as 'well-disposed to every person', and a servant, despite suffering under Stephen's anger, gave him 'a mervelows good name'.[70] His relationship with Fastolf was even more ambivalent, and like Worcester, with whom he had much in common, he frequently complained about the old knight, with less dignity but considerable psychological insight. Stephen would have made a difficult stepson and from the outset he must have compared Fastolf to the father he had lost so young. This understandable yet reasonable resentment was the crux of their relationship, and it is probable that Fastolf, a more stable and magnanimous man, could never fully comprehend Stephen's reaction to childhood experiences not too far removed from his own: his own mother remarried and this did not prevent him in his will from arranging for a marble image to be carved in St Nicholas' chapel, Yarmouth, depicting his mother with her arms and those of her three husbands.[71] Stephen probably enjoyed a good relationship with his father: in his will, made on 6 January 1406, Sir Stephen spoke affectionately of Stephen 'my precious son and heir',[72] and the son's idolization of his natural father would have been encouraged by the postumous chivalric reputation Sir Stephen enjoyed in England because of his victories in Ireland.[73] Millicent had played a conspicuous role in his Irish campaigns, and after his death she and her family continued to remember him in their prayers: in 1433, probably soon after the death of Stephen's younger brother, Robert, prayers were said by Fastolf's family for Sir Stephen and his son, Robert. The resentment Stephen felt towards his father's supplanter would have stemmed from the hastiness of his mother's remarriage within a year of his father's death; and Fastolf was probably eager to get this potentially difficult stepson out of the way by selling his wardship to Gascoigne.[74] However Stephen's fate was not unusual, for it was a convention among the English aristocracy to sell children and their inheritances to the family into which they would marry (Stephen's two aunts and his mother were brought up as wards of Richard Lord Scrope of Bolton with the intention that they would marry his sons); and this would in turn automatically involve the subsequent removal of prospective spouses into another household to prevent the children who were to marry growing up as siblings. The sale of wardships was also an important aspect of the educational system of the English aristocracy (anticipating the English public school) whereby children were provided with the sort of education and discipline necessary for their social advancement. In 1467 Stephen himself sold the wardship of his son and heir, John, to Richard Neville, the earl of Warwick, with the understanding that

---

[70] BL Add. MS 38692, fos 39–41; BL Add. MS 28212, fos 26, 32; C. Richmond, *The Paston Family in the Fifteenth Century*, Cambridge 1990, 179.

[71] *PL* iii (Gairdner), 147–60, FP 65.

[72] *TE* iii, 38–40.

[73] *CPR 1399–1404*, 507; *CCR 1409–13*, 208.

[74] BL Add. MS 28206, fo. 13v; Add. MS 29209, fo. 20.

he provide 'the said John Scrope, and her that shall be his wife, and his servants, competently and sufficiently in letters, nurtur, met, drinke, clothynge, beddynge and all other convenient fyndyng, during his nonage'.[75] The harshness of the system was observed by outsiders. In 1497 the Venetian ambassador in England remarked 'the want of affection in the English is strongly manifested towards their children, for having kept them at home till they arrive at the age of seven or nine years at most they put them out, males and females, to hard service in the homes of other people, binding them generally for another seven or nine years'.[76] Stephen's own son, John, must have cut a pathetic figure as a seven-year-old when arrangements were made before the Feast of the Apostle in 1467 to deliver him into the hands of the earl of Warwick or his second, Ambrose Cresacre, at St Katherine's by the side of the tower of London.[77] All he would have retained from his own father would have been his family coat of arms, and it is likely that many of the more adaptable children in such situations would develop stronger attachments to their prospective fathers-in-law. What is so interesting about Stephen is that he did have strong objections to the system; in the case of his own son he had little option but to make arrangements for his future security and education as he was by 1467 an old man; and he bitterly attacked his stepfather for forcing him into such poverty that around 1448 he had to sell the wardship of his daughter by his first marriage for much less than he had hoped, the proceeds of which he was still living on in 1452.[78] Behind his objections to the system were his own experiences of being delivered by Fastolf to a strange household as an eleven-year-old. Coming as it did so quickly after the loss of his father and his mother's remarriage, it had a disastrous effect on his personality which he fully appreciated forty-two years later when in 1452 he delivered to his stepfather a list of grievances headed by the complaint that 'in the first year that my mother was married to my father Fastolf he of his pleasure solde me to William Gascoigne, that time chief justice of this land for 500 marks the which he had in his possession for 3 years; through the wiche sale I tooke sekenesses that kept me 13 or 14 yere swyng, whereby I am disfigured in my persone and shall be whilest I lyve'.[79] Fastolf's reply, which presumably implied that Stephen exaggerated the effects of the transaction, did not satisfy Stephen and in a bill of charges against the estate of Fastolf (the Pastons) he described in detail his feelings of hurt, rejection and shame (perhaps the fact that his stepfather was now dead encouraged him to speak more openly) and claimed compensation. He asserted that when Fastolf married his mother 'he sold me for 500 marks without title or right' and such a sum could only be a partial recompense against a man 'who bought me and solde me as a beste, ayens al ryght and lawe,

---

75 BL Add. MS 28209, fo. 23v; G. Poulet-Scrope, *Castle Combe* 286.
76 *A Relation of the Island of England about the Year 1500*, Camden Soc. o.s. xxxvii, 1847.
77 BL Add. MS 28206, fo. 42v.
78 Schofield, 17.
79 BL Add. MS 28209, fo. 21.

to myn hurt'. In some of the the complaints we can hear echoes of the probable reactions of the dour Yorkshiremen to the sensitive youth under their care: 'I suppose it shull be founde be the reporte of some gentilmen of Yorkeshyre, that the summes were not soo grete as it rehersed – Notwithstanding how that ever it were I had the soor and felte the hurte'.[80] Stephen's response was to assert the unnaturalness of the taking of a boy of vulnerable age away from his mother: 'And where it is seyde that my seyde fader was nat bounden to finde me in my youthe, the lawe knowe I nat, but wel I wote that if a woman the which is to marry have many chylder, it is often seen that men be daungerous (afraid) to take sych women for the charge of theyre childer'. He further emphasised his helpless vulnerability when reproaching others involved in the transaction, including his father's executors who had allowed the sale of the estate of Bybury; and to Fastolf's claim that he, Stephen, was responsible he pointed out that 'every resonable man may conceyve that the suffraunce most nedes a been, for I was that tyme but X or XII yere of age, and fer loygned froo there be my seyde fader Fastolf thorugh hys forseyde sale made to the seyde Justice William Gascoigne, as at that time my seyde fader did with me as it plesed hym'.[81] Recriminations were also laid at his mother, Millicent, for while he claimed that his mother had denied Fastolf's charge that she had requested the sale of his wardship he added 'mesemeth that neyther he ne she had noon auctorite to selle me, wherefor I conceyve that I was wrongfully doon to'.[82]

This introspective man's obsession with compensation for these injuries dominated his personality and he probably lost no opportunity in reminding his mother and stepfather of their cruelty. Some of the myths in the *Epistle of Othea* would have served this function and many of the glosses to these legends warn Fastolf, the recipient of the letter, of the dangers of avarice; and one, describing the jealous attempts of Queen Ino, wife of King Athaneus, to disinherit her stepchildren and have them exiled, and the consequent punishment of the couple by the gods who drive the king mad and force him to kill his wife, depicts in an inverted form the roles played by Stephen's mother and stepfather. Another, possibly containing an element of ineffectual fantasy, warns the recipient of the letter that if he has wronged a father to beware of the son when, like Pyrrus son of Achilles, he comes of age.[83] In his preoccupation with the emotional injuries of childhood and his desire for compensation Stephen reveals that he possessed the retentive memory of an obsessive personality: in his replications he reminded Fastolf that he had promised him that if he became a

---

[80] Ibid., fo. 22; It is worth noting that there were wards who showed more independence and spirit than Stephen: Lord Grey of Hastings tried to arrange the marriage of his ward to Elizabeth Paston for a 400 mark dowry and the young ward declared that if he married the girl he would have the dowry himself. *PL* ii, 96, *PL* ii, 125.

[81] BL Add. MS 28209, fo. 22.

[82] BL Add. MS 28212, fo. 22.

[83] *Epistle of Othea* xvii, 27–8; xxxi, 42–3.

good son he would receive an annual income worth three times the value he would have received from the estate of Wighton: 'I can wel telle the place where it was seyde, that is to say, in a garden in the parke of Alaunsom'. Fastolf may have had the measure of Stephen in terms of business but he must have felt out of his depth when confronted by such a sensitive, introspective personality, and Stephen paraphrased his stepfather's somewhat callous expression of amazement that he could have 'akepte thees articles soo longe in my breste'.[84]

Stephen also felt that his own physical and emotional life had been blighted by this mistreatment and blamed his thirteen-year illness which disfigured him 'for ever' on the original sale of his wardship. It seem to have reoccurred whenever the issue of leaving Fastolf's household arose, for he fell ill during the dispute with his mother and stepfather over his joining the duke of Gloucester's service, describing himself when he rejoined Fastolf in France as 'beyng that tyme right seke'.[85] Spephen's poor health contributed to his lifelong interest in medicine, an interest he shared with William Worcester, whose physical appearance, like Stephen's, was not prepossessing (he had one eye and was described by Brackley as swarthy in complexion).[86] He served as Fastolf's personal physician and after his death he complained that he spent ten years continuously ministering day and night to his growing bodily needs.[87] It is probable that he also administered to Stephen Scrope, for Worcester kept medical notes from 1459 to 1478 in a tall paper volume from authorities such as Villanova, from doctors, barbers and friars, and from the recorded experiences of sufferers such as tanners, shepherds and clergy. Included in this volume were notes on Fastolf's last illness, a hectic fever (possibly asthmatic), and one of his informants was Stephen Scrope who gave him in 1459 a remedy for pain while urinating and in January 1466 a cure for palpitations of the heart. In the previous year Worcester obtained from Scrope a book that has been lent him by the abbot of Bermondsey providing instructions on treatments of hernias.[88] The emotional damage inflicted on Stephen by his childhood experiences was also manifested in an unnatural dependence on his mother and stepfather, something Fastolf's overbearing personality encouraged, a general unfitness for life and signs of emotional instability. Apart from his period in Gascoigne's household and his brief liaison with the duke of Gloucester, Stephen lived with his stepfather: he accompanied him to France, even though his physical disabilities prevented him from serving in a military capacity, and even after his quarrel with Fastolf over the marshal of Honfleur in 1427 he returned to England to live with his mother, objecting to his being obliged by his stepfather to pay for his food and drink. He was still living with her in 1432 when he was thirty-five and blamed

[84] BL Add. MS 28212, fo. 22.
[85] BL Add. MS 28209, fo. 21.
[86] BL MS Sloane 4.
[87] FP 72, m. 7.
[88] BL MS Sloane 4, fos 38v, 57v.

his stepfather for refusing to pay for his upkeep and forcing him into a disastrous marriage: 'God knoweth whate hynderaunce y hadde by that marriage with hys menys, the whiche hurte y canne well telle and y schalle,' and he proceeded to describe this marriage as a delivery into bonds through which he had lived 'in grete peyne and thoghte'.[89] After the death of his wife he presumably returned to live with his parents and he continued to live at Caister after his mother's death in 1446. He had a room (larger and more lavishly furnished than Worcester's) at Caister near his mother's room, which was preserved as she had left it. Stephen, according to John Paston I, was still living at Caister in 1454 and probably remained there until his marriage to Joan Bingham in 1456.[90] He was certainly regarded in the competitive society of East Anglia as an unpredictable, difficult personality. In 1454 Worcester wrote to John Paston I about Stephen warning him 'you need fare wyth hym, for he ys full daungerous (*proud and aloof*) when he wille'; and the reason Fastolf gave his stepson for failing to take his side in the dispute with the marshal of Honfleur was 'that myn outrageousnes caused moche thyng'.[91] Stephen certainly wrote intemperate, offensive letters to his stepfather, to one of which Fastolf replied: 'I wold that ye wrote to none othir man for the wordys be unfyttyng but if they be betwene countre parties as betwene an englishman and an armanake'.[92] Stephen's friendship with his father-in-law also proved to be full of suspicion, for he and Bingham were at loggerheads in the courts over Stephen's attempts to sell his paternal inheritance in Yorkshire, which Bingham had worked hard trying to secure for his son-in-law between 1456 and 1459. Stephen also seems to have been incompetent and unworldly to an alarming degree: in 1459 Elizabeth Paston, after ascertaining that Stephen had a livelihood of 350 marks a year, expressed a willingness to consider him for marriage despite being told that 'his persone is symple';[93] and he may have been prone to bouts of depression: in 1454 Worcester, writing to Paston about the rent of £8 from the township of Batham Wyly, added that though he had given Scrope full evidence of the rent 'he can not know it'.[94] Stephen appears to have been aware of this reputation and concluded his replications by saying to Fastolf: 'If I have seyd in thees forseyde replications other wyse than reson and conscience wold of necligence, simplenes, or unkonnynge, I ask pardon and grace'.[95] Unlike other literate members of Fastolf's household, such as Worcester or Spireling, it is hard to know exactly what he did outside his spell as an accountant in Honfleur and his translating. He seems to have failed in most of his undertakings. On his own

---

[89] BL MS Add. MS 28209, fo. 21.
[90] *PL* i, 154.
[91] *PL* i, 134; BL Add. MS 28212, fo. 22.
[92] Vale, 'The Scropes', 223.
[93] *PL* ii, 31.
[94] *PL* ii, 134.
[95] BL Add. MS 28212, fo. 22.

admission he was naive in matters concerning the law and his own landed interests, especially in 1433 when in an attempt to secure the necessary 500 marks for his marriage he signed over to Fastolf the life interest in his inheritance, which meant that he had no legal claim to his estates while his stepfather lived, an action he regretted when his mother died in 1446, and he could only respond by writing to his stepfather 'the sotilte of lawe is no clere conscience'.[96] It is therefore possible that Fastolf attempted to retain control of Stephen's inheritance because he believed him to be irresponsible and incapable of sustaining and defending it. After all, he impulsively sold a manor to buy a horse and armour with which to impress the duke of Gloucester (and when Stephen reproached his stepfather for failing to provide the necessary financial assistance Fastolf sensibly and logically replied that while he wanted to help him, if he insisted on joining the duke's service then this would become his new master's responsibility). It is furthermore unlikely that Stephen could have been able to control Bentley in Yorkshire, described by Worcester 'as a goodly manor but notoriously difficult to manage' and which needed to be frequently visited by Worcester and Geoffrey Spireling, Fastolf's accountant.[97] Fastolf was ultimately proved right in his assessments. After his stepfather's death Stephen, in expectation of receiving something from the estate controlled by the Pastons, got into debt with a number of men and by July 1462 he was waiting in London for a reply from John Paston I to his repeated requests for money.[98] Furthermore, in an effort to solve his financial problems he was prepared to sell the bulk of his inheritance, his father's estates which had been the cause of much of the ill feeling with Fastolf, and he eventually relinquished his interest in his mother's estates in return for an annuity and hunting rights.

The miserly way Fastolf dealt with his stepson did not therefore necessarily preclude genuine affection, and there is evidence that this was to some extent reciprocated. From the moment of Millicent's remarriage they would have needed one another. Stephen needed a father, and it would have soon become apparent to Fastolf that his wife, who was forty-one or two at the time of her marriage, would have no more children. He frequently expressed paternal concern and affection in his letters. His reaction from Calais to Stephen's sudden departure to join Humphrey duke of Gloucester's service is characteristic of the temperamental differences between the two men: 'I can not see by my feble wytte in whete wise it myght be more profitable for you there than it was here all things considered';[99] and he seems to have enticed Stephen from Gloucester's service because be genuinely wanted his company, so much so that even Stephen had to admit 'when I was comyn to hym, it plesed hym than of his grace to showe me so good faderhode, that I was right glad to wayte upon hym

---

[96] BL Add. MS 28209, fo. 21.
[97] *PL* i, 86.
[98] *PL* i, 279, 284.
[99] BL Add. MS 28212, fo. 23–4.

to do hym servyce'. After Stephen had remonstrated with him over his siding with the marshal of Honfleur around 1428 and failing to provide him with the financial assistance necessary to join Gloucester's retinue, Fastolf expressed his and Millicent's wish to see Stephen happily and prosperously married and until that time offered him his lordship: 'come againe unto me, and I wol do unto you as I ought to do, be kind as wel or better than ever I do, so that ye shal find me alwey good fader unto you as unto my feble power'. Despite Stephen's recriminations he claims: 'I take aworth whate ever ye wyte unto me for I must tendre both youre person and worship'.[100] As late as October 30 1457 Fastolf, seeking his stepson's good offices with Bingham, addressed Stephen as 'worshepful and right wel beloved sone' thanking him for his 'right well avysed lettres to me sent from tyme to tyme. and concluded by asking that his own letter 'may recomaund me to my doghtir your wyf, be sechyng the blissed Trinite to sende yow the acomplyshment of your good desyre'.[101] Stephen likewise expressed his desire to prove a good son and replied to Fastolf's accusation concerning the unkind recriminations in his bill of complaints: 'where there is thought moch unkindeness in me symple persone; I dare saufelye seye, and my seyde fader had a son of his owne body begeten, he shold nat have had better wylle to adoon hym servyse and plesir than I had had'.[102] It is perhaps indicative of the misunderstandings between them that Stephen got his father-in-law, Bingham, to write a letter to Fastolf (which Stephen kept) that attempted to reassure the older knight of the sincerity of his stepson's wish to prove himself a good and loyal son. The two men were opposites (Fastolf was a successful, self-made man of business and a soldier; Stephen was a sickly, introverted intellectual) and they were therefore attracted to one another and quarrelled like many a father and son, with Millicent probably acting as a mediator until her death. Around 3 July in the year of Fastolf's death they were not on speaking terms, for Fastolf informed John Paston I that he had appointed Yelverton to deal with Scrope and his father-in-law, Bingham, over the matter of the control of Wighton because he desired to bring the matter to an end 'so that I hafe no cause to trouble wyth hym'.[103] It is therefore hardly surprising that Stephen was ignored in Fastolf's controversial nuncupative will, along with Worcester, another surrogate son with whom Stephen had much in common, and that the sole heir of the estate was John Paston I, a wealthy lawyer and landowner who was much more a man in Fastolf's image.

The cruel ironies of Stephen's life and his treatment at the hands of Fastolf were widely known in the second half of the fifteenth century among the English aristocracy, especially among the Scropes of Bolton who took special precautions to safeguard the interests of their heirs. It is tempting, when

---

[100] BL Add. MS 28209, fo. 23.
[101] *PL* iii (Gairdner) 121.
[102] BL Add. MS 28212, fo. 22.
[103] *PL* ii, 181.

considering how so many aspects of this singular story (a mother's hasty remar-riage, a son's disinheritance and the tense, ambivalent relationship between this moody, unpredictable stepson, an ineffectual Pyrrhus, and his father's worldly supplanter) seem to have found their way in Skapespeare's *Hamlet*, to suggest that the story may have reached the playwright through oral transmission. Such a possibility is strengthened when it is considered that the origin of the ex-pressive accounts of father-son conflicts that Shakespeare was to transform into powerful myths were anecdotes of a man closely associated with Stephen Scrope's father. James le Botillere, the fourth earl of Ormund (d.1452) was in 1407 the deputy in Ireland of Sir Stephen Scrope (who features in Holinshed's Chronicle); he was probably a first-hand witness to the marriage of Millicent and Sir John Fastolf, and a contemporary with Stephen Scrope Esq. and Fastolf at the siege of Rouen, and he may have circulated accounts of Stephen's disin-heritance and subsequent conflicts with his stepfather. Botillere was certainly responsible for telling his own son, the sixth earl of Ormond (who died aged ninety-one in 1515) about Henry V's riotous youth, the rifts between the prince of Wales with his father, and the death-bed reconciliation, to which he had been an eyewitness as the young friend of Thomas of Lancaster. These were incorporated into Shakespeare's *Henry IV, Parts I* and *II*, dominated incidentally by Hal's alter father, Falstaff, who was partially drawn from anecdotes about Sir John Fastolf.

Family quarrels over land and inheritance and the complex personal relation-ships that often underlay such disputes were undoubtedly neither new nor unique to Stephen and his circle; but the evidence of these grievances survives because of the high degree of literacy and culture that was encouraged in Fastolf's household, a culture to which Stephen Scrope made important con-tributions. An important stimulus to the broadening of the intellectual horizons of Fastolf and his servants was the French war which brought exposure to the culture of the court of Charles VI, the father-in-law of Henry V. Fastolf's interest in astrology was stimulated here, for the astrologer Fusieris was promi-nent in the French court at the beginning of the fifteenth century and Fastolf had his horoscope (6 Nov. 1380) made by a French astrologer. The court of the Valois kings had since the thirteenth century been a source of patronage of literature, especially the translation of histories of Greece and Rome into French; and with the opportunities of conquest came the acquisition of cheap books, many of which brought into Fastolf's circle a deeper awareness of classi-cal literature in French translations. Fastolf, as lieutenant and steward of John duke of Bedford in 1423, would have been party to the purchase of the French royal library in 1425 for 1200 francs, and this was used as the basis of a library at Rouen in 1433 where Fastolf was captain.[104] Some of these books would have

---

[104] M.J. Barber, 'The Books and Patronage of Learning of a Fifteenth-Century Prince', *The Book Collector* xii, 1963, 308–18.

found their way into Fastolf's library at Caister. It is significant that one of the two surviving manuscripts belonging to Fastolf is a French medical compilation by Allobrandinus of Siena which contains Fastolf's motto *me fault faire*; and French works, especially translations of classical literature, figure prominently in the surviving list of books in the stew house at Caister. They include chronicles of France, the *Book of Julius Caesar*, the *Institutes of the Emperor Justinian*, the *Chronicles of Livy* and the *Problemata Aristotelis*.[105] After his retirement in 1439 Fastolf also brought back to England French translations of Latin classics that had been made in the second half of the fourteenth century, such as Cicero's *de Senectute* and *Le Dicts Morlaux*, a French version of a collection of sayings attributed to ancient philosophers made by Guillame de Tigonville, the chamberlain of Charles V. The most important French influence on the Fastolf circle was Christine de Pisan, a friend of Thomas Montacute, the fourth earl of Salisbury and husband of Alice Chaucer. Christine, who was brought up in the Valois court, quickened interest in this court in classical ethics, philosophy and history.[106] Around 1440 Fastolf possessed a *de luxe* volume containing *Livre des quatre vertus cardinaulx*, a translation of portions of John of Wales' *Breviloquium de virtutibus*, which was probably by Christine de Pisan, and her *L'Epitre d'Othea*, a letter of moral instruction based on classical teaching and that of the church fathers which she originally dedicated to Louis of Orleans.[107] This work, transcribed by Ricardus Franciscus, had been illustrated with pictures of classical deities under Christine's direction, and Fastolf arranged for this manuscript and its illustrations to be copied, using the services of a French artist who in the 1420s ran a flourishing shop in Rouen where Fastolf was captain, before he accompanied Fastolf to England.[108]

The member of Fastolf's circle who most profoundly absorbed classical culture was William Worcester. Worcester was educated at Oxford at Fastolf's expense, and from 1438 until Fastolf's death in 1459 he repaid him with resolute service as secretary and surveyor while somehow managing to combine the travelling between his master's various estates with collecting books, copying and annotating manuscripts, and compiling his own books from extracts, especially from classical works either in the original Latin or in French translations.[109] One such

105 Bodl. Lib. MS 179; FP 43, fo. 10.
106 For Christine de Pisan see S. Hindman, *Christine de Pizan's 'Epitre Othea'*, Toronto 1986.
107 Bodl. Lib. MS 179; Bodl. Lib. MS Laud 570; R. Tuve, 'Notes on the Vices and Virtues', *Journal of Warburg and Courtauld Institutes* xxxvi, 1963, 264–303; C.C. Willard, 'The Manuscript Tradition of the *Livre des Trois Vertus* and Christine de Pisan's Audience', *Journal of History of Ideas* xxvii, 1968, 435ff.
108 J. Plumer, *The Last Flowering, French Paintings in Manuscripts, 1420–1530, from American Collection*, Pierpont Morgan Library, New York 1982; Bodl. Lib. MS Laud. 570; O. Pacht and J.G. Alexander, *Illuminated Manuscripts in the Bodleian Library*, Oxford 1966, 695; C.F. Buhler, 'Sir John Fastolf's Manuscripts of the *Epitre d'Othea* and Stephen Scope's Translation of the Text', *Scriptorium* iii, 1949, 123–8.
109 Smith, 'Fastolf', 56ff; K.B. McFarlane, 'William Worcester, a Preliminary Survey', in

tall, narrow paper book contains the rubrics he copied from Chretien de Troyes's French translation of Ovid's *Metamorphoses*, and Worcester also provided sensitive outline drawing (the equal of the work of the Fastolf Master) illustrating the legends, and notes for their colouring, which suggests he studied Chretien's original manuscript.[110] In this same book Worcester copied extracts from Seneca's *de Beneficiis*;[111] extracts from Cicero (with notes from the Latin text), Seneca and Terence under such thematic headings as virtue and friendship; and a list of the works of Cicero from Bruni's *Cicero Novus* sent to Worcester by a correspondent.[112] Another of Worcester's books contains a compilation he made from a volume Fastolf obtained in Paris[113] consisting of extracts from the chronicle of Orosius on the Carthaginian wars and extracts from the accounts of Lucan and Suetonius of Julius Caesar's and Pompey's campaigns.[114] Worcester even purchased a volume from the library of John Free of Bristol containing three plays each of Sophocles and Euripides, which he may have tried to read with the help of Greek lessons under the tuition of William Selling of Canterbury.[115] Members of Fastolf's circle, with their master's active encouragement, also wrote books; and Roman didactic literature, especially the writings of Cicero, was the most important single influence, which implies Fastolf's pedagogic desire to form and influence young minds and to establish his household as an educational institution. William Worcester led the way with an English translation of a French version of Cicero's *de Senectute*, which was undertaken 'by the ordenaunce desyr of the noble knyght Syr Johan Fastolf' and presented, as *Tullius of Olde Age*, to Bishop Waynflete in 1473; and an English translation of Cicero's *de Amicitia*, translated from the Latin and printed by Caxton in 1481 as *Tullius of Friendship* to accompany *Tullius of Olde Age*.[116] Among the strongest and most consistent of classical influences on Worcester was military history, ethics and biography, and these are reflected in his original writings, especially *The Boke of Noblesse*, an analysis of the causes of the failure of the English occupation of Normandy, with many comparisons drawn from Roman history and illustrations from Worcester's favourite Roman writers; this was commenced soon after 1451, and Fastolf contributed reminiscences of his military

McFarlane, *England in the Fifteenth Century*, Guildford 1981, 199–225. For description of these books see McFarlane, 'Worcester', 221 n.

110 BL MS Cotton Julius FVII, fos 6–11.
111 Ibid., fo. 48–48v.
112 Ibid., fos 74–91v.
113 BL MS Royal 13 C1, fo. 143.
114 Ibid., fos 135–135v, 141v–146.
115 McFarlane, 'Worcester', 223 Bodl. Lib. MS Auct, F3 25.
116 *The Prologues and Epilogues of William Caxton*, ed. W.J.B. Crotch, EETS xliv. Caxton attributed the Tullius of Olde Age to John Tiptoft the earl of Worcester; but it was probably William Worcester's version for Caxton also says it was composed at the ordinance of Sir John Fastolf; R.J. Mitchell, *John Tiptoft*, 173.

experiences.[117] Another work strongly influenced by Fastolf was Worcester's biography of his master, the *Acta domini Johannis Fastolf*, commenced the year of Fastolf's death and no longer extant. Another contributor to this work was a poverty stricken servant of Fastolf, John Bussard who, according to John Davy, wrote for Worcester over twenty quires on a Chronicle of Jerusalem and the journeys his master made in France.[118] Worcester also contributed to an account of the French war which was dedicated to Fastolf. The other three contributors, who were were also servants of Fastolf, were: Luke Nantron, a French dependent who followed Fastolf to England (like the Rouen artist) and who initiated the work; Christopher Hanson, who collected Fastolf's rents in 1453–4 and remained in Fastolf's service with Nantron until Fastolf's death; and Peter Basset, who served Fastolf in Maine and Anjou.[119]

Worcester's education at Oxford from 1432 to 1438 would have stimulated his initial interests in astrology, medicine, history and geography (his first notebook was compiled between 1437–8) and disciplined him in the scholarly precision he showed in his annotation of manuscripts and references to sources, both authors and libraries;[120] but his literary activities and intellectual interests flourished in Fastolf's service. All his surviving works were written for Fastolf, serving his private needs or his military propaganda. His researches into the descents of East Anglian families, begun around 1449, his interest in English antiquities and geography, were facilitated by his travels to and from his master's estates and properties in London, Wiltshire, East Anglia, Kent and Yorkshire; and it was as Fastolf's surveyor and secretary that he took over the military and diplomatic papers and estate archives that he handed over to Bishop Waynflete in 1472.[121] Perhaps his most personal interest, contemporary poetry, also developed in Fastolf's household: in 1458 he brought books and took lessons from the London Italian Carlo Gigli 'in poetre or els in Frensh' saying that he 'would be as glad and as feyn of a good boke of Frensh or of poetre as Maister Fastolf would be to purchase a faire manoir'.[122] It was perhaps from Gigli that he purchased Boccacio's *de Casibus Illustrium Virorum*.[123] Some of these interests, such as the conservation of written records, Roman history and literature and contemporary poetry were shared by Fastolf's lawyer, John Paston I, and his family. The Pastons preserved their voluminous correspondence, and an inventory taken by John Paston II before 1479 shows that the family owned such books as Cicero's *de Amicitia* and *de Senectute* (the latter certainly and the former

---

117 *The Boke of Noblesse*, ed. J.G. Nichols, Roxburghe Club, 1860. Worcester in *The Boke of Noblesse* refers to Fastolf as 'mine auctor'. BL MS Royal B xxii, fo. 32v.

118 *PL* iii, 253–4; BL Add. MS 28206, fo. 19v; FP 72, m. 2.

119 Smith, 'Fastolf', 56ff; McFarlane, 'Worcester', 210–11.

120 Bodl. Lib. MS Laud Misc 674; J.I. Catto, 'Scholars and Studies in Renaissance Oxford' in Catto, ed., *The History of the University of Oxford*, iii, (publication forthcoming).

121 These became the Fastolf Papers.

122 *PL* ii, 175, no. 574. (Henry Windsor to John Paston I).

123 Catto, 'Renaissance Oxford'.

probably Worcester's translation), Stephen Scrope's *Epistle of Othea*, Lydgate's *Siege of Thebes*, Chaucer's *Parlement of Fowles*, and a collection of writings on knighthood and chivalry known as *The Grete Boke*.[124] Another who can be considered as part of Fastolf's literary circle was the Norwich scrivener, Geoffrey Spireling, Fastolf's deputy receiver 1448–52 and auditor in the 1450's, who later copied Chaucer's *Canterbury Tales*.[125]

Such was the intellectual environment that Stephen Scrope enjoyed, and he was closely associated with all of the above writers, especially William Worcester: they lived in Caister in adjacent rooms and Worcester tried to help Stephen in various ways, such as organising opposition to Fastolf's will, and acting as Scrope's literary executor. They probably collaborated to some extent on *The Boke of Noblesse*: Stephen, who was with Fastolf on many of his military campaigns, may have provided Worcester with some of the military anecdotes concerning Fastolf, and he used the title of Worcester's book as the subtitle to his own *Epistle of Othea*. Christopher Hanson, along with Bingham, tried after Fastolf's death to help Stephen to obtain money from Fastolf's estate; Spireling, as the accountant at manors such as Bentley that constituted Stephen's inheritance, was serving his interests. The Pastons were for a number of years prospective in-laws and even in the 1460s Stephen, despite his opposition to Fastolf's will, remained on friendly terms with William Paston.[126] Stephen's life in Fastolf's service in France and Norfolk therefore brought him into close contact with soldiers, accountants, scibes, lawyers and local gentry who read books on warfare, chivalry, romance, classical literature and history (and it is possible that he was attracted to the duke of Gloucester's service because of his reputation as patron of letters). All of these interests can be seen in his activities as a translator. He probably acquired his knowledge of French early in childhood (his father, Sir Stephen, wrote to his grandfather, Richard Lord Scrope, in French) and his fluency in the language would have improved with his spending his adolescence in France.[127] Stephen's first work of translation was the *Epistle of Othea*, which he undertook around 1440 at Fastolf's request for his retirement, using the same manuscript that was used to make the copy illuminated by the artist known as the Fastolf Master.[128] Scrope's translation was in turn illuminated by someone who closely followed the work of Fastolf's artist.[129] *The Epistle*

---

124 *PL* ii, 516–18; Bennet, 'Caxton and his Public' *Review of English Studies* xix, 1943, 115; S. Moore, 'Patrons of Letters in Norfolk and Suffolk in 1450', *Publ. Mod. Lang. Assoc. of America* xxvii, 1912, 188–207; xxvii 1913, 79–105.

125 J.M. Manly and E. Rickert, *The Text of the Canterbury Tales*, Chicago 1940, i, 183–8.

126 William Paston was a feoffee of John Lord Scrope of Bolton in 1464 (Bodl. Lib. Norfolk Charter a, 8. 734; Richmond, *The Paston Family*, 183) and John Paston II was in 1462 a prospective husband to a daughter or ward of Lord Scrope.

127 Poulet-Scrope, *Castle Combe*, 132; BL Add. MS 28212, fo. 7.

128 C.F. Buhler, 'Sir John Fastolf's Manuscripts of the *Epitre D'Othea*', 123–8.

129 M.R. James, *A Descriptive Catalogue of the Manuscripts in St John's College, Cambridge*, Cambridge 1903, 238–40; St John's Coll. Camb. H. 5, fo. 1.

*of Othea* was influential in the aristocratic and gentry circles in which Scrope moved. Besides dedicating his *Epistle of Othea* to Fastolf, Scrope presented other copies to Humphrey duke of Buckingham between 1444 and 1460 and a 'high princess' of unknown identity (perhaps Buckingham's widow, Anne Neville or his eldest daughter, the widow of Reynold Cobham of Sterborough with whom Scrope was acquainted, or Gloucester's widow Eleanor Cobham). Before 1485 William Worcester revised *The Epistle of Othea*, and a Warwickshire gentleman, Sir John Astley, K.G., owned a copy which was transcribed into a collection of writings related to chivalry and warfare including a challenge issued to Astley by a French squire Piero Massy (the combat took place in Paris in 1434), Lydgate and Benedict Burgh's *Governance of Princes* and a translation of the *Epitoma Rei Militaris* of Flavius Vegetius. Many of these items, including *The Epistle of Othea*, were copied by the scribe, William Ebesham, into Sir John Paston II's *Great Boke of Knyghthode*, although the *Epistle of Othea* was subsequently omitted and preserved by the Pastons as a separate work.[130] Another copy of the *Epistle of Othea* was owned in the second half of the fifteenth century by the Bramshotts, a gentry family of the Isle of Wight, and occurs in a manuscript containing the same illuminations that occur in Fastolf's French version and an illustration of Stephen presenting his book to duke of Buckingham.[131] It is possible that the Scropes of Bolton may have possessed a copy, for Richard Scrope of Bentley, a younger son of the fourth lord Scrope and Stephen's successor as the lord of Wighton, left a French book to Margaret duchess of Norfolk in 1484 and the remainder of his French books to his brother.[132] Stephen Scrope also translated for Fastolf a compilation of the sayings of ancient philosophers originally compiled around 1053 by Abu'l Wefa Mubeschschir ben Fatik of Damascus, which had been translated into French at the end of the fourteenth century by Guillame de Tigonville, the provost of Paris, and which Stephen translated into English in 1450 as *The Dicts and Sayings of the Philosophers*. This work was equally influential in the same circles. William Worcester 'correctid and examyned' Scrope's translation by March 1472 'for more opyn and redye undre standing'.[133] A third prose translation of *Le Dicts Morlaux* connected with Fastolf was undertaken after 1473 by Anthony Woodville, earl Rivers. Woodville was a member of the Fastolf circle: he had fought in France as Fastolf's steward, had become his debtor by 1428, and was a friend of Sir John Paston and Sir John Astley. Thirteen manuscripts survive of the English translations of *The*

---

[130] New York Pierpont Lib. MS 775; G.A. Lester, *Sir John Paston's Grete Boke*, Woodbridge 1984; A.I. Doyle, 'A Fifteenth-Century English Scribe, William Ebesham', *Bulletin of John Rylands Library xxxix*, 1957, 306–7.

[131] James, *Catalogue of Manuscrips in St John's College*, 238–40.

[132] TE iii, 297–300.

[133] Colophon of CUL MS Dd ix 18. Another manuscript corrected by Worcester is Emmanuel Coll. Camb. 1. 2. 10. See M.R. James *The Western Manuscripts in Emmanuel College Cambridge*, Cambridge 1904, 29–30.

*Dicts and Sayings of the Philosophers* and River's version became the first printed book in English to emerge from Caxton's press in 1478.[134]

Such literature is important because Scrope and his fellow writers in Fastolf's household were amateurs: they were active (albeit unsuccessfully in Stephen's case) as soldiers and administrators, and their writings provide important evidence about the culture of a fifteenth-century gentry household and the attitudes of its members towards the French war, classical antiquity, private morality and changes in codes of chivalry and religious sensibility. Stephen's early experiences were all of a military and imperial nature. He grew up in two English imperial possessions, Ireland and Normandy. His father was famous for his conquests in Ireland and Fastolf was even more successful in France. He played a part in the major victories of Henry V's campaigns including the battle of Agincourt and the captures of Harfleur and Rouen; he was elevated to the position of the duke of Bedford's lieutenant in 1418, and knighted in 1419. As regent of Normandy and governor of Anjou and Maine he played a crucial role in the campaigns of the first decade of Henry VI's reign: in 1424 he was an influential figure at the battle of Verneuil which established England's hold on the province of Normandy,[135] and he was at the subjection of Maine and Le Mans in 1425 and in charge in 1429 of the relief of Orleans, where he achieved a notable victory in the Battle of the Herrings. In 1435, while still in Bedford's service, he was a negotiator at the peace of Arras and he drew up a report for the management of the war, urging its continuance; and even after his retirement in 1449 he was still urging stronger military pressure in Normandy to retain and consolidate the English conquests.[136] Fastolf's educational programme for his household included the inculcation of military, heroic ethics. Worcester argued in *The Boke of Noblesse* that there was a need to school those of noble blood in all forms of armed combat from jousting to wrestling to make them 'hardie, deliver, and wele brethed', and ready to defend England; and he quoted Fastolf who had contrasted his own time, when the children of knights and esquires preferred to learn and practice common law, with the time of Edward III when Henry the first duke of Lancaster brought up in his court the high-born from Spain, Portugal, Navarre and France in the school of arms and courtesy.[137] We can still hear the echoes of Fastolf's lectures to his young charges at his tables in Rouen, Southwark and Caister in Worcester's marginal reminiscences of his conversation; one note beginning, 'I hafe herde myne auctor Fastolfe sey, whan he had yong knyghtys and nobles at hys solasse' records Fastolf's definition of courage, a distinction between the 'hardy man' who sacrifices his soldiers for the

---

134 *The Dicts and Sayings of the Philosophers*, ed. C.F. Buhler, EETS, 1941, xl–xlvi; McFarlane, 'Worcester', 218–19.

135 FP 9.

136 *Letters and Papers Illustrative of the Wars of the English in France during the Reign of Henry VI*, ed. J. Stevenson, 2 vols, RS 1864, ii, 223ff, 585–90; i, 433, 575.

137 *The Boke of Noblesse*, 76–7.

sake of great adventure, and the 'manly man' who always has a strategy before he advances and always discreetly ensures he has the advantage over his adversary and saves himself and his soldiers.[138] The charismatic appeal of his reminiscences of his conquests in the period from 1414 to 1435 is evoked in Worcester's marginal note recording his account of the defence of Harfleur: 'and as for wache and ward yn the wynter nyghtys I herd the seyd ser Johan Fastolfe sey that every man kepyng the scout wache had a masty hound at a lyes, to berke and warne yff ony adverse partye were commyng to the dykes or to aproche the town for to scale yt'.[139] It is ironic that Shakespeare created a paternalistic leader of youth who rejected chivalric values while the real Falstaff was in his dealings with the young conservative and austere. Such were the formative experiences of Stephen's youth and early manhood for, although he was an invalid, he accompanied Fastolf in France for most of the successful period of conquest, observing these campaigns. The other less important patrons in his life, Humphrey duke of Gloucester and the earl of Warwick, were also advocates of an aggressive foreign policy in France; and his friends in Fastolf's household shared the bellicose attitudes of their master. The writings of the Fastolf circle therefore express an imperialistic warrior ethic and hold up Fastolf and his ideas as the hope for a successful conquest of Normandy and the rest of France.

William Worcester gave an accountant's view of how this could be achieved, and so he made the hero of his *Boke of Noblesse* Sir John Fastolf, a knight who was no Hector but who combined soldiering with the shrewd administrative skills he used in administering his estates. For Worcester one of the main reasons for the failure of the English to hold on to Normandy was that the king and some captains did not pay their troops, forcing them to pillage from the inhabitants of conquered territory, alienating them from Henry VI's government (a point probably reinforced by Fastolf who never forgot the unpaid wages that Bedford owed him).[140] For Worcester the key to successful conquest and rule of Normandy was prudent husbandry: the adequate provisioning and equipping of English soldiers and garrisons with weapons and food would prevent the pillaging and extortion that made a conquering army so unpopular. This was probably Stephen Scrope's responsibility at Honfleur, ensuring that Fastolf's troops were supplied with herrings. Stephen would also have been aware of the significance of his mother's estate at Castle Combe (something Worcester pointed out) as a source of the annual woollen livery of Fastolf's troops.[141] Worcester saw Fastolf as a crucial figure who consolidated Henry V's conquests through prudent

---

138 Ibid., 64–5; BL MS Royal B xxii, fo. 32v.
139 *Boke of Noblesse*, 16.
140 Ibid., 30.
141 Ibid., 69–9. On the profitability of Castle Combe under Fastolf, see E.M. Carus-Wilson, 'Evidence of Industrial Growth in Fifteenth-Century Manors', *EcHR* 2nd ser. xii, 1955–66, 190–205.

husbandry, stocking every castle, fortress and town with corn and fish from England to such an extent that when the castle of the Bastille was under siege Fastolf was able to reassure the duke of Exeter that it had food to withstand a siege of six months. In a marginal note Worcester recalled that he had observed in the books of Fastolf's purveyors how he had provisioned every fortress, city and town with victuals, corn, beef and stockfish out of England in ships, and this policy was one of the reasons why the regent, Bedford, and the council, left him so many castles.[142] Stephen in *The Epistle of Othea* argued that the good knight needed to listen to the advice of old, prudent counsellors and Troy's failure to appoint such men caused its downfall.[143] This was advice endorsed by Worcester who, citing Cicero's *de Senectute*, advocated that for the future conquest of Normandy there be appointed a council of older, prudent men who were capable of steering and providing for the ship of state, and counsellors who were soldiers, accountants and astrologers capable of calculating the yield of their own nation and that of their enemy and the yields of future harvests.[144] Worcester, while acknowledging the important part played by English heroes such as Sir John Chandos and the Black Prince, introduced, through his emphasis on prudence, an element of human responsibility into military success and failure, instead of glorifying the knight's bravery in the face of fortune. He described the rapid capitulation of fortresses in Normandy in 1449 and 1450 and observed that the wheel of fortune would not have turned against the English if they had been adequately stocked.[145] A similar insistence on the importance of prudence occurs in *The Epistle of Othea*. In the earliest illustrations of this work, which were done under Christine de Pisan's direction, the authoress (in the disguise of Othea) addressed her letter counselling prudence to Louis of Orleans (Hector) in an attempt to inspire responsible leadership of France that would restore the unity and dignity of the monarchy. Stephen Scrope in his translation applied the same advice to Fastolf, the recipient of his letter and one who, though retired, was the focus of the hopes of many soldiers who still urged the reconquest of Normandy. The recipient of Othea's letter is advised not to trust in fortune or her promises, not to rely on his castle in time of war unless it is full of provisions and soldiers, and not to fight with those who are stronger.[146] Such advice was particularly pertinent in the light of Fastolf's strategic retreat from superior forces at Beaugenay in 1429; this was a strategy that caused Talbot (the English Achilles) to bring charges of unbecoming conduct against him, charges that cost Fastolf his Garter stall until he was reinstated in 1441 after an enquiry in which Worcester participated. A narrative of tragic dimension unfolds in *The Epistle of Othea* as Hector's vulnerability, his

---

[142] Ibid., 68.
[143] *Epistle of Othea*, lxxx, 98.
[144] *Boke of Noblesse*, 62–3.
[145] Ibid., 51–3.
[146] *Epistle of Othea*, liii, 65–6; lxxxix, 108.

lack of prudence, leads to the downfall of Troy; he refuses to listen to counsel, is distracted into taking soldier's arms, and ostentatiously displays his own coat of arms, allowing Achilles to identify and kill him.[147] Scrope's *Epistle of Othea* was conceived as an expression of hope in the conquest of Normandy through a redefinition and rejuvenation of English chivalry achieved with the virtue of prudence. In the prologue addressed to Fastolf the old knight's martial exploits in France and Normandy are linked with the battle over spiritual enemies in which the aid of the four cardinal virutes, and especially prudence, are enlisted.[148] The same moral, imperial message was transmitted in the illustrations commissioned by Fastolf to accompany the original French manuscript used by Scrope. The artist (the Fastolf Master), after illuminating the cardinal virtues in the treatise preceding *The Epistle of Othea*, depicted on the letter handed by Othea to Hector the cross of St George, the patron saint of the English soldiers in France, thus acknowledging the importance of the Guild of St George to members of Fastolf's circle: Fastolf, Geoffrey Spireling, John Paston I and Stephen Scrope's kinsman, the hermit Richard Scrope/Bradley (an illegitimate son of Richard Scrope the first lord of Bolton) were all members of the Norwich Guild of St George.[149]

By rationally analysing the reasons for military failure and appealing to prudent men of whom Fastolf would have approved, such as accountants and estate managers (men for whom discretion was the better part of valour), Scrope and Worcester introduced a code of moral responsibility to chivalry and questioned the conventional code of honour which held that virtue was inherited in the lineage and that personal and family honour was established through the unflinching conviction of the rightness of a course of action; attitudes which had been expressed by Scrope's ancestors in the court of chivalry in 1386 when they defended their honour against the Grosvenor family. An important aspect of the moral dimension to chivalry as conceived in Fastolf's circle was a sense of England's imperial destiny; this was emphasised in Stephen Scrope's implied comparisons between the Trojan wars and the Normandy campaigns and Worcester's claims that the English were descended from the Trojans. Fastolf and his servants began to conceive this destiny in strongly ethical, moral terms after they were exposed during their years of military service to French translations of the political, moral and historical writings of the Romans. Worcester, in his *Boke of Noblesse*, compared unfavourably England's failure to hold onto its territories in Normandy with the successes of the Romans in conquering and subjugating Gaul and other territories for so long. He attributed this to the fact that the Roman emperors ruled justly with the common weal in mind and that the English did not: 'sensualite of the bodi now a daeis hathe most reigned over

---

[147] Ibid., xci, 110.
[148] Ibid., Appendix A, 120–24.
[149] Bodl. Lib. MS Laud 570, fo. 25v; N.P. Tanner, *The Church in Late Medieval Norwich, 1370–1532*, Toronto 1984, 80.

us to oure destruction we not having consideracion to the generalle profit and universalle wele of a comynalte'.[150] Using Christine de Pisan's *Faits d'armes et de Chevalerie*, he advocated the notion of war as a struggle of virtue against fortune and exhorted the English to emulate the Romans who, after having lost Carthage, redoubled their efforts and reversed their defeat at the hands of Hannibal to regain their empire. He provided instructive examples of how the Romans achieved this through daily exercise in arms, military discipline, and by following the advice of old experienced counsellors such as Cato or Apulius who exhorted courage and prudence in war. Worcester also expounded from Cicero's *de Republica* the concept of public service for the common good; he provided examples of Roman senators and consuls ready to sacrifice gold, land and even their lives for the common weal, including Actilius who remained a prisoner in Carthage rather than be exchanged for enemy prisoners.[151] Worcester was undoubtedly alluding to the brief period of English conquest when the English army aspired to Roman ideals of empire: Henry V promised never to allow himself to be ransomed if taken prisoner and introduced a new element of discipline into his armies and was respected by those he conquered for the justice of his rule. Worcester may also have had in mind the imperial ideals that underlay Bedford's regency: in 1432 Bedford reduced his allowance as regent in Normandy, and in a roll in which Worcester set down all the offices Fastolf held while overseas from 1412–39, Fastolf is credited with the idea of founding a university at Caen in Normandy to train a new class of administrators.[152] Fastolf also applied a Ciceronian notion of public responsibility in his concern with corruption in Norfolk and Suffolk. In 1450 he was in correspondence with Sir Thomas Howys and Justice Yelverton about the extortions of Tuddenham and Heydon and their oppression of the poor, and urged that 'as ferre as justice, reson and conscience do that justice may be egallie mynistered'.[153] The imperial ideals in Fastolf's circle can be explained by exposure to Roman literature that Fastolf brought back from France and the common experience of the campaigns of Henry V and Bedford, and it is therfore appropriate that Worcester, in urging the English to fulfil their potential as descendants of the Trojans, made Bedford's former lieutenant, the prudent yet bellicose chancellor, the English Nestor, a focus of his hopes for a revival of the English empire in Normandy.

The experience of war in France and contact with classical literature in French translation did more than provide members of Fastolf's circle with a sense of imperial mission, it gave them a philosophy of life. Cicero had transmitted the practical, ethical philosophy of Socrates (who equated virtue with knowledge or reason) to Roman society and these instructions on *ars vivendi* were in turn adapted by William Worcester in his translations of Cicero for

---

[150] *Boke of Noblesse*, 52–3.
[151] Ibid., 57, 65.
[152] FP 69, mm. 4–7; McFarlane, 'Worcester', 212.
[153] *PL* ii (Gairdner) 195–6.

Fastolf's circle. Stephen Scrope also participated in this popularisation of classical philosophy. In his *Dicts and Sayings of the Philosophers* he provided succinct biographies of leading Greek and Roman statesmen and philosophers including Socrates, Plato and Cicero, and sayings attributed to them that provided guidance on how to live according to the dictates of reason to achieve mastery of self and one's fate. Hermes claimed 'the noblist thinge that God hathe maad in this world is man, and the noblist thyng that is in this worlde is reeson,' and Aristotle said of reason 'this prerogative þat God hath yeueven to men to regard of other beestes' and described the purpose of life as the acquisition of wisdom and knowledge: 'konnyng is lif and ignorance is dethe; therefore he that knowithe is lif, for he undrestandithe whate he dothe, and he that knowithe not is dethe, for he undrestandithe noo thing he doth'.[154] In Fastolf's household there seems to have been a conscious attempt to follow the ethical teachings of antiquity, and especially Cicero, and to live a prudent, rational life. Fastolf's Rouen artist illuminated a treatise on *The Four Cardinal Virtues* in a manuscript containing the French version of Christine de Pisan's *Epitre d'Othea* and depicted Prudence standing on spilled coins to reject avarice and holding a sieve of circumspection. Her sister, Temperance, stands on a windmill mastering the passions and moods.[155] Perhaps Fastolf set Stephen the task of translating the *Epitre d'Othea* to teach him the virtue of prudence. Othea was goddess of wisdom and prudence and Stephen in his prologue explained how a chivalric gloss and spiritual allegory of her letter (which consisted of extracts from Ovid's *Metamorphoses* and illustrations from Trojan history) could teach readers how to relate Greek mythology to ethical behaviour and to confront the world of fate and the inner passions with reason and prudence. Pyramus, who commited suicide after assuming that Thisbe had been devoured by a lion, is condemned for disobeying his parents and allowing his emotions to overcome his reason and the careful weighing of evidence. Similarly, the story of Hero and Leander demonstrated the dangers of surrendering to passion; and courtly love conventions are undermined in the gloss on the story of Pygmalion creating an image with which he is infatuated: the gloss interprets this as a warning for a knight not to fall in love with the artificial constructs of his imagination.[156]

Underlying such claims for reason or prudence was a belief in the lessons taught by common sense and the experience that came from observing human behaviour, the fruits of which were recorded in *The Dicts and Sayings of the Philosophers*. This source book of proverbial wisdom provided such aphorisms as Pythagoras's advice: 'if thou wolt that thi son or thi seruant doo no defauts, thou desirest that whiche is out of nature', and Diogenes' words to Alexander the Great: 'Whanne thou seist that oon hounde hathe left his maister for to followe

---

154 *Dicts and Sayings*, 24, 174.
155 Bodl. Lib. MS Laud. Misc. 570, fos 9v, 16v.
156 *Epistle of Othea*, App. A, 121–6; xxxvii, 49–50; xlii, 53–4; xii, 34.

the, cast stoonys at him and dryue him a-way, for euen so will he leue the'.[157] This pragmatic, practical philosophy would have appealed to such a self-made man and dominant personality as Fastolf, the inspiration behind the translation. Some of his own pronouncements were repeated by his servants: when his confessor, Friar Brackley, insisted on John Paston I's reliable behaviour in the past the old knight replied: 'show me not the meat show me the man'. Doubtless many such conversations would have been recorded in Worcester's lost life of his master. Stephen Scrope ironically referred to his stepfather's love of quotation when replying to Fastolf's charge that he had never disclosed to him all the complaints listed in his replications, claiming that Fastolf was a man of such wit, truth and gentility that he would know 'full wele what was for to doo: 'for an oolde proverbe seyth, a wyse man be the halfe tale wote what the hoole tale meneth'.[158] This admiration for the wit and brevity of the epigram indicates a high level of urbanity and sophistication in the conversation and correspondence of the Fastolf circle. Table talk at Caister may well have been enlivened by the sort of jokes provided in *The Dicts and Sayings of the Philosophers*: for example Diogenes' observation to a painter who became a physician that men would no longer be able to see his mistakes so clearly as they would be buried underground; or Theosophilis's words to a fat man 'thou doost greete peine to breeke the walles of thi prisone'.[159] Worcester collected such aphorisms and recorded in his *Itinerarium* a collection of the proverbs of ancient philosophers made by the master of King's Hall, Cambridge, John Hall, including Epimenedes's 'Fear not harsh words but soft ones' and Plato's 'He who accepts a kindness loses his liberty'.[160] Evidence that the Fastolf circle consciously used such proverbs in their conversation and correspondence comes from the Pastons. Fastolf's lawyer, John Paston I, wrote in 1454: 'euery thing must haue ende'; his accountant, Geoffrey Spireling, wrote on the wrapper of Fastolf's inventory 'Never trust entryed', and in 1469 John Paston II quoted a phrase attributed to Socrates from Scrope's *Epistle of Othea* 'thou that arte a man, thou shouldest not be hevy ne to mery for no cause'.[161]

The emphasis that members of Fastolf's household placed on reason or prudence went beyond simple observation of behaviour and worldly wisdom and had important implications for their interest in and understanding of individual psychology. Worcester and Scrope's interest in medicine and astrology was probably directed towards these ends. Scrope, who attributed his physical sufferings to emotional causes, provided in *The Dicts and Sayings of the Philosophers* a discussion of the development of ancient medicine, and in this work and in *The*

---

157 *Dicts and Sayings*, 58, 66.
158 BL Add. MS 28212, fo. 22.
159 *Dicts and Sayings*, 66, 254.
160 *Itineraries*, 365.
161 N. Davis, 'Review of *Proverbs, Sentences and Proverbial Phrases from English Writings Mainly Before 1500* by B.J. Whiting and H.W. Whiting', *Medium Aevum*, xli, 1972, 164–6.

*Epistle of Othea* he emphasised the need for medicine to be based on reason, observation and experience and not magic (the sort of methods shown by Worcester in his medical notes). He also provided in *The Epistle of Othea* a discussion of the attributes and composition of the planets, their identification with metals and their influence on behaviour, advising the knight to model himself on the heavy, considered wisdom of Saturn, the strength and bravery of Mars, the tempered mercy of Jupiter, and the silver eloquence of Mercury, while eschewing the inconstancy of the moon and idleness of Venus.[162] For Worcester astrology was both a way of explaining behaviour and determining future plans. His expertise in the subject is shown in the table of 1,022 fixed stars verified him to 1440 at the command of Fastolf.[163] He would frequently take a reading before going on a journey and often signed himself with the sign of Saturn, identifying his antiquarian interests, his propensity to measure distances and the dimensions of buildings and his moodiness with the melancholy inspiration of this planet. Brackley seems to have endorsed this when he described Worcester as of dark complexion.[164] Worcester, a mercurial and gregarious man, certainly had his black moods, especially after Fastolf's death. To John Berney III, 'a fellow sufferer', he complained in 1460 about the years of sacrifice he made for Fastolf and his treatment at his funeral: 'All myne aduersyte, trouble yn my spyryttes, thought and hevynesse that I susteyn, ye know well whom I do and may wyte it';[165] to a servant of Waynflete (the sole administrator of Fastolf's estate after 1472) he confessed that his poverty and the dead man's debtors and creditors 'make me noyed and werye'.[166] Both Scrope and Worcester were interested in sickness of the mind and the question of psychological health and happiness. *The Dicts and Sayings of the Philosophers*, in a saying attributed to Diogenes, defined heaviness as a prison to the soul as sickness is to the body; Worcester, in a copy of the work subsequently owned by him after Fastolf's death, added his own note to a saying of Plato on heaviness and sorrow which defined heaviness as a passion for things past and sorrow for things to come.[167] *The Dicts and Sayings of the Philosophers* provided guidance on how to attain self mastery and overcome unhappiness and the vagaries of fortune. Life, it was claimed, was the end product of sensuality and lust, whereas peace was the product of a soul subject to discipline acquired by rejecting vices which seem sweet but turn bitter, and developing virtues that are initially sharp and bitter but turn out pleasant.[168] Such self-mastery resulted in esteem of self and others: 'how shulde one loue another that can not loue himself – a man may not haue

---

[162] *Epistle of Othea*, vi–xii, 16–23.
[163] Bodl. Lib. MS Laud Misc. 674, fos 81–99v.
[164] *Itinerarium*, 300; BL MS Sloane 4, fo. 57; BL Add. MS 39848, fo. 47 (in 1458).
[165] *PL* ii, 539.
[166] Magdalen College, Titchwell 120.
[167] Emmanuel College Cambridge MS 1. 2. 10, fo. 11b.
[168] *Dicts and Sayings*, 146.

felicite in himself if he do not wele to other'. This was a happiness or detachment that could not be negated by misfortune or grief and as Boethius expressed it, 'Who-so is quietede is saued'.[169] Scrope's version of *Dits moraulx des philosophes* was dedicated to Fastolf, and like Worcester's translations of Cicero's *de Amicitia* and *de Senectute* it reflects the problems of Fastolf's old age, his increasing avarice and the tension and anxieties felt among members of his household as the master approached death with no heirs. Worcester, in a copy of the work made before 1459 and subsequently owned by him after Fastolf's death, added a number of marginal notes 'pro Johanne Fastolf' reflecting on the spiritual limitations of spending an old age acquiring wealth when there is no immediate family on which to bestow it. Such reflections were of particular relevance to both Worcester and Scrope, who felt they were morally entitled to some of Fastolf's wealth but who knew their master too well to have any real expectation of assistance. To the question 'whi olde peple enforceth theym to kepe their Ritchesse' Worcester gave Plato's answer: 'bi-cause that after theire dethe thei had leuer leue it to their ennemyes than to be in daunger to theire freendes'; in another marginal note 'for John Fastolf, a wealthy knight who acted against advice' (pro Johanne Ffastolff milite ditissimo qui egit contra concilium) Worcester provided his own rejoinder and alluded to Fastolf's schemes for Caister by warning him against erecting great buildings that others would inherit, and asking him what use it was for a man to build up property and to leave it to strangers.[170] Many of the quotations in Scope's *Dicts and Sayings of the Philosophers* go further and offer psychological insights into Fastolf's compulsive avarice, and when Fastolf read in his stepson's translation 'men be more enclined to couetice than to reson, for couetice hathe felawshipped with hym of childehood, and reson comythe not to theyme to that thei haue perfite age', he would have recognised that this vice was the greatest obstacle to a serene old age, especially when he could also read in this work a quotation on the paradoxes associated with compulsive hoarding: 'it is harde for a man that is mery to be wrothe, and oon envious man liberal, ne a couetouse man may not be riche'.[171] Worcester recorded similar sayings in his *Itinerarium* such as that of Epicurus: 'The miser lacks what he has as well as what he has not'.[172] Fastolf was too intelligent a man not to notice the applicability of such sayings to himself, and it is probable that this father figure who loomed large in the imaginations of his stepson and secretary was no less introspective. One quality they all valued above others and reflected upon was friendship, which probably made the jealousies and rivalries among Fastolf's servants all the more intense. Worcester recorded many quotations on the pleasures and pitfalls of friendship from Cicero

---

[169] Ibid., 172, 106.
[170] Emmanuel College, Cambridge, MS 1. 2. 10, fos 44b, 72b. M.R. James, *The Western Manuscripts in Emmanuel College, Cambridge,* 1904, 29–30.
[171] *Dicts and Sayings,* 174, 166.
[172] *Itineraries,* 365.

and Seneca; [173] and it was perhaps to preserve the cameraderie of the household as Fastolf's death drew nearer that Worcester presented his translation of Cicero's *de Amicitia* to the man around whom these friendships and rivalries revolved. Their disintegration after his death in the competing claims for a share of the estate caused Worcester and the others a great deal of pain. As early as the funeral he felt snubbed by Paston's men and wrote to a member of the household, who like him was an opponent of the nuncupative will, claiming that it was he who had brought Fastolf and Paston together and quoting Cicero's *de Amicitia*: 'A very frende at nede experience will schewe be deed – thangyng you for olde contynued frenship stidfastely grounded'.[174] Stephen Scrope, who also opposed the will and had claims to part of the Paston's inheritance, struck up a friendship with William Paston, who made efforts to mediate between Stephen and John Paston, writing: 'I can thynk and he were here he wold be a feythful frynd to yow'.[175]

This introspective, moral dimension to the lives of these active administrators and ex-soldiers implies that they had a degree of religious piety. Stephen Scrope's mother, Millicent, a member of the confraternity of Our Lady at Langley, had, according to her husband Fastolf, 'a singular affection and love of devocion for the prayers of that place'. Stephen, describing the sufferings he underwnet during his first marriage, said 'it myght not wele a ben as it is of myn labour withoute the grete grace of God', and said he 'endured III yere with oute any refuge save of god.'[176] Fastolf, who consulted his confessors before conducting business affairs involving the church, wrote to Stephen saying 'God keep you ever in his blessed governance'; during his illness Fastolf (who owned a copy of Bernard's *Meditations*) described himself as visited by the hand of God, and fourteen days before his death he made an orthodox definition of faith before his confessor, acknowledging his great fear of death and judgement.[177] However, there is little evidence in his circle of asceticism or ideological conviction. Worcester admired on his travels the beauty of church architecture, the holiness of certain places and shrines, and the hospitality and civilised conversation of certain monks. What he, Scrope, and probably others in Fastolf's household did achieve was to broaden the source of moral, spiritual edification for the aristocracy in the mid-fifteenth century. Whereas Stephen's ancestors, Henry the third lord Scrope of Masham and Richard Scrope, the archbishop of York, consulted the Bible, the writings of the Fathers, the lives of the Saints and the writings of the Yorkshire mystics, they read Cicero and Greek mythology. Worcester in his *Itinerarium* endorsed the theory that 'all eloquence and every kind of study that strive with the light of wisdom has been derived from Greek sources and

[173] BL MS Cotton Julius vii, fo. 74.
[174] *PL* ii, 203.
[175] *PL* i, 167.
[176] BL Add. MS 28209, fo. 21.
[177] FP 85, m. 2.

practised in their tongue by the Christians and I see that in all the liberal arts they have followed the Greeks footsteps'.[178] The central figure of Scrope's *Dicts and Sayings of the Philosophers* was Socrates who, like Christ, taught a circle of disciples, but counselled a wisdom based on common sense and prudence. These were the sort of values celebrated by Fastolf's artist, who, despite his having previously illuminated books of hours in Rouen, proceeded in Fastolf's service to illustrate the Cardinal Virtues by showing the goddesses of classical mythology usurping the traditional roles of the saints. Temperance and Prudence (as the accompanying plates demonstrate) were shown displaying, like patron saints, their traditional emblems: a delicate clock, representing the balance and harmony of the emotions, the spectacles of discernment and the spilled bag of coins symbolizing the rejection of avarice.[179] Scrope, in *The Epistle of Othea*, achieved an integration of classical myth and Christian morality in allegories that explained the myths of Ovid in terms of traditional penitential teaching on the Ten Commandments and the Seven Deadly Sins. The significance of this achievement was the transmission of a different sort of Christian teaching from that endorsed by such ancestors of Stephen as Henry the third lord Scrope of Masham, a patron of solitaries and hermits in Yorkshire and a trend-setter in devotional fashions. Writers such as Richard Rolle, the author of *The Prick of Conscience*, and Walter Hilton evoked in varying degrees the pain and misery of the world, the individual's insignificance in the face of death, the fallibility of human will, the dependence of the individual on God's grace and the attractions of the eremitic life. Scrope and Worcester, however, used classical literature, especially the works of Cicero, to give a new emphasis to free will and a rational aproach to such questions as guilt and death, and a confidence in the individual's capacity to triumph over fortune through the use of reason. Socrates, in *The Dicts and Sayings of the Philosophers*, says of the fear of death (which dominates *The Prick of Conscience*): 'dispreise not dethe for it hathe no grete bitternys bot the fere of it'.[180] Worcester in *The Boke of Noblesse* asserted that prophecies derived from heavenly constellations were contingent rather than of necessity and could be interpreted as heavenly warnings that a change of direction and disposition was necessary to avoid a certain fate. If such warnings were heeded men could be 'sovereign over the stars'. Worcester also opposed the fatalistic acceptance of the defeats in France which he claimed should be interpreted, like astrological configurations, as warnings from God, marks of his disapproval of the imprudence and injustice of the English rule of Normandy

---

178 *Itinerarium*, 251.
179 Bodl. Lib. MS Laud 570, fos 9v 16r. Tuve, 'Vices and Virtues' 278–84. Fastolf's particular affection for prudence probably influenced his decision, near the end of his life, to ask Bishop Waynflete to obtain a cheap licence in mortmain in recompense for his services to the crown to found a college at Caister of seven Benedictine monks and seven poor men.
180 *Dicts and Sayings*, 96–8.

and exhortations for a renewal of English manhood.[181] In their enthusiasm for the moral teachings of antiquity, and their implied rejection of the pessimistic religious teachings of the second half of the fourteenth century, the servants of Fastolf had something in common with earlier classical enthusiasts in the episcopal households of Bishop Burley and John Grandisson. Burley himself used *Le Dicts Morlaux* in his *Liber de Moralibus Philosophorum*, a similar collection of ancient sayings, and William Nassington adapted a moral guide based on the Cardinal Virtues, the *Somme le Roi* (a copy of which was obtained in France for Bedford and another version of which, *The Book of Vices and Virtues*, was owned by Fastolf).[182] More significant is the way Fastolf's lay servants (only two clerics, Kirtling and Howes, were employed in his household) and especially Worcester, integrated with their active lives of soldiering and administration a love of scholarship and antiquity and a belief in practical wisdom inductively based on experience; this was a secular outlook similar to that of the humanist scholars of Italy. It was most forcibly demonstrated in Worcester's intellectual curiosity about all aspects of his world, from the influences of the stars to the functioning of the human body, the rivers, landscapes, flora and fauna of England and Wales; the affairs of cities and towns like London and Yarmouth; the voyages of discovery undertaken from his native Bristol; the architectural beauties of churches and city skylines and the workings of such social institutions as parish churches and great families. Worcester also had a strong sense of historical perspective which he shared with other members of Fastolf's circle as they sought to place England's military destiny in conext: Fastolf in 1449 gave a series of proposals for securing Normandy which show that he had reflected on his own war-time experiences, had closely studied the war, and appreciated the differences between the campaigns of the 1420s and the 1440s.[183] In *The Boke of Noblesse* Worcester discussed Anglo-French relationships within the context of the Norman conquest, the establishment of the Angevin empire and the contribution of Edward I's campaigns in Wales and Scotland to Edward III's military successes. He appreciated the differences between Edward III's *chevauchées* and Henry V's campaign of conquest by siege warfare, comparing the latter's conquest of Normandy with the Roman conquest of Gaul, and expressed a philosophy of history that imposed a cyclical pattern of achievement and decadence in all empires from those of the Greeks, Romans, Saxons, and Normans to that of the English in the fifteenth century.[184] It is with this friend of Stephen Scrope, who showed such curiosity about the natural world and shared Stephen's aesthetic appreciation of literature and art and a belief in England's imperial destiny, that we can see the beginnings of the English renaissance.

---

181 *Boke of Noblesse*, 50–53.
182 *Dicts and Sayings*, xi.
183 Stevenson, *Letters and Papers*, 585–90.
184 *Boke of Noblesse*, 52–3, 30–40.

# Peace and War in Early Eleventh-Century Aquitaine

## JANE MARTINDALE

> The name of peace is splendid indeed, and beautiful is
> the idea of unity, which Christ left for his disciples when
> He ascended into heaven.[1]

These words form the introduction to the decrees of a well-known council held in the city of Poitiers during the late tenth or early eleventh century, and the bishops who met there were gathered together for the avowed purpose of ensuring the 'restoration of peace and justice'. 'Endeavours to propagate peace' characterized the activity and pronouncements of many ecclesiastical assemblies during the late tenth and earlier eleventh centuries; almost all are marked by the 'lavish ideological overtones' commented on by John Cowdrey in his masterly discussion of the 'Peace of God'.[2] Understandably, historians have come to regard the council of Poitiers as merely one of a long series of meetings which

---

[1]  *Speciosum quidem nomen est pacis, et pulcra est opinio unitatis, quam Christus ascendens in caelum reliquit suis discipulis*, Acta Conciliorum, ed. Ph. Labbe and G. Cossart, 12 vols, Paris 1714, vi part i, cols 763–4 (henceforth *Acta Conciliorum*); *Concilia Sacrorum Nova et Amplissima Collectio*, ed. J.D. Mansi, 31 vols, Venice 1759, xix, cols 265–8 (henceforth Mansi, *Concilia*) reproduces the text of the earlier edn. and is based on the same MS. The text is undated except for (i) references to a council held five years previously at Charroux, and (ii) to this council's being convened *idibus Januarii*; on the dating-problems see additional note, below 175.

[2]  H.E.J. Cowdrey, 'The Peace and Truce of God in the Eleventh Century', *P and P* xlvi, 1970, 42–67 (54, and 52 for a slightly different translation of the quotation cited at the beginning of this paper). My purpose in taking up this topic once more is essentially different from his, and I should like to thank John Cowdrey for his encouragement and help at Strawberry Hill. Since the first draft of this was composed, I have also benefited from the generosity of Patricia Morison who has allowed me to consult and use her unpublished Oxford D.Phil. thesis on 'French Society and the Miraculous, c.950–1100'. My debt to both of them will be obvious, and I hope that I have not distorted their work to suit my own narrower concerns. I should also particularly like to thank both the editors of this volume.

147

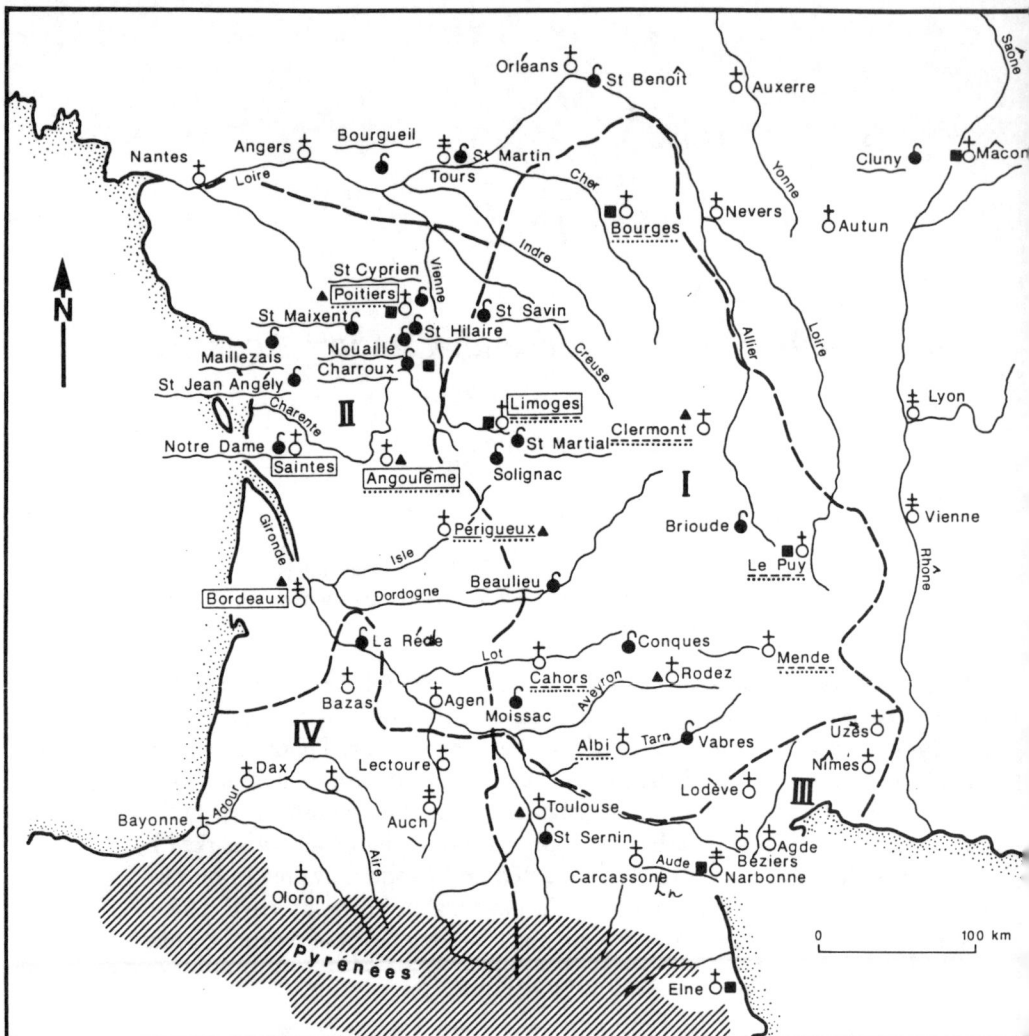

Orléans ⚲ ⚲ St Benoît    ⚲ Auxerre

      Saône

Nantes ⚲    Angers ⚲   Bourgueil    Cluny ⚲ ⚲ Mâcon

     Loire     ⚲ St Martin

      Tours    Cher

      Bourges ⚲   ⚲ Nevers    ⚲ Autun    Yonne

      Indre    Aller    Loire

St Cyprien ⚲

Poitiers ⚲   Vienne    ⚲ Lyon

St Maixent ⚲   St Hilaire ⚲   ⚲ St Savin

Maillezais ⚲   Nouaillé   Charroux    Creuse

St Jean Angély ⚲   Charente    II    Limoges ⚲    Clermont ⚲ ▲

Notre Dame ⚲   ⚲ St Martial    ⚲ Vienne

Saintes    Solignac    I

Angoulême ⚲ ▲    Brioude ⚲

     Périgueux ⚲ ▲    Le Puy ⚲

     Isle    Beaulieu ⚲

Bordeaux ⚲   Dordogne

     La Réole ⚲    Conques ⚲    Mende ⚲

     Lot    Cahors ⚲ ▲ Rodez

     Bazas ⚲   Agen ⚲   Aveyron

IV    Moissac ⚲

     Albi ⚲   Tarn   Vabres ⚲    Uzès ⚲

Dax ⚲   Lectoure ⚲    Nîmes ⚲

     Auch ⚲   Lodève ⚲    III

Bayonne ⚲   Adour   Aire   Toulouse ▲ ⚲

     St Sernin ⚲    Agde ⚲   Béziers ⚲

     Carcassonne   Aude   Narbonne ⚲

Oloron ⚲

Pyrénées

     0      100 km

     Elne ⚲

⚲ Bishopric (civitas)    ⚲ Archbishopric    ⚲ Principal religous houses

⌐ ECCLESIASTICAL BOUNDARIES

I AQUITANIA PRIMA (BOURGES)    II AQUITANIA SECUNDA (BORDEAUX)

III NARBONNENSIS PRIMA (NARBONNE)    IV EAUZE (AUCH)

■ SITE OF "PEACE COUNCIL" c990's–1040

☐ Bishop attending both the COUNCIL OF CHARROUX (c990) and the COUNCIL OF POITIERS (c1000–1014)

── Bishop attending only the COUNCIL OF CHARROUX

--- Bishop attending the COUNCIL OF BOURGES, 1031

......... Bishop mentioned in the proceedings of the COUNCIL OF LIMOGES, 1031

⚲ St-Hilaire = named religous house founded, endowed, or protected by the Poitevin Dukes of Aquitaine c mid tenth cent. – c 1050

▲ CIVITAS with COUNT during these years (NB Not all counties retained their secular rulers).

N.B. Distances close to the major Bishoprics are schematic.    The coastline is modern.

were held throughout the confines of the Capetian kingdom and beyond: together they have been viewed as making up a single great movement for the establishment and maintenance of 'Peace'.[3]

This 'movement' has normally been interpreted as an essentially religious and ecclesiastical phenomenon, for its origins have been attributed to the direction and control which members of the higher clergy could legitimately exercise within their dioceses. In the late tenth century, for instance, a man like Bishop Guy of Le Puy justified his involvement in the curbing of violence with the assertion that 'we know that without peace no one will see the Lord'.[4] Roger Bonnaud-Delamare, whose varied regional studies gave a new direction to historical investigation of the early medieval 'peace phenomenon' within the Capetian kingdom, went so far as to conclude that 'the eleventh century [more than any other historical epoch helped] to establish the foundations of a solid belief in peace. . . by which men should once again succeed in finding the order laid down by God'. In a broad survey of the idea of peace in the eleventh century Bonnaud-Delamare expressed the view that during these years peace

---

[3] Contemporaries rarely employed the phrase 'pax Dei' as such, although it has been extensively used by historians, see the comment of H.-W. Goetz, 'Kirchenschutz, Rechtswahrung und Reform: zu den Zielen und zum Wesen der früheren Gottesfriedensbewegung in Frankreich', Francia xi, 1983, 193–239 (193, n. 1). New critical editions of many of the texts of 'peace councils' are needed, for the compilation most widely used is still that of L. Huberti, Studien zur Rechtsgeschichte der Gottesfrieden und Landfrieden, Ansbach 1892, vol i (no more published, henceforth Huberti, Studien); see comments of Cowdrey, 'The Peace', 42 (with good bibliography), and cf. G. Duby, 'Les laïcs et la paix de Dieu', in Hommes et structures du moyen âge, Paris 1973 (first pub. 1966 – henceforth 'Les laïcs'), 231, 239. The most comprehensive recent study has been by H. Hoffmann, Gottesfriede und Treuga Dei (Schriften der Monumenta Germaniae Historica), Stuttgart 1964, (henceforth, Hoffmann, Gottesfriede); cf. the earlier discussion by B. Töpfer, Volk und Kirche zur Zeit der beginnenden Gottesfriedensbewegung im Frankreich, Berlin 1957; and the article by Goetz noted above. Rather different approaches are contained in Essays on the Peace of God: the Church and the People in Eleventh-Century France, ed. T. Head and R. Landes, Historical Reflections xiv, 1987. One of the most influential assessments of the wider implications of the 'peace' was made many years ago by C. Erdmann, The Origin of the Idea of Crusade (transl. M.W. Baldwin and W. Goffart), Princeton 1977, 57–94. The German edn contains material not included in the translation, which will be cited where necessary, Die Entstehung des Kreuzzugsgedankens, Stuttgart 1935 (2nd edn 1965 – henceforth both cited as Erdmann). Two wide-ranging and stimulating recent works also lay great emphasis on the importance of the 'peace of God': J. Flori, L'idéologie du glaive, préhistoire de la chevalerie, Geneva 1983, 135–50; L'essor de la chevalerie, XIe-XIIe siècles, Geneva 1986, 25–6 (henceforth respectively L'idéologie and L'essor).

[4] See the text of that so-called Charta de treuga et pace, Huberti, Studien, 123–4 (citation from 123); Hoffmann, Gottesfriede, 13, 16–23; Cowdrey, 'The Peace', 43–4. Cf. on the role of Bishop Guy of Le Puy, B. Bachrach, 'The northern origins of the peace movement at Le Puy in 975', in Essays on the Peace of God, 405–21.

---

*Figure 1*

Aquitaine: Councils, Bishops and ' Peace of God' in the early eleventh century. (Jane Martindale)

was envisaged as 'manifesting the order of Providence on earth and in heaven'. Furthermore, he criticised comparisons which placed such an elevated conception on the same plane as any peace which was merely established through the agency of human convention – still less one achieved by the 'arbitrary impositions of a conqueror'.[5]

Although he wrote in slightly less lofty terms, Hartmut Hoffmann, too, began his study of 'God's peace and the truce of God' with the assumption that these peace councils were inaugurated by the higher clergy because that was the only group whose members recognised how desperately peace was needed in the contemporary world. It was their aim to enforce order in the temporal world throughout territories where (it is normally assumed) violence was endemic and no secular power was able to guarantee peace; however that aim – as is suggested by the introductory quotation – could only be achieved through the proclamation of an other-worldly peace. Because no conception of public order survived, peace inevitably became the particular concern of bishops and their clergy throughout the region described by Hoffmann as southern France (*Süd-Frankreich*). Where kings once exercised authority in a direct and immediate fashion, it has been argued that the Church attempted to substitute its own power for that of inadequate 'temporal sovereigns': that was essential if ecclesiastics' efforts were to be effective in enforcing prohibitions against the wrongdoing of 'feudal nobles'. Indeed, for Georges Duby the 'ecclesiastical inspiration' and 'episcopal direction' of the movement could be regarded as self-evident; nevertheless, in his important study on 'Laymen and the peace of God', Duby speculated on the impact made on the laity by this conciliar movement.[6]

The 'peace of God' now occupies a central place in broad accounts of social and political change during the medieval era; but all the same, when the 'peace movement' is invoked in that context, the manifestations of the late tenth and

5 The particular objects of his criticism were 'les erreurs des juristes allemands, classant les textes et les comparant abstraitement entre eux comme des plantes mortes dans un herbier', R. Bonnaud-Delamare, 'Fondement des institutions de paix au XIe siècle', in *Mélanges Louis Halphen*, Paris 1951, 19–26 (esp. 26 – and for references to nineteenth-century works in French, 19); idem, 'Les institutions de paix en Aquitaine au XIe siècle', in *Recueils de la Société Jean Bodin* xiv, 1961, 415–87.

6 D.F. Callahan, 'Adémar de Chabannes et la paix de Dieu', *Annales du Midi* lxxxix, 1977, 21–43 (22); Duby, 'Les laïcs', 228; Hoffmann, *Gottesfriede*, 1–45. Cf. also Duby, *Les trois ordres ou l'imaginaire du féodalisme*, Paris 1978, 162–9. The assertion that 'the Peace of God can accurately be dubbed episcopal in view of the nature of the Peace's means and ends' has also been made by T. Renna, 'The Idea of Peace in the West, 500–1150', *Journal of Medieval History* vi, 1980, 143–67 (154). Note also the attitudes implied by the inclusion of this topic in the chapter entitled 'La direction morale de la société laïque' of the standard 'Fliche et Martin' *Histoire de l'église*: vii, E. Amann and A. Dumas, *L'église au pouvoir des laïques (888–1057)*, Paris 1948, 482–503; cf. two excellent 'manuals' in the series *L'histoire et ses problèmes*, J.-P. Poly and E. Bournazel, *La mutation féodale (Xe–XIIe siècles)*, Paris 1980, 220–74; J. Paul, *L'église et la culture en occident*, 2 vols, Paris 1986, ii, 564–74; and the invigorating discussion by J. Dunbabin, *France in the Making, 843–1180*, Oxford 1985, 150–5, 167–9.

earlier eleventh centuries are frequently viewed teleologically. Even in the 1930s, Leon MacKinney thought that the 'popular religious' emotionalism provoked by the peace assemblies during the first part of the eleventh century provided a 'dynamic influence in stimulating a public movement for social progress'. On the other hand, since he also considered that 'social progress' could not be achieved without the leadership provided by a strong monarchy and the revival of the idea of a 'public law', there was no easy way forward. As far as this interpretation of the impact of the 'peace of God' was concerned, the French kingdom stagnated until the thirteenth century.[7] Ingeniously – but somewhat paradoxically – it has also been argued that the 'peace movement' helped medieval writers and thinkers evolve 'a more precise justification of war'; thus, according to Frederick Russell, attempts made to limit the use of force during a time when levels of violence were high actually contributed towards the eventual transformation of attitudes towards non-combatants. The habits and ideas inculcated by means of the 'peace of God', it has been argued, made a significant contribution towards the formulation of theories of a 'Just War'. Ecclesiastical dominance of the peace movement, too, enabled the Church to devise a policy for directing warlike activity against non-Christian targets. Carl Erdmann's highly influential *Origin of the Idea of Crusade* prompted discussion of the view that 'the Peace of God and parallel phenomena reveal a new attitude of the church toward war and the profession of arms'. The cumulative efforts made by ecclesiastical authorities to curb violence within their own territories enabled churchmen to divert aggression and warlike activity against external targets.[8]

Discussions of the social implications and repercussions of the 'Peace of God' have been based on the hypothesis that there were deep identifiable divisions within early medieval society: the clergy and the unarmed (lay) populace have been distinguished from a military élite (also of course presumed to be composed of laymen), which is viewed as hostile to the pacific outlook of its ecclesiastical and rural opponents. So in Russell's view those who were drawn together to implement the peace councils' decrees were 'local churchmen, peasants and merchants'.[9] Individuals who made up these groups were after all the most likely to be damaged by the indiscriminate attacks of marauding warriors, whether or

7 L. Mackinney, 'The people and public opinion in the eleventh-century peace movement', *Speculum* v, 1930, 181–206 (192). This should be compared with the view that after a period during the eleventh century when 'the whole people within the Church' aspired to the organisation of a common life, God's peace made its contribution to a deeper movement of ideas and attitudes which would culminate in the liberation of the individual, Y. Congar, 'Les laïcs et l'ecclésiologie des *ordines*', in *Etudes d'ecclésiologie médiévale*, Variorum Reprints 1983 (first published 1966), 115.
8 F. Russell, *The Just War in the Middle Ages*, Cambridge 1975, 34; Erdmann, 67 (transl. ). The problems connected with formation of a 'crusading' ethos cannot be considered here; however, note the incident mentioned below, 174.
9 *The Just War*, 34–5 – an analysis based on a long view in which 'peace' and 'truce' of God are assimilated, and contrasted with the emergence of ideas justifying war against non-Christians; cf. Erdmann, 57–94 (transl.). For the distinction between 'peace' and 'truce',

not those warriors were regarded by their contemporaries or by historians as 'feudal nobles'. And since the purpose of peace councils is held to have been the curbing of these attacks, their pronouncements must have had an impact on the 'knights' whose position and activities provide the main focus of papers presented at this conference. Historians may differ on what they consider the nature of that impact to have been, but it has been authoritatively asserted that 'the church hierarchy . . . appears to have gone over the head of the formally constituted secular authority to deal directly itself with the knighthood'.[10] For Jean Flori, on the other hand, the chief problem for historians lies in deciding whether the attitudes expressed in the peace gatherings of the eleventh century helped shape the ideal of 'chivalry' which – under many guises – has also been a major concern of this conference. Some of the difficulties involved in tracing such a historical development are revealed in Flori's assertion that, 'the Peace of God did not forge a chivalric ethos, but it made a great contribution towards the creation of a mentality common to all those who are – more and more often – called *chevaliers*'.[11]

The dramatic descriptions of the Burgundian chronicler Rodulf Glaber were surely initially responsible for the importance attached by historians to the Aquitanian 'peace' councils. Glaber's account stated categorically that the movement for peace began when councils were summoned *in Aquitaniae partibus*: these were then imitated in the 'province of Arles and Lyon', before eventually being exported to 'the furthest parts of France'. It is Glaber's vivid picture of bishops raising crosses to heaven and of whole congregations shouting, 'Peace, peace, peace' which has created the best-known and most enduring 'image' of these councils; but his account has also been extremely influential for its insistence that the movement was led and directed by ecclesiastics. This chronicler, too, laid great emphasis on the highly charged atmosphere of these gatherings, and on the religious fervour aroused when 'bodies of saints and countless coffers of relics' (*corpora sanctorum et innumerabiles apoforete reliquiarum*) were brought to the meetings.[12]

This paper is concerned with Aquitaine and – in the first instance – with a number of the topics which have been raised during recent scholarly discussions of the significance of the 'peace' movement. The reason for returning to the well-worked topic of 'peace' during the late tenth and early eleventh centuries is not to offer a resolution of the historiographical differences which have been

Cowdrey, 'The Peace', 44, 52; and for reservations about the 'popular' origins of the Peace, Flori, *L'idéologie*, 152–5.

[10] 'The peace movement had a positive and active side, for the peace councils sought to do more than merely restrict violence', M. Keen, *Chivalry*, New Haven 1984, 47. The contribution made by peace legislation to the formation of an ethos of chivalry is also stressed (but with rather different emphasis) by Flori, *L'idéologie*, 135–57; *L'essor*, 161–90.

[11] Flori, *L'idéologie*, 157.

[12] *Rodulfus Glaber, Opera: Historiarum Libri Quinque*, ed. J. France, OMT, Oxford 1989, 194–196; 236–8 (for the *treuga Dei*); see below 154, 174.

rather crudely outlined here. Indeed, the primary purpose of this paper is to suggest that the social implications of the 'peace of God' can be rewardingly approached by rather different methods from those which have already been employed.[13] In the first place, more attention should be given to the regional setting of the peace movement, and in particular to the local structures of power and authority which have sometimes been presented in an over-simplified or anachronistic fashion. The prominence attributed in a number of recent studies to the 'peace of God' as a catalyst of social change seems to provide ample justification for reconsidering the regional setting in which the first councils took place.[14] With the exception of the meeting summoned by the bishop of Le Puy, the territorial framework of the 'movement' in Aquitaine was circumscribed by the boundaries of the Poitevin dukes' authority as much as by the 'ecclesiastical geography' of dioceses and provinces.

An enquiry into the regional setting of the councils held in Aquitaine between the late tenth and the first half of the eleventh century inevitably leads to further speculation on the part played in the 'peace movement' by the secular ruler and the greater laity – that is by the Poitevin duke of Aquitaine and perhaps by other counts. Since the impression left by a number of specialist studies is that the peace movement was predominantly ecclesiastical – operating in a vacuum left by the withdrawal of royal authority – any reassessment of the power wielded by a secular ruler has interesting implications for the relationship between the orders of *oratores* and *bellatores* within Aquitaine. One of the principal aims of this discussion is to show that the relative positions of the clergy and laity at this time were far more complicated than is suggested by the stereotypes established in the wake of Gregorian reform, or by the clear-cut ideology of the *ordines* which has been so elaborately developed by historians.[15] Another aim is to argue that any revision of the significance of early manifestations of the peace movement entails a further consideration of war, for – like peace at this time – war also had a place in the 'cosmic order'.[16]

Before examining a number of these interrelated aspects of peace and war in

<hr>

[13] The semantic analysis of the vocabulary of 'knighthood' – e.g., *miles*, *eques*, *caballarius* and related terms for warrior, *bellator*, *pugnator* – is vital for an understanding of the emergence of 'knighthood' or 'chivalry'. However, the argument of this paper is that there is a preliminary need to reconsider the regional foundations of political authority in Aquitaine around the turn of the tenth and eleventh centuries.

[14] These topics will be discussed at greater length in a study of the politics and government of the Poitevin dynasty, 'Aristocracy and Politics in Medieval Aquitaine: From Carolingian Kingdom to Poitevin Duchy (ninth century – 1137)' which is to appear shortly. The Poitevin counts began to use the title of *dux Aquitanorum* in the late tenth century, see n. 27 below.

[15] Ecclesiastical historians have understandably tended to assume that the ideals invoked during the course of a movement for reform involved 'absolute' standards applicable throughout the western world during a period of many centuries. There is, however, abundant evidence to show that there could be wide divergences of opinion even within different parts of the Capetian kingdom about moral and ethical 'priorities'.

[16] See below, 168–74.

Aquitaine it still seems necessary, however, to return to the most important ecclesiastical and religious features of the peace movement in the tenth and early eleventh centuries. These can be listed and summarised in the following manner without too much distortion. In the first place, the movement's decrees are held to proclaim cosmological convictions which constituted a distinctive ideology: in Bonnaud-Delamare's words, 'peace expressed the cosmic order ruled by Divine providence'. Undoubtedly that was a profoundly Christian notion, since peace is recorded in the Gospel as the central message of Christ's legacy to His followers – 'Peace I leave with you, my peace I give unto you' (John 14, 27-Vulgate). Peace was also a recurrent theme in the liturgy: the salutation Pax tibi et ecclesiae reveals peace to be the highest state to which the individual Christian and the Church collectively could aspire. It was a divine gift to the faithful. Furthermore, as we are reminded by Cowdrey, peace was a topic of considerable concern in religious writing at this time.[17]

The importance of the 'irrational' elements in religion have also been increasingly recognized by today's historians. Glaber's account of the movement conveys this very well, while the Chronicle and other works by the monk Adémar de Chabannes also dwell on the efficacy of relics and of the bodies of the great saints of the region in times of trouble. Perhaps because of this shift in emphasis, considerable attention has been paid to Adémar de Chabannes' contribution to the formulation of ideas associated with the peace movement. Like Glaber, Adémar dwelt on the protection afforded by the presence of the saints: at one meeting summoned not because of human violence, but because the region was plagued by disease, 'all the bishops of Aquitaine' brought the bodies of saints (or other less complete relics) to the city of Limoges. Only when Saint Martial (the patron of Adémar's own monastery) 'was lifted out of his tomb . . . everybody was filled with immense joy, and everywhere all sickness ceased'. Despite the fact that the pestilentia ignis had not been directly caused by human agency, the chronicler described this as an occasion when a 'pact of peace and justice' was concluded in his city.[18] For Duby, Adémar's account shows that 'in the mind of the writer there existed a direct relationship between the epidemic, the prophylactic intervention of relics and the proclamation of the reformatio pacis'.[19] In an evocative and powerful passage, the saint's reliquary (la châsse) has

[17] Bonnaud-Delamare, 'Fondement des institutions de paix', 22; Cowdrey, 'The Peace', 42, 50–1. For the Pax Domini (which is found at rather different places in the Roman and other ordines of the liturgy) and for the salutation, J. Jungmann, The Mass of the Roman Rite: its Origin and Development (transl. F. Brunner), 2 vols, New York 1955, ii, 321–32.

[18] Adémar de Chabannes, Chronique, ed. J. Chavanon, Collection de textes pour servir à l'étude et à l'enseignement de l'histoire, Paris 1897, 158 (henceforth Adémar, Chronique). For references made to the peace by Adémar in his sermons, Hoffmann, Gottesfriede, 27–9; Callahan, 'Adémar de Chabannes et la paix de Dieu', 27–8; Duby, Les trois ordres, 172. On the epidemic of the much discussed pestilentia ignis or 'mal des ardents', Cowdrey, 'The Peace', 48, n. 22; and Morrison, 'The Miraculous and French Society', 123–5, for the prevalence and significance of such mass-meetings when the saints were used to stave off disaster.

[19] G. Duby, 'Les laïcs', 235; in subsequent work he came to regard 'Adhémar de Chabanne' as

recently been described as forming the centrepiece (*la pièce maîtresse*) of those early peace councils.[20] Fear of an individual saint's wrath and of divine retribution might, therefore, be more effective in securing temporal peace than appeals of a more intellectual or 'rationalist' character; moreover, even when no miracle occurred, these ceremonies associated with the 'very special dead' created the 'emotional atmosphere propitious for knightly renunciations'.[21]

The penalties and sanctions employed or threatened by the clergy have also been regarded as essentially religious in character. Anathema, commination, and excommunication were all designed to create a powerful impression on those who contravened a council's decrees; the rituals associated with these sanctions appear to have been carefully orchestrated, and are for the most part described in more detail than any deterrent or sanction to be imposed by human agency. Most striking of all is the episcopal commination of the *milites* and their helpers (*adiutores*) in the bishopric of Limoges: this ends, 'their arms [are] accursed, their horses [are] accursed'.[22] A man who contravened a council's decrees was also threatened with the ultimate religious sanction – refusal to give an individual a Christian burial or the funerary rites which preceded interment. As voiced emphatically by Bishop Guy at Le Puy, this meant that no *raptor* should be be allowed to be buried *ad ecclesiam*;[23] and – even if that were not an

the theorist of the early peace movement, *Les trois ordres*, 168–73; cf. Bonnaud-Delamare, 'Les institutions de paix en Aquitaine', 432. Adémar's testimony has always been somewhat suspect because of his unjustified advocacy of the elevation of St Martial to the ranks of the apostles; and this has provoked considerable debate. These problems were recognised many years ago by L. Delisle, 'Notice sur les manuscrits originaux d'Adémar de Chabannes', *Notices et extraits des manuscrits de la Bibliothèque Nationale et des autres bibliothèques* xxxv, 1896, 241–358 (see esp. 277–96). For the great revival of interest in the problem of Martial's 'apostolicity', and for its relevance to the topics of this paper, see below 159.

20 Poly and Bournazel, *La mutation féodale*, 248; cf. for a discussion of the practice of '*ostension*', N. Herrmann-Mascard, *Les reliques des saints, formation coutumière d'un droit*, Paris 1975, 193–234, and esp. 221–5.

21 'Le saint au fond apaise les colères chevaleresques comme il guérit la démence des possédés du Démon,' Poly and Bournazel, *La mutation féodale*, 248; in general P. Brown, *The Cult of the Saints*, Chicago and London 1981, 69. There is often a critical problem associated with the texts which extol the virtues of a saint, or promote a particular cult, as was the case with Adémar's 'promotion' of the apostolicity of St Martial, as was shown by Delisle (see above, n. 18). The most recent detailed treatment of this topic (which appeared after a first draft of this paper had been completed) is by R. Landes, 'La vie apostolique en Aquitaine en l'an mil, paix de Dieu, culte des reliques, et communautés hérétiques', *Annales* lxiv, 1991, 573–93 (esp. 577).

22 *Acta Conciliorum* vi, col. 874; Mansi, *Concilia* xix, col. 530 – from the proceedings of the 1031 council held at Limoges. (The implication appears to be that the bishops at Limoges were imitating a ritual evolved only a short time before at Bourges, see Additional Note below, 175). The commination was accompanied by the extinction of all lights and the 'humiliation' of the relics, see Herrmann-Mascard, *Les reliques des saints*, 225–8; P. Geary, 'L'humiliation des saints', *Annales* xxxiv, 1979, 27–42; and on the real and symbolic value attached to horses in saints' lives and miracle collections, Morison, 'The Miraculous and French Society', 166–8. In general Duby, 'Les laïcs', 233; Paul, *L'Eglise et la culture* ii, 571–2.

23 Huberti, 124. At the council of Narbonne in 1054 it was enjoined that anyone who had

effective deterrent against a delinquent *miles* killed on a marauding expedition – it could be a powerful threat to hold over his kin and companions. The effect which this prohibition was intended to have is recorded in an anecdote preserved in the account of the 1031 council held at Limoges. The bishop of Cahors regaled his fellow-bishops with the tale of how, despite an episcopal veto on the burial of an excommunicated *eques*, the latter's *milites* had interred him on Church land. On the day after the burial the naked body was found 'far away from the cemetery' above ground; and, although the corpse was immediately reburied 'under an enormous weight of earth . . . closed with stone', the grave was unquiet. Only after further dramatic incidents (allegedly occurring five times) were the *principes militiae* 'struck with terror, and they then did not delay any more over confirming the peace [regulations] for us – just as we desired'.[24]

Faced with anecdotes like this one, it is scarcely surprising that it has been assumed that the purpose of the peace of God was to put an end to 'the cruel sport of knights' (*le jeu cruel des chevaliers*); moreover, it is understandable that the upsurge of reaction against secular violence could be interpreted as shaping ideas which eventually contributed to the formation of the idea of Crusade, through the reiteration of the decree that no Christian should kill another.[25] At the same time, historians struggling with the historiography of the peace movement need to recognise that there now exists a 'revised version' of the movement's social significance, for a growing pre-occupation with the socio-economic position of the marauders condemned in these councils has inevitably raised semantic questions about men described (in the Latin sources) as *milites* and *equites*. Duby's view – most forcefully expressed in *Les trois ordres* – is that the 'project' for a peace of God eventually resulted in the construction of an 'ideological model . . . serving the interests of the dominant class'. So now – instead of fostering an alliance between clergy and the unarmed populace *against* an aristocratic military élite – the ideas and methods of the 'peace movement' are presented as a catalyst which facilitated the emergence of 'chivalry'. And (in another of Duby's striking phrases) 'with chivalry, oppression became incarnate'.[26]

---

transgressed the detailed peace regulations and then failed to make amends would be denied communion, burial, or the benefits to be obtained from the singing of Mass: *cl.XXVIII . . . presbyter ei missam non cantet, nec ullum sacrum officium, neque communicet eum, vel sepeliat, se sciente*, ibid., 321. Cf. the text of the synod of Toulouges in the diocese of Elne, Mansi, *Concilia* xix, col. 484; Hoffmann, *Gottesfriede*, 73–9.

[24] *Quo terrore perculsi principes militiae pacem nobis, velut optabamus, firmare nequaquam distulerunt, Acta Conciliorum* vi, cols 884–5; Mansi, *Concilia* xix, cols 541–2. Note the interest of the assumption that an *eques* would have *milites* who would be his warriors-in-arms, but also his subordinates.

[25] Although otherewise not so bluntly stated, this was enunciated in 1054 at Narbonne, Hoffmann, *Gottesfriede*, 95; Duby, 'Les laïcs', 237; Paul, *L'Eglise et la culture* ii, 573. For the quotation, Bonnaud-Delamare, 'La paix', 25.

[26] *Les trois ordres*, 198, 191 for the quotations. In a an elaborate reassessment of traditional material, Duby argued that originally (193) 'les institutions de la paix de Dieu furent forgées

During the years between the late tenth and the first three decades of the eleventh century the counts of the Poitevin dynasty assumed an increasingly prominent political role in Aquitaine. By the third quarter of the tenth century these counts also employed the title *dux Aquitanorum* echoing the style previously borne by Carolingian kings of the region. The rulers of this 'principality' never imposed their control throughout all the territory included in the two ecclesiastical provinces of Aquitaine (Bourges and Bordeaux – respectively the metropolitan cities of *Aquitania prima* and *secunda*); although in ecclesiastical terms ducal authority can to some extent be measured by the numbers of bishops who attended the duke's courts, gave him counsel, and carried out the commands of the secular ruler.[27] The Poitevin duke of Aquitaine either inaugurated – or was at least closely involved with – most of the 'peace' assemblies held within his sphere of political influence; but the wider significance of these meetings in secular and political terms has not always been fully appreciated. For instance, the assertion that presiding bishops assumed the 'eminently royal mission' of legislating for the 'restoration of peace and justice' when they gathered in the city of Poitiers, overlooks the fact that this council had been 'convoked' by the duke. Additionally, it was the duke and 'other princes' rather than the bishops who are mentioned as 'confirming' the 'restoration of peace and justice' made on that occasion.[28] The canons of the council of Charroux (specifically confirmed at Poitiers) were admittedly enacted only by the bishops 'of second Aquitaine' (*secundae Aquitaniae*) presided over by the archbishop of Bordeaux; but the subsequent ducal intervention suggests that the bishops gathered at Charroux had not been able to eradicate 'the evil things' against which that earlier council had inveighed, and had eventually called on the lay power to help them.[29]

At an assembly called to meet in the city of Limoges during the last decade of

---

contre elle [i.e. la chevalerie] par les prélats et les princes, par les bons *bellatores*, amis des moines les plus purs . . . &c'; but that eventually – in order to preserve their economic resources – clerics were almost inevitably bound to confuse 'seigneurs' and 'chevaliers'. And through the elaboration of the tri-functional explanation of social divisions with their inbuilt inequalities, clerics were even able to justify 'le mode de production seigneurial' on which their wealth was based, 194–8.

[27] Cf. A. Richard, *Histoire des comtes de Poitou (778–1204)* 2 vols, Paris 1903, i, 1–220; W. Kienast, *Der Herzogstitel in Frankreich und Deutschland*, Munich/Vienna 1968, 175–203. In the book in course of preparation the formation of the Poitevin dynasty's 'territorial principality' will be discussed in detail, together with probable shifts in meaning attached to the ducal title. For an extended discussion of the use of royal diplomas as a means of assessing the changed nature of a secular ruler's power, J.-F. Lemarignier, *Le gouvernement royal aux premiers temps capétiens (987–1108)*, Paris 1965, 44–166.

[28] See n. 1 above. *Igitur idibus Januariis, Guillelmo Pictavense duce convocante concilium, Pictavo convenerunt episcopi numero quinque,* [for names see below, n. 33] . . . *& abbates duodecim* [names not given in the text], *pro restauratione ecclesiae. Firmaverunt per obsides & excommunicationem dux, & reliqui principes, huiusmodi pacis & justitiae restaurationem . . .*

[29] The text of the council held at Charroux *'per longam tarditatem concilii'* is drawn up in the first

the tenth century, the duke (as has already been seen) took a prominent role in concluding a 'pact of peace and justice'. Perhaps about twenty years later the duke also took the initiative in summoning a second council to meet at Charroux to consider the dangers posed by the presence of Manichees within his territories. The clergy undoubtedly played an important part on all those occasions (and they may have been responsible for initiating the meetings, or explaining the un-orthodoxy of the Manicheans); but at Limoges the 'peace pact' was only concluded after the bishop of the city and the Abbot of St-Martial had first consulted the duke,[30] while it is of considerable importance that Adémar de Chabannes should portray the secular ruler as the appropriate leader to summon and preside over an assembly on an occasion when the suppression of heresy was also associated with the 'confirmation of peace' and the 'veneration' owed to the Church.[31]

Even when conciliar deliberations are portrayed as almost exclusively eccle-siastical – as was the case with the rather rambling account of the proceedings of yet another council later held at Limoges in 1031 – the duke was still present, and his intervention was demanded by the council fathers when that was judged necessary. At Limoges in 1031 the duke's participation is known from the details of a tricky ecclesiastical affair which in practice could not easily be resolved by the assembled bishops and abbots. This concerned the abbey of Beaulieu – a wealthy monastery to the extreme south of the diocese of Limoges – which had been founded by a ninth-century archbishop of Bourges; however, since being taken over by the count of Toulouse at an unspecified date, it had remained under lay control. The interests of two further laymen (the count of Périgord and the viscount of Comborn) are mentioned; furthermore, at this stage in the eleventh century the abbot was not even a professed monk, but 'great by birth and secular nobility'. So, although the council bishops had an armoury of religious sanctions at their disposal for use against the offending laymen and their clerical stooges, it was agreed by the assembled clergy that the duke of Aquitaine must help the bishop of Limoges settle the affair.[32]

person, 'in nomine Domini & salvatoris nostri Jesu Christi, Kalendis Junii: ego Gunbaldus archiepi-scopus secundae Aquitanie . . .'

30 See above, n. 18; Hoffmann, Gottesfriede, 27. No decrees have survived for this council.

31 Adémar, Chronique, 194: His diebus concilium adgregavit episcoporum et abbatum dux Willelmus apud sanctum Carrofum propter extinguendas haereses, quae vulgo a Manicheis disseminabantur. Ibi adfuerunt omnes Aquitaniae principes, quibus precepit pacem firmare et aecclesiam Dei catholi-cam venerari . . .; cf. 173, 184–5, 206, 210 (a list of the errors by which simplices were turned away from the true faith). Adémar certainly implied that eruptions of 'heretical' belief were subversive of the established order and potentially disruptive of society; and, for an interpre-tation of the significance of this emergent heresy in the early eleventh century, Landes, 'La vie apostolique en Aquitaine', 579–84.

32 Duke and bishop were allotted six weeks to find a suitable pastorem secundum regulam for Beaulieu. The early eleventh-century abbot was apparently the nephew of a former bishop of Cahors, Acta Conciliorum vi, cols 880–81; Mansi, Concilia xix, cols 536–7. On the wealth and resources of this abbey, Martindale, 'The nun Immena and the foundation of the abbey of

Episcopal attendance at the councils in question is extremely revealing, as are the locations chosen for the meetings of the 'peace councils'. Both throw light on the authority exercised by the secular ruler in Aquitaine. An analysis of the names of bishops recorded in the surviving *acta* of councils, or in narrative sources (principally the *Chronicle* of Adémar de Chabannes) show that Charroux (I) and the council summoned by the duke to meet in Poitiers had a virtually identical membership. This was indeed made up of bishops from the province of *Aquitania secunda*. It included the archbishop of Bordeaux, the bishops of Poitiers, Saintes and Angoulême; but the bishop of Périgueux was not present at Poitiers, although he had been a signatory to the Charroux proceedings.[33] On both occasions there was an important additional member in the person of the bishop of Limoges – whose diocese was part of *Aquitania prima*, subject to the archbishop of Bourges. The scribe who transcribed the text of the Charroux decrees therefore made an error when he wrote that the composition included 'all the provicial bishops' of 'second Aquitaine'. Unfortunately the twelve abbots who also allegedly attended the council of Poitiers are unnamed, and the *religiosi clerici* who took part in the proceedings at Charroux (I) are equally anonymous.[34] The lengthy account of two councils held successively at Bourges and at Limoges refers to a considerable number of bishops from *Aquitania prima*; while those present at Bourges in November 1031 were listed in an account of those who heard the 'council fathers' agree to the proclamation that Martial was henceforth to be included in the ranks of the apostles.[35]

Beaulieu: a woman's prospects in the Carolingian church' in *Women in the Church*, ed. W. Shiels and D. Wood, SCH xxvii, 1990, 36–8.

[33] At Charroux the names were added to the foot of the proceedings in the form *Ego . . . subscripsi*, and the bishops of *Aquitania secunda* included *Gunbaldus* of Bordeaux, *Gislebertus* of Poitiers, *Frotarius* of Périgueux, *Abbo* of Saintes and *Hugo* of Angoulême. (These names should provide valuable means of dating this gathering, but the episcopates of very few are precisely dated. The best indication of a limiting date is the death of Hugo of Angoulême in 990, L. Duchesne, *Fastes épiscopaux de l'ancienne Gaule*, II, *L'Aquitaine et les Lyonnaises*, 2nd edn, Paris 1910, 66 n. 9.) The names of the bishops attending the council held at Poitiers were mentioned as being convoked by the duke: only the bishop of Poitiers was identical, whereas the archbishop of Bordeaux was *Siguinus*, the bishops of Angoulême and Saintes *Grimoardus* and *Islo* respectively; cf. n. 34 below; and Map (fig. 1).

[34] At Charroux and Poitiers the bishops of Limoges were named respectively as *Hildegarius* and *Hilduinus*. The death of Hilduinus provides the limiting date of c.1014 for this council, J. Font-Réaulx, in *Bulletins de la Société archéologique et historique du Limousin* lxviii–ix, 1919–20, 200, nn. 13–14. In neither case is there any indication that the archbishop, the duke, or the draftsmen of the proceedings were aware that the archbishop of Bourges was the metropolitan of the bishop of Limoges; although that relationship was later to provoke a conflict of jurisdiction and the excommunication of the whole diocese of Limoges by Archbishop Gauzlin, Adémar, *Chronique*, 183. By far the best and clearest guide to the importance of, and changes to, the 'ecclesiastical geography' of Aquitaine is still Duchesne's *Fastes épiscopaux* , 1–88. The Poitevin dukes' authority never extended to the following bishops of *Aquitania prima*: Albi, Cahors, Clermont (= Auvergne), Mende, Rodez, Velay (i.e. Le Puy). The implications of these limitations for an understanding of the title *dux Aquitanorum* and the duke's authority will be discussed in the study already mentioned.

[35] *Acta Conciliorum* vi, col. 879. They were Archbishop Aimo of Bourges, and the Bishops

Only if the ecclesiastical composition of these councils is related to the structures of secular power does their full importance emerge. Had the higher clergy been summoned solely on the basis of ecclesiastical allegiance and 'geography' the presence of the bishop of Limoges would be inexplicable, since Limoges did not form part of the province of Bordeaux. On the other hand, once it is realised that the city of Limoges had been one of the earliest political acquisitions made by the Poitevin counts, the membership of these early councils is invested with a rather different meaning. Bishops of Limoges are found alongside diocesans from the province of Bordeaux because the geographical basis of the council was the territory of the 'Poitevin duke' of Aquitaine, not the ecclesiastical provinces of Aquitaine.[36] Indeed, all the bishops who attended the councils of Charroux (I) and Poitiers were either regularly active in the circle of the dukes of Aquitaine during these years, or were drawn into that circle on important occasions. Even the archbishop of Bordeaux – whose city in the early eleventh century lay outside the region ruled by the Poitevin dynasty – seems in some sense to have been a ducal client; in particular, Duke William intervened in the election of a new archbishop in the year 1028. There is a strong case in fact for supposing that control of Bordeaux was one of the chief political objectives of these decades, at a time when the Poitevin ruler had no direct authority south of the Garonne.[37]

With the exception of the archbishop of Bordeaux, all the bishops who attended the two councils of Charroux and Poitiers are found in the ducal entourage on other occasions, or are named as subscribers to ducal charters. The documentary evidence for their presence in the ducal circle ranges from a handful of references for the bishops of Angoulême, Périgueux and Limoges respectively, to eight for the bishop of Saintes, and forty-one for the two bishops of Poitiers who occupied that see during the years between the later tenth and the mid-eleventh century.[38] Another indication of the closeness of the ties between the higher clergy and great laity in Aquitaine is provided by the

Stephanus of Le Puy, Renco of Clermont, Ragamundus of Mende, AEmilius of Albi and Deusdedit of Cahors. Rodez was said to be sede vacante, and Jordan of Limoges was not present, ibid. cols 851 and 854.

36 Ebles, brother of Count William Tête d'Etoupe of Poitou, was appointed Bishop of Limoges soon after 944 (dating to be considered elsewhere), while also holding important abbacies in the diocese of Poitiers, Adémar, Chronique, 146–7, 201–2; Richard, Histoire des comtes de Poitou i, 83, 92–8.

37 The election and ordination are noted as having taken place at Blaye – an important fortified site which virtually controlled the mouth of the Gironde from the north bank, Adémar, Chronique, 194; cf. the rather different wording of the note included in Leiden, MS. Vossius. lat. oct. 15, ed. Delisle, 'Les manuscrits originaux d'Adémar', 317–18. The duke's second wife had been the sister of the duke of Gascony (also present at this election of an archbishop for Bordeaux), Chronique, 162.

38 The supporting evidence will be cited in detail elsewhere in the study already mentioned. The analysis of subscriptions, or witness-lists, to charters has been increasingly employed as a method of assessing the range and importance of a secular ruler's subordinates, or the attraction exercised by his 'court'.

evidence for episcopal election in the region. One of the most detailed accounts of secular intervention is provided by Adémar de Chabannes, and concerns the appointment of the *prepositus* Jordan to the see of Limoges. The duke was apparently present himself at the election of Jordan as bishop of Limoges; and Adémar records that Jordan was freely (*gratis*) invested 'with the pastoral staff' by Duke William. The latter also made sure that there would be no local resistance when Jordan (who had been a layman before his election) made his ceremonial entry into his episcopal city of Limoges. This ruler was unable to monopolise the election of the archbishop of Bordeaux in quite such a blatant fashion, but he still had a role to play on at least one occasion, as he probably did for some other bishoprics.[39]

The most illuminating information about the dependence of the regional episcopate on the duke at this time is provided by a letter written by Isembert of Poitiers to his co-bishop Hugh of Angers in which he refused the latter's invitation to attend the consecration of Angers cathedral (16 August 1025). 'Our lord (*domnus noster*) Count William has taken counsel with the Italians and has ordered (*precepit*) me and my co-bishops, the lords Islo and Roho [bishops of Saintes and Angoulême], to take care of some serious business which cannot be delayed.' At least three of the 'conciliar fathers' from the councils of Charroux and Poitiers can therefore be seen acting here in a curial capacity: the commands of the secular ruler were to take priority over a solemn religious ceremony.[40] All in all, the higher clergy's dependence on the secular ruler throughout much of Aquitaine certainly ought to be taken into account in the interpretation of the activity of the early 'peace councils'. It seems obviously misleading in these cases to represent these gatherings as symbolising episcopal autonomy, or the subordination of secular to ecclesiastical authority.[41]

The significance of the sites chosen for the meeting of 'peace' councils in Aquitaine also needs emphasis. The first point of interest is a negative one. The avoidance of Bordeaux as a meeting-place must strike all historians concerned with the politics or social organisation of Aquitaine because, if ecclesiastical considerations had been dominant throughout these years, Bordeaux – the metropolis of *Aquitania secunda* – would surely have been chosen as the place for

---

[39] *Chronique*, 182–3 (but the installation of the bishop was entrusted to the duke's son *prudentissimo adolescenti*); cf. 172 for the consecration of Gerald, the previous bishop, at Poitiers (thus also suggesting secular influence and the Poitevin duke's protection). The connection between bishop and count at Poitiers was also very close (evidence to be discussed elsewhere), but there is insufficient evidence to suppose that all bishops in Aquitaine were appointed by the duke, Imbart de la Tour, *Les élections épiscopales en France du IXe au XIe siècle*, Paris 1891, 250, 358.

[40] *The Letters and Poems of Fulbert of Chartres*, ed. F. Behrends, OMT, Oxford 1976, no. 102 (translation slightly modified); cf. no. 110 (addressed to the archbishop of Tours by Bishop Isembert, regretting his inability to send an escort to bring the latter to Poitiers, because of the count's absence *in expeditionem*), and introduction, lxxxvi–viii.

[41] As has been done by historians interested in the 'long term' significance of the peace councils, see above 150–1, 155–6.

at least one of these gatherings. By contrast, the presence of a number of bishops from *Aquitania secunda* in the city of Limoges (as has already been seen, a *civitas* of *Aquitania prima*) supports an impression that the sites chosen for the 'peace councils' often corresponded with the places where the Poitevin duke's regional control was strong, or where there was some particular political point to be made. The case of Limoges has already been considered in a slightly different context, and it is interesting that Charroux (which had to a great degree fallen under the control of the upstart count of La Marche) should have been the only monastic site chosen. There can be no doubt, however, that this abbey was a pilgrimage site with at least one powerfully attractive relic, while the duke's choice of Charroux as the place where a council should meet to consider the problem of the Manichean heresy has political as well as ecclesiastical and religious significance. It may even have been intended to draw attention to the duke's own reform of the abbey.[42] The choice of Poitiers must have been understood as making a straightforward political statement because that was the city which since the early tenth century had been the heart of the territory controlled by the Poitevin dukes. It was the city where this ruler had his chief 'palace' or 'hall': any gathering held there would be under ducal protection, even if the secular ruler did not entirely dominate its proceedings.[43]

Three successive dukes of the Poitevin dynasty were involved in the activities of the 'peace' councils between the late tenth century and the 1030s, but it was the ruler known as William 'the Great' whose involvement has received the most attention.[44] His career is presented in fulsome terms by the chronicler Adémar de Chabannes for whom this secular ruler's interventions in ecclesiastical affairs were invariably worthy of praise. He was 'defender of the poor, father

---

[42] Duke William restored '*regularem disciplinam*' there through the ejection of Abbot Peter (described as a simoniac), and his replacement by *Gunbaldus* (probably a monk of St-Savin de Gartempe), cf. Adémar, *Chronique*, 184 and Behrends, *The Letters . . . of Fulbert*, no. 96 (dated 1023 x mid-1025). Charroux was not a *civitas* with its own bishop or count, although since Carolingian times the monastery had exercised a great attraction for pilgrims. This is normally attributed to the relic of the Holy Cross, but by the early eleventh century it also possessed a more personal Christ-relic, 'la sainte vertu', Morison, 'The Miraculous and French Society', 63 n. 2.

[43] Adémar's remarks that after a fire in Poitiers the duke allegedly restored the cathedral *maiori decore*, together with other churches, *suumque palatium*, are proof of his dominance of that city, Adémar, *Chronique*, 182. At this time, too (as I hope to show), the majority of ducal charters which have any note of enactment were dated from Poitiers.

[44] The three rulers are William 'Fier-à-bras', his son 'the Great', and the latter's son known as '*le Gros.*' The dating of these dukes' successions, like the dates of the 'peace' councils, can often only be approximately established, and the problems will not be discussed here. The chief problems relate to the succession of William the Great which almost certainly did not occur until c.995, although cf. Richard, *Histoire des comtes de Poitou* i, 139–40. This Duke would therefore have been responsible for convoking the council at Poitiers and for subsequent gatherings described by Adémar, whereas the meeting at Charroux must have taken place during his father's lifetime. If the dating is correct, the duke present at Limoges in 1031 was presumably the eldest son of William the Great.

of monks, builder and lover of churches, and above all lover of the holy Roman church . . .'; and it is against that background of eulogy that Adémar's complaisance about the duke's replacement of abbots and bishops, or his involvement in the promotion of relic-cults needs to be placed. But the duke could not have protected or defended the clergy if he had not also wielded great secular authority: Adémar's description acknowledges that authority with two epithets, *gloriosissimus* and *potentissimus*. The quasi-royal power commented on by this chronicler was marked by some form of religious ritual as well as by the splendour of the ducal entourage, and by the status of the men whom the duke could attract to his service. It is known from other sources as well as Adémar's chronicle.[45] Charters issued in the name of Duke William the Great, his immediate ancestors and his successors, suggest that over a number of generations members of the dynasty attached great value to the quasi-religious position which they held as abbots of the chapter of St-Hilaire de Poitiers. There is a nice irony in the fact that it was 'William, duke of the Aquitanians . . . seen to preside over the abbey of St-Hilaire' who prohibited the canons of this community from alienating the property of their house; and that it should have been a layman who expressed a fear that some canon might even be prompted to use violence to seize possession of the chapter's lands because of his own *potencia vel nobilitate*.[46]

An extended reconsideration of the relations between the secular ruler and higher clergy within the territories ruled by the Poitevin dukes of Aquitaine is more relevant to the theme of 'knights and knighthood' than this survey may perhaps suggest. In the first place, this discussion shows how distorted is any generalisation based on the view that the ethos of knighthood or chivalry can be directly attributed to the influence which the episcopate wielded over '*milites*' or '*equites*'. Whether or not the ruler's intervention is judged by modern historians to have involved a usurpation of what in the past had strictly speaking been royal 'rights', it is incorrect to suppose that in Aquitaine the episcopate alone was responsible for taking measures against laymen who made indiscriminate attacks on people and property. The view that 'peace councils' were directed by men of religion against the laity of '*un siècle de fer*' is scarcely acceptable in the case of Aquitaine.[47]

---

[45] *Chronique*, 163 (also remarks on the duke's conviction of the need to undertake annual pilgrimages whether to Rome, or to St James); cf. 207–8; 166, 179 (enthusiasm for relics); 183 (reception by the monks of St Martial *cum textu evangeliorum et timiamatherio sicut semper ab eis dux solet excipi*).

[46] *Documents pour l'histoire de St-Hilaire de Poitiers* ed. L. Rédet, Mémoires de la Société des Antiquaires de l'Ouest xiv–xv, 1847–52, no. 71, datable to 1015 x 1016 (the dating-problems cannot be discussed here). The charter was subscribed by the bishop of Poitiers who threatened to excommunicate those who contravened 'this privilege' – methods also employed by bishops at the 'councils' of this region. But for a different interpretation of the significance of this document, Landes, 'La vie apostolique', 529, n. 29.

[47] Hoffmann, *Gottesfriede*, 10.

The early peace gatherings included measures of a secular character which were intended to enforce peace, although these have attracted less interest than the dramatic ceremonial religious and ecclesiastical sanctions. Canon I of the council of Poitiers states categorically that disputes over '*res invasae*' and '*de ipsis rebus*' shall be settled 'before the prince of . . . the region': the same clause makes provisions for enforcing the decisions of the secular authority. Admittedly, if justice cannot be secured by the local prince or judge, a larger body of 'princes *and* bishops' shall pursue the wrongdoer to 'his destruction and confusion'; nevertheless, a literal reading of the text leaves the impression that all con-cerned were in fact eager to ensure that offences committed should initially be settled by 'ordinary' judicial methods.[48] Although sanctions of a religious char-acter were undoubtedly important, and may be interpreted as in some sense compensating for the limitations of human judicial procedure, clearly provisions were made for those who broke the peace to be pursued by secular authorities. As under the Carolingians, peace could be '*en même temps la loi civile et l'ordre du salut*'. Both laity and clergy should continue to be involved in the fulfilment of the conditions for 'salvation', as well as for 'civil order', in the tenth and the early eleventh centuries.[49]

In a further respect too, there is little support for the view that this conciliar legislation was specifically directed against men who were already envisaged as forming a uniform or homogeneous body of *chevaliers* or *milites* holding a com-mon set of values. The canons of Charroux (I) in fact condemn 'anyone' who uses violence against *ecclesiam sanctam*, or who plunders the stock of the poor or of peasants. The second topic is not treated in abstract terms (liberty, rights), but gives an extremely down-to-earth list of the animals which must not be seized (sheep, ox, ass, cow, nanny- or billy-goat, pigs).[50] The most probable culprits would be likely to be armed men, who make their appearance as 'preda-tors' in both saints' lives and miracle books; but that is not quite the same as supposing that this 'peace legislation' was specifically aimed at a named group of offenders, condemned for their membership of a particular social order. The

---

[48] The crucial part of the text is . . . *si ex contendentibus de ipsis rebus unus alium interpellaverit, veniant ante principem ipsius regionis, vel ante aliquem ipsius pagi iudicem, et stent in iusticia pro ipsis rebus: & qui sub districtione iustitiae stare noluerit, principes vel iudex, ipsius rei aut iusticiam faciat, aut obsedem perdat* . . . The judicial methods are further elaborated, and referred back to the decrees, *sicut in concilio Karrofensi constitutum est.*, Acta Conciliorum vi, col. 763 (punctuation of seventeenth-century edn).

[49] Paul, *L'Eglise et la culture* ii, 565. The problem for modern historians is that the topic of peace is so all-embracing, that the emphasis on one aspect rather than any other seems bound to involve distortion.

[50] *Acta Conciliorum*, col. 718 (the poor and *agricolae* do not have horses). It scarcely seems possible to generalise about the prohibitions of this type. Over a number of years great variation was shown in the protection extended to the rural population: cf. e.g. the provi-sions enacted at Le Puy (Huberti, *Studien*, 123) with those of a Catalan council of 1033, emphasizing the importance of plough beasts, Hoffmann, *Gottesfriede*, 260–1; Bachrach, 'The northern origins', 420.

terminology of the early councils held in Aquitaine does not identify the guilty parties as an order of *bellatores*, or describe them generically as *milites* or *equites*: the chief distinction appears to be between those entitled to wield 'public' authority and others who were not so qualified.[51]

Interestingly enough, the sections of the earliest Aquitanian councils which refer most uncompromisingly to armed warriors are *not* concerned with any specific group of laymen, but with ecclesiastics carrying 'secular arms'. This has never received the attention it deserves, although the condemnation of attacks on the clergy and the pronunciation of 'anathema' against anyone who showed violence to priest, deacon or 'anyone at all belonging to the clergy' was a feature of all early peace councils.[52] The insistence that the clergy form a privileged class – by virtue of their status exempt from violent attack – undoubtedly anticipates the attempts made at a later date by theorists and lawyers to classify groups of non-combatants: the Charroux prohibition against attacking clergy may be interpreted as proving that this body of men was already regarded by contemporaries as 'ministers of God' whose attackers would immediately be judged 'sacrilegious'.[53] However, the immunity granted to the clergy was conditional, as can be seen from a careful analysis of the terms of the Charroux decree. In particular, no cleric bearing arms would be covered by the terms of the decree – a qualification which indicates that sometimes the clergy in Aquitaine could not be distinguished from the laity. The detailed character of the decree enacted at Charroux is extremely unusual.

It was traditional to condemn clerks who engaged in warlike pursuits. From the mid-eighth century onward it had been laid down in Carolingian capitularies that ecclesiastics ought not to bear arms: councils enacted more general prohibitions against clerics following a military profession. These prohibitions are repeated in some form or another in the surviving decrees of most peace councils. At Le Puy, for instance, this took the form of a general prohibition: 'clerks shall not bear secular arms (*saecularia arma*); no man shall do injury to monks . . . nor to those who travel with them who are not carrying arms'. Considerably later a Catalan peace which was 'confirmed' in the year 1033 was less categorical in ordering that '. . . no man shall attack or do an injury to any clerk who is not bearing arms, or to monks or nuns'.[54] But the Charroux decree

---

[51] The prohibitions of Charroux (I) all begin '*Si quis* . . .' and end . . . '*anathema sit*'. The wording of Poitiers (I) is less uniform, but never mentions the profession or occupation of laymen – apart from the *princeps ipsius regionis* and the *iudex ipsius regionis*, *Acta Conciliorum*, ibid. Thus 'knights' or 'horsemen' were not the specific objects of condemnation. Cf. the regulations of the Catalan 'peace': '*Si vero exercitus militum super inimicum ospitatus fuit* . . .', Hoffmann, *Gottesfriede*, 261.

[52] Canon 1 of the Council of Charroux (I) – but for the important qualifications, see n. 57 below.

[53] Bonnaud-Delamare, 'La paix en Aquitaine', 423; Russell, *Just War*, 34–5; Amann and Dumas, *L'église au pouvoir des laïques*, 492. Interpreted literally this prohibition appears to prove that there was already an unbridgable gulf between clergy and laity.

[54] Cf. the terms of the oath composed by the bishop of Beauvais, Huberti, *Studien*, 123, 166;

on this topic was far more specific because, having extended immunity from attack to any member of the clergy 'not bearing arms', the clause then continues with a definition of 'arms' as 'shield, sword, mailcoat, helmet'. This is the strangest – and perhaps the most interesting feature – of the Charroux canons; all the most important items of a contemporary professional warrior are included (no reference is made to a horse or horses, however). Inevitably the wording of this clause raises the question whether such a definition would have have been considered necessary if members of the regional clergy did not engage in warlike pursuits, travelling in full military gear.[55] In any case the weapons listed were unlikely to have been intended solely for defensive purposes, while taken together with the body-armour they would have been formidably expensive. This clause (confirmed at Poitiers) serves as a reminder that the 'militarized' clergy of the ninth century probably had many successors during the tenth and eleventh centuries.[56]

Altogether, the significance of this canon of the Council of Charroux seems to be double-edged. In broad terms, it certainly offered the clergy protection from attack, but it also conveys an unequivocal threat against any clerk who does not live according to the desired norms of his own 'order'. Presumably any priest or deacon who was found bearing secular arms ought to have been deprived of the protection to which he was entitled by virtue of his status or 'order'. This condemnation is surely directed as much *against* the clergy as against the laity who might be expected to attack the clergy as an easy target. It is directed against ecclesiastics who adopted the way of life of a military aristocracy or who (we may suppose) used their churches' resources to buy arms and wargear. But that is not the interpretation normally placed on this clause; while in the majority of general discussions of the 'Peace of God' this important reservation is not even mentioned.[57]

Hoffmann, *Gottesfriede*, 261 (free translation of the clause). In 895 the Council of Tribur (col. 27), referring back to the Council of Chalcedon, prohibited engagement in any warlike activity (*militia*) to those who had become clergy, *Acta Conciliorum* vi, col. 447. For an interesting recent discussion, J.F. Benton, 'Nostre Franceis n'unt talent de fuïr: the Song of Roland and the enculturation of a warrior class', in *Culture, Power and Personality in Medieval France*, ed. T. Bisson, 1991, 147–65 (153).

55 *Acta Conciliorum* vi, col. 718: *Si quis sacerdotem, aut diaconum, vel ullum quemlibet ex clerico, arma non ferentem, quod est scutum, gladium, loricam, galeam, sed simpliciter ambulantem aut in domo manentem, invaserit, vel ceperit, vel percusserit, nisi post examinationem proprii sui, si in aliquo delicto lapsus fuerit, sacrilegus ille, si ad satisfactionem non venerit, a liminibus sanctae Dei ecclesiae habeatur extraneus.* A regulation of about a century later from the northern diocese of Soissons offered protection for all those who travelled in the company of clerics – as long as the latter bore no arms except a sword (*praeter ensem*), Bonnaud-Delamare, 'La paix en Flandre pendant la première croisade', *Revue du Nord* xxxix, 1957, 147.

56 For specific regional examples, see below, 169–71; cf. F. Prinz, *Klerus und Krieg im früheren Mittelalter*, Stuttgart 1971, 115–200. For contemporaries' criticism of 'militarized' clergy during the eleventh century, Erdmann, 74–80.

57 However, the prohibition was deliberately framed to exclude abbots and bishops, according to Bonnaud-Delamare, 'La paix en Aquitaine', 423. In his view it should be interpreted as

Is it perhaps possible to go even further than this? Although references in narrative sources like Adémar's *Chronicle* or Glaber's *Histories* associate the maintenance of peace in Aquitaine with a general veneration for 'the catholic church of God', a careful analysis of the few surviving *acta* of the councils shows that these were as much concerned with standards of clerical life and discipline as with violence committed by the laity against the clergy and church property. At Poitiers, for instance, the two decrees added to the Charroux canons both reveal the importance attached to religious or spiritual matters. One prohibits the sale of a sacrament (penance), while the other concerns clerical relations with women – a topic which of course recurs frequently in contemporary ecclesiastical legislation. As with the Charroux prohibition against the wearing of arms by clergy, words are not minced in the Poitiers decree relating to clerical morals: 'That no priest or deacon shall keep a woman at home, nor allow one to enter a cellar or secret place for the sake of fornication. For he shall know that, if he should be tempted to do this, he shall be degraded, and shall not celebrate the sacred mystery in the presence of others ( *cum aliis hominibus*)'.[58]

Many thinkers of the late tenth and earlier eleventh centuries idealised peace in the temporal world as a reflection of 'cosmic order'. That vision was expressed publicly at times of crisis, when the Church was faced with what appeared to be symptoms of a deep social and political disorder, or of God's wrath at the sinfulness of His people. Thus widespread disease and famine might be assessed by reference to the same standards which were used to condemn heresy, or human violence and breaches of the peace. But, where detailed accounts of 'peace councils' survive for Aquitaine, it can be seen that these gatherings were not simply employed to impose 'social control' upon subversive elements within society – for instance, those who threatened to undermine the clergy's privileged position and resources. Any desire to establish on earth the 'cosmic order' which formed the vision of another world, made particular demands on the clergy. Laymen who plundered the poor and the rural population, or who detracted from the dignity and honour of the clergy by capturing or wounding

---

being directed against 'the lower clergy' who would be allowed to carry knives and staves (characteristic of '*vilains*'); but it seems unlikely to me that priests or rural clergy (whose economic resources probably resembled those of their humbler parishioners) would have been able to afford chain-mail and the other military equipment listed at Charroux. It seems far more likely that this was intended to be directed against the wealthier ranks of the clergy, who would be unlikely to be simple parish priests; and for the continuing evaluation of the clergy throughout this period in terms of their 'nobility', Martindale, 'The French aristocracy in the early Middle Ages: a re-appraisal', *P and P* lxxxv, 1977, 5–45 (35–6).

[58] *Acta Conciliorum*, ibid. These clauses relating to the prevailing moral and ethical standards of the clergy are normally discussed under a different heading from that of the 'peace' councils; a notable exception is Goetz, 'Kirchenschutz, Rechtswahrung und Reform', 229–34. It is also surely of some significance that the canons of the 1031 Bourges council do not contain a single decree relating to the promulgation, or enforcement of the peace, ibid., cols 847–52 (largely concerned with different aspects of clerical marriage, discipline and with the marriage of the laity).

them, or making attacks on their property were strongly condemned; but priests who shed blood, cohabited with women, or used their sacramental powers to extract money from their flock (it was assumed) could be just as offensive to God as the laity. During these years around the turn of the tenth and eleventh centuries, issues relating to the reform of religion – like the 'purification' of the clergy – do not seem to have been regarded by contemporaries as distinct from secular problems of the peace, although historians have often not treated these as interdependent issues. A failure by members of the clergy to conform to the norms established for their order could be just as harmful to the 'divine peace' as attacks by layman on clerics and the Church, and it is anachronistic for historians to assess the issues of the late tenth and early eleventh centuries by the standards of a 'post-Gregorian' world. During these earlier years the promotion of peace, it seems to have been felt, depended on the definition and imposition of clerical norms and standards, as well as on the realisation of temporal peace; but neither as yet had been achieved.[59]

War, like peace, had a sacral character in the early Middle Ages. It is valuable for historians to be reminded that during the early Middle Ages, if contemporaries thought of a duality of 'peace and war', peace was not necessarily perceived as being the positive term of a related ' sistema linguistico-concettuale'.[60] The implications of this are perhaps difficult to grasp for individuals born into a modern world in which an outbreak of war would inevitably be interpreted as involving both the failure, and the extinction, of peace. The sacral quality (or associations) of warfare are revealed through liturgical formulae for the blessing of armies and weapons, as well as through the magical and talismanic associations with which warriors surrounded their swords. Furthermore, these differing signs that war had a religious dimension apparently preceded the creation or diffusion of any liturgical *ordo* for the 'creation' of a knight by many years – possibly even by centuries.[61] Early medieval political and social historians neglect this point at their peril.

---

[59] During these years violence and unrest were undoubtedly matters of great concern, but explanations of the causes of human violence would have been more far-reaching than is likely to be the case to-day. Divine wrath and human sin might be more readily invoked than, for instance, the breakdown of 'central government' or an oppressive social organisation which might today be diagnosed as the chief failings of late tenth-century society. Not to recognise this distorts views of the prevailing '*mentalités*', in which so much interest has been professed by historians.

[60] Gina Fasoli, 'Pace e guerra nell'alto medioevo', in *Ordinamenti militari in occidente nell'alto medioevo*, 2 vols, Spoleto 1968 i, 17. The interdependence of peace and war in the minds even of clerics praising a secular ruler is conveyed by the poetic reference to the Emperor Charles the Great as a lover of 'the lilies of peace mixed in the rosebeds (*rosetis*) of war', also cited by Fasoli, 45.

[61] In her stimulating paper Fasoli makes comparisons with Hebraic and Roman practices, and refers to the widespread and recurrent view held in many traditional societies that the vanquished should be treated as sacrificial victims to the victors' gods, 'Pace e guerra', 21, 26, 28–47. The view that by the eleventh century there already existed a formula '*d'entrée en*

The effects of the peace movement on warriors' attitudes, together with the paradoxical impact which a religious conception of peace eventually had on ideas of the 'just war' have been widely studied by historians. By contrast, the possibility that a 'sacralised' view of war might co-exist with a religious conception of peace during these crucial decades of the late tenth and early eleventh centuries does not seem to have been seriously explored. And yet, there seem to be good grounds for arguing that this was the case in Aquitaine. Moreover, the chief exponent of that point of view was Adémar de Chabannes, the same ecclesiastic who has recently been regarded as the chief intellectual spokesman for the ideology of a religious peace. In his historical work Adémar undoubtedly supplies a great deal of detailed information about military activity, but as far as the present argument is concerned, it is not the events or the *diachronique* which are being considered, but the possibility that peace and war were both seen as being subsumed within a divine purpose. Warfare needed to be accommodated into a scheme of existence in which obtaining the 'palm of victory' could be interpreted as a sign of God's approval, so that the laity – and indeed occasionally even the clergy – might be praised for involvement in conflict. References scattered in his *Chronicle* show that Adémar considered that God ought to be invoked to further the aims of war as well as the end of peace.[62]

In the early medieval West the associations between religion and warfare had been widely accepted by clergy and laity alike. These associations must have helped contribute to the increasing 'militarisation' of the clergy which characterised the the later Carolingian era, and they account for the perpetuation of a number of inconsistencies in the attitudes towards armed or warring clergy. Within Aquitaine around the turn of the tenth and eleventh centuries, for instance, there are a significant number of references to the involvement of bishops in warlike activities, such as the building or destruction of castles; and it seems likely that – whatever had been laid down at the Council of Charroux – this would have necessitated the wearing of armour and the carrying of weapons. It is all the same a little surprising to find that Adémar, the tireless exponent of peace, did not always condemn such activity.

Adémar's ambivalence towards the involvement of clergy in war emerges most clearly from two rather different cases, the first concerning the same bishop of Limoges who put his subscription to the *acta* of the council of Charroux, and the second (of slightly later date) the abbot of 'the canons of Le Dorat'. Bishop Hilduin/Alduin is described as building fortifications to protect the abbey of St-Junien, in the company of the duke, but he also later provided armed support for his brother Guy, and the wording of the passage leaves little

---

*chevalerie*' has recently been strongly criticised by Flori, *L'essor*, 51, 369–86; idem, *L'idéologie*, 112–18. For an interesting exploration of the continuing importance attached to weapons, Emma Mason, 'The Hero's Invincible Weapon: an Aspect of Angevin Propaganda', *ante* iii, 1990, 121–37.

[62] See below, 171–4.

doubt that this meant participation in a military engagement which took place 'in the bitterest part of winter'.[63] Abbot Peter, on the other hand, through a series of genealogical mishaps was left alone in charge of the administration of La Marche, where he seemed 'terrible as a lion' and suppressed all opposition to his will. After a chequered career during which he seems to have granted *beneficia* to a whole troop of *milites*, and after a pilgrimage to Jerusalem, he eventually renounced his secular way of life. But Adémar does not directly criticise his earlier actions, or his fulfilment of a secular role – indeed, he notes that the duke appointed Abbot Peter as defender of the region during the minority of a young count of La Marche.[64]

The contemporary duke of Aquitaine is presented in an idealised fashion by Adémar de Chabannes in his *Chronicle*: 'he was thought to be king rather than duke' – and the attributes of royalty included leadership in war, followed by victory.[65] It would be going too far to suppose that Adémar presented all the ducal conflicts as 'just wars', but he occasionally comes remarkably close to such a position in emphasizing that Duke William 'the Great' subdued all those who attempted to rebel against his authority. For instance, the defeat of Count Boso of La Marche after the duke had 'engaged [him] strongly in battle' (*commisso fortiter bello*) was attributed to God's granting him the 'palm of victory'. It was ducal policy not only to subdue regional magnates and take their castles but also to extract oaths from them and to ensure that no one dared lift a hand against him.[66] Adémar's narrative history provides tantalising glimpses of the campaigns and sieges in which the duke engaged with allies and opponents, but – despite the monastic standpoint of the chronicler – this was still the violent world of secular conflict and antagonism which is presented elsewhere – say in the '*Conventum*' eventually agreed between this duke and Hugh of Lusignan, 'the leader of a thousand'. It is instructive also that on a number of occasions Adémar should record that the duke should exercise clemency and refuse to mutilate or execute those who fell into his hands. Although violence might be justified, and the duke 'stirred up by a great anger' to take revenge, he is

---

[63] *Chronique*, 165–6: . . . *Episcopus, adgregata armatorum inmanitate, habito in auxilio fratre Widone, ocurrit ei, et grave ortum est praelium tempore durioris hiemis.*

[64] *Chronique*, 167–8. The details of the account probably came to Adémar from a member of his own family, for his mother was the sister of one of the *consiliarii* of Abbot Peter.

[65] Adémar, *Chronique*, 163. Whether or not Adémar was presenting a balanced or factually correct account of this duke's career is not the issue here. For the view that 'often if not frequently . . . ecclesiastical intellectuals presented their wishful thinking or even their fantasies as reality', B. Bachrach, '*Potius rex quam esse dux putabatur*: some observations concerning Adémar de Chabannes' panegyric on Duke William the Great', *The Haskins Society Journal* i, 1989, 11–21 (12, n. 5); and cf. in particular Bachrach's earlier paper, 'Towards a re-appraisal of William the Great Duke of Aquitaine (995–1030)', *Journal of Medieval History* v, 1979, 11–21. For a more favourable view of this duke as 'politician', J. Dunbabin, *France in the Making*, 173–6.

[66] *Chronique*, 163–6, 207–8.

nevertheless portrayed as wishing to settle hostilities 'peacefully and reasonably'. But Adémar does not condemn the original display of fury.[67]

Adémar's attitude to war is most strikingly illustrated in his account of a pitched battle fought between Duke William the Great and a body of Norman marauders (possibly c.1015–16, although the conflict is difficult to date). He wrote (and, because of its importance it is necessary to cite the account fairly fully):

> At that time an infinite multitude of Norsemen from Denmark and the Irish region crossed the sea in a fleet too great to number. Confident in their arms they landed in this hostile multitude at an Aquitanian port close to the frontiers of Poitou. And, just as their ancient pagan ancestors had depopulated the countryside of Aquitaine, so again as a [force] of mixed pagans and Christians they tried to set fire to our villages, castles and cities, to exterminate or capture a Christian people by the sword, and to lay waste God's churches and monasteries. Then Duke William, undismayed and counting on Christ's victory, soon treated their great strength as nought. He sent orders throughout the monasteries of Aquitaine that all should beseech the Lord's mercy with fasts and litanies, so that He [i.e. God] should consume the strength of the enemy and should make His people victorious.[68]

The eventual outcome of battle did not really justify Adémar's conviction that God favoured the Poitevins rather than their opponents; however, the significance of the account lies in the picture which it gives of the two faces of peace and war in eleventh-century Aquitaine. But first it is necessary to return to the battlepiece. The scene is set with the duke's recruitment of a 'numerous and very strong force of picked warriors of Aquitaine', and in the *Chronicle* it is assumed that he was in complete control both of military preparations, and of the conduct of the battle. For instance, he is described just before nightfall making sure that his camp was ranged near the seashore, and his men prepared for battle on the morrow (*ad bellum*). Unfortunately the engagement which is described does not cast a very favourable light on the duke's tactical sense or military intelligence (in any sense of that term), since even divine inspiration did not prompt anyone to reconnoitre or to discover that the Normans for their part had spent the night digging ditches and covering them with stakes and

---

[67] For a very different view of the way in which ducal authority was expressed and implemented, *Conventum inter Guillelmum Aquitanorum comitem et Hugonem Chiliarchum*, ed. Martindale, *EHR* lxxxiv, 1969, 528–48.

[68] Adémar calls them *Normanni*, which I have translated 'Norse' to distinguish them from the 'Normans' of Normandy, *Chronique*, 208 (and see Delisle, 'Les manuscrits originaux', 332–41); for a less elaborate account given by Adémar, 176. The dating problems associated with this conflict are considerable. Although Adémar follows the incident with an account of the death of King Aethelred of England and Cnut's succession 'by treachery' (*dolo-* 177–8, correctly c.1015–16), the conflict has been attributed to the years c.1010–13, Richard, *Histoire des Comtes de Poitou* i, 173 n. 1, 174.

turves 'so that the warriors, unaware, should be brought down' (*ut ignorantes bellatores delaberentur*).

The inevitable therefore occurred soon after the first charge. The duke rode:

> on a very swift horse, [but] . . . soon the horses with their riders were brought down by the ditches. And because the weight of their arms made them heavy, many were captured by the Normans. But divine piety snatched the duke away . . . [Although] When he suffered a fall, he was almost captured by the Normans, and in spite of the great weight of the helmet on his head and the cuirass on his shoulders (?), employing very great strength he leapt a long way beyond the ditch, and rejoined his own men.[69]

As a battle this engagement was something of an anticlimax, because, according to Adémar, the duke then retired from the field:

> for fear of those men who had fallen first and were now held captive (thirty were among the noblest), lest they might be slaughtered by the Norsemen . . . The duke ransomed his men who had been captured, [and after] he had sent ambassadors to the Norsemen and paid over a huge weight of gold and silver . . . he received them safe.

It is interesting to find that a lord was expected to ransom his men captured in battle; but otherwise Adémar seems to have been putting the best interpretation possible on a rather ignominious defeat when he commented that the Normans never again returned 'to our shores'.[70]

The account given by Adémar de Chabannes of the duke's attempt to repel the Norse marauders from the Atlantic seaboard of Aquitaine describes a military engagement in which the army collected from ducal territories certainly fought as 'cavalry'. No information is given about the tactics employed by the *'multitudo Normannorum'*, but it seems unlikely that they fought on horseback.[71] However, even if the ducal army was relying on more 'advanced' tactics than their opponents', Adémar's vocabulary in describing this 'prepared force of

---

[69] *Chronique*, 209 – a free translation which admittedly has not solved all the problems of an originally difficult passage. The Latin seems to me to state that the duke was unhorsed and clambered out of the ditch on foot, although Richard's narrative account implies that the ducal horse only stumbled and then (because of its rider's admirable horsemanship) leapt clear, *Histoire de Comtes de Poitou* i, 172–4.

[70] . . . *nec amplius apposuerunt venire in nostros fines*, ibid. However, this was also an accurate statement, and the author was possibly looking back at an event which occurred about twenty years earlier.

[71] For references to Scandinavian military engagements of the eleventh century in Ireland and elsewhere see the interesting survey by L. Musset, 'Problèmes militaires du monde scandinave', in *Ordinamenti militari* i, 245–53. The tactics employed on the Poitevin shore would hardly have been appropriate for a battle in which the *Normanni* expected to fight on horseback; furthermore, it seems unlikely that on this occasion the Norsemen could have had time to raid inland to obtain horses.

Aquitanians' is resolutely traditional and old-fashioned. For him the army was composed of *pugnatores* or *bellatores*; and the only distinctions which he introduced were social rather than military or professional, as can be seen from his reference to the 'nobler' captives taken when the duke's horsemen were brought down by the enemy's carefully placed ditches. Despite the obvious dangers involved, the ruler and his noblest men had fought in the frontline – and Adémar's account was seemingly designed for readers who would have expected such leadership as a sign of *noblesse oblige*.[72]

Adémar's portrayal of warfare is instructive, and its religious dimensions seem to reflect and complement his presentation of peace. Peace was highly valued, and descriptions of the means employed to secure peace certainly often occupy the foreground of his densely packed narrative; but war in itself is not criticised or condemned, for it provided the only available means of 'subjugating' magnates and other men who might be unwilling to accept the superior political authority of the duke and a number of his counts. War also had to be employed to drive off the force of 'part Christian and part pagan' Norsemen from Denmark and Ireland who had revived memories of the long years when their entirely pagan ancestors 'depopulated the countryside of Aquitaine'. It is too often assumed that by the early eleventh century there was no longer any need in Western Europe for defence against a 'heathen' enemy sweeping down unpredictably on a rural population; but, although the number and intensity of attacks certainly decreased during the course of the tenth century, it must have been a long while before a region's inhabitants could be convinced that they were rid of the danger of sudden attack. In Aquitaine there was still a need for defence against opponents who could be presented as the enemy common to to all Christians.[73]

Against enemies like the Norsemen it was necessary to call on religious invocation, in addition to relying on the military support of the trained warriors of Aquitaine. During the same decades that the the English population was being ordered by king and bishops to fast so that God might avert His wrath – manifested through the Danish attacks on Æthelred's kingdom – the Poitevin duke of Aquitaine also hoped to secure protection from Norse attacks through religious intercession for the inhabitants of his territories. As has been seen, Adémar's account of the military engagement is preceded by a reference to the ducal command ordering all the monasteries in Aquitaine to call on the Lord's mercy with 'fasts and litanies', and prayers for victory. '*Quod et factum est*', wrote Adémar, as apparently convinced by the sequence of cause and effect, as he was

---

[72] The use of the rather awkward phrase *equi cum sessoribus suis* (ibid.) perhaps implies that there would have been ambiguity at this time in employing even a term like *equites* to denote a body of armed horsemen.

[73] Thus it would be misleading to suppose that through the 'peace movement' ecclesiastics could divert the attention of the laity to problems of internal violence because warriors had now turned to quarrelling among themselves – the 'diachronic' was not so simple.

by the therapeutic effect which was operated by St Martial during the *pestilentia ignis*. His chronicle provides a further example of closeness of the associations between warfare and religion during these decades, although this second incident refers to the Mediterranean, rather than to the Atlantic, coast. It is concerned with the descent of a naval force of 'Moors from Cordoba' who poured by night onto the land around Narbonne, in the hopes of taking that city by storm. In the account of this conflict the supernatural forces invoked by the 'Christian' and 'Saracen' opponents are given greater weight. A modern reader might almost interpret Adémar's account as part of a magical conflict, for certainly Adémar attributes greater fortifying power to the Eucharist (which was offered to the Christians by their priests), than he does to the 'spells' available to their opponents. The Christians, provided with 'the body and blood of Christ', were victorious against all the odds. The Moors, on the other hand – at least according to Adémar – had been duped by the false spells of their 'soothsayer' who had promised them success in battle: their fate was death or captivity.[74]

The oblique approaches to the topics of knights and chivalry in this paper were adopted because it seemed desirable to draw attention to some of the problems resulting from making too close a connection between the peace councils of the early eleventh century and the emergence of a chivalric order. The political organisation and the social structure of Aquitaine at this time were far more intricate than has normally been supposed and, unless the account of these is revised, it is unlikely that views on the shaping of 'knighthood' in this region of Aquitaine will be much further advanced. In particular, the wider context of the 'peace councils' needs to be borne in mind, as do the ambiguities of the relationship between clergy and laity at this period. In some respects at least the activity of the higher clergy at this time seems to hark back to the warrior clergy of the late Carolingian era – and forward to the battling Archbishop Turpin of the *Song of Roland*. Moreover, it may be misleading to separate the issues of peace from those of war as completely as many historians have done. Certainly God's aid, His saints and their relics would be invoked for both war and for peace.

[74] *Chronique*, 175. Although the Christians had gone into battle expecting death, instead they gained a complete victory – and 'much booty' (*multis spoliis*). It seems strange that neither of these two incidents was noted by Erdmann, although he comments on Adémar's interest in Norman attacks on Muslim Spain and also on Normanno-Byzantine relations, 110 (Eng. edn). On the 'miraculous' and the Eucharistic sacrament, Morison, 'The Miraculous', 16–18 and for 'the consecrated elements themselves . . . as a permanent focus of power', B. Ward, *Miracles and the Medieval Mind*, revised edn London 1987, 16.

NOTE ON THE DATING OF THE EARLY PEACE COUNCILS HELD IN
DUCAL TERRITORIES IN AQUITAINE.

As a sequence of regional councils which need to be related to contemporary
secular and ecclesiastical affairs, one of the chief problems associated with the
early 'peace' meetings held in Aquitaine is the absence of firm dates. Those
which have been attributed by historians have often become conventional over
the years, although they are not necessarily any more convincing through being
endlessly repeated. When this paper was first presented this problem was
avoided in the hopes that these difficulties would already have been discussed in
the necessary detail in the more extended study of ducal government already
mentioned (see above, 153, n. 14). Since this has not yet been completed, the
following observations are intended as a summary to draw attention to difficulties which have a bearing on the regional interpretation of the peace councils'
material.

1. The dates now frequently ascribed to the two councils held at Charroux
and Poitiers can be traced back to early printed editions. (a) The text of the
Charroux canons bears the heading *Concilium . . . celebratum Kal. Iuniis, anno
Christi circiter DCCCCLXXXIX, Acta conciliorum* vi, cols 717–18 (see above
n. 1. (b) The council of Poitiers is headed *Concilium Pictavense . . . celebratum,
Idibus Ianuarii, anno Christi circiter millesimo, Acta conciliorum* vi, cols 763–4 (also
see above n. 28). Very few subsequent commentators on these councils have
troubled to return to the question of where Labbe obtained the sources for his
editions (both were described as being taken *ex codice Engolismensi Joann. Tilii*);
although Erdmann identified the MS as Vatican *Reginensis* lat. 1127 – a compilation whose contents are otherwise relatively well-known (but cannot be discussed here). There can be little doubt that Vat. Reginensis is the Angoulême
MS because it contains an episcopal list for this *civitas*, brought up to date by
different hands, Duchesne, *Fastes Épiscopaux* ii, 64–6, above n. 33). The significant point is that Erdmann drew attention to the absence of any dating within
the body of the text apart from the record of the day and month, and noted that
the only means of accurately dating the councils was by means of the *Bischofs-
namen*, Erdmann, 336 (Exkurs II, *Zur Überlieferung der Gottesfriedens-Konzilien*,
German edn only).

2. Between the *acta* of these two councils and the late 1020s–1031 no further
accounts have survived of conciliar proceedings held at the command, or within
the orbit, of the dukes of Aquitaine; although the sermons and historical works
attributed to Adémar de Chabannes include fairly frequent references to 'peace'
gatherings in Limoges and elsewhere. Either no decrees survive for these meetings, or none were ever enacted.

3. (a) The council held at Bourges is dated to 1 Nov. 1031, by a synodal letter
drawn up in the name of Archbishop Aymo of Bourges, *anno incarnationis
dominicae MXXXI, indictione xv, in concilio Bituricensi quod actum est Kalendis*

175

*Novembris, Acta conciliorum* vi, col. 852. The *capitula* pronounced during the council are printed, ibid., cols 840–51. (b) The Limoges council proceedings are incomplete and, in their present form, preserve a would-be *verbatim* account of sessions held on the 18–19 November, *XIV Kalendas Decembris* and *XIII kalendas Decembris*, ibid., cols 854, 875.

The problems relating to the councils of Bourges and Limoges bear some resemblances to those connected with the earlier councils already considered; although critical attention has chiefly been attracted to the question of whether the accounts of these gatherings were 'contaminated' by Adémar de Chabannes in the interest of promoting the cause of St Martial's 'apostolicity' since, in the form in which these texts survive, a considerable amount of time must have been spent during both councils debating that issue, *Acta conciliorum* vi, cols 848–9, 853–73, cf. above, 159. The texts for both councils derive from a single MS, Bib. Nat. lat. 2469; but complications arise from the fact that the Bourges canons form part of a 'council within a council', although generally edited as though they had an existence independent from the Limoges proceedings, see Delisle, 'Les manuscrits originaux', 282–4. The interrelationship between the later and earlier councils is made plain by a reference within the account of the council of Limoges to the archbishop's calling for the reading of the *capitula Bituricensis concilii* (which had taken place at an earlier date), ibid., col. 879 = fo 107, the account of the later council begins fo 97).

# Perversion of an Ideal

PETER NOBLE

Romance is not a safe guide to the realities of twelfth- and thirteenth-century knighthood.[1] By definition Arthurian romance is set against a background of the court of a legendary Celtic hero in lands which were either fantastical or at least strange to many in the audience. Many of the main characters, Arthur, Guinevere, Gawain, Kay and Perceval had already existed in Celtic literature and came into French Arthurian Romance with established characters which had to be adapted to the new audience and the new social setting. Nevertheless, these heroes did all belong to the knightly class (and if they were not already knights, like Cligés in Chrétien de Troyes, they quickly became knights) and, as Maurice Keen has pointed out: 'From a very early stage we find the romantic authors habitually associating together certain qualities which they clearly regarded as the classic virtues of good knighthood; prouesse, loyauté, largesse (generosity), courtoisie, and franchise (the free and frank bearing that is visible testimony to the combination of good birth with virtue). The association of these qualities in chivalry is already established in the romances of Chrétien de Troyes (written c.1165–85), and from his time on to the end of the middle ages their combination remains the stereotype of chivalrous distinction.'[2] The romances are, however, providing 'an ideal of knighthood culled from what appears so often to be essentially a literature of escape . . .',[3] and Marie-Louise Chênerie has shown how the fabliaux give a more realistic glimpse of contem-

---

1 For further information about the twelfth century see T. Hunt, 'The Emergence of the Knight in France and England 1000–1200', and L. Paterson, 'Knights and the Concept of Knighthood in the twelfth-century Occitan Epic', in Knighthood and Medieval Literature, ed. W. H. Jackson, Woodbridge 1981, 1–38. See also P. Rousset, 'La description du monde chevaleresque chez Orderic Vital', Moyen Age lxxv, 1969, 427–44, especially 431–33 where details are given of the chevalier pillard.
2 M. Keen, Chivalry, New Haven and London 1984, 4.
3 Keen, 5.

porary life, especially with regard to the tournaments where physical and financial damage could be serious.[4] In addition, these gatherings inevitably attracted
criminals of all sorts, but particularly loose women, to relieve the knights of any
winnings as quickly as possible (p. 347 and p. 355) and were denounced by, for
example, Jacques de Vitry.[5] Even in romance, however, there are hints of this as
Chênerie shows (p. 348), citing texts from *Le Conte du Graal* and *Guiron le
Courtois*, and the real world can be seen in other circumstances as well.[6] Heroes
need villains to defeat so that they can prove their heroism. Wars against
foreigners which dominate the pages of Wace and Geoffrey of Monmouth can
supply only part of the challenge in their successors, who, from Chrétien on,
focus much more on the individual and thus need individualised enemies, most
of whom have to be identified, as a succession of nameless opponents becomes
boring. Similarly, too many supernatural or other-worldly challenges risk destroying any belief in the character by the audience, so that other knights must
frequently be the enemy.

There are three main areas in which a knight can fall from the ideal, so that
he is branded as evil. These are politics, sex and lack of chivalry. Politics covers
the rebellion of the knight against his lord so that he becomes a traitor, whether
the lord is Arthur himself or another, and thus breaks his oath of loyalty. Sex
covers two different acts, either rape or betrayal by abandoning a lady in pursuit
of another. Lack of chivalry means the way that knights behave to each other
and how far they respect chivalrous standards, such as granting mercy to a
defeated opponent who asks for it or treating guests with hospitality, whoever
they may turn out to be. None of these is confined to the thirteenth-century
romances, of course. The treason of Mordred seems to be as old as the Arthurian
legend itself,[7] and in Chrétien's *Cligés* Count Angrés rebels against Arthur
during the latter's absence in Brittany.[8] In *Perlesvaus* Kay, normally one of
Arthur's closest friends and supporters, is a traitor and a rebel.[9] In sex, too, the
twelfth century provides examples of both rape and betrayal. Even if the rapes of
Helena of Brittany and her aged nurse by the giant in Wace and Geoffrey are set
aside, Enide is on the point of being raped by Count Oringle in *Erec et Enide*
when he forces her to marry him and there is the burlesque scene in the
*Chevalier de la Charrete* when Lancelot sees his hostess stripped to the waist and
about to be raped by two knights.[10] Although not quite as reprehensible as some

[4] M.L. Chênerie, ' "Ces curieux chevaliers tournoyeurs . . .". Des fabliaux aux romans',
*Romania* xcvii, 1976, 327–68.
[5] Chênerie, 347 and 355.
[6] Chênerie, 348.
[7] K.H. Jackson, 'The Arthur of History', in *Arthurian Literature in the Middle Ages*, ed. R.S.
Loomis, Oxford 1959, 4–5.
[8] *Cligés*, ed. A. Micha, Paris 1957.
[9] *Perlesvaus*, ed. W.A. Nitze and T.A. Jenkins, Chicago 1932.
[10] *Erec et Enide* ed. M. Roques, Paris 1952. *Le Chevalier de la Charrete*, ed. M. Roques, Paris
1958.

of the later examples, Yvain in the *Chevalier au Lion* betrays Laudine by forget-ting his promise to her to return by a fixed date, with the result that she casts him off as a faithless, worthless lover and knight. An obvious example of a knight who fails to observe the chivalrous code in his treatment of other knights is Meleagant in the *Chevalier de la Charrete*, who poisons Kay's wounds which his father is trying to heal and later treacherously captures and imprisons Lancelot in the hope of preventing Lancelot from attending the duel arranged between them. All these examples, Yvain excepted, are of characters who are seen to be evil or outsiders, men on the fringes of the Arthurian world, who are punished deservedly by the knights of Arthur's court who thus reassert the standard of behaviour and the moral code expected from true knights.

In the thirteenth century, however, a change can be detected in that some of the miscreants are members of Arthur's court or ancestors of the hero and therefore are not censured to the same extent for their behaviour. As already mentioned, Kay becomes a murderer and a traitor in *Perlesvaus*, while in *Yder* Arthur himself, in the ungrateful role of the jealous husband, plots the murder of Yder.[11] In the *Prose Lancelot* Arthur is an adulterer sleeping with both the pagan Saxon enchantress Camille, and the false Guinevere, who successfully usurps the place of the true Guinevere.[12] In *La Mort le roi Artu* Lancelot and the whole of the kindred of King Ban find themselves reluctantly forced into open war against King Arthur as a result of the discovery of the adultery of Lancelot and Guinevere.[13] Thus, from the early years of the thirteenth century, the elite knights of Arthur's court and Arthur himself are seen to fall far short of the ideal.

This slippage in standards can be seen in three texts from later in the century, the *Tristan en Prose*, dating from between 1215 and 1235 according to Renée Curtis (at least as far as the first part is concerned, which is the part discussed here) but, since it is heavily influenced by the *Prose Lancelot*, the date seems likely to be towards the end of that period;[14] *Claris and Laris*, which is after 1268 according to Micha, a vast 30,000 line romance by an unknown poet, and *Escanor* by Girart d'Amiens, which is dedicated to Eleanor of Castile, wife of Edward I of England, and dating from 1279–80.[15]

Examples of treason can be found in all the texts under consideration. In the *Prose Tristan* two knights who are close kin to King Melyadeus, the father of Tristan, plot to murder the baby Tristan whom they find in the forest where his mother has just given birth to him before dying. With the queen dead and the king lost, bewitched by an enchantress, they realise that only the baby stands

---

11 *The Romance of Yder*, ed. A. Adams, Cambridge 1983.
12 *Le Roman de Lancelot en Prose*, ed. A. Micha, Geneva 1978–83.
13 *La Mort le roi Artu*, ed. J. Frappier, 3rd edn, 1964.
14 *Le Roman de Tristan en Prose*, ed. R.L. Curtis, Munich 1963.
15 *Claris et Laris*, ed. J. Alton, Tübingen 1884, reprinted Amsterdam 1966. *Escanor*, ed. H. Michelant, Tübingen 1886.

between them and the throne of Lyonnesse. Only the frantic pleading of the queen's lady-in-waiting, who promises that she will keep the baby hidden where he can never be found, saves the life of the infant Tristan. The plot is frustrated by the intervention of Merlin who reveals the guilt of the two knights to the people of Lyonnesse and also tells them how to rescue Melyadeus. Without this supernatural intervention, however, there would have been a sordid coup d'etat by two knights, members of the royal family, who would not have shrunk from murder to achieve their treasonable end. In *Claris et Laris* the king of Northumberland is one of the knights of Arthur's court who is making his way to Denmark to help Laris rescue Marine, the sister of Yvain, with whom Laris is desperately in love. As he stops at a castle for the night, the old castellan who owns it tells him that he is a subject of the king of Northumberland to whom he is loyal. A neighbouring duke has killed his two sons (lines 25219–23) and is now trying to make the castellan swear fealty to him instead of his true lord, the king. Sagremor, who is travelling with the king, undertakes to fight the duke on behalf of his host and rapidly defeats him (line 25342). He demands that the duke go to seek peace from the king of Northumberland but the duke immediately recognises the king and throws himself on his mercy there and then. The king treats him with remarkable courtesy, considering the way in which the duke had been oppressing the castellan.

> 'Certes, bons dus, frans, gentis sire!
> Fait il, 'roy sui ge voirement
> Et ai en mon comandement
> Norhombelande, la contree,
> Qui est en mainz leus renonmee;
> Quite vous claim vostre mesfet,
> Que encontre moi avez fet;
> Ja mes nen orrez plus parler
> En quel leu que doiez aler. (25385–25393)

> 'Certainly, good Duke, noble, well-born lord,' he said, 'I am really the king and have in my power the country of Northumberland which is well-known in many places; I pronounce you absolved of your crime which you did to my harm; never again will you hear it mentioned in whatever place you may go.'

The castellan and the duke both do homage to the king (line 25408), and the incident is closed. What is striking is the way in which the very serious offences of the duke are just dismissed. The episode is a chance for Sagremor to add to his conquests, for the king of Northumberland to right an injustice on the way to Denmark and to display his clemency to another great noble. No moral is drawn from the episode.

In *Escanor* treason is one of the major themes of the romance. Andrivete, princess of Northumberland, is heiress to her father's kingdom, but when he dies leaving her unmarried her position is vulnerable. The principal suitor for her hand is Kay, the seneschal of King Arthur, who had won the tournament of Bauborc, which her father had arranged to find a suitable husband for her. Kay, however, was too shy to press his suit at the appropriate moment, although he and Andrivete are in love. This lack of a powerful male protector gives Andrivete's uncle, Ayglin, the chance to seize power despite the support for her from the people of the towns. Ayglin is determined to prevent the marriage to Kay, who has too many powerful friends as well as being a mighty warrior himself. At first he keeps Andrivete a prisoner but then he plots to marry her to a man of no rank.

> et la voloit par mariage
> meller a .i. povre lignage,
> qui n'eust force ne puissance
> vers lui de nulle chose nee.   (9312–16)

> and he wanted to join her in marriage to a poor family
> who would have no strength or power against him in any
> way at all.

Only the escape of Andrivete frustrates this plan. The poet blames 'covoitise' (line 9300) as the cause of the trouble. Ayglin had intrigued before the death of the old king to prevent the marriage of Kay and Andrivete. Now that the king is dead, there is no-one sufficently powerful in Northumberland to resist Ayglin, although Yonet, an honest knight and castellan, remains loyal to Andrivete. Ayglin sends forged letters to make Kay believe that Andrivete has deserted him, but in the end his lengthy resistance is in vain. As Arthur and his forces approach Northumberland to put Andrivete on her throne, Ayglin finds that his support melts away (lines 23991–93), and Kay and Andrivete are established as rulers of her country. The story illustrates well, if at great length, the vulnerability of a great heiress with powerful and unscrupulous male relations. Once her father is dead, Andrivete is helpless in the face of Ayglin's intrigues. He is aiming at the throne for himself and is described as one:

> ... qui ert maus
> et traitres et desloiaus.   (6736–37)

> ... an evil man and treacherous and disloyal.

Despite his patent treachery and the covert opposition of many who are loyal to Andrivete, he is able to control the kingdom with his armed followers and overawe any potential opponents. It takes outside intervention to defeat this act of treason by one of the rightful heir's own family and someone who is of the highest rank in the country.

In cases of sex there are almost too many examples to choose from. The

*Tristan en Prose* opens with a lengthy introduction establishing the ancestry of the hero and tracing his family back to the nephews of Joseph of Arimathea. One of them, Sador, prefers to choose his own bride rather than have a bride selected for him by Joseph. He marries a beautiful ship-wrecked Babylonian princess, Chelinde. One day while Sador is hunting, his brother, Naburzadan, rapes Chelinde. Sador then kills his brother and has to flee with Chelinde. This is only the start of a series of adventures in the course of which Chelinde is married to Canor of Cornwall, Pelias of Lyonnesse and eventually her own son by Sador, Apollo of Lyonnesse. Because of Chelinde's beauty Pelias seduced her while he was staying at the court of Cornwall where she was Canor's queen. Pelias tried to murder Canor and then, believing him dead, made war on the defenceless kingdom. Later, after the deaths of Canor, Sador and Pelias, Apollo, now king of Lyonnesse and unaware of who his parents are, has to choose a wife from amongst the widows and maidens of the kingdom. The most beautiful is Chelinde and he marries her, his own mother. Chelinde has been raped by her brother-in-law, undergone a forced marriage with Canor and been seduced unwittingly by Pelias whom she mistook for Canor. Naburzadan is condemned in the words of Chelinde and Sador for the rape which has brought shame on them, but Sador certainly sees it as a feudal insult to be avenged. He accuses Naburzadan of having shamed him without first challenging him and so, before he kills Naburzadan, he takes care to challenge him. The rest of Chelinde's adventures seem to be attributed to her beauty and although the men may not be behaving creditably, they are not severely censured except in so far as the disasters which follow their surrender to lust are punishment.

The *Tristan en Prose* reveals a different attitude to love from the earlier Tristan poems in which the hero was faithful to Iseult and in which there is no suggestion of any earlier love for Tristan. In the prose version Tristan is the object of the affections of Belide, daughter of the king of France, who, when he spurns her, first accuses him falsely of attempted rape and then, when Tristan wisely decides to leave France, commits suicide. Tristan is too young, aged twelve or thirteen at this time, to respond but when he is at the court of Mark of Cornwall, his uncle, the most beautiful woman there is the wife of Seguradés, one of Mark's knights. Mark himself is in love with her, but to his fury she prefers Tristan who this time is not so unresponsive, although he has to survive an ambush by Mark to reach her and make love to her as arranged. The affair comes to an end when Bliobleris, a knight of the kingdom of Logres (one of Arthur's men) comes to the court to claim a boon from Mark. The boon is granted and he chooses the wife of Seguradés, easily defeating the attempt of Seguradés to rescue her. Tristan dare not move because of the enmity of Mark but two days later he does overtake the couple and challenge Bliobleris. After a savage but inconclusive fight they agree to leave the choice to the lady who is put half way between them. To Tristan's dismay she chooses Bliobleris, saying tartly that she has no opinion of Tristan since he let her be removed from Mark's court without resistance. In other words, in her eyes he betrayed her and thus has forfeited any claim to her love. The episode is one of gallantry, but it diminishes the effect of Tristan the singe-minded lover. He is a courtly knight, a seducer of other men's wives on a par with the gallant knights of Arthur's court such as Gawain. Of course, it is a narrative device to get rid of a lady who would have been an obstacle to his love for Iseult and the whole affair is there to deepen the enmity between Mark and Tristan, rivals for the same woman, but it is not essential to the development of the plot. Its presence changes the character of Tristan and not for the better.

In *Claris et Laris* Claris twice saves girls from rape. In one episode Gauvain and his *amie* are attacked by four knights who want to avenge their cousin, killed by Gauvain. Gauvain is unarmed and so is captured by two of the knights while the other two pursue the girl to rape her. Laris rescues Gauvain while Claris goes after the girl and reaches her just as she is trying to fight off her attackers (lines 2566–68). The second attempted rape takes place when Claris is riding through a dark forest. He comes across a knight on top of a girl who again is trying to fight him off. Claris intervenes, the knight hastily pulls on his armour and mounts his horse to defend himself but is quickly unhorsed and left with a broken arm, to the great joy of his intended victim. These are nameless knights but Gauvain's own brother Mordret tries rape (line 23905) and is captured by the brothers of his victim. He is rescued by an extremely angry Gauvain, who does, however, make his peace for him. Gauvain denounces Mordret.

> 'Gars', fet il, 'trop eus grant tort,
> Qu'ainsi honnir la voliez;
> Certes, se mes le faisiez,
> Le chief m'i leriez en gage ...' (24020–3)

> 'Wretch', he said, 'you do far too great a wrong when you want to shame her in this way; certainly, if you were ever to do it, you would leave your head as a token with me ...'

Mordret, of course, has had a bad reputation since the beginning of the legend, but he is a knight of the Round Table and Gauvain's reaction shows just how seriously he views the offence.

It is one of the heroes, Laris, who is guilty of the most obvious act of betrayal. He and Claris are trapped in a town in a valley enchanted by Morgain la Fee and her companions, one of whom, Madoine, falls desperately in love with Laris. He seduces her and learns how to escape from the town and the valley, which he and Claris do, leaving her pregnant. She remains faithful and attempts to win him back, but the poet assures us that Laris is not to be blamed for rejecting her:

> Mes Laris ne la puet amer,
> De ce ne le doit nus blamer,
> Car a force le veult avoir ... (10141–43)

> But Laris cannot love her, for this no-one must blame
> him for she wants to have him by force . . .

Be that as it may, he rejects her with increasing brutality as the poem continues and his own love for Marine, the sister of Yvain, develops. He shows no interest in the child which Madoine is to bear him and appears selfish and heartless, despite the effort of the poet to defend him. He is even prepared to betray his own sister for the love of his friend, Claris. Laris's sister, Lidoine, is married to the king of Gascony and Claris falls desperately in love with her. Although she loves him too, Lidoine is virtuous and rejects him which causes him to fall ill. Laris is furious and threatens to burn her if Claris dies (lines 8094–95). He insists that she put herself at the disposal of Claris (*a son comandement*) but Lidoine holds firm, describing it as *outrage*, and she will consent to nothing more than a kiss which, fortunately, is enough. A sister's honour was of little importance to Laris when his friend was the suitor.

In *Escanor* Mordret and Dinadan rescue a girl from Brunz sans pitié who has just killed her *ami*. Brunz is a notorious oppressor of women and is clearly bent on rape but he has no stomach for a contest with the two knights of the Round Table. After a fruitless chase Mordret explains to Kay, who has just arrived, the wickedness of Brun to any woman he encounters (lines 1012*ff.*).

Knights suffer at the hands of other knights almost as much as women do. In the *Tristan en Prose* Mark of Cornwall is rebuked by his brother Pernehan for failing to resist the Morholt, who has arrived from Ireland to claim the tribute due from the Cornish. He threatens to take over the kingdom from Mark, but, although Mark is a coward, he is not a fool and he murders Pernehan a few days later. In this way Mark confirms his unsuitability to be a king but he also secures his throne against any challenge. Mark's character in the *Prose Tristan* is consistently blackened and right from the start he is shown to be a coward, a murderer and unfit to be a king. As a result, of course, there is no chance that the audience will feel any sympathy with him in his role as a deceived husband.

In *Claris et Laris*, on the death of the king of Gascony, the king of Spain invades his lands to avenge a previous defeat. Lidoine is betrayed by her men to the king of Spain and is sent to Spain as a prisoner. Arthur condemns the actions of Savari of Spain.

> Li rois d'Espaigne d'autre part
> Ne fait pas bien, se dieux me gart,
> Quant vostre seror fait outrage,
> Ge le tieng a molt grant folage.  (13622–25)

> 'The King of Spain on the other hand is not acting hon-
> ourably, so God help me, when he attacks your sister, I
> consider him to be utterly crazy.'

Savari has acted wrongly towards both the dead man and his widow and in the end is defeated. Only the intervention of a mighty external power brings this about, however. Otherwise he would have conquered Gascony and held Lidoine.

In *Escanor* Gauvain is accused before Arthur's court of treacherously killing his challenger's cousin. The challenger remains incognito and Gauvain reacts very badly to this. Overcome with worry and depression, he prepares for the combat in a very downcast state. His comrade Girflet is so upset that he discusses with his younger brother, Galentivet, who is still a squire, what is to be done. Without anyone's knowledge, Galentivet prepares an ambush for the challenger and in the missing part of the poem wounds him so badly that his followers think that he is about to die. The challenger is, in fact, Escanor, but Gauvain's reputation suffers even more as a result of the ambush, because two of Escanor's maidens denounce Gauvain before the court of Arthur. The attempted murder is never solved, although Girflet has his suspicions. Because it is his brother, he never voices them and with the recovery of Escanor the matter fades into the background. Nevertheless it is a scandalous breach of the knightly code and of the laws of hospitality which reflects very badly on Arthur's court. Girflet is one of the leading knights. That his younger brother should stoop to murder to try to help a friend shows the deterioration in knightly standards.

The episodes cited are only a sample of the possible examples of rape, murder, betrayal and non-knightly behaviour to be found in the three works under consideration. A comprehensive survey of such episodes in thirteenth-century prose and verse romances is obviously outside the scope of this article. Nevertheless it is clear that in the thirteenth century authors could easily visualise members of the court of Arthur, which was supposed to incarnate the virtues of chivalry, behaving in ways which completely negated everything which they were supposed to defend. It is possible to argue in the case of the *Tristan en Prose* that the court of Cornwall and Cornish knights were a byword for cowardice and evil so that they are deliberately contrasted with the knights of the Round Table, of which Tristan eventually becomes a member, but some of the knights of the Round Table are shown to behave extremely badly. It can also be argued that the ancestors of Tristan and Mark were alive before knightly standards were devised, but the author does not advance this excuse. Love and lust are shown to be so powerful that they override all scruples. In *Escanor* Girard d'Amiens shows naked political ambition at work as an uncle cheats a niece out of her inheritance. The call of friendship is such that a young man will try to murder the unknown opponent of his friend who is preparing to meet that opponent in open and fair combat. In *Claris et Laris* the brother will sacrifice the honour and reputation of the sister to the health and lust of his friend. Betrayal, murder and rape are all part of the life of the thirteenth-century Arthurian characters. In addition, there are minor examples of the code of the knight being breached, as when Lamorat decries the beauty of Queen Iseult in front of her, comparing her unfavourably with the queen of Orkney. Iseult's rebuke is dignified but Lamorat, though a mighty warrior and lover, is shown, not for the last time, to lack courtesy. Claris and Laris kill some knights who have asked for mercy. The rebels in Brittany (in *Escanor*) slander Gauvain to an enchantress as a sodomite (line 1847) so that she will use her magic arts against him.

The prevailing impression is of a life of violence with the knights only partially defending the cause of justice. To be sure, most of the knights uphold righteous causes most of the time but lust, ambition, and even masculine friendship can all lead them astray. The diatribe at the beginning of *Claris et Laris* on the difference between the standards of the age of Arthur and the contemporary period (a time of *Honte*, *Avarice* and *Guerre* waged by the great barons, according to the author) sounds ironic in view of the contents of the poem; all the more so as the thirteenth century was less turbulent and anarchic than the twelfth as the power of central government increasingly asserted itself.[16]

[16] I would like to thank Dr Anne Curry for pointing this out to me.

# Arms and the Men: War, Loyalty and Lordship in Jordan Fantosme's Chronicle *

MATTHEW STRICKLAND

The Anglo-Norman poem of Jordan Fantosme must be ranked with the *Histoire de Guillaume le Maréchal* as one of the most important sources for the study of the *mentalité* of Anglo-Norman knighthood. Yet although the poem has long been known – it was edited for the Rolls Series by Howlett complete with an accompanying translation[1] – its study has been almost wholly the preserve of scholars of literature and prosody.[2] Historians have quarried the poem piecemeal for details concerning the great war of 1173–4 or for contemporary statements concerning the conduct of warfare, but there has been no sustained analysis of

* I would like to thank Bill Zajac and Professors Jim Holt and Archie Duncan for their helpful comments on this paper. Errors of detail and eccentricities of style remain mine alone.

1  *The Metrical Chronicle of Jordan Fantosme*, in *Chronicles and Memorials of the Reigns of Stephen, Henry II and Richard I* (hereafter *Chronicles and Memorials*), ed. R. Howlett, 4 vols, RS 1884–90, iii, 202–377.

2  For predominantly literary studies of Jordan see P.A. Becker, 'Jordan Fantosme, La Guerre d'Écosse: 1173–4', *Zeitschrift für romanische Philologie* lxiv, 1944, 449–556; I. Macdonald, 'The Chronicle of Jordan Fantosme. Manuscripts, Author and Versification', *Studies in Medieval French Presented to Alfred Ewart*, Oxford 1961, 242–58; D.M. Legge, *Anglo-Norman Literature and its Background*, Oxford 1963; R.C. Johnston, *The Versification of Jordan Fantosme*, Oxford 1974; R.C. Johnston, 'Jordan Fantosme's Experiments in Prosody and Design', *Mélanges de langue et littérature français du Moyen Ages offerts à P. Jonin*, Aix-en-Provence 1979, 355–67; *Jordan Fantosme's Chronicle* (hereafer JF), ed. and trans. R.C. Johnston, Oxford 1981, xxiii–xliii.

This article was read at Easter 1990 and completed before I became aware of the recent contribution by A. Lodge, 'Literature and History in the *Chronicle* of Jordan Fantosme', *French Studies* xliv, 1990, 257–270, though it is reassuring to find that Dr Lodge and myself have arrived independently at similar conclusions. I would like to thank Mr David Sherlock of English Heritage for drawing my attention to this paper.

Jordan as a source or discussion of the light he throws on attitudes to the Young King's rebellion and the self-perception of Henry II's baronage.[3]

Such neglect is remarkable given the unique nature of the poem. Unique, of course, is a dangerous word, but in many respects Jordan's poem stands *sui generis*. It is not a *chanson de geste*, a *lai* or a romance. The events and characters it describes are not only factual but strictly contemporary. Though far shorter than the *Histoire*,[4] it focuses less on the biography of a single protagonist, which in the case of William the Marshal dominates the content and focus of the work, but rather concerns the interactions of several important figures. Its chronology and subject matter are clearly defined; the revolt of Henry the 'Young King', eldest surviving son of Henry II, and the war of 1173–4, seen almost wholly from an insular standpoint and focusing particularly on the northern border.[5] Other than tantalizing inferences garnered from internal evidence, we possess virtually no conclusive evidence concerning the author – to whom I will return – but the poem can be dated with some confidence to between 1174 and 1183, and in all probability was composed shortly after the

---

[3] Jordan's poem has been drawn on, for example, by F.M. Powicke, *The Loss of Normandy*, Oxford 1913, 300–2; R.A. Brown, *English Castles*, 3rd edn, 1976, 194–8; and J. Gillingham, 'Richard I and the Science of War in the Middle Ages', *War and Government. Essays in Honour of J.O. Prestwich*, ed. J. Gillingham and J.C. Holt, Woodbridge 1984, 83–6. Fantosme is briefly discussed by A. Gransden, *Historical Writing in England c.550 to c.1307*, 1974, 236–8.

[4] Jordan's poem consists of only 2065 lines compared with the 19214 lines of the *Histoire de Guillaume le Maréchal* (*L'Histoire de Guillaume le Maréchal* (hereafter HGM), ed. P. Meyer, 3 vols, *Société de l'Histoire de France*, 1891–1901).

[5] The poem largely avoids Henry II's campaigns in Normandy, Anjou and Poitou. Thus we hear nothing of the siege of Verneuil by Louis VII or its successful relief by Henry which resulted in a humiliating flight for the king of France, events which dominated the campaigns of 1173. The siege of Drincourt and the defeat and capture of Ralph of Fougères and the earl of Chester at Dol in the opening stages of the war are briefly sketched (JF, lines 87–108, 119–239), but only as a dramatic background to the intervention of William the Lion. Thereafter, Jordan ignores the continental dimension of the war, and concentrates exclusively on hostilities on the Scottish border, on Robert of Leicester's invasion of East Anglia in 1173, and the war in the Midlands in 1174. For Jordan, the capture of William the Lion at Alnwick and the surrender of his brother, Earl David, at Leicester (ibid., lines 2033–2040), mark the effective end to the war. The siege of Rouen by King Louis, the count of Flanders and the Young King, which represented the chief allied effort of 1174, receives but three lines (ibid., lines 2045, 2062–2064).
The best succinct modern narratives of the war of 1173–4 are given by W.L. Warren, *Henry II*, 1973, 117–142, and J. Boussard, *Le Gouvernement d'Henri II Plantagenet*, Paris 1956, 474–88. Aspects of William the Lion's campaign's are discussed by M.J. Strickland, 'Securing the North. Invasion and the Strategy of Defence in Twelfth-Century Anglo-Scottish Warfare', *Anglo-Norman Studies* xii, 1989, 177–98. The war receives mention in many contemporary sources, but the fullest treatment is afforded by the *Gesta Henrici* of Roger of Howden (formerly attributed to Benedict of Peterborough), (*Gesta Henrici secundi Benedicti abbatis* (hereafter GH), ed. W. Stubbs, 2 vols, RS 1867, i, 41–82); by Ralph of Diceto (*Radulphi de Diceto decani Lundoniensis opera historica* (hereafter Diceto), ed. W. Stubbs, 2 vols, RS 1876, i, 355–98; and William of Newburgh, *Historia rerum Anglicarum* (hereafter WN), ed. R. Howlett in *Chronicles and Memorials* i, 169–98.

end of the war.[6] The poet repeatedly claims to be an eye witness to much of what he describes, including the capture of William the Lion at Alnwick in 1174,[7] and the validity of such claims has been accepted by the poem's most recent editor, R.C. Johnston.[8]

That Jordan's work is not merely versified history, a 'metrical chronicle' as Howlett misleadingly labelled it, is readily apparent, and Johnston has only kept the title as *Jordan Fantosme's Chronicle* for convenience.[9] Johnston's own work on the versification of the poem, however, has led him to make some pertinent comments on the nature of the work as a historical source which must be addressed. Briefly, Johnston's contention is that hitherto Fantosme's 'veracity has been assumed to have been guaranteed by the author's ingenuousness and technical weakness', that is to say that historians have regarded the poem essentially as a factual source rather than a literary piece because of his seemingly inept use of metre.[10] Johnston, however, has been at pains to rehabilitate Fantosme as 'a highly competent and innovative prosodist', arguing that his use of metre, once properly understood, reveals the poem as one of great sophistication, in which mood was subtly conveyed by changing metres and the whole built up from carefully arranged patterns of rhyming stanzas.[11] This realisation,

---

6  The poem ends abruptly with Henry's relief of Rouen, which occurred in August, 1174 (GH i, 74–6; Diceto i, 387; WN, 195–6). The peace treaty between Henry and his sons, ratified between Tours and Amboise at a conference beginning on October 11th (GH i, 77–9; Diceto i, 394–5), receives no mention, but the tenor of the poem strongly suggests a rapprochment between Henry and the Young King had already been effected. The *terminus ante quem* cannot be later than 1183, when the Young King died, once again in revolt, at Martel on June 11th (Diceto ii, 19; GH i, 300–1), but internal evidence points to a considerably earlier date. It is perhaps significant that Fantosme makes no mention of the Treaty of Falaise, which imposed far-reaching terms on William the Lion, or the great ceremony at York where the Scots king and his men performed homage to Henry II and the Young King (GH i, 94 9; *Anglo-Scottish Relations, 1174–1328*, ed. and tr. E.L.G. Stones, OMT 1965, 1–5). Legge, *Anglo-Norman Literature*, 75, suggested the composition date as 'most likely 1175 or even the end of 1174', a view with which Johnston is in full accord (JF, xxiii).

7  Speaking of the Scottish invasion of 1174 he notes: 'It was after Easter, as well I may remember, when the king of Scotland began his return to Northumberland to ravage and lay low. Ah! God! what great harm I saw come to them!' (JF, lines 1139–1142). Of the surprise at Alnwick he states, 'I relate no fable as one telling from hearsay, but as one who was on the spot, for I saw it all myself', and again says explicitly of William the Lion's capture 'this I saw with my own two eyes' (JF, lines 1669, 1804).

8  JF, xix. Johnston firmly rejects Legge's assertion that 'wild statements have been made that Fantosme was a sort of war reporter, partly owing to various clichés having been misinterpreted to mean that Fantosme was an eye witness to some of the events' (*Anglo-Norman Literature*, 75).

9  JF, xiv, where he suggests a more suitable title might be *Estoire del viel rei Henri*.

10  R.C. Johnston, 'The Historicity of Jordan Fantosme's Chronicle', *Journal of Medieval History* ii, 159–69, 162.

11  Ibid., 159–162. Johnston demonstrates that his mixture of decasyllabics, Alexandrines and a metre of his own devising was a deliberate and skilful artifice, not, as had been thought, the main indication of his lack of poetic ability. In the use of this mixed metre he appears as the successor to Elias of Winchester's *Afaitement Caton* and the precursor of Matthew Paris's *Vie*

189

he argues, forces a fundamental re-appraisal of Jordan as a source, for once his skill is recognised 'it makes a great deal of difference to the view we take of some of the vivid glimpses conveyed to us by Fantosme with little or no support from the Latin chroniclers'.[12] He points out incidents in the poem that smack of literary fabrication for didactic purposes[13] and challenges historians to distinguish between a 'truth of *Dictung* and a truth of *Wahrheit*'.[14]

That genre affects content, that art conceals art and that literature should not be quarried without due consideration of overall purpose and construction are clearly important caveats. Nevertheless, Johnston does not himself attempt to re-evaluate the historical, as opposed to the literary, importance of Jordan in the light of his own admonitions, nor are his assumptions of critical naivety on the part of historians wholly warranted.[15] That Jordan was writing poetry and not a metrical counterpart to William of Newburgh or Roger of Howden is as obvious to the reader now as it was to the thirteenth-century copyists who, in the two surviving manuscripts, placed the work after Wace's *Brut* and Gaimar's *Estoire des Engles*.[16] All three works treat historical subjects in literary forms, and thus in the loosest sense share a genre. But Jordan's poem differs from those of Wace and Gaimar in several important ways. Gaimar's historicity is often dubious, that of Wace currently in the process of being rehabilitated, but whatever their respective degrees of accuracy, both were writing about events considerably distanced from their own times.[17] Fantosme, by contrast, was a strict contemporary, and can be substantiated on many important points by chronicle material.

---

*de Seint Auban*, which includes lines in his own 'Jordanian' metre. See also Johnston, *The Versification of Jordan Fantosme*.

[12] Johnston, 'The Historicity of Jordan Fantosme's Chronicle', 162. Cf. JF, xvi:
> Because it is the work of a medieval 'historian' whose purposes include moral instruction . . . and an attempt to view the deeds of human beings as subject to the laws of God . . . its words cannot always be taken at their face value. Neither can its conception as a work of literature, owing much to the *chanson de geste*, be neglected when one assesses the value and purpose of the many striking vignettes liberally scattered through the work.

[13] Johnston, 'The Historicity of Jordan Fantosme's Chronicle', 165–6. Hence the capture of Petronelle, countess of Leicester, after the battle of Fornham, with her unseemly fall into a ditch and the loss of her rings demonstrates the fickleness of fortune's wheel (JF, lines 1064–71); the failure of William the Lion's siege engine before Wark castle, which only succeeds in knocking down a Scottish knight, is symbolic of the futility of an attack on Henry II, which must of necessity rebound on the aggressor (lines 1235–53); the heroic defence of the lone knight at Brough is either imitation or gentle mockery of heroic convention (lines 1493–5).

[14] Johnston, 'The Historicity of Jordan Fantosme's Chronicle', 168.

[15] Few present-day historians would, I suggest, regard Fantosme's poem as 'unvarnished histori-. cal fact' nor fail to to appreciate that, for example, the dramatic dialogue between Henry II and Richard of Ilchester 'has passed through a poetic imagination' (Johnston, 'The Historicity of Jordan Fantosme's Chronicle', 162, 164).

[16] Macdonald, 'The Chronicle of Jordan Fantosme: Manuscripts, Author and Versification', 243.

[17] Gaimar's *L'Estoire des Engleis* (ed. and trans. T. Duffus Hardy and C. Trice Martin as *Lestoire*

This is not, of course, to deny the inherent importance of convention and literary form, and their potentially distorting effects. The poem contains hyperbole, embellishment and didactic 'parables', and is shot through with epic themes – loyalty and lordship, courage and folly, piety and sacrilege, the fall of a great man (William the Lion) through hubris. But what needs to be stressed is that such themes are not necessarily incompatible with a framework of essentially factual material. Where it can be checked, much of Jordan's material, such as William the Lion's itinerary or overall chronology, is largely sound.[18] If his treatment of a given incident is matched against chronicle accounts, Jordan can be seen to have indulged in elaboration, exaggeration or moralisation, but rarely if ever complete invention.[19] Indeed, if one compares Fantosme's account of the

*des Engles solum la Translacioun Maistre Geffrei Gaimar*, 2 vols, RS 1888–9; with a more recent edition by A. Bell, *L'Estoire des Engleis*, ANTS, xiv–xvi, 1960) was written shortly before 1140, but his narrative stops with the death of William Rufus. On Gaimar in general see Gransden, *Historical Writing*, 209–12. For Wace, whose *Roman de Rou* was written between 1160 and 1170, see *Le Roman de Rou de Wace*, ed. A.J. Holden, 3 vols, *Société des Anciens Textes Français*, Paris 1970–73, and M. Bennett, 'Poetry as History? The Roman de Rou of Wace as a Source for the Norman Conquest', *Anglo-Norman Studies* v, 1982, 21–39, and idem, 'Wace and Warfare', *Anglo-Norman Studies* xi, 1988, 37–57.

18  Jordan's chronology is largely in agreement with that of Howden, Diceto and others. He wrongly places the fall of Norwich to the rebels in 1173 instead of 1174, but he openly admits his information concerning this area was limited. Speaking of the capture of Norwich, and adding the detail absent from other accounts that it was 'taken by surprise because a traitor from Lorraine let the enemy in', he notes, 'I was not in that region when it was besieged' (JF, lines 839–891). To place such inaccuracy in perspective, it should be noted that even so scrupulous a chronicler as Howden might confuse his chronology of the war (see, for example, GH i, 60, n. 12).
   Where Jordan's account can be corroborated, it is basically accurate. Hence although stylized, his account of the battle of Fornham, receives confirmation from chroniclers in details such as Bury St Edmunds forming the royalist mustering point, the names of many of the lords present, the capture of Earl Robert, his wife and Hugh de Chastel, and the rout and ruthless treatment of the Flemings (GH i, 61–2; Diceto, 377–8). Notwithstanding the 'effectively planned contrast' between the stubborn defence of Robert de Vaux at Carlisle and the rapid surrender of Gospatric fitz Orm (JF, xvi–xvii), his insistence that Appleby was poorly garrisoned is fully born out by the Pipe Rolls (*The Great Roll of the Pipe for the 22nd Year of the Reign of King Henry II, AD 1175–1176*, ed. J.H. Round, 1904, 119–20). The same Pipe Roll entry records that Gospatric fitz Orm was amerced 500 marks *'quia reddidit castellum regis de Appelbi regi Scottorum'*, showing that Henry II shared Jordan's opinion about the unseemly speed of the castellan's capitulation (ibid.; see also Strickland, 'Securing the North', 182 and n. 32). Similarly, Jordan's insistence that Robert de Vaux was in dire straits in 1174 through shortage of supplies (JF, lines 1568–9, 1586–94) is born out by Howden's statement that Robert sought conditional respite from William the Lion *'victu sibi et burgensibus, qui intus erant, deficiente'* (GH i, 65). The roll-call of lords loyal to Henry given by Jordan in dramatic dialogue between Henry II and Richard of Ilchester (JF, lines 1526–1612) again finds corroboration in large measure with a list of Henry's supporters given by Howden (GH i, 51, n. 4).

19  A good instance is provided by Jordan's description of the massacre by the Scots of the inhabitants of Warkworth in 1174. Clearly much moved by this atrocity, he indulges in sensationalism, inflating the numbers slain, and attributing William the Lion's ultimate downfall to divine retribution (JF, lines 1700–4, 1785, 1893–1903). Yet the incident is reported in detail by Howden, who may have had access to first-hand information, as later in 1174 he had been sent on a diplomatic mission to Galloway in the company of Robert de

battle of Alnwick with that of William of Newburgh, who can be shown to have used Jordan's poem,[20] it is Fantosme who emerges as the more sober and reliable and Newburgh as guilty of extensive distortion and fabrication for literary purposes. It is Newburgh who has the Anglo-Norman force riding headlong through thick fog and stumbling on the king of Scots wholly by accident, or rather by divine providence. Such embellishments are completely absent from Jordan's account, from which it appears that the capture of William was no accident but a carefully planned and professionally executed military strike by Glanville's 'task force'.[21]

Despite the literary form of his work, the basic accuracy of Jordan's poem should not be surprising. For Jordan was addressing a courtly audience of Anglo-Norman nobles about specific events that were still fresh in the minds of his listeners.[22] They would doubtless have accepted his use of hyperbole with wry smiles as being an integral element in the maker's art, but they would not have tolerated wholesale distortion and misrepresentation of events in which many of them had been personally involved.

Jordan's work is essentially a courtly praise-poem, designed at once both to laud the knightly virtues of Henry's supporters and to serve as a *speculum principis* for the Young King. This didactic purpose is achieved, as I hope to show, less by directly criticising young Henry for his part in the revolt against his father than by holding up William the Lion as an exemplar of a ruler who, though possessing many admirable qualities, is led astray by rash counsel and pays a heavy penalty for embarking upon an unjust war. As a work intended for recitation at court, one may apply to Jordan's poem arguments similar to those that have been adduced by scholars of Viking history for the veracity of material contained in skaldic verse of the tenth and eleventh centuries, despite their most elaborate forms and verbal conventions.[23] For the recitation of actual

Vaux, castellan of Carlisle (GH i, 66, 80). Howden places the number of slain at over 100, and like Jordan, mentions the violation of the church of St Lawrence (ibid., 66).

[20] For Newburgh's use of Jordan see Gransden, *Historical Writing*, 264, and below, n. 21.

[21] Compare Fantosme's sober and detailed account of the ambush at Alnwick (at which he claims to have been present), with its stress on the English force having good military intelligence and making full use of scouts (JF, lines 1722–4, 1738–40, 1758–61), with Newburgh's dramatic but clearly erroneous re-rendering (WN, 183–5). Newburgh's elaborations and the importance of Jordan's poem for revealing the professionalism of Glanville's force is dicussed by Strickland, 'Securing the North', 195, n. 116.

[22] Jordan's repeated naming and praising of individual lords throughout the poem can only mean that he intended the poem to be recited or circulated among a courtly audience which was comprised at least in part of these men.

[23] See, for example, the dicussion of skaldic verse by M. Magnusson and H. Pálsson in their translation of *King Harald's Saga*, Harmondsworth 1966, 23–8, who quote the apt comments on the value of skaldic verse by the great thirteenth-century saga writer, Snorri Sturluson, in his preface to the *Heimskringla*:

> With Harald [Fine Hair, king of Norway] there were Court Poets, and even now their poems are known, as well as the poems about all of the kings who have reigned in Norway since then. And the best evidence which we have is

deeds, as opposed to those of legend, must be executed within fairly narrow parameters of truth, unless what is intended to praise and magnify instead invites ridicule and disbelief from an informed audience. Thus while being fully alive to the problems of interpretation inherent in vernacular literature, one must also avoid confusing the literary treatment of a subject with fabrication for the purposes of literature. Despite the topos, Jordan's claim that his own work is 'verai histoire' is more than justified.[24]

The debate on Fantosme's historicity, however, has largely served to obscure the true value of the poem. Whether we regard Fantosme as accurate or not as to factual detail, we can learn as much, if not more, from his approach to the great war, from his assumptions and prejudices, and from the way in which he chooses to praise or criticize both kings and nobles. It provides us with an invaluable insight into the thought-world of the Anglo-Norman aristocracy at a point frozen in time, in the aftermath of a bitter two-year war and in the search for reconciliation between Henry II and the Young King.

Jordan's poem may be said to have two main purposes, both closely inter-woven: to further the reconciliation between father and son, and to praise the loyalty and bravery of the old king's nobles during the war. Here the contempor-ary nature of Jordan's poem becomes of paramount importance. For unlike the accounts of the quarrels between the Young King and his father furnished by Howden, Diceto, Newburgh, Map, the Histoire and others, Jordan's poem was not written with hindsight in the knowledge of the Young King's death in 1183. Jordan was not to know that the old king would outlive his son, and he therefore composed his poem in the full expectation, doubtless shared by his audience, that the younger Henry, already consecrated as a king, would be the next ruler of England and head of the Angevin house.[25] The circumspection this

that which is contained in the poems which were composed for the kings themselves or their sons. We accept as true everything which is to be found in these poems concerning their journeyings and their battles.

It is, of course, in the way of Court Poets to lavish the most praise on the people for whom the poems were composed; but no one would dare to tell the king himself that which everyone present, including the king, would know to be nonsense and lies; that would be mockery, not praise . . . (24–5).

[24] JF, line 1. Despites his valuable caveats, Johnston himself notes: 'While Fantosme's preoccu-pations and presentation are essentially literary, it is surprising how coherent and basically accurate his story, his estoire, is' (JF, xviii).

[25] For the role envisaged by Henry II for the Young King in relation to his brothers and the partition of the Angevin 'empire' see Warren, Henry II, 109, 229–230; and J. Gillingham, The Angevin Empire, 1984, 29–33.

As an infant, he had been acknowledged as heir to the crown by the nobility in 1155, should his elder brother William die (Chronica Roberti de Torigneio, abbatis monasterii Sancti Michaelis in Periculo Maris (hereafter Torigny), ed. R. Howlett in Chronicles and Memorials iv, 184; The Historical Works of Gervase of Canterbury (hereafter Gervase), ed. W. Stubbs, 2 vols, RS 1879–80, i, 162), and his crowning had been envisaged as early as 1162, when the barons of England swore him fealty and did him homage (Diceto i, 306). The following year saw homage to him performed by the king of Scots and the Welsh princes (Diceto i, 311; cf. JF, lines 5–12). Henry the younger was crowned at Westminster in May, 1170 (GH i, 5–6;

enjoined on Fantosme is clear, but as a piece of living diplomacy, reflecting at least to a degree the opinions of both sides in the war, his poem becomes of the highest value, getting us closer than any extant source to the relationship between the Young King and his father as seen by an informed contemporary, intimate with Henry's court and yet divorced from the wisdom of retrospection.

To urge reconciliation within the context of a poem both celebrating Henry's victory in the war and censuring the folly of the Young King in raising rebellion was no easy matter. Jordan, nevertheless, achieves this unenviable task with considerable skill and, given the political circumstances, a surprising degree of even-handedness. This he does principally by concentrating on William the Lion's invasions, the resistance to him by the Northumbrian and Cumbrian castellans, and on rebel activity in East Anglia and the Midlands. For these were a series of campaigns which did not involve either Plantagenet father or son directly, and for which Fantosme could draw on his close personal links with both the nobility of northern England and with the Scottish court.[26] Using William's invasion as a vehicle, Jordan could celebrate Henry's triumph, laud the courage and constancy of those who had stood by the old king and censure the disloyal without directly offending the Young King, while simultaneously weaving into his narrative a plea for a rapprochment. While unequivocally condemning their recourse to war against Henry II, Jordan acknowledges the grievances of both the Young King and William the Lion and in some measure seeks to set out their respective positions.[27] Jordan lavishes much praise on Henry, and would leave the listener in no doubt as to where his sympathies lay, but he was no blind sycophant, and to deliver several of his remarks must have required a cool nerve.

William of Newburgh, writing in retrospect, dwelt on Henry's folly in having his son crowned prematurely.[28] Whatever Jordan may have felt about the wisdom of this act, he passes no judgement on the coronation itself, but rather he

---

*Chronica Rogeri de Hovedene* (hereafter *Chronica*), ed. W. Stubbs, 4 vols, RS 1868–71, ii, 4–5; Torigny, 245; Gervase i, 219–20), then again with his wife Margaret at Winchester in August 1172 (GH i, 31).

[26] Thus, for example, Jordan seems particularly knowledgeable about Odinel II de Umfraville, being aware of his connections with Earl Henry, son of David I and William the Lion's father, and of William's subsequent hostility towards Odinel for siding with Henry II against him (JF, lines 591–597; cf. lines 1650–1655). He twice mentions Odinel's horse, Bauçan, (the only horse named in the poem) and is eager to stress both the brave defence of the garrison of Prudhoe and Odinel's role in the battle at Alnwick (JF, lines 1643–1690, 1705–1707, 1719–1720, 1727–1735, 1742, 1772, 1891). On Odinel see L. Keen, 'The Umfravilles and the Castle and Barony of Prudhoe', *Anglo-Norman Studies* v, 1982, 165–85. If Jordan's claim to be an eye-witness at Alnwick is true, then he must have accompanied Odinel, William de Vesci, Bernard de Balliol, Roger fitz Richard, the Stutevilles and other northern lords in the host that attacked William the Lion. For Jordan's intimacy with the Scottish court, see below, pp. 208–12.

[27] See particularly JF, lines 5–24, 248–382, 669–678, 740–745.

[28] WN, 172: '*Tunc demum vidit rex senior, sic enim vulgo dicebatur, quam inconsulte, immo quam stulte egerit, praemature creando sibi successorem*'. Cf. ibid., 170. Ralph of Diceto, by contrast,

boldly criticizes Henry for having made the Young King a monarch in name alone. In raising his son to the royal dignity but denying him any effective power, Henry must take much responsibility for the outbreak of war. As he frankly tells the old king:

> 'After this crowning and after this transfer of power (*aprés icest curunment, e aprés ceste baillie*), you took away from your son some of his authority (*surportastes a vostre fiz auques de seignurie*), you thwarted his wishes so that he could not exercise power (*n'en pot aver baillie*). Therein lay the seeds of pitiless war. God's curse be on it!'
> A king without a realm is at a loss for something to do: at such a loss was the noble and gracious Young King. When through his father's actions he could not do what he wished, he thought in his heart that he would stir up trouble for him.[29]

Jordan clearly empathized with young Henry's sense of frustration and impotence, and in these lines can be seen the poet's most overt attempt to steer a difficult path between pleasing his present patron and his patron to be. Jordan never seeks to condone the Young King's revolt, but by placing such a forthright statement at the very beginning of the poem, he ensures that the audience keep in mind the grievances that have underlain the conflict. With this important statement made, Jordan thereafter upholds the essential justice of Henry's war. His son and his enemies do him wrong in trying to deprive him prematurely of his rights, when he is still in his prime and a fine warleader. 'I am not so overcome with age', Jordan has Henry say to his barons, 'nor so burdened with years, as is well known to many people, that I should lose my realm.'[30] To this he receives their reply:

---

felt moved to provide a lengthy catalogue of filial rebellion culled from biblical, classical and more contemporary western historical sources (Diceto i, 355–66).

[29] JF, lines 17–24. The immediate cause of the estrangement between father and son was Henry II's proposed treaty with Count Humbert of Maurienne, which sought to marry his youngest son John to Humbert's daughter and heiress. Henry, however, promised to provide John with the traditional appanage of an Angevin cadet, namely the three castles of Chinon, Loudun and Mirebeau, which were currently in the possession of the Young King. The latter, however, utterly refused to countenance their surrender to John (GH i, 41; Warren, *Henry II*, 117–8). But fuelling young Henry's bitterness was the fact that although he had been crowned king of England, his father had denied him any effective power, had dictated the composition of his household which included several of the old king's *familiares*, and kept him starved of funds. Cleverly exploiting his grievances, his father-in-law, Louis VII, urged him to demand from Henry II real control of either England, Normandy or Anjou (GH i, 41; *Chronica* ii, 41–5; WN, 169–70; Torigny, 255–6; Gervase i, 242). In addition, it was generally – and rightly – believed that Eleanor was a principal agent in sparking off the revolt, particularly by setting her two younger sons, Richard and Geoffrey, against their father (Diceto i, 355; WN, 171; Gervase i, 242). Jordan avoids any reference to either the queen or the Young King's brothers throughout his poem.

[30] JF, lines 135–6.

'You are full of martial fervour (*pleins estes de buntez*). Luck has turned against your enemies. The land is yours, defend it well! Your son is in the wrong to make war on you.'[31]

Judiciously brief and well separated comments gently remind the Young King of the essential folly of his war, but the majority of Jordan's criticism is oblique or carefully tempered. Thus, for example, within a single stanza he reminds the audience that Henry II is an injured father whilst concurrently seeking to excuse the Young King as he has been led astray by evil counsel:

The lord of England is heavy at heart, since his son, whom he had nurtured from infancy, is waging war upon him, and he sees that the count of Flanders and his kinsmen have led him astray, promising him for a certainty the land of England.[32]

Similarly, in describing how the Young King had tried to suborn the citizens of London, Jordan balances censure with a plea for reconciliation, and lays the blame once more upon evil counsellors:

'Noble king of England, do what I desire; love those whose wish it is to serve you faithfully. It is not right that any evil should befall the Young King, since his better nature made him regret bringing in foreigners to bring shame on his countrymen who after his father's lifetime are to support him. Before this world approaches its end many strange thing can come to pass. You never had to sustain a war so bad that your son may not have a worse one on his hands. Now let him think of improving the lot of his own people!'[33]

The theme of an essentially good man led astray by evil counsel, particularly by that of foreigners, lies at the heart of Jordan's poem, and is given its most extensive treatment in relation to William the Lion. In those passages concerning the Young King, however, Jordan goes directly to the heart of a crucial political issue. Despite their resounding victory in the war of 1173–4, Henry II's lords and *familiares* were confronted with an acutely difficult position in the

---

[31] JF, lines 149–52.

[32] JF, lines 77–80.

[33] JF, lines 931–40. Immediately prior to this statement, Jordan had noted, with the same balance between censure and a stress on reconciliation;

'Your own son – whom you should love greatly since his innate feelings have made him draw closer to you – urged them [the Londoners] by letter and by envoy to aid him in making war on his father in such terms as you will hear me state; that he would esteem them all the days of his life, would love them and cherish them, and much he wanted to give them. But they would not fall in with his wishes or even consider them, if it meant driving you out of your kingdom or exiling you therefrom' (JF, lines 918–26).

196

aftermath of hostilities. For in suppressing the Young King's revolt, they had warred not only against an anointed king, but against the heir to the majority of the Angevin lands, and their own future sovereign. Though legally their position was entirely correct, for their homage performed to the Young King at his coronation in 1170 had been conditional on ultimate loyalty to Henry II,[34] the peace treaty of 1174 reflects these men's fear of reprisals following the succession of the new king. A general pardon issued by Henry II to the supporters of his rebellious sons was followed in the treaty by a reciprocal pardon of Henry's men by the Young King:

> And in a like manner, the king his son has put aside all malice towards all, both clerks and laymen, who were with his father, and has pledged in the hands of the king his father that he will not for this reason do, nor seek to do in all his life, any evil or harm to those who obeyed him.[35]

The Young King's status made it essential that Henry II demand a pardon and guarantee of future security from reprisal for his men, and his grant to the Young King of two castles in Normandy and £15,000 Angevin per annum was specifically 'pro hac conditione'.[36]

Jordan could choose no more powerful a lever to urge reconciliation than by an explicit reminder to the Young King that his father's men will soon be his. He will doubtless have his own wars, so he should see to it that these men will be his supporters. Indeed, the praise of Henry's faithful lords which forms the core of the poem must be seen in the light of these considerations. Jordan is telling the Young King that loyal vassals are the greatest resource a king can have, and he must remember that should he in turn merit their devotion, these lords will support his cause in the future with equal loyalty.

Jordan himself neatly summarizes one of his principal themes when, speaking of the brave defence of the town of Dunwich against the rebel earl of Leicester, he says:

> You have often heard the proverb which says: he who acts falsely towards his rightful lord or does any wrong which causes him annoyance can be sure of getting his merited punishment: and he who serves him loyally is greatly to be esteemed.[37]

---

[34] GH i, 6. Their oaths were made expressly 'salva fidelitate sua' [to Henry II]. This is stressd by Jordan with special reference to William the Lion at the very start of the poem: 'Noble king of England . . . do you not remember that when your son was crowned you made the king of Scotland do him homage, with his hand placed in your son's, without being false in his fealty to you (senz fei aver mentie)?' (JF, lines 5–8).

[35] GH i, 77–8.

[36] GH i, 78.

[37] JF, lines 845–9.

One of Jordan's main purposes was to remind Henry who his most loyal supporters had been during his absence from the kingdom, and to recount their exploits so as to enhance their esteem in the eyes of both their king and their peers. He concentrates his attention primarily on two groups of men. The first, with whom Jordan seems to have had the closest links, consisted of the castellans of Northumbria and Cumbria; Roger de Stuteville, Robert de Vaux, William de Vesci, Roger fitz Richard and Odinel de Umfraville, Bernard de Balliol and Walter de Bolbec.[38] The second, more amorphous grouping contains Henry's leading *familiares* such as Richard de Lucy, the justiciar, Rannulf de Glanville, Richard of Ilchester, bishop of Winchester, and Hugh de Creissi together with the most prominent of his supporters from the greater nobility: William, earl of Arundel, Humphrey de Bohun, Roger Bigod, loyal son of the rebel earl Hugh.[39] Other loyal lords receive passing mention, such as Walter fitz Richard, Robert and Thomas fitz Bernard, William de Humez, the constable of Normandy, Bertram de Verdun and Geoffrey, bishop elect of Lincoln, Henry II's natural son.[40] In addition, the citizens of London are repeatedly singled out for extravagant acclaim.[41] In his lavish praise for these men, Jordan allows us to see

---

[38] For Jordan's references to Roger de Stuteville, constable of Wark and sheriff of Northumberland, JF, lines 482–529, 1143–5, 1171–2, 1191–1314, 1558–61, and for collective praise of the Stuteville family, lines 1547–9, 1773; for Robert de Vaux, castellan of Carlisle and sheriff of Cumberland, JF, lines 587–90, 645–668, 759–64, 1350–1457, 1506–22, 1566–69, 1586–89, 1628–42; for William de Vesci, castellan of Alnwick, JF, lines 537–58, 1171–4, 1592–3, 1770, 1888–9, and *Complete Peerage*, xxii (2), 274–5. Contrary to Johnston's statement (JF, 213) that the *jofne Willame* of line 555 was the illegitimate son of William de Vesci, Professor Holt has suggested that 'the father' here referred to may in fact be Eustace de Vesci, and that all Jordan's references are to the William de Vesci who had been sheriff of Northumberland from 1157–1170. See *Early Yorkshire Charters*, 12 vols, vols i–iii, ed. W. Farrer (Edinburgh, 1914–16), vols iv–xii, ed. C.T. Clay, (*Yorkshire Archaeological Society*, Record Series, 1935–65), xii, 91–2.

For Roger fitz Richard, lord of Warkworth and constable of Newcastle, JF, lines 563–68, 1742; for Odinel de Umfraville see above, n. 26; for Bernard de Balliol, JF, lines 1713–14, 1734–5, 1771, 1861–65; and for his brief mention of Walter de Bolbec, JF, lines 1891.

For Vesci, Stuteville and de Vaux, and their close family connections see J.C Holt, *The Northerners*, Oxford 1961, 202, and for the later fortunes of these families under John, 17–34. See also *Early Yorkshire Charters*, and *Early Yorkshire Families*, ed. C. Clay and D. Greenway, *Yorkshire Archaeological Society*, 1973.

[39] For all these men see the index in Warren, *Henry II*, and especially 304–16 for a discussion of Henry's *familiares*.

[40] For Walter fitz Richard, see below n. 41: for William de Humez, who was to suceeded his father Richard as constable of Normandy in 1180, and Bertram de Verdun see Warren, *Henry II*, 308, n. 2 and 310.The fullest account of the role of Geoffrey Plantagenet in the war of 1173–4 is furnished by Gerald of Wales in his *De vita Galfridi archepiscopi Eboracensis*, in *Giraldi Cambrensis Opera*, ed. J.S. Brewer, J.F. Dimock, and G.F. Warner, 8 vols, RS 1861–91, iv, 364–8.

[41] JF, lines 906–30, 1916–43. Jordan's repeated insistence on the unwavering loyalty of the Londoners and their devotion to Henry smacks of intercession. In 1173, the Young King had tried to suborn the citizens to declare for his cause (JF, lines 918–24), and although the city remained loyal, Jordan may have been attempting to allay any suspicions which Henry II may still still harboured. Other than the obvious strategic and political importance of the capital,

those virtues with which his aristocratic audience most wished to see themselves endowed. His poem might almost be said to be a *speculum militis*, if one can venture such a phrase, holding up an ideal of knighthood, yet expressing such ideals not through the superhuman figures of romance but through actual individuals.

In a poem composed in the aftermath of the great rebellion it is unsurprising to find that loyalty takes precedence among such virtues. Almost all of Henry's supporters who are named in the poem receive some formulaic statement of their unswerving allegiance to Henry. Thus Roger Stuteville, for example, 'who was never a friend to treason or to the work of the devil' (*ki unkes n'ama traïsun ne servir al diable*), is a 'wise knight who loved his liege lord' (*le sage chevalier, ki sun seignur ama*),[42] while Richard de Lucy 'affords great help to his liege lord in the prosecution of his war'.[43] Indeed, one of the highlights of the poem is a dramatic dialogue between Richard of Ilchester and Henry II, couched in the form of question and answer, whereby the king enquires about the loyalty of a series of lords in turn and receives fulsome confirmation of their steadfastness.[44] A typical stanza with royal question and episcopal reply runs thus:

'Now tell me truly of my land up north: has Roger Stuteville had any truck with the enemy?' 'Sooner would a thousand men, sire, be overwhelmed by sudden death than that Roger, be the cause right or wrong, do you any hurt.'[45]

Similarly, the bishop tells Henry that William, earl of Arundel, 'is one of your loyal supporters and one of the foremost in anything that concerns you'.[46] Humphrey de Bohun is 'one of the most faithful of those who stand by you', Richard de Lucy 'would let himself be roped to a stake' rather than submit, while 'no treacherous deeds ever came from the Stutevilles'.[47] The ties between

---

the reasons for Jordan's championing of London and his forthright call on Henry to reward its citizens are unclear. He singles out Henry le Blunt and Gervase de Cornhill for special mention (JF, lines 1928, 1936). On the latter see C.N.L. Brooke, assisted by G. Keir, *London, 800–1216: The Shaping of a City*, 1975, especially 1210–15, and S. Reynolds, 'The Rulers of London in the Twelfth Century', *History* lvii, 1972, 346ff. Brooke and Keir deal only very briefly with London's role in the war of 1173–4, but argue that contrary to Jordan's implication that the Clares had sided with the rebel Gilbert de Montfichet in threatening London (JF, lines 1609–10), the powerful Clare lord Walter fitz Robert held Baynard's castle for Henry II, and may have commanded the city militia (JF, 215–16). Jordan in fact notes that it was Walter fitz Robert who struck the first blow against the rebels at Fornham (JF, lines 1010, 1032–5). His statement that Gilbert de Mountfichet claimed the support of the Clares concurs with Diceto's comment that Henry II suspected Richard de Clare of collusion with the rebels (ibid., lines 1609–10; Diceto, I, 385).

42 JF, lines 482–4, 524.
43 JF, line 767.
44 JF, lines 1526–1616.
45 JF, lines 1558–61.
46 JF, lines 1540–1.
47 JF, lines 1545, 1536–7, 1549.

lord and man are portrayed as being intensely personal. When Roger de Stuteville realizes he cannot hold Wark with the forces at his command, 'he thinks sadly of his liege lord, valiant King Henry, his tears course down his cheeks',[48] while William de Vesci, the castellan of Alnwick 'thinks more longingly of his absent lord than does a knight of his mistress'.[48] Doubtless Jordan intended this latter comment to be gently humourous, invoking conventions of courtly love, but the ultimate purpose of the remark, to emphasize de Vesci's devotion to Henry, could not have been more serious. In turn the king himself, with epic exaggeration, is moved to tears by the desperate plight of his barons in the north in 1174.[49] Even rebellion is couched in terms of loyalty to one's lord. Speaking of the Young King, the earl of Leicester is made to say: 'I am delaying too long before striking a blow for my liege lord and taking revenge on his father, the old king, for the ills I have suffered'.[50]

Jordan seeks to highlight the loyalty of such '*pruedhumes*',[50] particularly the Anglo-Norman lords of Cumbria and Northumbria, by the insistence that in their lord's service they have suffered great material loss at the hands of the Scots. Nevertheless, as loyal vassals they willingly undergo such self-sacrifice for Henry's cause. Speaking of William's invasion of 1173, Jordan comments:

> The barons of this land will pay a grievous price for his folly – alack that it was ever seen. Before he departs he will bring such misery on them that, outside their defensive walls, they will not be left with an ox to their plough. But the barons' feelings towards their position of lordship are deep-seated (*mes li barun sunt naturel vers lur seignurage*): they hold their wealth no dearer than they do wild animals that are nobody's property. Rather would they die with honour than suffer shame, or abandon their liege lord, whatever they might lose. They will endure and wait patiently, acting wisely in so doing, but they will not surrender their castles no matter what harm may come.[51]

Extending this concept, Jordan notes that Robert de Vaux's commitment to Henry's cause is so deep that he uses the booty gained in the pursuit of the Scottish army from Carlisle in 1173 not for his own enrichment, but to further strengthen his castle against the king's enemies.[52] Yet in Jordan's repeated statements about the barons' financial loss there is an implicit suggestion that Henry should make good this drain on their resources by royal largesse, and reward those who have saved his throne in direct proportion to their suffering on his behalf.

The most obvious way Jordan chooses to demonstrate loyalty is by describing

[48] JF, lines 496–7, 548.
[49] JF, line 1596.
[50] JF, lines 970–1.
[51] JF, lines 572–80.
[52] JF, lines 759–62.

the stubborn defence of castles, principally those of Wark, Carlisle, Brough and Prudhoe, and the prowess of Henry's barons in the battles of Fornham and Alnwick.[53] In Jordan's highly stylized account of Fornham, Walter fitz Robert, Humphrey de Bohun, William, earl of Arundel, Roger Bigod, Robert fitz Bernard and Hugh de Creissi are all lauded for their eagerness to be first into the attack and their skill at arms when in the affray.[54] Their feats of arms occasionally assume epic proportions. There were 'enormous numbers' against Walter fitz Robert, while before other royalist lords 'could strike their fill, Humphrey de Bohun had captured more than a hundred'.[55] The ubiquitous leitmotif of loyalty again emerges: Walter fitz Robert urges on William of Arundel by saying, 'You are one of my lord's men, do not hang back! You see his enemies going to overthrow him, clap spurs to your horse, my lord earl, and come with us!'[56] Prior to the attack on William's retinue at Alnwick, Bernard de Balliol is made to say, 'He who is not bold and resolute now does not deserve to have a fief or anything belonging thereto!'[57] There could hardly be a more explicit statement of the intimate connection in the minds of contemporaries between tenure, military service and martial prowess. Jordan implies that bravery in war and loyal service should form the ultimate title-deed.

Such sentiments are still more forcefully expressed in relation to siege. Robert de Vaux, for example, in rejecting William the Lion's bribes and threats to obtain Carlisle, is made an exemplar of vassalic propriety. He tells the Scots messenger that if he receives his lord's explicit command to yield the fortress, he will do so, but if not he will fight to the death to defend Carlisle: 'We here in this castle are loyal men and secure (*bone gent asseure*); cursed be he who surrenders as long as his food lasts out!'[58] Similarly, the people of Dunwich reply to the earl of Leicester's demand for their surrender on pain of death:

---

[53] JF, lines 645–668 (Carlisle, 1173), 1185–1316 (Wark, 1174), 1338–1455 and 1632–42 (Carlisle, 1174), 1475–1505 (Brough, 1174), 1658–82 (Prudhoe, 1174). Conversely, lack of martial prowess is used to belittle certain rebels; Earl Ferrers is mocked as 'a simple knight, more fitted to embrace and kiss fair ladies than to smite other knights with a war-hammer' (JF, lines 947–949).

[54] JF, lines 1008–85.

[55] JF, lines 1036, 1049–50.

[56] JF, lines 1040–3.

[57] JF, lines 1736–7.

[58] JF, lines 1411–12. It is interesting to note that by the sixteenth century, the term 'assured men' had assumed a very different, and often pejorative meaning. 'Assuring' was a process, particularly common in the Borders, whereby contracting parties formally agreed not to molest each other for a specified period of time. Such assurances were entered into by English and Scottish wardens of the marches, and were common between Scottish nobles themselves. During the English crown's attempt to secure the marriage of Henry VIII's son Edward to the young Mary Queen of Scots known as 'the Rough Wooing' (1543–50), the English systematically used assurance to create a band of Scottish collaborators (M.H. Merriman, 'The Assured Scots. Scottish Collaborators with England during the Rough Wooing', *Scottish Historical Review* xlvii, 1968).

'A curse on him who gives twopennce for your threats! Our good and rightful king, who will speedily bring your war to nought, is still alive. As long as we live and can still stand on our feet, we shall not surrender the town no matter what assault we have to fear.'[59]

Such statements represented the ideal of heroic defence. Yet despite his own rhetoric, Jordan is equally at pains to define the limits of a vassal's duty in war. For Anglo-Norman warfare, and siege in particular, was carefully regulated by an amorphous but extensive body of custom, designed to ensure that both attack and defence usually stopped well short of suicidal heroism. Chief among such conventions was that of conditional respite, whereby hard-pressed defenders might seek a truce for a pre-determined period (often forty days) in which to seek relief from their lord. If no such help was forthcoming within the allotted time, the garrison surrendered with honour and were normally allowed free egress with horses and arms.[60] Thus in Jordan's poem, the importance of reciprocity of aid and support, of the lord's loyalty to his men and his duty to rescue them in their time of need finds clear expression. Roger de Stuteville, for example, when petitioning William the Lion for conditional respite in 1173, is made to address his absent lord King Henry:

'Since you are now powerless, what will it help you that once you were strong? You cannot give aid to your vassal! I shall go to the king of Scotland and ask him for a truce, a breathing space of forty days, so that I can cross the seas. If then I cannot procure help, from then on you will certainly and rightly have lost the whole of Northumberland.'[61]

The implication was clear. A vassal should put up the best resistance he can on his lord's behalf, but should the lord then fail to bring him relief, the vassal can surrender without any slur on his loyalty and honour. Hence when in 1174 the Scots fire the keep at Brough, its garrison 'will act as knights should and will surrender to the king, for they see plainly that no help is coming to them'.[62] Similarly, it was necessary for Jordan to vindicate the conduct of Roger fitz Richard, who had abandoned Warkworth in 1173 because it was too weak and fell back on Newcastle. Jordan first stresses the inadequacy of Warkworth's defences, then is quick to dispell any hint of cowardice: 'I must say a word about Roger fitz Richard: he was master and lord of Newcastle upon Tyne. He was so

---

59 JF, lines 856–60.
60 Conventions governing siege warfare and notions concerning the extent of resistance expected from garrisons are discussed in detail in M.J. Strickland, *The Conduct and Perception of War under the Anglo-Norman and Angevin Kings*, Ph.D. thesis, Cambridge 1989, 50–87.
61 JF, lines 498–503.
62 JF, lines 1488–9.

afire with daring and wrath that he would not speak of peace with the king of Scotland or make light of it'.[63]

It is not merely prowess in arms in battle or siege that distinguishes the best of knights, but also qualities of leadership and experience in the art of war. Jordan takes Roger de Stuteville, castellan of Wark, to exemplify the knightly ideal. Roger 'was no coward, nor wrong-headed about the art of war, nor less than chivalrous in his conduct (*ne fud mie lanier, në abobéd de guerre, ne vilain chevalier*); no wiser, more balanced, more noble warrior was ever heard of (*unkes de plus sages n'en oistes parler ne plus mesurable ne plus gentil guerrier*)'.[64] When the Scots lay siege to Wark in 1174, Roger addresses his men with words of practical advice:

> 'Shoot your arrows only in cases of greatest need: we do not know what they propose to do or what they are thinking. They control highways and roads and paths, they have wine and beer, plenty to eat and drink, and they are well supplied with arms and swift chargers. And we, serjeants and soldiers, are inside, and we too have food – let us look after it carefully. Do not waste your weapons, it is to you, bowmen, that I address these words, but when an emergency arises and when there are full scale attacks, then defend yourselves like noble knights.'[65]

After the Scots withdraw in the face of a stubborn resistance from Wark's garrison, Roger instructs his men not to taunt the retreating Scots – less, one imagines, from chivalric sensibilities than from fear of provoking a fresh assault:

> 'Make no opprobrious remarks, let us eschew all such things, and do not shout or whoop at the men of Scotland. It is meet that we should all praise God, our Father; as he has preserved our lives from the king of Scotland and his bold array, it is our bounden duty to offer him thanks.'[66]

Even in victory after a hard fought siege, Roger is made to behave with perfect decorum, and to have praise to God as his first thoughts.

This practical wisdom in war extended to skill in diplomacy, the ability not simply to fight but to recognize when to parley and to seek truces or respite when needed. Thus Roger, 'a model of discretion' (*senz faire nul desrei*), succeeds in gaining from William a respite for the relief of Wark 'wisely and humbly' (*sages par humilité*), thereby preventing much loss.[67] Humphrey de Bohun is 'a

---

[63] JF, lines 565–8. For Warkworth's lack of strength, lines 562–4, and Strickland, 'Securing the North', 181–2.
[64] JF, lines 1287–90.
[65] JF, lines 1224–33.
[66] JF, lines 1293–7.
[67] JF, line 505.

man of great sagacity' (*est de mult grant cuintise*).[68] In particular, Jordan associates this quality of wisdom with the justiciar, Richard de Lucy, 'that man of wisdom and good sense' (*le sage, le sené*): 'He is skilled at seeking truces and peace in case of need, when he sees that desperate measures are required'.[69] He receives special praise for obtaining a vital truce from William the Lion late in 1173 which enabled the royalist forces to march south to contain Robert of Leicester's landing in East Anglia without fear of the Scots taking them in the rear. To gain this essential respite, news of Leicester's landing had to be concealed from the Scots king and the truce negotiated as if from a position of English military strength. Jordan's account clearly reveals that dissimulation and diplomatic guile, when used for the right ends, were qualities to be admired in a warrior-statesman.[70] Similarly, it was by judicious use of military intelligence that the English lords were able to surprise and capture William at Alnwick.[71]

On a more metaphysical level, Jordan endows many of the nobles he seeks to praise with a sense of piety. Several lords are made to invoke the aid of God, the Virgin or the saints before combat, or to give thanks after their successful resistance. Hence when faced with the arrival of William the Lion before Wark in 1173, Roger de Stuteville 'addresses this prayer to the God of Glory and to His true Mother: "Give me such guidance as will maintain my honour for the Scots are waging war mercilessly against me" '.[72] William de Vesci often calls 'in loving faith on his Heavenly Father for help', while following the relief of Carlisle in 1173, Robert de Vaux 'bends his knee, stretches out his pointed shoe behind him, and gives thanks to God, praying Him to enfold him in His love'.[73] At the battle of Fornham, the earl of Arundel is made to say 'Let us go and strike them [Leicester's army] for the honour of God and Saint Edmund who is a true martyr!', reflecting the fact that the royal army, which had mustered at Bury St Edmunds, had carried the banner of St Edmund into battle as a potent source of spiritual power.[74] Though often couched in conventional and formulaic terms, such attributions of piety were clearly an integral element in the self-perception of Jordan's aristocratic audience.

To Jordan himself, the reward for such piety was success in war. Speaking of the relief of Carlisle in 1173, Jordan notes: 'Aid will speedily come to those in

[68] JF, line 782.
[69] JF, lines 722, 768–9.
[70] JF, lines 764–832. Cf J. Gillingham, 'War and Chivalry in the *History of William the Marshal*', *Thirteenth-Century England ii. Proceedings of the Newcastle Upon Tyne Conference, 1987*, ed. P.R. Coss and S.D. Lloyd, Woodbridge 1988, 1–14, 5, where the Marshal is praised by Henry II for his advice to ravage Philip's lands having first lured him away by a diversionary attack.
[71] JF, lines 1718–24, 1758–61; Strickland, 'Securing the North', 195.
[72] JF, lines 488–90.
[73] JF, lines 547, 763–4..
[74] JF, lines 1026–8; Howden notes that the royalist army set out for battle '*praeferentes sibi vexillum Beati Edmundi regis et martyris; et ordinatis aciebus suis, in virtute Dei et gloriosissimi martyris Sui Eadmundi percusserunt aciem in qua comes Leicestriae erat*' (GH i, 61–2).

the castle. That is the outcome for people who trust in the Lord God'.[75] When Wark is invested by the Scots in 1174, Roger de Stuteville is made to say, 'God Himself will defend us', and so he does, for when the Scots try to fire the castle, 'Jesus, the King of Glory, by whom all things are made, turned the wind against the King of Scotland'.[76] Similarly, Jordan ascribes William's capture at Alnwick to the intervention of God and St Thomas, and in so doing is one of the first of many sources that would highlight the miraculous correlation of Henry's penance at Becket's tomb and the overthrow of the king of Scotland.

On 8 July 1174, Henry II had crossed from Normandy to Southampton, and the next day made directly for Canterbury, walking the last part of the journey barefoot and in penitential garb. Having been scourged by the monks, he spent the day and night of 12 July in fasting and prayer before Thomas's tomb, where he gave lavish offerings to the martyr's shrine.[77] Referring to this display of humility, which struck a deep impression on contemporaries, Jordan notes: 'The king was truly reconciled with Thomas the Martyr and to him he confessed his guilt and his sin and his sorrow, and he underwent the penance imposed upon him – it was no light one!'[78] Jordan clearly felt that Henry had gravely sinned concerning Becket's death, and was not afraid to say so publically. When Richard of Ilchester brings Henry news of the plight of his barons in England in 1174, Jordan has the king remark, 'St Thomas . . . guard me my realm! I admit to you my guilt for which others bear the blame (*a vus me rent cupable dunt li autre unt le blasme*)'.[79]

Yet as with his admonition of the Young King, Jordan exercizes restraint and discretion, tempering overt criticism and again stressing above all the theme of reconciliation. This he does by emphasizing the fact that William the Lion's capture at Alnwick on 13 July occurred the very day following Henry's penance at Canterbury, and on the morning when he ended his night's vigil at the tomb:

> Speaking with full knowledge of the facts I assure you that you are hearing the truth: the king of England has landed while these events [in the north] were in train and made his peace with St Thomas on the very morning when the king of Scots was made prisoner and led away.[80]

The victory of Rannulf de Glanville and his force over William the Lion had important strategic consequences, since it neutralized the Scottish threat and deprived the rebel lords of the Midlands of the aid on which they had counted. Yet of far greater consequence was the psychological impact of the correlation

[75] JF, lines 703–4.
[76] JF, lines 1222, 1260–3.
[77] Diceto i, 382–4: GH i, 72; R.W. Eyton, *The Court, Household and Itinerary of King Henry II*, 1878, 180.
[78] JF, lines 1912–15.
[79] JF, lines 1599–1600.
[80] JF, lines 1904–7; for the date of William's capture, GH i, 67.

between Henry's act of contrition and the Scots king's capture. For it seemed to contemporaries a clear manifestation of both Thomas's forgiveness of and reconciliation with the king, and of divine support for Henry's cause against the rebel coalition. When Henry hears the news of William's capture at Alnwick, Jordan has him exclaim, 'Thanks be to God and to St Thomas the Martyr, and to all the saints of God!'.[81] Earlier in the war, Henry's opponents had attempted to harness Becket's murder as a propaganda weapon against the king; the hymn *Novus miles sequitur* invokes the aid of Thomas on behalf of the Young King and the earl of Leicester.[82] The correlation of events at Alnwick and Canterbury put paid to any further rebel exploitation of the cult of St Thomas, and may well have served to further undermine the morale of those in England in arms against Henry, who quickly capitulated *en masse*.[83] Most telling of all is the reaction of the man who was the principal victim of this divine intervention: when William the Lion came to build his royal abbey at Arbroath, he dedicated it to St Thomas.[84]

In his portrayal of knightly ideals, Jordan extends the concept of piety from personal devotion to actual conduct towards Holy Church in war. Whereas most contemporary ecclesiastical writers were concerned to vilify knightly despoliators of churches during hostilities, Jordan stresses the praiseworthy behaviour of one lord in particular. His choice of Earl David, younger brother of William the Lion, at first seems most surprising. David had played an active role against Henry II in the war of 1173–4, harassing the royalist garrisons of the Midlands from his bases at Leicester and Huntingdon.[85] To Jordan, however, he is the embodiment of restraint and respect:

> Earl David, no matter what anyone else may tell you, was the noblest of warriors (*le plus gentil guerrier*), as God give me blessing; Holy Church was never robbed by him nor was any abbey, and no one under his orders would do any wrong to a priest.[86]

---

JF, lines 2011–12. A similar sentiment is ascribed to Henry by Howden: '*Quod cum audisset rex, gavisus est gaudio magno valde, et gratias inde egit Omnipotenti Deo et beato Thomae Martyri*' (GH i, 72). Both Diceto (i, 384) and Newburgh stress the intervention of God in the capture of William, with the latter chronicler deliberately reworking the story of the engagement at Alnwick to make it seem as if the English had stumbled across the Scots king by accident, thus stressing further the hand of Providence (WN, 183–5: Strickland, 'Securing the North', 195, and n. 195).

[82] D. Stevens, *Music in Honour of St Thomas*, 1973, 10–11; A. Duggan, 'The Cult of St Thomas Becket in the Thirteenth Century', *St Thomas Cantilupe, Bishop of Hereford. Essays in his Honour*, ed. M. Jancey, Hereford 1982, 32 and n. 73.

[83] GH i, 72–3.

[84] *Early Sources for Scottish History*, collected and trans. A. O. Anderson, 2 vols, Edinburgh 1922; republished Stamford 1990, ii, 298.

[85] JF, lines 1107–30; GH i, 45, 68; WN, 180. On Earl David see K.J. Stringer, *Earl David of Huntingdon, 1152–1219*, Edinburgh 1985, especially 20–29 for his role in the war of 1173–4.

[86] JF, lines 1096–9.

Jordan's clear enthusiasm for Earl David strongly suggests that Jordan had close ties with the earl, either through his connections with the Scottish court, or in relation to the honour of Huntingdon. Indeed, his treatment of David bears a marked similarity to the fulsome praise lavished on his father Earl Henry, son of King David I of Scotland, by English writers such as Henry of Huntingdon and Ailred of Rievaulx a generation earlier.[87] Both Earls Henry and David are painted as the apogee of chivalry and decorum and their martial feats are extolled, irrespective of the fact that they had been erstwhile enemies of the kings of England. There was very much the sense that as cadets, they could win glory in war without sharing the ultimate responsibility for its inception, or reproach for the atrocities perpetrated by the Scots during its prosecution – factors which by contrast gravely compromised the reputation of David I and William the Lion in the eyes of the English.[88] Such a comparison certainly underlies Jordan's treatment of David, for he holds him up as a mirror of virtue to his errant elder brother:

> David fought well in the heart of England. But the king of Scotland's war went badly. Urged on by his evil councillors (*ses malveis cunseilliers*) he engaged on a venture which in the event turned out disasterously for him. David was wise as well as nobly born. He defended Holy Church, for it was never his will to do wrong to priest or canon possessed of book learning, or to cause displeasure to any nun from an abbey.[89]

Not so William. Whether he wishes it or not, his men burn churches and slaughter men, women and children.[90] It is divine vengeance for such sacrilege

---

[87] Thus both Henry of Huntingdon and Ailred praise Earl Henry's prowess at the battle of the Standard in glowing terms, making him out as one of the heroes of the day (Henry of Huntingdon, *Historia Anglorum*, ed. T. Arnold, RS 1870, 263; *Relatio venerabilis Aelredi, abbatis Rievallensis, de Standardo* (hereafter *Relatio*), ed. R. Howlett, *Chronicles and Memorials* iii, 196–8. In addition, Ailred provides a eulogy of the wisdom, bravery and piety of his boyhood companion, attributing to him all the qualities expected of both a prince and a knight; humility, yet the ability to inspire fear of his authority, affability, chastity, sobriety in council, generosity to the poor, reverence for Holy Church and her ministers, and bravery and prudence in war (*Relatio*, 190–1).

[88] For a full discussion of the question of Scottish 'atrocities', and the extent of the complicity or otherwise of David I and William the Lion in their execution see Strickland, *Conduct and Perception of War*, 280–329.

[89] JF, lines 1131–38.

[90] Jordan is ambivalent as to William's complicity in the excesses of his native Scottish troops. Speaking of his campaign in 1173, Jordan notes:
> He orders that peace be kept in regard to Holy Church; and metes out stern justice to those who break it. But that does not do him the slightest bit of good. That miserable race, on whom be God's curse, the Gallovidians, who covet wealth, and the Scots who dwell north of the Forth have no faith in God, the son of Mary: they destroy churches and indulge in wholesale robbery. (JF, lines 681–88).

In his account of the invasion of 1174, however, he has William explicitly order his Galwegians to slay all the men found in the lands of Odinel de Umfraville (JF, lines 1689–

207

that causes William's downfall. When at the engagement at Alnwick, William's horse is slain and traps him beneath it, Jordan adds 'The sin of the Scots weighs him down.'[91] As he goes on to explain, the Scots have in particular incurred God's wrath for their massacre of the inhabitants of Warkworth:

My lords, do not marvel if they are routed. On that day the Scots cruelly ill-treated more than a thousand, and death has separated sons from their fathers. When you think of the grief, the tears, and the lamentation of those unhappy people in St Lawrence's church, some of them with their bodies and breasts slashed open, and even tonsured priests not guaranteed from harm, you have no need to ask if God is angered and if he is roused to hatred of King William. Misfortune has come upon many because of his sin, and he himself was that day overthrown.[92]

But if the war has led William to commit sin, then it was the advice of evil counsellors that led him to embark upon the war. Jordan's treatment of William and his cause is complex and ambivalent. In personal terms, Jordan praises his courage and prowess as a knight. It is William who wishes to turn and fight the English army advancing to the relief of Carlisle in 1173, but who is compelled by his cowardly advisers into a precipitous and shameful flight.[93] The following year, when taken by surprise before Alnwick, William is first to take up arms and engage Glanville's force.[94] He is 'merveillus e hardi', a 'chevalier bon e de grant vasslage'.[95] His claim to Northumbria, which had been the principal casus belli for the Scots, is treated at length by Jordan and with considerable sympathy.[96]

That such empathy stemmed from a close personal connection with the Scottish court is suggested not only by his praise for Earl David but by the detailed knowledge concerning William's familiares that Jordan displays in his poem. Thus in reporting at some length William's diplomatic moves prior to the war, he cites by name some of the leading Scottish envoys such as the Hospitaller William de Olpen, William of St Michel and Robert de Husville,[97] while he

---

90), and focuses on the massacre of the inhabitants of Warkworth (lines 1700–4, 1893–1903).

91  JF, line 1785.

92  JF, lines 1893–1903.

93  JF, lines 1718–58. For general surveys of the reign of William the Lion see A.A.M. Duncan, *Scotland: The Making of the Kingdom*, Edinburgh 1975, 174–215; *Regesta Regum Scottorum ii. The Acts of William I* (hereafter *RRS* ii), ed. G.W.S. Barrow, Edinbugh 1971, 3–27.

94  JF, lines 1774–83.

95  JF, lines 1766, 709.

96  JF, lines 271–420, 740–6. On the nature of William's claims see Duncan, *Scotland: The Making of the Kingdom*, 216–55, and cf. M.O. Anderson, 'Lothian and the Early Scottish Kings', *Scottish Historical Review* xxxix, 1960, 92–12. Jordan's sympathy is shared by Ralph of Diceto, who notes that the Northumbrian lands sought by William 'avo suo David regi fuerant donata, tradita, cartis confirmata, quae etiam ab ipso tempore longo possessa' (Diceto i, 376).

97  JF, lines 322, 421. Brother William de Olepen attests a confirmation (1166 x 1170) by William the Lion of land in Midlothian held by Geoffrey de Melville, and another confirm-

warmly praises the valour of four Anglo-Scottish knights during the engagement at Alnwick.[98] Most significantly of all, Jordan seems to align himself strongly with an element of William's court, headed by Bishop Ingram of Glasgow, who had been Malcolm IV's chancellor, and Waltheof, earl of Dunbar, which had in vain counselled against the declaration of war against England in 1173.[99] His association with this peace party, the 'doves', against the 'hawks' urging war, dictates Jordan's whole approach to William. The Scottish king is essentially a brave and good man, who has an important grievance, but who is led astray by the evil counsel of aliens. As Fantosme declares:

> Ah God! What sorrow about noble King William! He will incur King Henry's deadly reproach; by the noble St James this grieves me, for never did a more honourable man govern any realm. Fantosme says and pledges you his faith on it, that William would never on any occasion in his life have thought of waging war against Henry, duke of Normandy, the son of Matilda, him of the bold mien. But by evil counsel and the

ing the property and privileges of Cambuskenneth Abbey (1166 x1171) (*RRS* ii, nos 59 and 60). A biographical note is given by Barrow, *RRS* ii, no. 60. For William of St Michael see ibid., nos 498 and 577. Robert de Huseville does not seem to feature in William's surviving *acta*.

[98] Thus Jordan notes of Alan de Lascelles that he
> was very old and a most excellent knight, it was a good thirty years since he had last encountered an adversary. But he was a good and knowledgeable knight; if the king had followed his advice, he would have been in a far better plight. (JF, lines 1852–5)

Similarly, William de Mortimer 'sweeps through the ranks like a wild boar. He deals a succession of great blows and takes as good as he gives', while Richard Maluvel, who 'was bold and chivalrous', 'performed courageously' and Ralph Ruffus 'fought well' (JF, lines 1858–60, 1872–6, 1868). Alan de Lascelles appears as a witness in *RRS* ii, nos 28 and 137, while the prominence of William de Mortimer (or Mortemer) is revealed by his frequent attestations of King William's charters (ibid., nos 42, 79, 80, 82, 83, 86, 107, 129, 137, 147, 149, 150, 151, 152, 170, 172, 195, 197, 207, 236, 243), including one also attested by Odinel de Umfraville, who fought on the opposing side at Alnwick (ibid., no. 80). Ralph Ruffus was the beneficiary of a grant (1172 x 1174) of the lordship of of Kinnaird, and also witnesses several of William's *acta* (ibid., nos 135, 140, 175, 338, 339, 355, 356 (the last three being grants to Arbroath abbey) and 358; cf. nos 470, 471). Ralph Maluvel is mentioned but once, as a benefactor to St Andrews cathedral priory (ibid., no. 333). Cf. G.W.S. Barrow, 'The Beginnings of Military Feudalism' in his *The Kingdom of the Scots*, 1973, 279–314.

[99] JF, lines 383–8:
> Now the king of Scotland hears his men upbraiding him. But they do not carry with them Bishop Engelramm, the best of his clergy, nor does Earl Waltheof thrust himself forward to counsel war; he plainly sees that this is a foolish course; and it comes about that the king himself many times opposes him, lured on by those who are given over to folly.

Bishop Ingram of Glasgow (1164–1174), whose career had begun in the royal household, was one of the few prominent ecclesiastical councellors at William's court (*Regesta Regum Scottorum i. The Acts of Malcolm IV* (hereafter *RRS* i), ed. G.W.S. Barrow, Edinburgh 1960, 17; *RRS* ii, 6.

deadly sin of envy (*par cunseil e par malveis' envie*), a wise man can be pushed into disastrous folly.[100]

And Jordan was clear in his own mind from whence such evil counsel came:

The king of Scotland was skilled at warfare (*bien sout li reis d'Escoce adunkes guerreier*) and in inflicting damage on the enemies he fought; but he was too much in the habit of seeking new advice. He cherished, loved and held dear people from abroad (*la gent estrange*). He never had much affection for those of his own country (*la sue gent*), whose right it was to counsel him and his realm (*ki lui e sun reaume deveient cunseillier*). In a very short time it became evident – you will hear me tell of it – how his war developed because of bad advice (*par malveis cunseiller*).[101]

Such protestations against the 'bad advice' of 'aliens' were to become commonplace in England during the first half of the thirteenth century, epitomized by the richly abusive writings of Roger of Wendover and Matthew Paris, who saw a '*gent estrange*' as excluding the king's 'natural' – that is to say native – counsellors from their rightful position of influence. The St Albans chroniclers fulminated first against John's foreign mercenary captains and officials, then against the Poitevin and Savoyard favourites of Henry III.[102] Jordan's poem, which anticipates these writers by a generation, is thus an important foretaste of nascent nationalist sentiments forged by resentment of foreign cliques, seen by a 'native' baronage to be monopolizing the king's favour and patronage to the exclusion of his 'natural' advisors.

Just who these *gent estrange* were, however, is far from clear. For despite his invective against them, Jordan consistently, and one must infer deliberately, refrains from naming any of them. As a result of both a sustained policy of enfeoffment of Franco-Norman settlers begun by David I and continued by his successors, and of close political and cultural links with the Anglo-Norman kingdom, the Scottish court had, by the time Jordan was composing his poem, come to be dominated by a new, imported, aristocracy.[103] By the early thirteenth century, the Barnwell annalist, using the blanket term 'Frenchmen' to mean

---

[100] JF, lines 669–78.

[101] JF, lines 637–44.

[102] On such views, and on the question of nationalism see M. Clanchy, *England and its Rulers, 1066–1272. Foreign Lordship and National Identity*, 1983, especially 241–62; cf. V.H. Galbraith, *Roger of Wendover and Matthew Paris*, The David Murray Lecture, Glasgow 1944; reprinted 1970). Clanchy points out that the antipathy of early thirteenth-century chroniclers towards the king's Poitevin and Savoyard favourites had been anticipated by writers such as William of Malmesbury, who complained bitterly about the exclusion of native English from high office by the Normans (*England and its Rulers*, 241).

[103] See G.W.S. Barrow, *The Anglo-Norman Era in Scottish History*, Oxford 1980; G.W.S. Barrow, 'Scotland's Norman Families', and 'The Beginnings of Military Feudalism', in *The Kingdom of the Scots*, 315–336, and 279–314; Duncan, *Scotland. The Making of the Kingdom*, 135–42.

Anglo-Norman, Flemish and other non-native lords, could write: 'the modern kings of Scotland count themselves as Frenchmen in race, manners, language and culture; they keep only Frenchmen in their own household and following, and have reduced the Scots to utter servitude'.[104] Only two native earls, Waltheof of Dunbar and Duncan of Fife appear as regular witnesses to William's *acta*, while there is evidence that the king was attempting to impose a feudal character upon these and other native earldoms.[105] Yet though Jordan clearly favours Bishop Ingram of Glasgow and Earl Waltheof as counsellors of peace, it seems most unlikely that he regarded all Franco-Norman settlers as parvenu foreigners. An important element of William's baronage had served under David I and Malcolm IV, lords such as David Olifard, one of the king's justices, Richard de Moreville, the constable, Walter fitz Alan, the steward, Walter de Bidun, the chancellor, and others. These men were hardly parvenu, and must have been well known to the northern English lords (and doubtless by others of Henry's court) who attest several of William's charters with them.[106] It is inherently implausible that a poet writing in Anglo-Norman for a predominantly Anglo-Norman audience considered all non-native Scots to be 'evil counsellors'. Jordan, indeed, has much praise for several Anglo-Norman lords who fought for William at Alnwick and distinguished themselves in battle despite their ultimate capture. Each is lauded for his bravery, with Jordan stressing that it is William's folly that, against their advice, has brought low these noble men.[107]

Geoffrey Barrow has suggested that these 'Anglo-Norman hotheads' may have included exiles such as Adam de Port, stirring up William against Henry II.[108] Such a view, however, does not accord with Jordan's own treatment of Adam, which, despite his status as a rebel, is far from hostile.[109] Possibly Jordan had in mind a group of more recently arrived lords, such as Bernard fitz Brien,

---

[104] *Memoriale Fratris Walteri de Coventria*, ed. W. Stubbs, 2 vols, RS 1873, ii, 206.
[105] Barrow, 'Beginnings of Military Feudalism', 283, 288; Duncan, *Scotland. The Making of the Kingdom*, 138–42. Barrow notes that similarly, only Duncan II of Fife and Cospatric III of Dunbar, the father of the Earl Waltheof of Jordan's poem, had frequented the councils of Malcolm IV (*RRS* ii, 6).
[106] *RRS* ii, 6, and for William's justices, 42–7. For the connections of Northumbrian lords with William's court see above, n. 141.
[107] JF, lines 1850–85. See above, n. 91.
[108] *RRS* ii, 7 and n. 19a, which gives details concerning Adam de Port and his relations with William the Lion.
[109] Despite the fact that in 1172 Adam had been attainted '*de morte et proditione regis*' (GH i, 35) and had fled to Scotland, Jordan is remarkably sympathetic to him. Speaking of the rout of the Scots at Alnwick, he notes:

> Lord Adam de Port, a most valiant baron (*un barun mult vaillant*) fled with him [Roger de Mowbray]. Off they go at full speed. It is well for them – God is their protector – that they were not caught up with by anybody. Truly if Adam de Port had not taken a good lead, he would have lost everything that day; but that was not God's will, God who is the omnipotent king; it would have been too much to bear, for he is a very valiant man (*mult vaillant*). (JF, lines 1840–7).

211

Philip de Valognes, chamberlain from 1165 to c.1171 and one of the king's most influential barons, and the brothers Robert and Walter de Berkeley, the latter succeeding Philip de Valognes as chamberlain from c.1171 to c.1193.[110] It is these who may well be the 'young and untutored men' (le gent jufne et salvage).[111] Jordan's unwillingness to name names is clearly significant, but his reticence makes it ultimately impossible to pinpoint the gent estrange with any degree of certainty. What does seem clear is that Jordan's criticism of William's evil counsellors is intended to apply by extension to the parallel case of the Young King. He too had fallen under the sway of foreigners, and in Jordan's eyes, his revolt constituted nothing less than the waging of war on his natural subjects, that is those lords who had remained loyal to the old king.

Jordan elaborates this theme in relation to William. It is the outsiders, acting from self-interest, who are responsible for urging the Scottish king to embark upon the war that was to bring about his downfall. In championing the opposing peace party, Jordan provides a vivid glimpse of court bitterly divided about the wisdom of taking up arms against Henry II, and of the pressures that might force a king down the road to war. William had not rushed into open hostilities. He had tried first to force Henry's hand by blackmail, offering the old king loyal support against his son provided only that Henry restored his rightful inheritance of Northumbria. Should this request fail, William proposed to settle the issue by single combat.[112] When, however, Henry rejected all such proposals outright,[113] William found himself in a difficult position. He had threatened force against the English king, and now had to fight or to lose face completely by a humiliating climb down. Jordan has the younger knights leave him in no doubt as to the consequences to his prestige and authority unless he fulfils his primary role as a war-leader:

> Then you should have heard the knights, those young and untutored men (ces chevaliers, la gent juefne et salvage), swearing mighty oaths and making a show of boldness: 'If you do not make war on this king who treats you thus curtly, you are not fit to hold lands and overlordships, rather should you serve Maud's son in bondage (en servage).'[114]

War is thus seen by Jordan as the policy of the young and inexperienced, of the juventus about whom Duby has written so perceptively. Duby has demonstrated how in the eleventh and twelfth centuries, these groups of young knights, eager for lands, wealth and heiresses, represented a highly volatile political force, 'the spearhead of feudal aggression', an ever-present catalyst for

---

[110] RRS ii, 6, and for the office of chamberlain or camerarius regis Scottorum, 33–4; Barrow, 'Beginnings of Military Feudalism', 287–90; 'Scotland's Norman Families', 328ff.

[111] JF, line 378.

[112] JF, lines 271–337.

[113] JF, lines 338–47, 365–77.

[114] JF, lines 378–82.

the inception of war and an important element in its prosecution.[115] Membership of the *juventus* generally lasted until a knight married, became enfeoffed, and in his turn assumed the responsibilities of the head of a family grouping. Such a process might take many years: though perhaps an extreme case, William the Marshal was still technically a 'youth' until his acquisition of Isabel, the heiress of Richard, earl of Pembroke, in 1189 when he was forty-five.[116] 'Youth' might thus extend well beyond early manhood: it was essentially a state of mind and a social condition. It is therefore of considerable significance that by this definition, William the Lion was still a *juvenis* in 1173, for although he was now thirty, he was as yet unmarried.[117] Like his father, Earl Henry, William regarded himself as an Anglo-Norman knight, and was anxious to make his mark in the chivalric society south of the Tweed. As a prince, he had accompanied his brother Malcolm on Henry II's expedition to Toulouse, and had participated enthusiastically in the tournament circuit of north-west France.[118] In his dealings with the northern English castellans in the forthcoming war of 1173–4, he was anxious to display his adherence to the knightly conventions of conduct to a degree that ultimately undermined the success of his campaigns.[119] Given these factors, and his overwhelming desire to recover what he saw as his lost inheritance of Northumbria, it is unsurprising that William was swayed by the heady counsel of the *juventus* at his court. In what was almost a ritualistic preliminary in the milieu of a warrior aristocracy, the urging of war was accompanied by the boasting of the knights as to the martial deeds they would perform – highly reminiscent of the pre-battle vows of Byrhtnoth's warriors, made from the safety of the mead-benches, before the battle of Maldon in 991.[120]

---

[115] G. Duby, 'Youth in Aristocratic Society', in G. Duby, *The Chivalrous Society*, trans. C. Postan, 1977, 112–22.

[116] For William's marriage and the rich lands and titles it brought him see S. Painter, *William Marshal. Knight-Errant, Baron and Regent of England*, Baltimore 1933, 74–9; D. Crouch, *William Marshal. Court, Career and Chivalry in the Angevin Empire, 1147–1219*, 1990, 57, 60–4. By comparison, Arnold of Ardres, son of Baldwin count of Guisnes, was knighted in 1181 and married in 1194 (Duby, 'Youth', 113).

[117] It was as late as 1184 that William sought the hand of Henry II's granddaughter, Maud, daughter of Henry the Lion, after the two kings had become reconciled after the war of 1173–4. The marriage, though granted by Henry, was forbidden by the pope on grounds of consanguinity (GH i, 313–4, 322). Henry later found William a bride, Ermengard, daughter of the viscount of Beaumont and a great-granddaughter of Henry I by an illegitimate line. The marriage was celebrated at Woodstock at Henry II's expense in 1186 (GH i, 347, 351).

[118] For William's presence on the 1159 campaign to Toulouse see RRS i, 11–12, and no. 155; Anderson, *Early Sources* ii, 240–3. In 1166, William crossed to France to indulge in 'certain feats of chivalry' (ibid., ii, 263 quoting the *Chronicle of Melrose*), and in 1175 had fought in a tournament near Le Mans, where Philip de Valognes, his chamberlain, was captured by the young William the Marshal (HGM, lines 1303–29).

[119] Strickland, *Conduct and Perception*, 65–69.

[120] JF, line 379. Cf. ibid., lines 43–58; *The Battle of Maldon*, ed. E.V. Gordon, Manchester 1976, lines 211–15; 'Aelfwine said; "Remember the words we uttered many a time over the mead, when on the bench, heroes in hall, we made our boast about hard strife. Now it may be

Jordan vividly shows how in such a tense and emotionally charged atmosphere, those who cautioned against war might easily be accused of cowardice. Thus Earl Waltheof, one of the leaders of the 'native' peace party, does not

> thrust himself forward to counsel war; he plainly sees that this is a foolish course; and it comes about that the king himself many times opposes him, lured on by those who are given over to folly. He [William] swears his oath: 'By God, the son of Mary, your cowardice will not prevent war being waged! You have great riches and wealth stored away: defend your land and seek to bring aid. And if you will not do so, you will not have any share in anything I gain as long as you live!'[121]

One may compare the account in the *Histoire de Guillaume le Maréchal* of the opposition by the Marshal to John's Poitou expedition of 1205. William's loyalty was more ambiguous than that of Waltheof, for he had sworn liege-homage to Philip Augustus for his continental lands, and therefore refused to accompany John.[122] When the king demanded judgement from his barons against the Marshal on a charge of felony, they refused, prompting the king to exclaim: 'By the teeth of God! I see that none of my barons are on my side. I know whom I can trust. I shall converse in private with my bachelors about this treason'.[123] According to the *Histoire*, John's bachelors, that is his household knights, agreed that a man who refused to accompany his lord to war was no longer entitled to hold land of him.[124] At this point, however, William's old friend, the distinguished lord Baldwin de Bethune, count of Aumâle, rounded on the bachelors: 'Be silent! It is not fitting for you or me to judge in court a knight of the Marshal's eminence. On all this field there is no man strong enough to prove in combat that he has failed his lord'.[125]

This incident once more highlights the tension between older lords, the barons, and those members of a household, in this case that of the king, the

proved which of us is bold!" '. Commenting on the flight of the coward Godric and his brothers the poet notes, 'It was as Offa had told them on the field when he held a council, that many were speaking proudly there who later would not stand firm in the hour of need' (lines 198–21). Offa himself is slain, 'yet he had compassed what he promised his chief, as he bandied vows with his generous lord in days gone by, that they should both ride home to the town unhurt or fall among the host, perish by wounds on the field', (lines 288–94).

121 JF, lines 385–94.
122 Painter, *William Marshal*, 138–42, from which the following translations (slightly abridged from the verse) are taken.
123 HGM, lines 13091–190, and lines 13184–90 for John's remark.
124 HGM, lines 13219–32.
125 HGM, lines 13233–44. The *familia regis* was not, of course, composed simply of landless younger knights, but might include men of some prominence. See J.O. Prestwich, 'The Military Household of the Anglo-Norman Kings', *EHR* xcvi, 1981, 1–37; and M. Chibnall, 'Mercenaries and the *Familia Regis* under Henry I', *History* lxii, 15–23. A detailed study of John's military household is currently being undertaken by Dr Stephen Church, and I am grateful to him for letting me have a copy of his forthcoming paper 'The Knights of the Household of King John: A Question of Numbers'.

majority of whom were not yet in possession of substantial landed wealth. The element of self-interest that might be present in the advice of landless younger men is neatly expressed by the reply Jordan gives to Waltheof in answer to William the Lion's charge of cowardice:

> 'Do not be carried away. I am your liegeman (*vostre liges huem*) as were all my kinsfolk . . . You must not let yourself be led astray by the ravings of foreigners (*la folie de aliene gent*). If all goes well with you they will profit, and they will not stand to loose much if things go wrong. There is a proverbial saying and a true one that: "When the crunch comes, one who cannot help can do harm". Do not think that I speak thus out of fear nor that, as long as life lasts, I shall let you down if war comes'.[126]

To Jordan, then, war was fuelled by young men seeking wealth and influence by catching the nearest way. And what was true for William the Lion's court was, by implication, still more so for that of the Young King, the prime example of the rash *juvenis*, surrounded by a *mesnie* of noble cadets, impatient for real power and willing to jeopardize Henry II's position and play into the hands of the Plantagenets' enemies to gain it. The themes expressed by Jordan find strikingly close parallels in Orderic Vitalis's treatment of Robert Curthose's rebellion against his father, William I, in the late 1070s. Describing Robert himself as a *tiro*, Orderic noted how he was stirred up against his father by 'factious young knights (*seditiosi tirones*)', who urged him to claim Normandy and Maine.[127] As with Jordan, the self-interest of such men was plain to Orderic, for real power meant the ability to distribute largesse to one's following. As he has the knights tell Robert:

> 'Royal prince, how can you live in such wretched poverty? Your father's minions guard the royal treasure so closely that you can scarcely have a penny from it to give to any of your dependants (*tuis clientibus*). It is a great dishonour to you and injury to us and many others that you should be deprived of the royal wealth in this way. Why do you tolerate it? A man deserves to have wealth if he knows how to distribute it generously to all seekers. How sad that your bounteous liberality should be thwarted, and that you should be reduced to indigence through the parsimony of your father, who sets his servants, or rather your servants over you.'[128]

In reply to Robert's demands, the Conqueror says that his son must wait, but that in due time he will receive his full measure of power. Meanwhile, he adds:

[126] JF, lines 395–406.
[127] *The Ecclesiastical History of Orderic Vitalis* (hereafter OV), ed. and trans. M. Chibnall, 6 vols, Oxford 1968–80, iii, 96–7, and for the course of the quarrel, 96–113.
[128] OV, iii, 96–7.

'Choose yourself better counsellors; have the sense to mistrust those rash spirits who have shamelessly goaded you on to lawless deeds . . . They provoke you to foolish ambitions, so that when order breaks down they may do as they please and commit crimes without fear of retribution. Pay no attention to the specious reasoning of wanton youths (*petulantum persuasionibus iuvenum*), but seek counsel from archbishops William and Lanfranc and other wise and experience lords (*et aliis sophistis maturisque proceribus*).'[129]

Though Orderic's own clerical bias shows clearly in having William recommend foremost the advice of the great churchmen, he here draws the same distinction as Jordan between the rash counsel of youthful knights and the wisdom of elder statesmen. His subsequent treatment of Curthose portrays the duke as the epitome of prodigality, dominated by avaricious counsellors.[130] If Henry II had ever read Orderic's *Ecclesiastical History* he would surely have found these pages prophetic, for they apply equally to the Young King. Both young men were seen by contemporaries as the epitome of reckless largesse, irresponsibly lavish with their fathers' money, reduced to knightly playboys because deprived of effective power. Both were caught in the same dilemma, for lacking the supporters that could be commanded by real political control, both needed to attract a retinue of followers by extravagant largesse in order to maintain their status yet lacked extensive demesnes or revenues from which to fund this. Though material is lacking for any comparative study, one imagines the exercise of patronage by Henry I when only lord of the Cotentin, or by Richard as count of Poitou, would have been very different.

It seems appropriate to conclude by returning to Jordan Fantosme himself, and by asking just who he was. The frank answer is that we do not know for certain. External evidence concerning the identity of the poet is limited and circumstantial. That he was called Jordan Fantosme cannot be doubted, as he names himself in the poem no less than five times, while a thirteenth-century hand in the Lincoln MS noted *auctor libri* after one of these mentions.[131] It is, however, only the rarity of the name which has led to general agreement that the author of the *Chronicle* is synonymous with a Winchester clerk, prominent first in the household of Henry of Blois, then that of his successor.[132] Both clerk

---

[129] OV iii, 98–99. Following Robert's rebellion, a group of leading magnates, some of whose sons had sided with Curthose, came to intercede with William I. Among the arguments put into their mouths by Orderic was that 'Young Robert has been led astray by the evil counsel of degenerate youths (*pravo perversorum monitu iuvenem Robertus iuvenis male deceptus est*)' (OV, lines 110–111).

[130] OV iv, 114–5; ibid., 118–19 and 119, n. 8, where Dr Chibnall notes that Robert's household consisted both of mercenary knights (*stipendiarii*) and 'the young men of noble birth and knightly training, many of them younger sons, who had no prospect of an adequate landed inheritance'.

[131] JF, xi.

[132] JF, xiii for suggestions as to the meaning of the name. The best critical study of the evidence

and poet have also been seen as synonymous with a pupil of the philosopher Gilbert de la Porée.[133]

Though there is no definite link between Jordan the poet and Jordan the clerk, it is worth briefly sketching the known facts about the latter. A letter of Archbishop Theobald to Pope Adrian, preserved by John of Salisbury and dated 1154–9, refers to a dispute 'between Master Jordan Fantosme and Master John Joicel, both clerks of the Lord Bishop of Winchester' over control of the city's schools.[134] From it, Jordan emerges as a man of some importance and holder of a recognized teaching monopoly, since in Theobald's words 'master Jordan's claim to the schools was indisputable'. He appears as aggressively litigious, being involved in a more serious case in 1171 in which he seems to have unscrupulously used papal appeals and attempted to play off the rivalries between secular and ecclesiastical courts in order to gain letters banning the prosecution witnesses from appearing.[135] Fantosme testified *viva voce* for Henry of Blois in 1160, and his house in Minster Street was regarded as a prominent landmark in contemporary charters.[136]

It has been suggested that poet and the *magister* of Winchester are linked

is Macdonald, 'The Chronicle of Jordan Fantosme: Manuscripts, Author and Versification', 242–58, which reviews all previous opinions, including that of Legge, *Anglo-Norman Literature*. The preface of Johnston's edition contains a synopsis of Macdonald's findings (JF, xi *ff.*).

[133] The connections between the clerk and the pupil of Gilbert de la Porré carry some weight. A twelfth-century St Amand manuscript of Gilbert de la Porré's commentaries on Boethius on the Trinity contains a miniature showing the master with the most distinguished pupils at his feet, including one Jordanus Fantasma, the gloss noting them to have been disciples '*sub pictavensi espiscopo*' (Macdonald, 'The Chronicle of Jordan Fantosme: Manuscripts, Author and Versification', 252–3; Johnston, 'The Historicity of Jordan Fantosme's *Chronicle*', 162–3, 167, where the illustration is reproduced). This pupilage links up well with references to Jordan as a '*magister*' (below, n. 134) and suggests that Jordan the clerk had studied at Poitiers, where Gilbert was bishop from 1142–1154, rather than at Chartres or Paris where the master had taught earlier. Both clerk and philosopher are fitting candidates for the authorship of a Latin poem on the incarnation of Christ, preserved in a thirteenth-century manuscript entitled '*Rithmus Jordanis Fantasmatis*' (JF, Appendix A, 196–199).

Links between philosopher and poet are more dubiously confined to the influence of Provençal lyric verse apparent in the poem (JF, xii) and the concurrence of the material with views of free will in the Porretanian tradition (Legge, *Anglo-Norman Literature*, 79).

[134] *The Letters of John of Salisbury*, ed. W.J. Millor, S.J. and H.E. Butler, revised by C.N.L. Brooke, 2 vols, 1955; re-issued OMT 1986, i, 95–6. The editors accept the link between clerk and poet without reservation (ibid., 95, n. 1), while P. Bourgain (*Lexicon des Mittelalters* iv, col. 283) believes the connection between poet, clerk and philosopher to be probable. My thanks are due to Dr Stuart Airlie for this last reference.

[135] Macdonald, 'The Chronicle of Jordan Fantosme: Manuscripts, Author and Versification', 250. The last known stage of the case involved the pope ordering Bartholomew, bishop of Exeter, to suspend Jordan and to deprive him if found guilty of active intimidation. If clerk and poet were one and the same, it is possible that Jordan's praise poem was an attempt to regain favour after the consequences of damaging litigation. The whole tenor of the work, however, suggests a man already close to the heart of the court, who could presume on a significant degree of intimacy with the king, his son, and their magnates.

[136] Macdonald, 248–50.

through the person of Richard of Ilchester, bishop of Winchester, who may have commissioned the poem from his clerk.[137] Yet internal evidence lends less support to this notion. For while Jordan portrays the bishop as a loyal and trustworthy minister on intimate terms with Henry, there is no dedicatory preface, Richard is never addressed directly, and features but once in the poem, in order to furnish the dramatic dialogue with Henry II concerning the plight of his realm. Equally, it is most implausible that Hugh du Puiset, bishop of Durham, who had close links with Winchester, may have been Jordan's informant on northern affairs: Jordan's only two references to the bishop of Durham openly accuse him of collusion with the Scots.[138]

In short, while the recurrence of the name Jordan with the very rare soubriquet Fantosme or Fantasma is striking, the external evidence connecting the author of the poem with the master of the schools at Winchester is at best circumstantial and is likely to remain so. What seems beyond dispute is the internal evidence of the poem as to the author's connections. The poem is clearly intended for recitation at Henry II's court, and Jordan implies a sufficient familiarity with the king and his son to venture both criticism and mediation. He displays a particular bias towards the city of London, lauding the citizens' loyalty to Henry as if he were acting as an intermediary. But it is the north which forms the focus of Jordan's poem. He clearly knew and respected William the Lion, and was on close terms with Earl David. Perhaps, as with Henry of Huntingdon's admiration for Earl Henry, these connections had been forged by virtue of David's possession of the honor of Huntingdon and other English lands, though there is no proof of this. Rather, the fact that Jordan claims to have been on the expedition to Alnwick in 1174 and his seeming intimacy with the lords of the northern border would suggest that his information came from direct contact both with these men and with members of the Scottish court.

He reveals a detailed knowledge of William's *familiares*, his diplomacy and his movements. He was clearly partisan to a faction at the Scottish court that represented both a native interest and that of long established Franco-Norman families against the preponderant influence of a *gent estrange*. Yet whatever his own origins, he associated himself primarily with the Anglo-Norman lords of

---

[137] Legge, *Anglo-Norman Literature*, 77. On Richard, who as itinerant judge, baron of the Exchequer, ambassador, reformer of the exchequer and bishop was the epitome of the omnicompetence expected from a minister in Angevin government see C. Duggan, 'Richard of Ilchester, Royal Servant and Bishop', *TRHS*, 5th series xvi, 1966, 1–21.

[138] As suggested by Macdonald, 'The Chronicle of Jordan Fantosme: Manuscripts, Author and Versification', 251. For Hugh's early career and his attempt to gain control in the north for the house of Blois see G.V. Scammell, *Hugh du Puiset, Bishop of Durham*, Cambridge 1956, 7 ff. Jordan is forthright concerning Hugh's attitude to the Scots. He has William the Lion say: 'The bishop of Durham – behold his messenger – writes to me that he has no stomach for war, and that I shall have nought to complain of in the way of interference from him or his forces' (JF, lines 534–6). Later, he has Richard of Ilchester state openly that 'He is hand in glove with King William' (ibid., lines 1597–8). Scammell, (*Hugh du Puiset*, 35–43) offers a more equivocal view of du Puiset's position in the war of 1173–4.

England. His work is essentially insular; he refers to Glanville's knights as '*noz chevaliers*'[139], and it is with the northern castellans that Jordan seems to have the closest connections. These personal links with Umfraville, Stuteville, de Vesci and others repeatedly hinted at throughout the poem, coupled with his informed stance on Scottish affairs, strongly suggest that Jordan's ambit was the northern march. In this context, it is perhaps significant that the earliest of the two surviving manuscripts of Jordan's poem comes from Durham.[140] There had been much interconnection between the Scottish court and the northern English lords, not least when Northumbria had formed part of the Scottish royal cadets' appanage. Several of the Northumbrian lords witness William's charters both as earl and then as king prior to 1173,[141] and it is possible that Jordan had shared in these ties.

If it is the case that Jordan the clerk, the philosopher and the poet are one and the same, then we have the striking image of a pugnacious master of the schools, who once may have sat at the feet of Gilbert de la Porée, riding with the knights of Rannulf de Glanville in the northern march in time of war. Such a scenario is not inherently implausible. The omnicompetence and multiplicity of function demanded from *familiares* such as Richard de Luci, Rannulf de Glanville and Richard of Ilchester is a marked feature of Angevin government.[142] If the dictates of war easily transformed justiciars or bishops into military commanders and chiefs of staff, royal or episcopal clerks, particularly those with keen interest in recording current affairs, could just as easily become diplomats and envoys. We know that in 1174, Roger of Howden, royal clerk and chronicler, was sent on a special mission to Galloway to prevent moves by

---

[139] JF, line 1758.

[140] Macdonald, 'The Chronicle of Jordan Fantosme: Manuscripts, Author and Versification', 243–7.

[141] Some of the Anglo-Norman families of northern England were bound very closely to the Scottish court. Thus, for example, Robert de Umfraville witnessed ten extant charters of David I and Earl Henry, while his son Gilbert was constable to Earl Henry and witnessed many charters in Scotland (Keen, 'The Umfravilles', 171–2). Jordan notes that Gilbert's nephew, Odinel, was brought up and held dear by Earl Henry, and must therefore have been a boyhood companion of William the Lion (JF, line 595). Many families, such as the Brus, the Umfravilles, Balliols, Vieuxponts, Bolbecs and Bertrams, held Scottish lands (J.C. Holt, *The Northerners*, 208–9). As J.C. Holt notes: 'Socially, the Border did not exist' (ibid., 208). These ties were intensified by the lordships held by the Scottish royal family in England. Prior to his accession to the earldom of Northumberland in 1152 on the death of his father, Earl Henry, William the Lion had witnessed a charter of Bernard de Balliol to Kelso abbey and had issued his own charter in favour of Nostell priory in the west riding of Yorkshire, styling himself 'William de Warenne, son of Henry, earl of the Northumbrians' (A.C. Lawrie, *Early Scottish Charters Prior to A.D. 1153*, Glasgow 1905, no. 258; RRS ii, no. 1). William de Vesci, 'father' of the castellan of Alnwick besieged by William in 1173, attests one of William's comital charters and was the beneficiary of the right to hold a market at Alnmouth, granted by William at Edinburgh (1152 x 1155) (RRS ii, nos. 2 and 3). Even after Henry II had deprived William of the earldom in 1156, he granted him the extensive Northumbrian lordship of Tynedale, so that close links continued with these families.

[142] Warren, *Henry II*, 301–16.

dissident Galwegians to remove themselves from the overlordship of William the Lion and to place themselves instead directly under the authority of Henry II.[143] Equally, while one need not posit any military function for Jordan at Alnwick, it was not exceptional for an ecclesiastic and man of letters to take to the field. Henry of Blois and still more Peter des Roches were the very models of warrior prince bishops despite the impact of Gregorian reform.[144]

Whether Jordan's own experience of the borders stemmed from a position as a long-term diplomat, or as an observer or clerk – if clerk he was – sent on a particular mission, it is impossible to say. Yet whoever Fantosme was, one thing seems clear. He is responsible for furnishing us with a poem of primary import- ance for the study of war, diplomacy and knighthood in the Anglo-Norman world. He not only gives us a vivid insight into the courts of Henry II and William the Lion, but also provides a mirror in which we can see reflected the self-perception of the Anglo-Norman warrior aristocracy.

[143] GH i, 79–80. Following the capture of William the Lion at Alnwick, the brothers Uhtred and Gilbert, rulers of Galloway, returned with their men to Galloway, expelled the king's officers, killed some Anglo-French settlers and destroyed their castles (ibid., i, 67–8). They then invited Henry to accept their allegiance. On this affair and its background see Duncan, *Scotland: The Making of a Kingdom*, 181–7.

[144] For Henry of Blois as a warrior see, for example, the *Gesta Stephani*, ed. and trans. K.R. Potter, with new introduction and notes by R.H.C. Davis, 1976, 156–7 and 156, n. 5, 210–11. Peter des Roches played a prominent role in the battle of Lincoln, 1217 (HGM, lines 16259–63, 16314–17, 16557–66, 16581–90, 16997–17006), and held other important military commands during his varied career (Clanchy, *England and its Rulers*, 184).

# A Bell-house and a Burh-geat: Lordly Residences in England before the Norman Conquest

## ANN WILLIAMS

I was recently conducting a tutorial with a student who had been asked whether or not William the Conqueror had introduced feudalism into England. The student maintained that he had, supporting his argument by the absence of feudal vocabulary in Old English. Knights, he declared, were unknown in England and in English before the Norman Conquest. When I remarked that the word 'knight' itself was Old English, he was, to use the vulgar parlance, gob-smacked. I don't say that his conclusion was thereby wrong (or indeed right) but introduce the anecdote simply to justify a paper on pre-Conquest England as suitable fare for a Knights Conference.*

I must make it clear at the outset that this is not a paper on the origin of English castles. The word 'castle', unlike the word 'knight', is not Old English. It first appears in an English context in the *Anglo-Saxon Chronicle* for 1051, when '*þa welisce menn gewroht aenne castel on Herefordscire*'.[1] In its Old English setting, the foreign word *castel* stands out, not least, alas, because it is now the one most familiar to modern ears. There were several native words which the chronicler could have used to describe a fortification – *burh, geweorc, herebeorg*; Old English had even borrowed, in the form *ceaster*, the Latin word *castrum* from which 'castle' itself is derived. The chronicler chose none of them. What King

---

* I should like to thank Professor H.R. Loyn, Dr David Roffe and Dr Stephen Church for reading and commenting upon a draft of this paper. Thanks are also due to the members of the Strawberry Hill Conference, especially Dr Richard Eales, Dr Jane Martindale and Mr Matthew Bennett for much helpful criticism and advice. I have thus been saved from many errors. Those which remain are entirely mine.
1 *Two of the Saxon Chronicles Parallel*, ed. John Earle and Charles Plummer, Oxford 1892, i, 173–4 (compare p. 175 for the *castel* of Dover). See also p. 217, where the 'feudal terminology' of the Salisbury Oath is rendered in Old English without recourse to French or Latin.

221

Edward's Normans had constructed was something new, to be described in the tongue of the *welisce menn* (foreigners) who built it.

The castles of the newcomers were seen by contemporaries as different from the residences of the native nobility. Leaving aside for the moment the question of where the differences lay, it should be remarked that there is a singular unanimity of opinion among modern historians on what English lordly residences were like. This opinion is epitomized in the description of Dorothy Whitelock, written in 1952:

> ... they were commonly built of wood, and in the early days consisted of a single-storied great hall, used for meals, entertainment and all the main daily business, and as sleeping-quarters for the retainers at night, with smaller, detached buildings, called 'bowers', for the bedrooms of the owner, his family and guests. The whole was surrounded by an earthwork and a stockade, and was known as a *burh*, that is, a fortified residence.[2]

It is unfortunate that the word *burh* inevitably conjures up images of an urban settlement. Its development into Modern English 'borough' stems from the fact that most (though not all) of the fortifications built by King Alfred and his successors were, or became, towns. The primary meaning of *burh* is, however, simply a fortified or defended place; its root is the verb *beorgan*, 'to protect'. In the formation of place-names, *burh* and its derivatives, *byrh* and *byrig*, are applied to a variety of defensive structures: prehistoric earthworks, Roman camps, Anglo-Saxon fortifications, castles, fortified houses and manors, market-towns and suburbs.[3] Only the context will determine the meaning intended in any given case. Concentration on the *burh* as walled town has obscured the *burh* as fortified house, yet it continued in use (at least in place-name formation) in this latter sense well after the Norman Conquest. Nobury, in Inkberrow, Worcs., means 'the new borough' and probably refers to a new manor-house built there in 1235.[4] Such work as exists on the *burh* as fortified house has tended to concentrate on its influence, or lack of influence, on the development of the English castle.[5] What is missing is a survey of English lordly residences for their own sake, rather than as the prelude to something else.

---

2  Dorothy Whitelock, *The Beginnings of English Society*, Harmondsworth 1952, 88; cf. H.R. Loyn, *Anglo-Saxon England and the Norman Conquest*, 1962, 220; Nicholas Brooks, 'The development of military obligation in eighth- and ninth-century England', *England before the Conquest*, ed. Kathleen Hughes and Peter Clemoes, Cambridge 1971 (henceforth Brooks, 'Development of military obligation'), 83; Kathryn Hume, 'The concept of the hall in Old English poetry', *Anglo-Saxon England* iii, 1974, 64; P.H. Sawyer, *From Roman Britain to Norman England*, 1978, 155–6; Eric Fernie, *The Architecture of the Anglo-Saxons*, 1983 (henceforth Fernie, *Architecture*), 29.

3  A.H. Smyth, *English Place-name Elements*, Cambridge 1956 (henceforth Smyth, *Place-name Elements*), i, 58–62.

4  Margaret Gelling, *Signposts to the Past*, 1978, 143.

5  The debate is exemplified in R. Allen Brown, 'An historian's approach to the origins of the

This paper is an attempt to redress the balance. It is based on what material I have been able to find, and is in no sense the fruit of any exhaustive (or even systematic) research. I have in the process strayed far out of my field and apologize in advance for my lack of skill in linguistic and archaeological sources. To compensate for these shortcomings, I have tried to confine my enquiries to the tenth and eleventh centuries, and to concentrate on examples of unambiguously aristocratic, as opposed to royal and ecclesiastical, residences, other than for purposes of comparison.

My first *burh* does, however, date from the pre-Alfredian period. It occurs in a memorandum from the archives of the church of Worcester.[6] In 822 or 823, King Ceolwulf I of Mercia asked the bishop and community of Worcester to give him the estate (*þæt lond*) at Bromsgrove, Worcs. The memorandum is not easy to interpret, but it seems that Bromsgrove was held of the church by the thegn Wulfheard of Inkberrow. The bishop therefore summoned Wulfheard, and asked him to relinquish his interest in Bromsgrove. Wulfheard agreed, on condition that the bishop would compensate him with some other estate (*swelce londare*), 'where he could live honourably and have his dwelling (*wic*) in the *burh* during his life'. *Burh* in this context clearly means the manor-house, to which the estate (*land*) was appurtenant. It emerges from the memorandum that what Wulfheard was after was Inkberrow itself. This estate had been bequeathed to the church of Worcester by Wulfheard's kinsmen, and had been the subject of an earlier dispute between the bishop and Wulfheard. It had ended (as was usual in such cases) in compromise; Wulfheard was to hold the estate for life, with reversion to the church. Now Wulfheard was trying to bargain his interest in Bromsgrove for outright possession of Inkberrow, but he was unsuccessful. From the present viewpoint the interest lies in the description of the residence which Wulfheard considered suitable to his status; a matter quite separate from what kind of structure actually existed at Inkberrow in the ninth century.

The description of Wulfheard's ideal residence can be contrasted with the highly undesirable dwelling in the Old English poem, *The Wife's Lament*. Like the Worcester memorandum, the poem is not easy to interpret, but it seems that the speaker is a lady who has been driven from her home and forced to live in a cave or barrow, under an oak-tree, in a woodland grove. To the modern reader comfortably ensconced by the fire it sounds romantic and charming, but the poem's heroine comes from a harder world, and complains bitterly:

'. . . *burgtunas brerum beweaxne, wic wynna leas.*'

___

castle in England', *Archaeological Journal* cxxvi, 1969 (1970) (henceforth Brown, 'Origins of the castle'), 131–48.

6  P.H. Sawyer, *Anglo-Saxon Charters: an annotated list and bibliography*, 1968 (henceforth S.), no. 1432, printed in A.J. Robertson, *Anglo-Saxon Charters*, Cambridge 1956 (henceforth Robertson, *Charters*) no. 4. For Wulfheard's previous claims on Inkberrow, see S. 1430. There had been a minster at Inkberrow, founded in the seventh century (S. 53).

'The *burhtunas* are overgrown with briars, and the dwelling (*wic*) is joyless.'[7]

The word *burhtun* is often found as a place-name, in the forms Burton, Bourton
and Broughton. Its meaning is 'fort settlement' and it has been interpreted in
various ways.[8] In this particular case, it seems that the meaning 'defensible
house' is intended: the wife is comparing the tangled undergrowth around her
miserable hole in the ground with the well-kept hedges surrounding the manor-
house where she used to live.

It is to such *burhs* that the Laws of Alfred refer, in the clause concerned with
*burh-bryce*, the crime of breaking into a fortified residence.[9] The fines are graded
according to the status of the *burh*'s owner; the king, the archbishops, the
bishops and ealdormen, the men with a 1200s wergild, and the men with a 600s
wergild. The clause makes it clear that a nobleman's house is intended, for it
ends with the fine for *ceorles edorbryce*, breaking through the fence surrounding
the residence of a ceorl. A famous and spectactular example of *burh-bryce*
occured in 786, when the ætheling Cyneheard surprised and killed King
Cynewulf of Wessex in the royal *burh* of *Meretun* (possibly Martin, Dorset),
where the king was visiting his mistress.[10]

A later estate similar to that specified by Wulfheard is described in a writ of
Edward the Confessor, issued between 1042 and 1046.[11] The king confirmed to
Westminster Abbey an estate in Essex, given to the abbey by Azur Swart (the
Black) and his wife Aelfgyth. It consisted of the *burh* of Wennington, with 4
hides of land belonging to it, the church and the churchsoke, and the land
called 'At the Lea'; this last tenement probably lay in the neighbouring vill of
Aveley, whose name (Aelfgyth's *leah*) preserves that of Azur's wife, Aelfgyth.
This estate can be compared with another at Burwell (*burh*-spring) in Cambridgeshire, which the thegn Aelfgar gave to Ramsey Abbey towards the end of
the tenth century.[12] It consisted of his house and court (perhaps the enclosure

---

[7] Bruce Mitchell and Fred C. Robinson, *A Guide to Old English*, Oxford 1964, 248–51 (lines
31–2); *burgtun* is glossed 'protecting hedge' (p. 294).

[8] Smyth, *Place-name Elements*, 62; Matthias T. Löfvenberg, *Studies on Middle English Local
Surnames*, Lund 1942 (henceforth Löfvenberg, *Middle English Local Surnames*), 29. Margaret
Gelling has argued that the pre-Alfredian *burh-tunas* were 'a system of defence posts', notably
on the borders of Mercia and Wales ('The place-name Burton and variants', *Weapons and
Warfare in Anglo-Saxon England*, ed. Sonia Chadwick-Hawkes, Oxford 1989, 145 ff); compare
the 'defensible houses' in Herefordshire discussed below, pp. 231–2.

[9] Alfred 40, repeating and refining Ine 45; see F.L. Attenborough, *The Laws of the Earliest
English Kings*, Cambridge 1922 (henceforth Attenborough, *Laws*), 83.

[10] ASC sub anno 757. The description of *Meretun* mentions the *bur* (bower, private room) in
which the king was being entertained by his lady-friend, while his hearthtroop was elsewhere
(presumably in the hall); and the gates of the *burh* which the aetheling's men locked against
the royal host, and around which the fighting took place.

[11] S. 1117, printed and discussed in F.E. Harmer, *Anglo-Saxon Writs*, Manchester 1952, no. 73,
pp. 492–3, 556.

[12] *Chronicon Abbatiae Rameseiensis*, ed. W. Dunn Macrae, RS 83, 1886, 51; C.R. Hart, *Early*

within which the house stood), along with 3 hides, 40 acres and a virgate of land, and the church of Burwell, of which Aelfgar was patron. Both Azur and Aelfgar were of thegnly rank, though perhaps not of the highest status. Azur Swart was remembered at Westminster as the donor of land at Leyton as well as Wennington, and is probably the father of Swein Swart, who in 1066 held land in Leyton, Upminster and Aveley amounting to 12½ hides.[13] Aelfgar was probably in the service of the lay patron of Ramsey Abbey, Ealdorman Aethelwine of East Anglia (d.992); he is described as *aldermanni familiaris et a secretis*.

Wennington and Burwell come close to the ideal thegnly residence described in the eleventh-century tract *Geþyncðo* (the so-called 'promotion law'). It occurs in the passage relating how a ceorl may thrive to thegnhood:[14]

And if a ceorl prospered so that he had fully five hides of his own land (*agenes landes*), [church and kitchen], bell [house] and *burh-geat*, seat and special office in the king's hall, then was he thenceforward entitled to the rank of a thegn.

The passage has been much discussed and doubts have been expressed whether it should be taken as a literal description of eleventh-century reality, rather than a nostalgic image of the mythical 'good old days'.[15] Given, however, that it comes from the pen of Archbishop Wulfstan of York (1002–23), whose deep knowledge of English law and custom is reflected in his drafting of the later law-codes of Aethelred II and those of Cnut, it would be unwise to dismiss the description as moonshine. The ideal residence of the tract is reflected not only in Wennington and Burwell, but in the twelfth-century estate of the Cockfield

---

*Charters of Eastern England*, Leicester 1966 (henceforth Hart, *Charters of Eastern England*), 238. For the use of *curia* in the sense of enclosure, see the case of Shalford discussed below, pp. 228–9. The customs of Oxford (below p. 238) speak of breaking into a man's *domus vel curia*.

[13] For Swein Swart, see *LDB* fos 78v, 91. He is not distinguished by his bye-name in the entry for Aveley (*LDB* fo 84v) and Swein is, of course, a common name but his tenure of Leyton, associated with Azur Swart, suggests he is the Swein who held Aveley, which preserves the name of Azur Swart's wife. A Swein Swart, described as Earl's Edwin's man, held Lamport, Bucks (*GDB* fo 147v). Sons could 'inherit' their father's bye-name; see Aethelmaer the Fat, son of Aethelwold the Fat and Esbearn Bigga, son of Aethelric Bigga (Robertson, *Charters*, 387, 436); and Aelfgar Meaw, son of Aethelweard Meaw (Ann Williams, 'An introduction to the Gloucestershire Domesday', *The Gloucestershire Domesday*, ed. Ann Williams and R.W.H. Erskine, 1989, 22). In the last case, the bye-name seems not to have descended to the third generation; Aelfgar Meaw's son, Beorhtric, is no-where called Beorhtric Meaw. For a possibly inherited toponymic, see Siward and Sired of Chilham, below, p. 237.

[14] F. Liebermann, *Die Gesetze der Angelsachsen*, Halle 1903–16 (henceforth Liebermann), i, 456; translated in Dorothy Whitelock, *English Historical Documents*, i, *c.*500–1042, 1955 (henceforth *EHD*), 431–2. The words in square brackets are found only in the *Textus Roffensis* version.

[15] Brown, 'Origins of the castle', 141; F.M. Stenton defended the reality behind *Geþyncðo's* image ('The thriving of the Anglo-Saxon ceorl', *Preparatory to Anglo-Saxon England*, ed. D.M. Stenton, Oxford 1970 (henceforth Stenton, 'Thriving of the ceorl'), 383–93.

family, described in the appendix to Jocelin of Brakelond's Chronicle, and consisting of 'the large messuage (in Bury St Edmunds) where the manor-house of Adam (I) of Cockfield formerly stood, with its wooden belfry 140 feet high'.[16] Adam I of Cockfield lived in the time of King Stephen, and was of English descent; his father bore the Old English name of Leofmaer.

Part of the unwillingness to accept Geþyncðo at face-value stems, I think, from the equation of ceorl with 'peasant'. This is, to my mind, misleading. In the late Old English period, the category ceorl, like the category thegn, covered men of widely differing status; it included all 200s men, as opposed to the 1200s men who made up the thegnly class. The term ceorl would describe the geneat Byrhtwold who fought beside his lord, Ealdorman Byrhtnoth, at the battle of Maldon in 991; or the cnihtas, Sexi and Leofwine, whom their lord sent to the archbishop of Canterbury, Eadsige (1038–50), to ask for a renewal of his lease on Halton, Bucks. Such men might hold land, and owe service, including agricultural service, in respect of it, as did the radmen and radknights of Domesday Book; but they are rather more than semi-servile peasants. They are best described as non-noble free men, who might, by the favour of their lords, advance their fortunes and aquire thegnly status. Indeed the line between such men and the lesser thegns is not easily drawn in practice.[17] It is men of this type, surely, that Geþyncðo has in mind.

The marks of thegnly status in Geþyncðo are four: land, church, burh-geat and royal service. The last stipulation shows that the status intended is that of a king's thegn, rather than the median thegn who serves a lord other than the king. This may also be the implication of the statement that the ceorl's five hides must be his own land, if agenes landes here means not demesne, but land held by charter, for such land (bookland) was the characteristic mark of a king's thegn.[18] The burh-geat (the gate of the burh) presumably stands for the whole manor-house. It is used in the same sense in the tenth- or eleventh-century tract on the king's personal peace, known as Be Griðe or Pax. In this tract the extent of the king's peace is defined as follows:[19]

> Thus far shall be the king's grið, from his burh-geat where he is dwelling, on its four sides; 3 miles, 3 furlongs, 3 acres' breadth, 9 feet, 9 palms, 9 barleycorns.

16 Jocelin of Brakelond, Chronicle of the Abbey of Bury St Edmunds, ed. Diana Greenaway and Jane Sayers, Oxford 1989, 123.
17 D.E. Scragg, The Battle of Maldon, Manchester 1981, 67, 108; Robertson, Charters, 174–5; Ann Williams, 'An introduction to the Worcestershire Domesday', The Worcestershire Domesday, ed. Ann Williams and R.W.H. Erskine, 1988, 6–7.
18 Stenton interpreted agenes landes as demesne ('Thriving of the ceorl', 389) but see the arguments of Richard Abels, Lordship and Military Obligation in Anglo-Saxon England, 1988, 141.
19 Liebermann, i, 390. The clause is repeated in the Leges Henrici Primi, ed. L.J. Downer, Oxford 1972, 120–1, where burh-geat is Latinized as porta. For a discussion of grið, see H.M. Chadwick, Studies on Anglo-Saxon Institutions, Cambridge 1905, 115; N.D. Hurnard, 'The Anglo-Norman franchises', EHR lxiv, 1949, 303–5.

Here the *burh-geat* presumably means the king's royal residence.[20] King Edmund, in his code regulating the blood-feud, lays down the penalties for attacking those who have sought refuge in a church or in his *burh*, here meaning not the fortified towns established by his father and grandfather, but the royal residences or king's *tunas* ('Kingstons'), whose role in articulating the royal administration has been described by Professor Sawyer.[21] Like *burhtun*, the word *burh-geat* occurs as a place-name, in the forms Burgate, Boreat and Buckhatch. The precise nature of the *burh* in such places needs to be established by the individual context, but some of the 'Burgates' may represent defensible manor-houses.[22]

The use of the word *burh-geat* to indicate the manor-house or residence suggests that the gate-house was the most prominent feature of the defences; a parallel appears in the Bayeux Tapestry, which represents Norman castles by their most obvious feature, their mottes. A gate implies a fence or hedge, and the enclosures were probably ditched as well. A *burh*-ditch occurs among the boundary-marks of an estate at Upper Winchendon, Bucks., in a charter of 1004, and topographical examination of the area suggests that the ditch of the estate's manor-house is intended.[23] The construction of such works was a duty laid on the peasants of the estate. The survey of Tidenham, Gloucs. (a manor belonging to Bath Abbey), which was made about 1050, prescribes that each *gebur* (or villan) should 'fence and dig one pole of the *burh*-hedge: *tyne 7 dicie i gyrde burhheges*'.[24] A similar obligation, 'to build and fence the *burh*: *bytlian 7 burh hegegian*', appears in the eleventh-century tract on the *Rights and Ranks of the People* (*Rectitudines Singularum Personarum*), though here the burden fell not upon the *geburas*, but on the higher-ranking free men, the *geneatas*.[25] The duties of the good reeve included 'to make good the hedges' (*hegan godian*) of the *burh*.[26] A *burh*-hedge may not sound a very impressive structure, but the same word is used in a tenth-century boundary-clause to describe the walls of the

[20] Maitland believed that the *burh-geats* of both Gepyncðo and Be Grið referred to the gates of fortified towns, but so far as Gepyncðo is concerned, he was using a faulty text; see W.R. Stevenson, 'Burh-geat-setl', *EHR* xii, 1897, 489–92, who showed that a manorial *burh* was intended.
[21] II Edmund 2, see A.J. Robertson, *Laws of the Kings of England from Edmund to Henry I*, Cambridge 1925 (henceforth Robertson, *Laws*), 8–9; P.H. Sawyer, 'The royal *tun* in pre-Conquest England', *Ideal and Reality in Frankish and Anglo-Saxon Society*, ed. Patrick Wormald, Donald Bullough and Roger Collins, Oxford 1983, 273–99.
[22] Smyth, *Place-name Elements*, 62; Löfvenberg, *Middle English Local Surnames*, 28.
[23] Margaret Gelling, *Early Charters of the Thames Valley*, Leicester 1979 (henceforth Gelling, *Charters of the Thames Valley*), 181–4.
[24] S. 1555, printed in Robertson, *Charters*, 204–7.
[25] Liebermann, i, 445.
[26] Liebermann, i, 454–5, translation in *Anglo-Saxon Prose*, ed. Michael Swanton, 1975, 26. For similar services in the post-Conquest period, see David Austin, ed., *Boldon Book: Northumberland and Durham*, Chichester 1982, 36–7.

royal city of Winchester, to whose upkeep 2,400 hides were assigned by the *Burghal Hidage.*[27]

Such services resemble royal rights to labour on the king's works, and indeed, where bookland is concerned, derive from those rights.[28] When land was booked, that is granted by a royal diploma or land-book, the public obligations due from it were remitted, with the exception of military service, geld, and some judicial rights. In practice this meant that the holders of bookland could intercept for their own benefit the services formerly due to the king. Tenure by book, once the preserve of the church, was by the eighth century extended to lay landowners, and by the tenth century was the characteristic tenure of the king's thegns. They discharged their service, which was primarily military, directly to the king; thus Tewkesbury, Gloucs., held in King Edward's reign by the rich nobleman, Beorhtric son of Aelfgar, was 'quit of all royal service and geld except the service of the lord himself whose manor it was'.[29] All other services were appropriated by Tewkesbury's lord, Beorhtric.

The services due from the estate were rendered to the hall (*heall, aula*) and the court (*curia*), the public part of the manor, which defined the identity of the land attached to it. Thus Thurstan son of Wine in his will (1043–1045) defined his two manors at Shouldham, Norfolk, as 'the estate at the north hall' and 'the estate at the middle hall' respectively, and when Ringulf of Oby, Norfolk, forfeited his land for rebellion after the Norman Conquest, his *terra et aula* were taken into the hands of the king's officials.[30] It is this aspect of the manor, its function as the collecting-point of seigneurial dues and services, that interested the Domesday commissioners. In Domesday Book the presence of a hall is one of the criteria used to identify a manor; indeed places without halls are called manors only in exceptional circumstances. A manor which lost its hall lost also its manorial status; at Irish Hill, Berks., Hugolin the steersman 'transferred the hall and other houses' to another manor, of which Irish Hill, once a manor in its own right, became a dependency.[31] In some cases the hall may be a notional concept rather than a physical building, as at Eaton, Notts., which was assessed at only 6½ bovates but held, before the conquest, by no less than 10 thegns, each of whom had his hall.[32] In such cases the 'hall' may only indicate the rights to a separate share in the profits of the estate. Conversely the entry for Shalford, Surrey, may indicate a joint-tenure, for the manor there was held before the conquest by two brothers, each of whom had his own house (*domus*) 'but

[27] S. 1560.
[28] Brooks, 'Development of military obligation', 71, gives examples of the services remitted.
[29] GDB fo. 163v.
[30] Dorothy Whitelock, *Anglo-Saxon Wills*, Cambridge 1930, 81; F.M. Stenton, 'St Benet of Holme and the Norman Conquest', *EHR* xxxvii, 1922, 227.
[31] R. Welldon Finn, *An Introduction to Domesday Book*, 1963, 50–1; GDB fo 63.
[32] GDB fo 284v.

nevertheless dwelt within one court (*curia*)'.[33] A single manor held in common seems to be implied.

It is at the time of Domesday that the variety of manorial estates can be most clearly seen. Some manors were co-terminous with the townships in which they lay, but some vills were divided between several manors or parts of manors, while some manors extended into several separate vills. The latter have been given many modern names, multiple-estates, composite estates, and the like. They did not necessarily consist of a contiguous block of territory; often their component parts were widely scattered. Tewkesbury, Gloucs., held before 1066 by Beorhtric son of Aelfgar, is a particulary well-defined example. It had been 'destroyed and dismembered' at some point between the Conquest and 1086, and its description in Domesday is in the past tense, probably deriving from a pre-Conquest, or at least pre-Domesday survey.[34] It was assessed at 95 hides, with another 5 hides in the manor of Oxenton, which, despite having its own hall, was part of Tewkesbury. The chief vill was Tewkesbury itself, where Beorhtric's hall and court were situated, and to this was attached 45 hides of land in seven vills, inhabited by the peasants who owed service to the hall. These holdings would have been described elsewhere as berewicks of Tewkesbury. A further 30 hides in four vills were held by tenants, probably on some form of leasehold tenure, and 20 hides in seven vills belonged to the church of Tewkesbury, an old minster situated at Stanway. Tewkesbury was a large estate and growing larger, for to the original 95 hides had been added another 32¼ hides in six vills, whose holders 'had submitted themselves and their lands into the power of Beorhtric'.

It is at the focal points of such great estates that we might expect to find the fortified houses of the Old English aristocracy. Only physical examination of likely sites will reveal their presence. For example, Edwin, earl of Mercia, had a hall at Laughton-en-le-Morthen, Yorks. (WR) on the eve of the Conquest.[35] The parish church of Laughton, dedicated to All Saints, has pre-Conquest fabric, possibly the remains of a *porticus*, at its west end. Given the relationship observed elsewhere between churches and seigneurial residences, it has been suggested that Edwin's hall may have lain on the site of the later motte and bailey castle, constructed to the west of All Saints.[36] Only archaeological excavation could confirm this suggestion and it is to the archaeological evidence for aristocratic *burhs* that we must now turn.

---

[33] GDB fo. 35v.

[34] GDB fo. 163–163v.

[35] GDB fo. 319. Laughton-en-le-Morthen, held by Roger de Bully in 1086, was an estate of 18 carucates, including a berewick in Throapham, to which was attached 36 carucates of sokeland in seven vills; compare the estates of Barton upon Humber and Earl's Barton, discussed below, pp. 234–5.

[36] R.K. Morris, *Churches in the Landscape*, 1989 (henceforth Morris, *Churches*), 258–9. Morris covers in detail many of the subjects touched upon in the present paper, and my debt to his work will be obvious.

Attenborough remarked, in 1922, that 'stones or earth can hardly have been used; otherwise such residences would frequently be traceable now'.[37] Since then matters have changed considerably. The dramatic discoveries at Goltho, Lincs., have shown what a pre-Conquest aristocratic *burh* was like.[38] Occupation layers from early Saxon to late medieval revealed the successive stages in the development of the site, which was abandoned towards the end of the middle ages. By the late ninth or early tenth century, a large hall (80 feet by 20) and its subsidiary buildings lay within a banked enclosure, surrounded by a ditch up to 7 feet deep and 18 feet wide. This *burh* went through successive rebuildings, and in the eleventh century occupied an area some 325 feet by 270, surrounded by a rampart still standing up to 5 feet high when excavated and a ditch up to 6 feet deep. After 1066, a motte and bailey castle was erected over the former *burh*.

Although no site has, as yet, produced the same volume of detailed material as Goltho, it is unlikely to be unique. A similar complex was excavated at Sulgrave, Northants. Here in the early eleventh century a large hall (80 feet long) and its outbuildings were associated with a contemporary bank and ditch. To the east stood a church, whose west door was aligned on the same axis as the hall, suggesting that the two buildings were associated. The hall of Sulgrave must have been an imposing structure:

This great house, of five square bays with an open, cobbled porch at one end, seems to anticipate the traditional medieval arrangement, having a service-end, separated by a screen and cross-passage from the hall proper, with its central hearth and benches. There was an L-shaped chamber-block at the other end, perhaps over-sailing the hall. Near the porch-end, on the axis of the hall, was a detached timber building, perhaps a kitchen. There was a free-standing stone building set to one side of the hall, later incorporated into the post-Conquest defences to serve as a gateway.[39]

Sulgrave's chamber-block may have been two-storied. On the Bayeux Tapestry, Earl Harold is shown feasting in the upper room of his hall at Bosham, which was reached by an outside staircase.[40] Doubts have been expressed whether the Tapestry is representing an English building, rather than reflecting continental

[37] Attenborough, *Laws*, 190.

[38] Guy Beresford, 'Goltho manor, Lincolnshire: the buildings and their surroundings', *Anglo-Norman Studies* iv, 1982, 13–36; *Goltho: the development of an early medieval manor*, 1987. Paul Everson ('What's in a name? Goltho, "Goltho" and Bullington', *Lincolnshire History and Archaeology* xxiii, 1988, 93–9) argues for a revision of Beresford's dating of the successive stages at Goltho.

[39] P.V. Addyman, 'The Anglo-Saxon house: a new review', *Anglo-Saxon England* i, 1972, 297; for the excavations, see B.K. Davison, 'Excavations at Sulgrave, Northamptonshire', *Archaeological Journal* cxxxiv, 1977, 105–14.

[40] D.M. Wilson, ed., *The Bayeux Tapestry*, 1985 (henceforth *Bayeux Tapestry*), plates 3 and 4; Fernie, *Architecture*, 22.

models, but some English halls had upper rooms. There was a spectactular accident at the royal residence of Calne, Wilts., in 978, when 'the leading councillors of England fell down from an upper story (*of anre upfloran*), all except the holy archbishop Dunstan, who alone remained standing on a beam'.[41] If the designer of the Tapestry really could distinguish between the details of English and Norman hair-styles and armour, he could perhaps tell the difference between English and continental building traditions.[42]

The excavations at Goltho are not only important in themselves, but show the possibilities of sites as yet unexplored. They also demonstrate the necessity for full and detailed excavation. A site which bears more than a passing resemblance to that at Goltho was recently destroyed to make way for a playing-field. It consisted of a group of earthworks in a field called Very (previously Berry) Croft, in the village of Hillesley, Gloucs.[43] The main mound was surrounded by a ditch, with a causewayed entrance; two smaller ditched mounds were associated with it, and a low bank to the south may have been the outer bank of a bailey. Three periods of building were identified in the rescue dig, the earliest associated with what may have been a timber hall. There was some indication that the site, classed as 'Saxo-Norman', had been in use before the construction of the earthworks, but no details were available. Whether the earliest defences were pre- or post-Conquest could not be determined, and no conclusions could be drawn about the nature or function of the earthworks.

Both Goltho and Sulgrave continued in use after the Conquest and were re-modelled by their later lords.[44] It is quite possible that the more heavily-defended castles of the post-Conquest period may overlie other pre-Conquest lordly residences. This hypothesis sheds some light on the nature of the two 'defensible houses' recorded in the Herefordshire folios of Domesday Book. One *domus defensabilis* lay at Eardisley, a manor situated 'in the midst of a certain wood', and the other at nearby Ailey, where there was 'a large wood used for

---

41 ASC sub anno 978. The same word, *upflor*, is used for the vantage-point from which the Norman archers (*cnihtas*) shot at the English monks in the infamous massacre in the church at Glastonbury (ASC 'E', sub anno 1083).

42 Nicholas Brooks and H.E. Walker, 'The authority and interpretation of the Bayeux Tapestry', *Anglo-Norman Studies* i, 1979, 19–20; but see also Ian Peirce, 'Arms, armour and warfare in the eleventh century', *Anglo-Norman Studies* x, 1988, 238.

43 Bruce Williams, 'Excavations of a medieval earthwork complex at Hillesley, Hawkesbury, Avon', *Transactions of the Bristol and Gloucestershire Archaeological Society* cv, 1987, 147–63. The 1086 tenant was Bernard, probably Bernard Pauncevolt, holding of Turstin fitzRolf; the 1066 tenant was a thegn with the ubiquitous name of Aelfric (*GDB* fo. 169v).

44 Goltho itself does not appear in Domesday Book. It lay in Bullington, a vill divided in 1066 between the holdings of Lambi or Lambakarl (*GDB* fos 349v, 351) and those of Aelfric (*GDB* fos 340v, 354, cf. 375v), whose family's lands had passed to the bishop of Durham. It was probably on Aelfric's manor that the manor-house of Goltho lay (Steven Basset, 'Beyond the edge of excavation: the topographical context of Goltho', *Studies in Medieval History presented to R.H.C. Davis*, ed. Henry Mayr-Harting and R.I. Moore, 1985, 24). Sulgrave belonged to Giles fitzAnsculf in 1086; its pre-Conquest holder is not recorded (*GDB* fo. 227).

hunting'.[45] Both manors were close to the borders of Wales, an area whose inhabitants were doubtless more conscious than most of the need for security. Indeed a castle was later built at Eardisley, when it became the *caput* of the Baskerville fee. In 1086, Eardisley was held by Robert (de Baskerville) of Roger de Lacy, and Ailey by Gilbert fitz Turold, as the gift of his former lord, William fitz Osbern, earl of Hereford.

It has been suggested that these two defensible houses, lying as they do in 'the long gap between Wigmore and Clifford castles', were part of the string of defences built by the Normans against the Welsh. The suggestion is an attractive one but does not explain the unusual terminology used to describe them.[46] Clearly they were not castles, not even little castles, like the *castellulum* at Sharpness, Gloucs.[47] Were they pre-Conquest aristocratic *burhs*?

It is true that in neither case does Domesday say or imply that the *domus defensabilis* was in existence before 1066. When we look, however, at the pre-Conquest tenants of Eardisley and Ailey, the possibilities are interesting. Eardisley belonged to Eadwig *cild*, an important local landowner, whose estates were the main source for Roger de Lacy's fee in Herefordshire; Eadwig's manor of Weobley became the *caput* of that fee, and the site of its castle. Eadwig's manor did not take up the whole vill of Eardisley; part of it was in the hands of a still greater lord, Harold Godwineson, who was *inter alia* earl of Herefordshire.[48] It was Earl Harold who held Ailey before the Conquest. Harold's responsibility for the defence of the Welsh borders might well provide a context for the construction of particularly strongly defended residences in exposed and outlying places, given especially the presence of actual castles in the region before 1066.

Identification of the vestigial defences of pre-Conquest *burhs* is problematic, but another indication of their presence has been longer lasting. The church of the manor may survive, even when the hall and its outbuildings, and the surrounding defences, vanish or are subsumed into a later structure. Churches formed part of the seigneurial estates at both Wennington and Burwell, quoted above; the church was an integral part of the thegnly estate described in *Geþynçðo*. In the only surviving pictorial representation of an English manor, that of Bosham on the Bayeux Tapestry, the lord's hall stands adjacent to the church.[49] The connection between church and manor-house has been very fully

---

[45] GDB fos 184v, 187; Frank and Caroline Thorn, *Domesday Book: Herefordshire*, Chichester 1983, entry 10, 42 note.

[46] See *Domesday Book: Herefordshire* (see previous note), Introductory Notes, 4. No other *domus defensabilis* appears in Domesday, but compare the entry of Eardington, Shrops., to which were attached a *nova domus*, and a *burgum* called Quatford; there was later a Norman castle at Quatford, eventually transferred to Bridgnorth (Frank and Caroline Thorne, *Domesday Book: Shropshire*, Chichester 1986, entry 4, 1, 32 and note; GDB fo 254).

[47] GDB fo. 163.

[48] For Earl Harold's land in Eardisley, see GDB fos 181, 187.

[49] *Bayeux Tapestry*, plates 3–4. Like Tewkesbury, Bosham was an estate divided between a lay lord, Earl Godwine, and the canons of Bosham.

explored by R.K. Morris, who has drawn attention to 'the frequency with which parish churches are found next to buildings or monuments of lordly status'.[50]

The relationship between churches and the lords on whose lands they were established long pre-dates the Conquest. Such 'estate-churches', though relatively rare in the period before Alfred, become more and more common in the tenth and eleventh centuries, with the break-up of ancient estates (usually royal) as their component vills were booked to the king's thegns. It can sometimes be shown that the discrete estates formed in this way bore the names of the thegns to whom they were granted. Woolstone, Berks. (*Wulfric's tun*) was once part of the great estate of *Aescesbyrig* (the *burh* in this name refers to the Iron Age hillfort known as Uffington Castle). Woolstone acquired its name after it was given to Wulfric by successive grants of the kings Edmund and Eadred in the middle of the tenth century.[51] On such estates the king's thegns built their residences, sometimes encouraging or compelling their dependent peasants to settle around the manor-house, and re-organizing the layout of their tenements in the surounding fields. Thus nucleated villages might be created out of previously scattered settlements and farmsteads. The estate churches were built to serve such 'new' villages, or, in places where such agglomeration did not occur, the needs of the lord and his family. This process, operating throughout the tenth, eleventh and twelfth centuries, gave rise to the parochial structure of the later middle ages.[52]

Already by the reign of Edgar (959–75) it had become necessary to regulate the relationship between such estate-churches and the old minsters on which the earlier parochial structure had been based. The main bones of contention were payment of tithes, and burial-rights, for which soul-scot (mortuary dues) could be charged. Edgar's Second Code, promulgated between 959 and 963, allowed 'the thegn who on his bookland has a church and a graveyard' to pay one-third of his demesne tithes to that church, the remainder going to the old minster in whose *parochia* the estate lay. If the thegnly church had no graveyard, the full tithe was to go to the minster, and the thegn could 'pay what he chooses to his priest from the [remaining] nine parts'.[53]

As we have seen, *Geþyncðo* envisaged that a church would form part of the ideal thegnly residence. Its use of the word 'bell-house' (the tower or loft in which the bell was hung) for such a church may not be merely symbolic. The word 'belfry' (from Middle English *berefrey*) has the root-meaning of a secure or defended place, like the 'wooden belfrey 140 feet high' which belonged to

50 Morris, *Churches*, 248.
51 S. 503 (dated 944), 575. If the date, 958, of S. 575 is correct, it cannot be a charter of Eadred, who died in 955; either it is a charter of his successor, Eadwig, or, more likely, the date is wrong (see Gelling, *Charters of the Thames Valley*, 36, 49, 53).
52 John Blair, ed., *Minsters and Parish Churches: the Local Church in Transition, 950–1200*, Oxford 1988, 1–19; Alan Everitt, *Continuity and Colonization: the Evolution of Kentish Settlement*, Leicester 1986, 198–205.
53 II Edgar 2, see Robertson, *Laws*, 20–1.

Adam of Cockfield (see above). The first element, bel-, bere-, is derived from the same verb beorgan ('to protect') which lies at the root of burh. Thus a church-tower associated with a defensive wall or hedge could itself form part of the defences of the lord's burh.[54] This is particularly true of turriform churches, which consisted of tower-naves with porches and small chancels attached.

One of the largest and most elaborate tower-churches still remaining is St Peter's, Barton upon Humber, Lincs. Archaeological and topographical examination of the site has revealed several stages in its development.[55] In the period before 900, the settlement was enclosed with a bank and ditch; the area within the bank was sub-circular in shape, with an average diameter of 820 feet, and covered twelve acres. By the tenth century, there was a graveyard to the west of the settlement, and presumably a church, though none has yet been found. When the tower-church was built, between 970 and 1030, the ditch was in-filled, 'leaving no significant physical boundary between the hall and the church'. The late Saxon and medieval manorial complex lay within the area defined by the bank and ditch.

The site at Barton upon Humber bears a strong resemblance to that at Earl's Barton, Northants. Here also is a pre-Conquest tower-church, dedicated to All Saints, and dating from the same period as St Peter's, Barton upon Humber.[56] It stands on the end of a spur of land, which falls away upon three sides; on the fourth side, to the north, the neck of the spur is cut across by a ditch, which cups a large mound lying partly within the present churchyard. Neither ditch nor mound have been investigated, and their dates are unknown.[57]

In the reign of Edward the Confessor, both Barton upon Humber and Earl's Barton were centres of large estates, held by rich and powerful king's thegns. At Barton upon Humber there were in 1066, besides the church and its priest, two mills, a market and a ferry which produced £4 a year. To Barton were attached lands in Horkstow and South Ferriby (where there was another ferry). The estate, assessed at just under 20 carucates of land, belonged to Ulf Fenman, whose extensive lands, the bulk of which lay in Lincolnshire, passed after the Conquest to Gilbert de Ghent.[58] Earl's Barton (whose church is not recorded in

---

54 Morris, Churches, 255; cf. pp. 250–5 for examples of churches used in a military context. Morris notes the frequent addition of towers to pre-existing local churches in the eleventh and twelfth centuries, and suggests that this 'might be explained as a result of the adoption by local lords of a status symbol which had its beginnings at a higher social level'.

55 Warwick Rodwell and Kirsty Rodwell, 'St Peter's Church, Barton upon Humber: excavation and structural survey, 1978–81', Antiq. Journ. lxii, 1982, 283–315, especially 308–9; see also Morris, Churches, 153.

56 The church is dated by the Taylors to the late tenth century (H.M. and J. Taylor, Anglo-Saxon Architecture, Cambridge 1965, i, 222); Fernie prefers a date in the early eleventh century, perhaps c.1030 (Fernie, Architecture, 143–4, 161, 178).

57 Historical Monuments in the County of Northampton, Royal Commission on Historical Monuments, 1979, ii, 39–40; see also Morris, Churches, 253–5.

58 GDB fo 354v. Ulf Fenman's land in Lincolnshire amounted to over 200 carucates of land; his other estates lay in Cambridgeshire and Huntingdonshire (22½ hides), Nottinghamshire and

Domesday) was the *caput* of a group of vills including Great Doddington, Wilby, Mears Ashby and (probably) Ecton, a total of 20 hides of land. It was held by Bondi the staller, with sake and soke, that is, as bookland, and by 1086 had passed to Countess Judith. Most of Bondi's estate, however, amounting to 110 hides in six shires, had gone to Henry de Ferrers.[59] Bondi's title implies that he held office in the royal administration and Ulf Fenman was one of the leading thegns of the Danelaw. It is tempting to see in Barton upon Humber and Earl's Barton the *burhs* of these two prominent pre-Conquest magnates.

Nor do Barton upon Humber and Earl's Barton stand alone. Another 'estate-church' with a graveyard has been excavated at Raunds, Northants. An extensive dig on the site of the medieval manor of Furnells, in the north of the present village, revealed occupation levels going back to the settlement period. From the seventh century onwards, a series of timber halls occupied the site, each with associated outbuildings. About 900, a small stone church was built to the east of the hall, and by about 930, this church had acquired a chancel and a cemetery. It was by then surrounded by a ditch, which linked with the ditch of the hall-complex.[60]

The whole village of Raunds has been subjected to intensive archaeological and topographical investigation over the last few years.[61] By the middle of the eleventh century, there were several distinct holdings within the vill. The major manor, associated with the Furnells site, was held by Burgraed, a thegn with a considerable estate in Northamptonshire, Buckinghamshire and Bedfordshire, where he and his sons, Edwin, Ulf and Wulfsige, had land assessed at over 160 hides. Burgraed was a benefactor of Peterborough Abbey, and had some connection with the abbey of St Albans. I have argued elsewhere that his family was of

Derbyshire (25½ carucates), and Yorkshire (at least one carucate and perhaps more): see GDB fos 197, 197v, 207, 277v, 280v, 290v, 298v, 354v, 355, 355v, 364v, 369v, 373v, 376v, 377. In Nottinghamshire, Derbyshire, Yorkshire and Lincolnshire, he was one of those who held full jurisdiction and in Cambridgeshire he is called a king's thegn (see Olof von Feilitzen, *Pre-Conquest Personal Names of Domesday Book*, Uppsala 1937, 400–1).

59  GDB fo 228. For the Earl's Barton estate, see David Hall, 'The late Saxon countryside: villages and their fields', *Anglo-Saxon Settlements*, ed. Della Hooke, Oxford 1989 (henceforth Hall, 'Late Saxon countryside'), 104–6. Bondi held about 110 hides of land in Berkshire, Buckinghamshire, Essex, Gloucestershire, Northamptonshire and Oxfordshire (*GDB* fos 60, 151, 157v, 166v, 225, 228, 228v; *LDB* fo 57). His title implies a position in the royal administration; in Oxfordshire he had charge of a wood attached to the royal manor of Bampton (*GDB* fo 154v) and he was probably reeve of the royal manor at Luton, Beds (*GDB* fo 218v). He witnessed several royal charters in the 1060s (S. 1033–4, 1036, 1042) and two private transactions (S. 1235 and S. 1426, in Bedfordshire and Gloucestershire respectively).

60  Brian Dix, 'The Raunds area project: second interim report', *Northamptonshire Archaeology* xxi, 1986–7, 18–9; W.J. Blair, 'Local churches in Domesday Book and beyond', *Domesday Studies*, ed. J.C. Holt, Woodbridge 1987, 268.

61  Graham Cadman and Glenn Foard, 'Raunds: manorial and village origins', *Studies in Late Anglo-Saxon Settlement*, ed. Margaret Faull, Oxford 1984, 81–100; Glenn Foard and T. Pearson, 'The Raunds area project: first interim report', *Northamptonshire Archaeology* xx, 1985, 3–21; Hall, 'Late Saxon countryside', 106–7, 111–3 and see note 60 above.

sufficient importance to provide a wife for Edward the Confessor's nephew, Ralph, and that this marriage was the prelude to Ralph's appointment as Earl of the East Midlands in 1050.[62]

It was Earl Ralph's wife, Gytha, who held the second major tenement in Raunds. Her land there was attached, as sokeland, to her manor of Higham Ferrers.[63] It can be identified as the later manor of Burystead situated just to the north of the parish church and facing Furnells across the valley in which the village of Raunds lies. Excavation is still in progress around Burystead, and it is not yet clear whether a pre-Conquest manor-house underlies the later structure, or whether the tenement only acquired manorial status, and therefore a hall, in the twelfth century.[64] The name Burystead means 'the site of a *burh*', but may be a post-Conquest formation, referring to the twelfth-century hall.[65]

Even if Gytha, like her kinsman Burgraed, had a manor-house in Raunds, it is another matter how often she was to be found there. The rich king's thegns held numerous manors and probably visited them in turn as occasion arose, just as the king and his court journeyed around the royal demesnes. Some traces of these aristocratic itineraries can be found in Domesday Book. At Eardisland, Herefordshire, which belonged to the earl of Mercia, the reeve 'had the custom . . . that on the arrival of his lady at the manor, he would present her with 18 *orae* of pence, so that she would be well-disposed'.[66] Earl Godwine had to buy his wife Gytha an estate at Woodchester, Gloucs., to live off while she stayed at Berkeley, whose produce she refused to consume, because of the destruction of its abbey.[67] Traces of favoured residences also appear from time to time. Aethelwine, ealdorman of East Anglia from 962 to 992 'had his hall and kept his court' at Upwood, Hunts.[68] Earl Godwine and his sons seem to have favoured Bosham, perhaps because its harbour was a convenient place to keep their ships in case of emergency.[69] Tovi the Proud, who held land both in Somerset and in Essex, chose to celebrate his wedding-feast in 1042 at Lambeth; it was on this occasion that King Harthacnut collapsed 'as he stood at his drink', and died soon afterwards.[70]

A few noblemen in the late Old English period were occasionally

62 GDB fo. 220v; see Ann Williams, 'The king's nephew: the family and career of Ralph, earl of Hereford', *Studies in Medieval History presented to R. Allen Brown*, ed. Christopher Harper-Bill, Christopher Holdsworth and Janet L. Nelson, Woodbridge 1989, 327–43.
63 GDB fo. 225v.
64 See note 60 above (first reference).
65 Smyth, *Place-name Elements*, 62; Karl-Inge Sandred, *English Place-names in -stead*, Uppsala 1963, 58.
66 GDB fo. 179v.
67 GDB fo. 164.
68 Hart, *Charters of Eastern England*, 231.
69 Ann Williams, 'Land and power in the eleventh century: the estates of Harold Godwineson', *Anglo-Norman Studies* iii, 1980, 185.
70 ASC sub anno 1042.

distinguished by the names of estates which belonged to them. Surnames are rare in pre-Conquest England, and toponymics very rare, so their use is of some interest. It has been said that 'an Anglo-Saxon toponymic will usually lead to a village', whereas a Norman toponymic leads to 'a lordship or castle'.[71] This I find somewhat misleading. The toponymics applied, albeit sporadically and rarely, to English thegns, do not indicate mere residence in a rural community, but the lords who owned the estates of which those communities were composed. Sired of Chilham did not simply live in the village of Chilham, Kent. He held the manor of Chilham *de rege Edwardo*, as one of the king's thegns who had full rights of jurisdiction in West Kent.[72] It may even have been his patrimony, if (as seems possible) he is related to Siward of (*aet*) Chilham, a member of the shire-court of Kent in the reign of Cnut.[73] Aristocratic *burhs*, no less than Norman castles, functioned as centres of lordship, to which dues and services were rendered.

That such places should be defensible is not surprising, given the conditions prevalent in the tenth and eleventh centuries. The struggle of the West Saxon kings against the Viking rulers of York was both bitter and prolonged. Though it ended with the incorporation of the north into the West Saxon hegemony, raiding from Scotland, Wales and the Norse colonies in Ireland did not cease. As late as the year 1000, Aethelred II was ravaging Cumberland and the Isle of Man to prevent incursions from Ireland. Raids from Scandinavia recommenced in 980, and the later part of Aethelred's reign saw the devastating campaigns which led to the Danish Conquest. Even in the reign of Edward the Confessor, the south-east was raided by a fleet from Scandinavia, and the assessment of Fareham, Hants, was reduced from 30 hides to 20, 'on account of the Vikings, because it is on the sea'.[74] The prevalence of war and violence might be expected to encourage the building of stronger defences around the halls of the English nobles. Such defences, however, were not primarily military in character or function. The *burhs* which figure so largely in the wars of the early tenth century, and again, to a lesser extent, in Aethelred II's time, were not defensible manor-houses, but the urban and quasi-urban fortifications built by Alfred and his successors. Fortification for specifically military purposes may have been a royal prerogative. Nowhere is private fortification actually forbidden, but the statement of William of Malmesbury that King Athelstan, when he took York in 927, demolished the *castrum* of the Viking kings 'so that there might be no place for disloyalty to shelter in', is suggestive.[75] The *castrum* cannot refer to the walls

71 J.C. Holt, *'What's in a Name?' Family Nomenclature and the Norman Conquest*, The Stenton Lecture 1981, Reading 1982, 10.
72 GDB fos. 1, 10.
73 Robertson, *Charters*, 170, 372, 419.
74 ASC sub anno 1048; GDB fo. 40v.
75 *Willelmi Malmesberiensis Monachi de Gestis Regum Anglorum*, ed. William Stubbs, RS 90, 1887 (henceforth GR) i, 197.

of York, and presumably means a smaller fortification within the city, perhaps on the site of the Viking palace in the area known as King's Court.[76] It might be objected that William of Malmesbury is attributing to Athelstan actions more appropriate to the twelfth century than to the tenth, but such internal strongholds are not unknown. Traces of a ditched enclosure were found under the site of Stamford Castle.[77] At York itself, the area of Marygate, around St Olave's Church, was once known as *Earlesburgh*, which suggests a fortified residence belonging to the earls of Northumbria; it was Earl Siward (before 1035–1055) who founded the church of St Olave.[78]

The defences of the *burh* in its manorial sense seem to be directed not against external enemies, but against neighbours. Successive West Saxon kings legislated against private violence, beginning with Alfred, who laid down the circumstances in which a man can besiege his enemy's house.[79] In the second code of Edmund (940–6) the crime of *hamsocn*, assault on a man in his own house, makes its first appearance. The penalty was forfeiture of the offender's property, 'and it shall be for the king to decide whether his life shall be preserved'.[80] *Hamsocn* was one of the pleas of the crown, whose judgement was reserved to the king. The *Institutes of London*, which date from Aethelred II's reign, decree that anyone slain while committing *hamsocn* 'shall lie in an unhonoured grave' and the customs of Oxford, preserved in Domesday Book, distinguish between *hamsocn* which results in injury to the householder and his family, and that which results in death; in the latter case, the offender's 'body and all his substance shall be in the king's power, except for his wife's dowry'.[81] Yet private violence was not rare, and was often abetted by those officials charged with its control. In the 990s, the widow of Wulfbald of Bourne 'went, along with her son, and slew Wulfbald's cousin, Eadmaer the king's thegn, with his 15 companions, on the estate of Bourne'.[82] At about the same time, three brothers in Oxfordshire, whose servant had stolen a bridle, were involved in a fight with the bridle's owners, in which two of them were killed, but the royal reeves of Oxford and Buckingham allowed the thieves Christian burial.[83] A particularly flagrant example of *hamsocn* on the part of a royal officer occurred in 1002,

---

[76] For the Viking palace see R.A. Hall, ed., *Viking-age York and the North*, Council for British Archaeology Research Report xxvii, 1978, 34.

[77] Christine Mahoney and David Roffe, 'Stamford: the development of an Anglo-Scandinavian borough', *Anglo-Norman Studies* v, 1983, 203–4.

[78] Alfred P. Smyth, *Scandinavian York and Dublin*, ii, Dublin 1979, 235; ASC sub anno 1055.

[79] Alfred 42, see Attenborough, *Laws*, 82–5.

[80] II Edmund 6, see Robertson, *Laws*, 10–11. Cf. Rebecca V. Coleman, 'Domestic peace and public order in Anglo-Saxon law', *The Anglo-Saxons: Synthesis and Achievement*, ed. J. Douglas Woods and David A.E. Pelteret, Waterloo (Ontario) 1985, 49–61. It was *hamsocn* that Eustace of Boulogne and his men committed at Dover in 1051 (ASC 'E', sub anno 1051).

[81] IV Aethelred II, 4, see Robertson, *Laws*, 74–5. The Oxford customs, see GDB fo. 154v.

[82] S. 877, printed Robertson, *Charters* 128–31.

[83] S. 883, translated *EHD* i, 526–7.

when Earldorman Leofsige slew the king's high-reeve, Aefic, 'in his own house, without warning' and was exiled. When Leofsige's sister Aethelflaed attempted to help him, thereby committing *flymenafyrmth*, the crime of harbouring fugitives, she lost her property.[84]

It is in this context that the fortified houses of the English nobles should be seen. More serious acts of defiance, against the king himself, took a different form. It was the private fleet, not the private *burh*, which was used in such cases. When, in 1009, the South Saxon thegn, Wulfnoth *cild*, was 'accused to the king', he took twenty ships from the fleet and went raiding along the Sussex coast. In like manner the staller, Osgod Clapa, when he was exiled in 1046, collected his fleet at Bruges, and three years later ravaged around the Naze in Essex. In 1051, to quote the most famous example, Earl Godwine gathered his men at Beverstone, a member of his manor of Berkeley, Gloucs., but when things came to the crunch, it was not to any manor-house that he turned, but to his fleet, lying in the harbour at Bosham.[85] It never seems to have occurred to a disgruntled nobleman to retire to his *burh* and fortify it against attack.[86] The bishops, abbots and lay noblemen who travelled the roads of Europe on their own or the king's business must have seen the castles rising, but they never felt tempted to build them on their own account.

This leads us to consideration of the difference, clear to eleventh-century commentators, between a castle and a private *burh*. On the continent, a distinction between castles and other fortifications and defences was as old as the ninth century. In the Edict of Pitres, 864, Charles the Bald ordered the destruction of all *castella et firmitates et haias* built without royal permission, because 'the villagers (*vicini*) and those dwelling round about suffer many depredations and impositions from them'.[87] The comments of Jean Dunbabin on this passage seem relevant to the English as well as the Frankish situation:[88]

> ... whether the large number of simple defended towers in which individual families lived ought to be considered castles at all and whether they posed any threat to public order must be doubted. ... It is only the ... castle, *the fortified administrative centre* (my italics), which is at issue.

---

[84] ASC sub anno 1002, S. 926; see F.M. Stenton, *Latin Charters of the Anglo-Saxon Period*, Oxford 1955, 76–80.

[85] ASC sub anno 1009, 1046, 1049, 1051

[86] An apparent exception is the occupation of Wimborne and Christchurch by the rebellious aetheling, Aethelwold, in 901 (ASC sub anno 901). Both may have been 'urban' *burhs* however; Christchurch appears in the almost contemporary *Burghal Hidage*, and Wimborne had burgesses by 1066. For Wimborne, see also John Blair, 'Minster churches in the landscape', *Anglo-Saxon Settlements*, ed. Della Hooke, Oxford 1989, 41–4.

[87] MGH *Legum*, i, 499. See also the similar distinction between *castelli* and *fortitudines* in cap. 4 of the *Consuetudines et Justicie* of 1091 (C.H. Haskins, *Norman Institutions*, New York and London, 1913, 1960, 281ff).

[88] Jean Dunbabin, *France in the Making, 843–1180*, Oxford 1985, 41.

Fortified administrative centres are precisely what aristocratic *burhs* were not. The public administration of the English kingdom was based upon the shire, the hundred and the vill, not on the manors of even the greatest lords. Even in those cases where whole hundreds had come into lay or (more usually) ecclesiastical hands, the king's officers could not be denied entry. However powerful the earls and king's thegns, or for that matter, the bishops and abbots might be, they were not allowed to slip through this net. The *burh* was the centre of its estate, and the men of that estate were justiciable, in lesser matters, in its court; the lord of the *burh* answered to the shire and hundred. The lord's *burh* remained a private house.

To quote the words of Allen Brown, 'there was no room, no occasion, no power-vacuum at the centre to promote the growth of local and feudal territorial power'.[89] It was the king's business to provide for the defence of the realm, and even in the darkest days of King Aethelred's reign, when 'one shire would not help the next', the local magnates did not take matters into their own hands.[90] The outrage against the Norman castle in Herefordshire was directed precisely against its encroachment on royal and comital power; it intruded into Earl Swein's district (*folgoð*) and its castellans 'inflicted every possible injury and insult on *the king's men* (my italics) in those parts'.[91] The language of the entry in the *Anglo-Saxon Chronicle* is strikingly similar to that in the Edict of Pitres, quoted above. The king was the unity of his folk, the guarantor of law and justice, the source of patronage and power. It did not occur to anyone to question this situation; the English, as William of Poitiers was to remark 'were accustomed to serve a king and wished only for a king to be their lord'.[92] In such circumstances it is not surprising that no castles arose on the estates of the Old English nobility. They preferred, as William of Malmesbury unkindly remarked, 'to consume their whole substance in mean and despicable dwellings' than to live frugally 'in noble and splendid mansions'.[93] After all, an Englishman's house is his castle.

[89]  Brown, 'Origins of the castle', 139.
[90]  *ASC* sub anno 1010.
[91]  *ASC* 'E' sub anno 1051.
[92]  R. Allen Brown, *The Norman Conquest*, London 1984, 37.
[93]  *GR* ii 305.

*Plate 1 (above)*
Bodiam castle (June 1970), S front looking W, showing: silt deposited since 1920, bulldozed; the impermeable bed of the moat; the bank (left-hand side) with postern bridge-pier facing diminutive cheek-wall barbican-platform; machicolation to part of flank only; the SE tower (right-hand side); SW tower beyond.

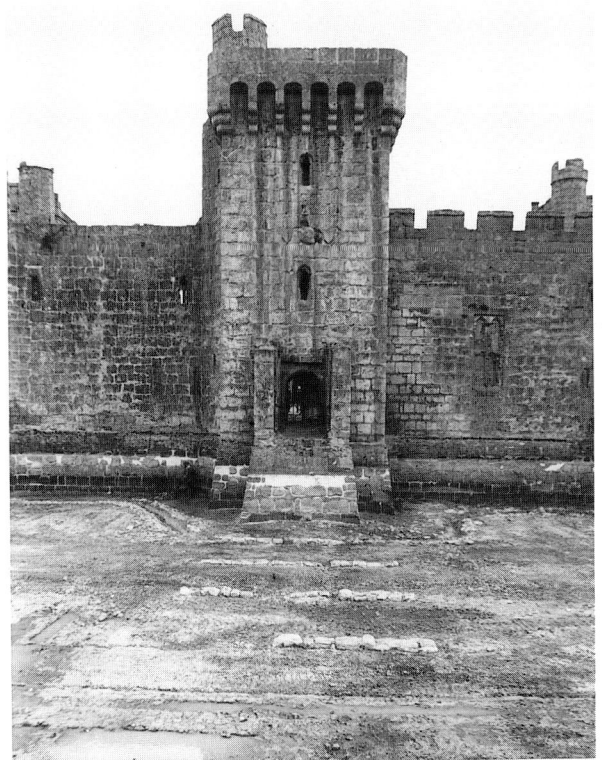

*Plate 2 (right)*
Bodiam castle (June 1970), postern tower from the S bridge-pier, showing: trestle-bridge footings; the moat water-level mark on the plinth (partly rendered by Curzon); hall lower window (right-hand side) in the SE curtain; the postern barbican, an afterthought (not bonded).

*Plate 3*
Bodiam castle (March 1991), detail of the postern archway, showing: no chain holes, pit or pivots, closure by thin portcullis and doors (early modern) lacking bar-hole(s) and socket(s); specious 'drawbridge' rebate; screens passage beyond.

*late 4*
:odiam castle (June 1970), E side looking N, showing: vulnerable E bank (right-hand side); large
ngle-light windows; small ground-floor lights to SE tower (non-defensive); hall window
eft-hand side); moat overflow to NE, lately restored with NE pond (see Fig. 2).

*Plate 5*
Bodiam castle (March 1991), detail of the SE-tower-base and curtain junction: note plinth; masonry detail; bevelled lights (right-hand side damaged, not modified for cannon); accessibility from boat in moat.

*Plate 6*
Bodiam castle (March 1991), NE tower and main gate E summits, showing: stair-well narrow lights; allure door; cap of stair projection below (dummy) turret; curtain parapet destroyed; machicolation not over allure junction with main gate flank.

*Plate* 8

Bodiam castle (June 1970), N front looking across original line of entry to octagon (left-hand side), showing: bridge gap; Barbican remnants; second gap; main entry; NW tower (right-hand side) and W tower; special treatment of N curtain parapets.

*Plate* 7 (*opposite*)

Bodiam castle (February 1989) from SSE near the stream (F.other), showing: raised central moat area; vulnerable SE angle of the embankment; hill slopes to W (left-hand side) and N (see Fig. 2). (RCHME copyright)

*Plate 9*

Bodiam castle (June 1970), site of main approach looking NE, showing: solid earthen N causeway with hedges, perhaps late-medieval (left-hand side: see note 60), lately replaced by timber catwalk; octagon; barbican; NW tower base; wall foundations, found to be shallow on silt pan.

*Plate 10 (below)*

Bodiam castle (February 1989) from NW, dominated by rising ground. Note: rivulet beneath the banks in the distance; semi-aerial overview from the 'viewing platform' higher up (Fig. 3); massing on N (show) front; the impact of alternating round and rectilinear towers. (RCHME copyright)

*Plate 11*
Bodiam castle (March 1991), main-gate central panel, showing: the large window over the portcullis slot and above consorts with oblique gunloop-form squints and heraldry; an *assommoir* (and also machicolation) overhead but no 'drawbridge' below, despite spurious recess.

*Plate 12 (opposite, top)*
Bodiam castle (March 1991), main entry W side, showing: the octagon edge, left-hand side foreground; above, remnants of the barbican, partly masking frontal main gunloop(s); small gunloop-form garderobe-chamber light (right-hand side) set in the recessed wing (design precludes flank defence).

*Plate 13 (opposite, bottom)*
Bodiam castle (March 1991), main entry W side: gunloop does not bear; none is in an ideal position in the NW tower (right-hand side); lesser 'gunloop' entirely masked by salient; 'dumb-bell' loop to apron-platform (far left-hand side, just apparent); awkward junction of curtain parapet to NW tower, showing afterthought alteration.

Plate 14 (right)
Bodiam castle (March 1991), main gate, showing: detail of W jamb of archway, with bevelled edge and (below) broach stop; 'dumb-bell' double-oillet loop, showing exaggeratedly thick 'plate front' design, from porters' lodge.

Plate 15 (below)
Bodiam castle (February 1989) from SE, showing: the view displayed to arrivals from the SW (Bodiam bridge) who would pass along the SE and E bank, around the N side to the NW entry point (see Fig. 2). Note inter alia the stair-capping turrets to the SW (left-hand side) and NE (right-hand side) towers. (RCHME copyright)

*Plate 16*
Bodiam castle (June 1970) from SE: without the magnifying and romanticizing effects of water, still impressive but prosaic and reduced in scale; once the centrepiece of an entire system of water features (Fig. 2).

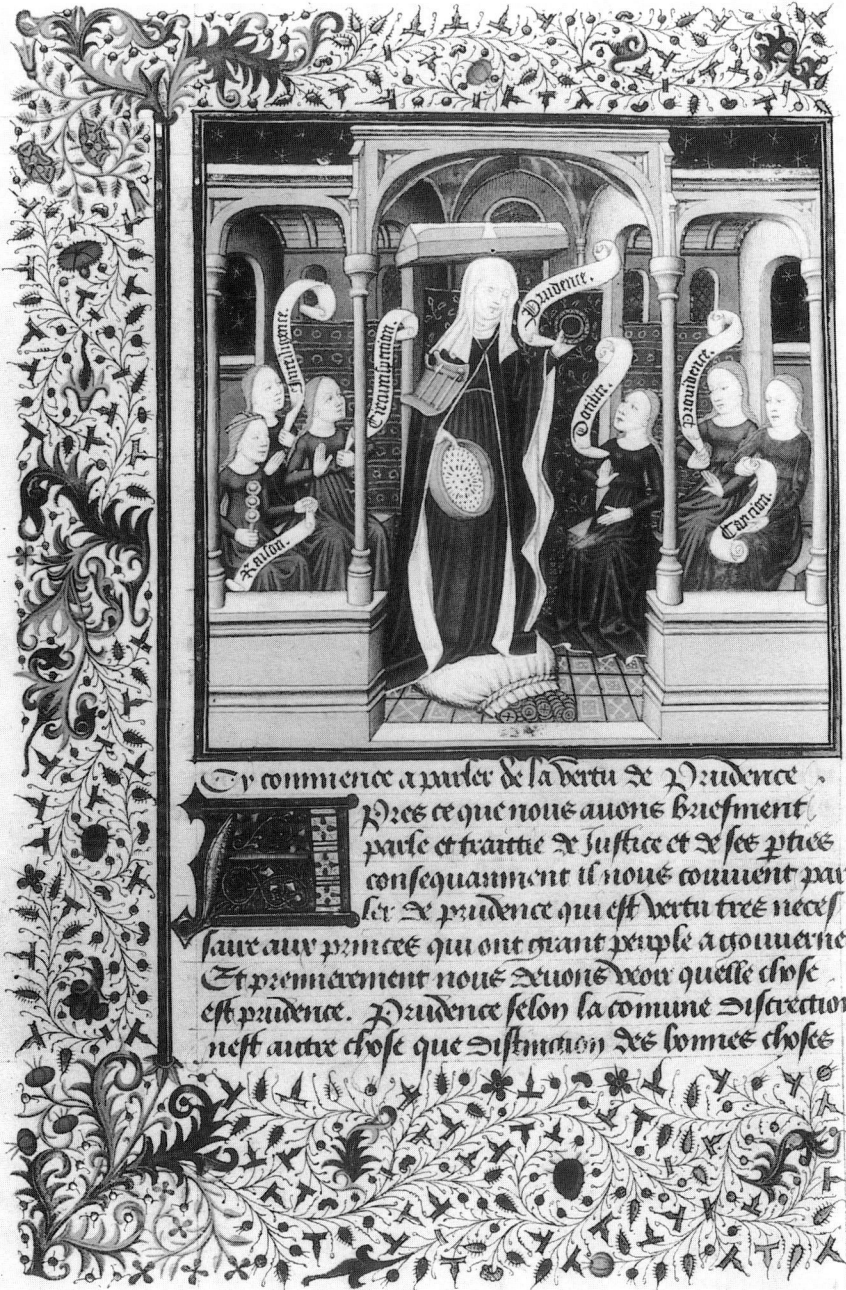

Plate 1  *Bodleian Library MS Laud Misc. 570, fo. 9v*

Prudence is depicted bearing a coffin on her head, holding a mirror in her right hand and looking into the future we must all prepare for; with her right hand she sifts the virtues from the vices. She stands on a bag of spilled coins: avarice rejected. The virtues necessary for these attitudes are represented by the accompanying handmaidens of: Raison, Intelligence, Circumspection, Doucilite, Providence and Caucion, identified in the scrolls they hold.

*Plate 2* Bodleian Library MS Laud Misc. 570, fo. 16r

Temperence has a clock on her head to show the harmonious working of the emotions. In her left hand she holds spectacles of discernment to distinguish enough from excess; and in her right hand she holds the head-harness which bridles the tongue or appetites. She stands on and masters with spurs the windmill that is obedient to every wind of passion. Her handmaidens are Continence, Clemence and Moderance.